This is a new and accessible study of the plays of Heinrich von Kleist (1777–1811), an author who ranks in importance with Goethe and Schiller in the nineteenth century and has been a major influence on contemporary German writers. In an attempt to resolve a number of long-running controversies in Kleist scholarship, Seán Allan shows how Kleist's plays expose the contradictions inherent in the transcendent aspirations of both Enlightenment and Romantic metaphysics. Central to this critique is the view that the attempt to embrace fictitious ideals of perfection forms an insuperable obstacle to genuine human progress. The book includes chapters on two works often ignored by scholars – *Das Käthchen von Heilbronn* and *Die Hermannsschlacht* – and contains concise summaries of the current state of research on all of Kleist's plays. All quotations appear in both German and English, and full references are given to published English translations of Kleist's work.

CAMBRIDGE STUDIES IN GERMAN

THE PLAYS OF HEINRICH VON KLEIST

CAMBRIDGE STUDIES IN GERMAN

General editors: H. B. NISBET *and* MARTIN SWALES
Advisory editor: THEODORE J. ZIOLKOWSKI

S. S. PRAWER
Frankenstein's Island: England and the English in the Writings of Heinrich Heine

BENJAMIN BENNETT
Hugo von Hofmannsthal
The Theatres of Consciousness

PHILIP PAYNE
Robert Musil's 'The Man without Qualities'
A Critical Study

ANNA K. KUHN
Christa Wolf's Utopian Vision
From Marxism to Feminism

LESLEY SHARPE
Friedrich Schiller: Drama, Thought and Politics

PETER HUTCHINSON
Stefan Heym: The Perpetual Dissident

ERNST BEHLER
Germanic Romantic Literary Theory

J. P. STERN
The Dear Purchase: A Theme in German Modernism

MICHAEL BUTLER (editor)
The Narrative Fiction of Heinrich Böll
Social Conscience and Literary Achievement

THE PLAYS OF HEINRICH VON KLEIST

Ideals and illusions

SEÁN ALLAN

Lecturer in German,
University of Reading

CAMBRIDGE
UNIVERSITY PRESS

Published by the Press Syndicate of the University of Cambridge
The Pitt Building, Trumpington Street, Cambridge CB2 1RP
40 West 20th Street, New York, NY 10011–4211, USA
10 Stamford Road, Oakleigh, Melbourne 3166, Australia

First published 1996

Printed in Great Britain at the University Press, Cambridge

A catalogue record for this book is available from the British Library

Library of Congress cataloguing in publication data

Allan, Seán D.
The plays of Heinrich von Kleist : ideals and illusions / Seán D. Allan.
p. cm. – (Cambridge studies in German)
Includes bibliographical references and index.
ISBN 0 521 49511 3 hardback
1. Kleist, Heinrich von 1777–1811 – Criticism and interpretation.
I. Title. II. Series.
PT2379.Z5A53 1996
832′.6–dc20 95-41083 CIP

ISBN 0 521 49511 3 hardback

SE

Contents

Preface

In the following study, I have dealt with all the plays of Kleist in chronological order. I have not, however, included an individual chapter on *Robert Guiskard* because of its fragmentary nature.

I am grateful to the *Deutscher Akademischer Austauschdienst* for financial assistance towards the completion of this work. In addition I would like to thank Yale University Press for permission to reproduce extracts from Heinrich von Kleist, *Five plays*, edited, translated and introduced by Martin Greenberg (New Haven and London, 1988) and to Penguin USA for permission to reproduce extracts from *An abyss deep enough: letters of Heinrich von Kleist with a selection of anecdotes*, edited, translated and introduced by Philip B. Miller (New York, 1982).

A great many people have offered assistance at various stages during the preparation of the text. I would like to thank Dr Katharina Brett, Alison Gilderdale and Hazel Brooks at Cambridge University Press for their constant help and guidance. Julia Allen, Dr Ian Roe and Dr Suzanne Stark also offered invaluable assistance and advice on numerous points of detail. In particular, however, I should like to thank Professor Roger Paulin, Dr Erika Swales, Professor Martin Swales and Dr Nicholas Boyle for their helpful suggestions and comments. Needless to say, any remaining errors are entirely my own responsibility.

Finally I should like to acknowledge a great debt of thanks to the late Mr Ralph Manheim, whose support and encouragement throughout the research for this study was instrumental to its completion. It is to his memory that this book is dedicated.

A note on the translations

In order to make the book accessible to those readers lacking any knowledge of German, I have provided translations of all the quotations. Unfortunately not all of Kleist's works are translated. There is an English translation of *Die Familie Schroffenstein (The feud of the Schroffensteins)* by M. J. and L. M. Price in the journal, *Poet Lore*, 27 (1916), pp. 457–576, but given the difficulty most readers would have in obtaining this, I have decided not to make use of it here. To the best of my knowledge there is no published translation of *Die Hermannsschlacht.*

Where there is no acknowledgement, the translation supplied is my own. In certain instances I have used my own translation rather than an available published version.

Abbreviations

In the text the following abbreviations for primary sources are used. In each case the abbreviation is followed by the volume number, page number and line/paragraph number (where appropriate).

E	Rousseau, Jean-Jacques, *Emile*, translated by Barbara Foxley and with an introduction by P. D. Jimack (London: Dent, 1911, reprinted 1989).
G	Kleist, Heinrich von, *Five plays*, translated from the German with an introduction by Martin Greenberg (New Haven and London: Yale University Press, 1988).
GA	Goethe, Johann Wolfgang, *Gedenkausgabe der Werke, Briefe und Gespräche*, edited by Ernst Beutler, 24 vols. (Zürich: Artemis, 1949).
GN	Gneisenau, Neithardt von, *Denkschriften zum Volksaufstand von 1808 und 1811*, Kriegsgeschichtliche Bücherei, Heft 10 (Berlin: Junker und Dünnhaupt, 1936).
KA	Schlegel, Friedrich, *Kritische Friedrich-Schlegel-Ausgabe*, edited by Ernst Behler with the collaboration of Jean-Jacques Anstett, Hans Eichner, and other specialists, 35 vols. (Munich, Paderborn, Vienna: Schöningh; Zürich, Thomas, 1958–).
KS	Tieck, Ludwig, *Kritische Schriften. Zum erstenmale gesammelt und mit einer Vorrede*, (Leipzig: Brockhaus, 1848–52. [Photomechanical reproduction, Berlin, New York: de Gruyter, 1974]).

L — Kleist, Heinrich von, *The Marquise of O . . . and other stories*, translated and with an introduction by David Luke and Nigel Reeves (London: Penguin, 1978).

Lebensspuren — Sembdner, Helmut, ed., *Heinrich von Kleists Lebensspuren: Dokumente und Berichte der Zeitgenossen* (Frankfurt: Insel, 1984).

M — *An abyss deep enough: letters of Heinrich von Kleist with a selection of anecdotes*, edited, translated and introduced by Philip B. Miller (New York: Dutton, 1982).

Nachruhm — Sembdner, Helmut, ed., *Heinrich von Kleists Nachruhm: eine Wirkungsgeschichte in Dokumenten* (Frankfurt: Insel, 1984).

P — Kleist, Heinrich von, *Kaethchen of Heilbronn*, translated by Frederick E. Peirce, in Frederick E. Peirce and Carl F. Schreiber, *Fiction and fantasy of German Romance: selections from the German Romantic authors, 1790–1830, in English translation* (London, Toronto, Melbourne and Bombay: Oxford University Press, 1927), pp. 248–344.

PF — Schlegel, Friedrich, *Philosophical Fragments*, translated by Peter Firchow; foreword by Rodolphe Gaché (Minneapolis: University of Minnesota Press, 1991).

SV — Goethe, Johann Wolfgang, *Selected Verse*, edited and with an introduction by David Luke (London: Penguin, 1986).

SW — Kleist, Heinrich von, *Sämtliche Werke und Briefe*, edited by Helmut Sembdner, 7th extended and revised edition, 2 vols. (Munich: Hanser, 1984).

Werke — Klopstock, Friedrich Gottlieb, *Klopstocks Werke*, edited by R. Hamel, 4 vols. (Berlin, Stuttgart: Speman, 1883).

WM — Goethe, Johann Wolfgang, *Wilhelm Meister's apprenticeship: a novel from the German of Goethe*, translated by R. Dillon Boylan (London: Bohn, 1855).

The following are used to refer to periodicals in the bibliography:

DVjs.	*Deutsche Vierteljahrsschrift für Literaturwissenschaft und Geistesgeschichte*
GLL	*German Life and Letters*
JbDSG	*Jahrbuch der Deutschen Schillergesellschaft*
OGS	*Oxford German Studies*
PEGS	*Publications of the English Goethe Society*
PMLA	*Publications of the Modern Language Association of America*

Chronology of Kleist's life and works

1777 Bernd Heinrich Wilhelm von Kleist born in Frankfurt on the Oder (18 October).

1792 Kleist taken on as a corporal in the king's Guards Regiment at Potsdam.

1793 Composition of earliest surviving poem, 'Der höhere Frieden' ('The higher peace').

1798 Travels to the Harz mountains in the company of Rühle von Lilienstern and two other fellow officers.

Composition of *Aufsatz, den sichern Weg des Glücks zu finden und ungestört – auch unter den größten Drangsalen des Lebens – ihn zu genießen!* (*An essay on the means whereby Man can be certain to attain and enjoy a state of lasting happiness under even the most adverse of circumstances!*).

1799 Discharged from the Prussian army at his own request (4 April).

Embarks upon the study of physics, mathematics and philosophy at the University of Frankfurt on the Oder (10 April).

1800 Engagement to Wilhelmine von Zenge.

Travels to Würzburg (*via* Leipzig and Dresden), in the company of Ludwig von Brockes (28 August).

Returns to Berlin (27 October). Attends the literary salons of Rahel Levin and Henriette Herz, as well as a number of sessions of the Technical Deputation.

1801 'Kant crisis' (see letters of 5 February and 22 March).

Departs for Paris (*via* Dresden) in the company of his sister, Ulrike von Kleist (15 April).

Arrives in Paris (6 July) in time to witness the Bastille Day celebrations.

Leaves Paris and travels – *via* Frankfurt, Darmstadt, Heidelberg, Karlsruhe, Strasbourg and Basel – to Bern (November–December).

1802 Sets up house on the 'Delosea Island', near Thun (February).

Works on the first drafts of *Die Familie Schroffenstein.*

Starts work on *Der zerbrochne Krug* and *Robert Guiskard.*

Breaks off all relations with Wilhelmine von Zenge (May).

Falls ill and has to return to Bern (June–July).

Travels to Jena and Weimar in the company of Ulrike von Kleist and Ludwig Wieland (October–December).

Spends Christmas in Ossmannstedt at the home of Christoph Martin Wieland.

1803 Anonymous publication of *Die Familie Schroffenstein* (spring).

Kleist leaves Ossmannstedt and moves first to Leipzig (March–April) and from there to Dresden (April–July).

Returns to Thun in the company of Ernst von Pfuel (July–August) and from there travels to Paris (October).

Burns the manuscript of *Robert Guiskard* (October).

Attempts (unsuccessfully) to enlist with Napoleon's armies in northern France. Returns to Germany (November).

Spends the winter recovering from illness at the home of Dr Georg Wedekind in Mainz.

1804 First performance of *Die Familie Schroffenstein* in Graz (14 January).

Leaves Mainz and returns, *via* Weimar, Frankfurt on the Oder and Potsdam to Berlin (June). Seeks a position in the Prussian civil service.

1805 Employed in the Prussian civil service under the supervision of Finance Minister Baron von Stein zum Altenstein.

Sent to Königsberg to study economic theory under Professor Christian Jakob Kraus (May).

Composition of *Über die allmähliche Verfertigung der Gedanken beim Reden (On the gradual construction of thoughts while speaking).*

1806 Obtains a six-week discharge from the civil service on grounds of ill health (August).
Prussian forces defeated by Napoleon at Jena (14 October). Prussian court moves to Königsberg.

1807 Kleist leaves Königsberg for Berlin and is arrested by French officials on charges of espionage (January). Imprisoned first in Fort de Joux and subsequently in Chalons sur Marne.
Publication of *Amphitryon*, with a foreword by Adam Müller (May).
Peace of Tilsit between France and Prussia (9 July).
Kleist released from prison (12 July) and travels, *via* Berlin and Cottbus, to Dresden.
Publication of *Jeronimo und Josephe* – an early version of *Das Erdbeben in Chili* (*The earthquake in Chile*) – in Cotta's *Morgenblatt für gebildete Stände* (September).
Attends lectures by Adam Müller and Gotthilf Heinrich Schubert in Dresden (October).
Manuscript of *Penthesilea* completed (December).
Kleist and Adam Müller found their own literary journal, *Phöbus* (17 December).

1808 First number of *Phöbus* published, including an extract from *Penthesilea* (23 January).
Second number of *Phöbus* published, including *Die Marquise von O . . .* (February).
Disastrous performance of *Der zerbrochne Krug (The broken jug)* in Weimar under Goethe's direction (2 March).
Third issue of *Phöbus* published, including extracts from *Der zerbrochne Krug* (April).
Fourth and fifth issues of *Phöbus* published, including extracts from *Robert Guiskard* and *Das Käthchen von Heilbronn* and a series of epigrams (June).
Publication of *Penthesilea* in book form (July).
Manuscript of *Das Käthchen von Heilbronn* sent to theatres in Dresden, Berlin and Vienna (August).
Sixth issue of *Phöbus* published, including extracts from *Michael Kohlhaas* (November).
Completion of *Die Hermannsschlacht* (December).

1809 Twelfth (and final) issue of *Phöbus* published.
Composition of a series of political articles (March).
Austria declares war on France and invades Bavaria (9 April).
Kleist leaves for Prague in the company of Friedrich Dahlmann (29 April).
Vienna occupied by Napoleon's forces (13 May).
Kleist observes the defeat inflicted on Napoleon's forces at the battle of Aspern (21 and 22 May).
Applies (unsuccessfully) for a licence to publish a patriotic journal, *Germania* (June).
Austrian army crushed by Napoleon's forces at the battle of Wagram (6 July).

1810 Kleist returns to Berlin (February).
First performance of *Das Käthchen von Heilbronn* in Vienna (17 March).
Completion of *Michael Kohlhaas* (May).
Feud with Iffland on account of the latter's refusal to stage *Das Käthchen von Heilbronn* in Berlin (August).
Publication of *Das Käthchen von Heilbronn* and the first volume of *Erzählungen* (September).
First issue of the *Berliner Abendblätter* published (1 October).
Publication of Adam Müller's article on national credit attracts the displeasure of both Hardenberg and the king and signals the start of a period of intense difficulties for the *Berliner Abendblätter* (16 November).

1811 Publication of *Der zerbrochne Krug* (February).
Publication of *Die Verlobung in St. Domingo (The betrothal in St. Domingo)* in *Der Freimüthige* (25 March).
Last number of the *Berliner Abendblätter* (30 March).
Second volume of *Erzählungen* – including *Der Findling (The foundling)* and *Der Zweikampf (The duel)* – published (August).
Kleist's cousin, Marie von Kleist, presents the manuscript of *Prinz Friedrich von Homburg* to Princess Marianne at the Prussian court (3 September).
Development of an intensive friendship with Henriette Vogel (November).

Kleist commits suicide (together with Henriette Vogel) at the Wannsee, Berlin (21 November).

1821 Publication of Kleist's *Hinterlassene Schriften (Posthumous writings)* edited by Ludwig Tieck, including, for the first time, *Prinz Friedrich von Homburg* and *Die Hermannsschlacht*.

SCHELTET, ich bitte, mich nicht! Ich machte, beim delphischen Gotte,
Nur die Verse; die Welt, nahm ich, ihr wißts, wie sie steht.

(*SW* I, 21)

CHAPTER I

Introduction

Ambiguity, paradox and self-contradiction have long been regarded as the hallmark of the Kleistian *œuvre*.[1] It is this formal complexity that has so aroused the interest of critics in the latter part of the twentieth century and has led some to see Kleist as a precursor of literary modernism.[2] Not for nothing did Franz Kafka name Kleist as one of his four 'blood' relatives.[3] At the same time, the rise of literary theory in the seventies and early eighties prompted a renewed and intensive interest in Kleist's work which has lasted up to the present day. Nor has this interest been confined to the world of literary criticism: many works by contemporary German authors, among them Christa Wolf, Heiner Müller and Christoph Hein, bear the unmistakable imprint of Kleist's influence. But although the volume of secondary literature on Kleist is increasing rapidly (and shows few signs of slowing down) critics still seem unable to reach any firm consensus even on some of the most basic issues. And as we shall see, not only has his work given rise to a wide divergence of critical opinion, but the critical debates it has provoked have been often bitter and uncompromising.

Few such debates can have been as fiercely contested as that between Wolfgang Wittkowski and Lawrence Ryan regarding the play *Amphitryon*.[4] Indeed the Wittkowski–Ryan exchange highlights many of the difficulties with which any critic dealing with Kleist's work is confronted, not the least among which is the fact that the text appears to offer readings that are, at first sight, diametrically opposed to one another. For Wittkowski, the play is an attack on conventional systems of morality grounded in the structures of religious authority and, at the same time, a plea for a more natural, autonomous system of ethics. Seen in this light, Jupiter's 'triumph' is a sham and it is Alkmene who emerges as the 'moral victor' at the end of the play.[5] For Ryan, the play shows how the 'natural spontaneity' of Alkmene's love has degenerated into nothing more than a 'contractual arrangement' between a married couple: accordingly, Jupiter is to be seen as a 'benevolent' deity who guides Alkmene to a better understanding of the true nature of the love relation.[6] Yet despite all appearances to the contrary, the basic positions of Wittkowski and Ryan are much closer perhaps than either would care to admit: each is concerned to show how the play offers a critique of authority and social convention. Wittkowski sees the play as a critique of conventional morality, Ryan as a critique of conventional love. From this perspective, the difference in their interpretative strategies is not so much one of substance as of emphasis, and further evidence of this can be seen in the way each assigns the play to a different genre. For Wittkowski, the play ends on a tragic note because Alkmene's 'Promethean resistance' is crushed by the forces of authority and results in the loss of her innocence.[7] For Ryan, the play is a genuine comedy that derives its effects from the inflexibility of the heroine's attempt to comply with the dictates of her society.[8] In short, resistance to authority is heroic, compliance with social convention is comic.[9]

The Ryan–Wittkowski exchange is remarkable for the vehemence with which each critic attempts to discredit the other's interpretation of the play. Indeed the typically Kleistian metaphor of the 'duel' ('Zweikampf') would not be out of place here. Yet the polemical character of the debate is symptomatic of what is at stake. For just as the characters in Kleist's plays and stories resort to force, both physical and rhetorical, in an attempt to resolve the paradoxical situations with which they are confronted, so too the vehemence of much Kleist criticism is symptomatic of the critics' efforts to sustain a position of interpretative coherence in the face of the often contradictory and paradoxical nature of Kleist's work. For although Wittkowski and Ryan correctly identify the contradictions inherent in conventional 'morality' and conventional 'love', each posits the resolution of these contradictions in idealised notions of, on the one hand, autonomous human morality (as represented by Alkmene), and on the other, unconditional love (as represented by Jupiter). Yet the paradoxical character of Kleist's writing embraces both these 'solutions', neither of which is unambiguously upheld in the play itself.[10]

The disagreements between Ryan and Wittkowski can be seen as the logical development of a dispute which has dominated Kleist scholarship ever since the publication of Gerhard Fricke's book *Gefühl und Schicksal bei Heinrich von Kleist* in 1929. For although few would now accept uncritically Fricke's view that Kleist's works demonstrate the superiority of human intuition over the rational intellect, the influence of his ideas on later scholarship is unmistakable.[11] Perhaps the best known attempt to come to terms with Fricke's thesis is Walter Müller-Seidel's book *Versehen und Erkennen: eine Studie über Heinrich von Kleist*, published in 1961, a work which has itself been highly influential in the development of Kleist criticism.[12] As the title of his book suggests, Müller-Seidel is concerned to show how Kleist's characters progress from a state of error ('Versehen') to one of genuine insight ('Erkennen').[13] To this end, he points out that these errors and misapprehensions are not simply the result of fate and chance, but are rooted in the personalities and beliefs of the characters themselves.[14] In the final analysis, however, Müller-Seidel's study fails to follow up the implications of his own insights and ends by reinstating the very categories that his own interpretative model has shown to be inherently problematic. This is most clearly revealed in his handling of the motif of intuition ('Gefühl') itself. For although he asks, quite correctly in my view, how we can endorse Kleist's faith in the supremacy of human intuition when it is shown to be so unreliable, he attempts to resolve this very real dilemma by drawing a distinction between 'different varieties of human intuition'.[15] In so doing, however, he merely postpones the problem. Faced with the impossibility of drawing a principled distinction between 'genuine intuition' ('wahres Gefühl') and 'illusory intuitions' ('der Schein des Gefühls'), Müller-Seidel has little choice but to revert once again to the notion of 'innermost feeling' ('innerstes Gefühl') as the one form of intuition 'that is incapable of being misled'.[16] And thus what began as a critical appraisal of Fricke's ideas ends up reinstating those same ideas, albeit at a higher level in the argument.

It is not hard to detect the presence of Kleist's essay *Über das Marionettentheater (On the puppet theatre)* as the main impulse behind

Müller-Seidel's interpretative approach. In his reading, the plays and stories depict a teleological process of development whereby human beings are said to progress from a condition of self-consciousness to 'a new state of innocence',[17] in which they will be guided solely by intuition. In this way, they are said to attain a state of 'infinite grace' that, in Müller-Seidel's view, is symbolised by the Kleistian marionette. This interpretation of Kleist's essay is well represented in the secondary literature[18] and has become the cornerstone of a number of studies of his works. Perhaps the best known of these is Ilse Graham's book *Heinrich von Kleist. Word into flesh: a poet's quest for the symbol*, published in 1977, in which she argues that Kleist's characters are prevented from experiencing 'the Absolute' as a result of their obsession with its embodiment in physical phenomena.[19] In short, she sees Kleist's works as a reflection of his engagement with Kant's philosophy, and as a representation of Man's struggle to transcend the world of phenomena and gain access to the noumenal world. But in her reading, this struggle is set within a specifically Christian framework, for as she writes, 'in Kleist's world, salvation is found, if at all, in a renewed, higher form of blindness which transcends physical perception in that it apprehends the invisible numinous realm by the disclosure of a new, religious organ of cognition'.[20] As we shall see however, this type of reading is open to objection on at least two accounts. Not only is it far from clear what such notions as 'infinite grace' and 'infinite consciousness' could mean when applied to the behaviour of concretely existing, finite human beings, but it is equally questionable whether the behaviour of Kleist's mechanical puppet can be accepted thus uncritically as the embodiment of an ideal state of human grace. This is an issue to which we will return when we look more closely at the most 'puppet-like' of all Kleist's creations, the 'ideal woman', Käthchen von Heilbronn.

The difficulties inherent in reducing Kleist's work to an unambiguous affirmation of one set of beliefs over another are explored at some length in John Ellis's highly polemical book *Heinrich von Kleist: studies in the character and meaning of his writings*, published in 1979. His commentary on the violent disagreements between Kleist's critics reads almost like a résumé of the Wittkowski–Ryan debate itself when he suggests that 'while the critics argue over who has the better case, they do not see that the story is *about that argument*, not about the particular interpretation they are trying to make the victor in the argument.'[21] At first reading, Ellis's approach seems most compelling, not least because, in his attempt to show how 'Kleist's writings are about the *process* of coming to terms with the world, of interpreting and then reinterpreting it',[22] he displays a keen sense of the subtleties and formal complexities of the texts themselves. But despite his insistence on the need for a more flexible critical approach, when he turns specifically to the task of interpreting the texts, he does not always live up to the high standards he has set himself. In his discussion of *Prinz Friedrich von Homburg*, for example, he starts by drawing attention to the 'numerous enigmatic episodes' in the play, yet contrary to his own stated aims, quickly sets about resolving these moments of textual indeterminacy in terms of his own psychological model of the rivalry between the Prince and the Elector. In short, Ellis appeals to the inherent ambiguity of Kleist's work in order to undermine one set of interpretations only to replace them with his own re-interpretation. And whilst he is never slow to castigate other critics for their willingness to adopt 'fixed rigid positions', in the end his own approach appears hardly less rigid than those he criticises.

Given Kleist's views on the inadequacy of language as a means of communication,[23] it is not surprising that many critics should have sought to account for the paradoxical and ambiguous nature of his work in terms of his apparent scepticism vis-à-vis language.[24] Indeed the frequency with which instances of faulty communication and linguistic misunderstanding occur in his plays and stories has prompted one critic, Hans Heinz Holz, to claim that the fundamental theme of his work is language itself.[25] But, as Anthony Stephens has pointed out, quite correctly, much of the critical literature on the role of language in Kleist's work suffers from the defect that 'critics have been all too willing to take up Kleist's observations on language in general without paying due attention to the fine distinctions the author draws between different forms of discourse.'[26] One of the first critics to draw attention to the presence of a multiplicity of different discourses in Kleist's work was Max Kommerell,[27] who, in his seminal essay of 1944, *Die Sprache und das Unaussprechliche: eine Betrachtung über Heinrich von Kleist*, suggests that we can evaluate these different discourses in terms of how far they correspond to the unconscious impulses ('das Unbewußte') of the individual protagonists.[28] For Kommerell these different discourses are arranged in a continuum extending between two extremes: on the one hand, there is conventional discourse, in which the feelings of the individual are articulated in accordance with certain preconceived forms; on the other, there is the discourse of authenticity that provides access to the 'inner self'.[29] In the light of this distinction, Kommerell attempts to show how the conflict between the public and private identities of Kleist's characters is both reflected and enacted in the discursive structure of the texts themselves. But as we have already seen in the case of Müller-Seidel's study, any attempt to identify the realm of the unconscious as the locus of authenticity is bound to raise at least as many difficulties as it resolves. Nonetheless, although Kommerell's claim to have identified certain points in the text where we are confronted with moments of authentic communication is often problematic, his views have been highly influential in the subsequent development of the critical literature relating to linguistic issues in Kleist's work.

In the late seventies and early eighties, a number of critics have turned their attention to the relationship between language, power and love in order to show how in his work, Kleist explores the possibility of the dialectical construction of the self in language. To this end, Helmut Arntzen, Gerhard Neumann and, most recently, Anthony Stephens, have all argued that Kleist's work constitutes both a critique of conventional forms of discourse ('konventionelle Sprache') and a quest for an ideal form of authentic discourse ('neue Sprache') free from the effects of convention and authority.[30] However, whereas Arntzen (in common with most who see Kleist as striving throughout his life towards a dialectical synthesis of Self and Other) posits the emergence of this 'new authentic discourse' ('neue Sprache') at the end of *Prinz Friedrich von Homburg*,[31] Neumann and Stephens are rather more cautious, suggesting that, at best, Kleist's work merely gestures in the direction of such a utopian condition. Indeed for Stephens, the fact that any such gesture is almost always thwarted by the forces of convention and authority is seen as symptomatic of Kleist's scepticism regarding the possibility of a 'fresh start' in the aftermath of the French Revolution.[32]

The fact that Kleist's work does not appear to uphold such metaphysical notions as 'absolute communication' and 'perfect selfhood' need not, however, be seen as indicative of a pessimistic cast of mind. As we shall see, in rejecting such notions, his work draws attention to their illusory and wholly artificial character. For just as the non-alienated 'consciousness' of the Kleistian marionette is the property of an artificial, man-made construction, so too perfect formal transparency is not a property of natural language, but a quality to be found only in artificial languages (such as perhaps mathematical logic). Moreover, the attempt to attribute a particular teleological view of history to Kleist – whether optimistic (as in Arntzen's case) or pessimistic (as in Stephens's case) – may well raise more problems than it solves. For it is precisely this tendency on the part of human beings to place reliance on metaphysical accounts of historical and personal development that is so ruthlessly called into question in his work. The absence of any such teleological perspective need not be seen as implying that Kleist did not believe in the possibility of human improvement. For whilst he presents us with an uncompromisingly realistic picture of human behaviour, his realism is such that he never portrays Man as 'inherently good' or 'inherently evil'. Accordingly, he imputes neither an optimistic nor a pessimistic teleology to the course of history. What he does show is that if we are prepared to confront the finite nature of human beings (which is what distinguishes real human beings from their fictional counterparts) we will discover that they do have a genuine capacity for self-improvement. Therefore it makes little sense to speak of Kleist's pessimism in respect of the possibility of 'fresh start' in history, since for him there can never be a clean break with the past, only a modification – possibly for the better, possibly for the worse – of what has gone before.

IDEALS AND ILLUSIONS

The aim of the present study is to show how Kleist explores the problems that arise when human beings look to metaphysical categories embodied in the prescriptive conventions of their society, in an attempt to protect themselves against the inroads of uncertainty in their everyday affairs. As we shall see, it is the uncritical acceptance of such metaphysical notions – 'perfect' justice, 'infallible' feminine virtue, the hero who is 'incapable' of fear, the 'irredeemably' wicked man and the like – that prevents Kleist's characters from discovering the true nature of their predicaments and hence from taking appropriate action. Thus in *Amphitryon*, Alkmene is led astray by her (mistaken) belief that she is so 'perfectly' in love with her husband, that she is, quite literally, 'incapable' of infidelity. In his other plays, Kleist shows us a number of societies dominated by ideologies masquerading as genuine insights into a 'natural' social order, but which are, for the most part, man-made conventions reflecting the interests of a dominant class. In *Die Familie Schroffenstein*, the juxtaposition of Rossitz and Warwand society draws attention to the particular ideology that underpins each of their contrasting views of 'human nature'. Likewise, in *Amphitryon*, the presence of Jupiter and Mercury allows the audience to see that the institutions and culture of Theban society are simply a series of *ad hoc* arrangements designed to sustain Amphitryon's bare-faced dictatorship.

In several of his plays, Kleist explores the possibility that true love, by excluding all considerations of self-interest, might enable lovers to break free from these elaborate systems of pretence that stand in the way of genuine self-knowledge and self-fulfilment. Thus for a moment it seems possible that in *Die Familie Schroffenstein*, the love affair between Agnes and Ottokar might offer a way out of the conflict between the two families; that in *Penthesilea*, the love affair between the queen and Achilles might provide a means of transcending the gulf between the culture of the Greeks and that of the Amazons. In the final analysis, however, these 'utopian idylls' are shown to be illusions, shot through with insincerities and irredeemably grounded in the social realities from which they seek to escape. In this way, Kleist reminds his audience that often it is where ideology appears to be positively absent, that it is most actively present. Even in a play, such as *Das Käthchen von Heilbronn*, in which the love affair between Strahl and Käthchen survives against all the odds, the kind of love involved is inimical to the problem presented in the play, and results only in the perpetuation of a social system that is manifestly flawed and desperately in need of radical change. Indeed in Kleist's works, such love affairs almost invariably signify not a fresh start in human affairs, but on the contrary, a continuation of the *status quo*.

Are we justified, then, in regarding Kleist's work as an unrelievedly pessimistic commentary on the human predicament? Is the real import of his work to point out the way in which human achievements are always bound to fall short of 'the ideal'? Does he really believe that the love between man and woman is necessarily doomed from the outset? I think not. For as we shall see, although Kleist sets up such 'idylls' of love only to demolish them, it is not his intention to discredit the notion of love itself, but to expose the extent to which the conception of love to which his characters subscribe is flawed, being little more than a conventional arrangement of sexual relations designed to serve the interests of a predominantly male-oriented culture in which the element of ownership is paramount. The same might be said of his presentation of another important area of human concern, namely justice. Thus although in *Der zerbrochne Krug*, he points out how far the prevailing conception of 'justice' serves the interests of a corrupt state, once again, it is not justice *per se* that he criticises, but rather the pretentious version of it that Walter and Adam serve. Nevertheless, in exposing these defects in the notions of 'love' and 'justice' as they appear in his plays, Kleist's aim is to not to discourage individuals from the pursuit of the ideal, but rather to argue the need for a new way of attaining the ideal, one which would take into account both the limitations of finite human beings and their positive capacity for self-improvement (a way more in line, perhaps, with his understanding of Kant). And it is in this that the genuinely emancipatory thrust of Kleist's art consists. For underlying the specific concerns of each play, we can discern a more general theme, namely the dangers for human progress inherent in a particular type of moral and aesthetic theory, the origins of which go back to Plato. This theory – which is remorselessly pilloried by Kleist – holds out the possibility that philosophers, visionaries, artists and writers have privileged access to a so-called 'transcendent' realm of existents – 'perfect love', 'perfect justice', 'perfect beauty' and the like. It is further claimed that by contemplating these 'ideal' forms, this privileged elite are in a position to fashion temporal versions of these great central concepts for the guidance of lesser mortals. This view is open to criticism on at least two counts, both of which Kleist rehearses in his correspondence and in his literary works. Firstly, there are no good grounds for believing that human beings have access to any such 'transcendent' realm. Kleist's reading of Kant would appear to have confirmed this. Secondly, this view appears increasingly suspect when we remind ourselves of the sinister regularity with which ruling elites throughout history have gained an advantage from this claim to have privileged access to a 'transcendent' realm and to have based what are merely class-biased conventions in the legal, moral and aesthetic fields on such 'perfect transcendent models'. In addition, Kleist is able to show that the application of this theory to everyday life causes many problems, even for its 'beneficiaries'. The prevailing concepts of love, morality and aesthetics being so obviously slanted in their favour (and not in fact derived from a 'transcendent' source) there is every chance that the fraudulent character of these 'ideals' will be unmasked. Because of this, the ruling elite is compelled to resort to increasingly grotesque acts of self-deception in an attempt to deny the obvious imperfections in the temporal human institutions over which they preside and thereby to maintain their privileged position. But as Kleist shows us time and again, human beings, no matter what their status, ignore reality at their peril.

The major appeal of such notions of 'perfection' and their 'transcendent' provenance lies in the illusion of certainty they provide. Yet as Kleist points out, such certainty is simply not available to finite human beings. In *Prinz Friedrich von Homburg*, for example, the Elector believes that if his perfect battle plan is followed to the letter, it must, of necessity, lead to total victory over the Swedes, and it is left to Kottwitz to point out that such seemingly 'infallible' master strategies have to be carried out with real soldiers on real battlefields and rarely fit these hard human facts. Not only are such allegedly 'transcendent' insights of little value as a guide to life: they also pose a serious threat to individual and social improvement. Blinded by the hazy rhetoric in which these fictions are peddled, even the sincere seeker after truth is distracted from readily available gradual reforms by the vain hope of attaining, *via* some glorious metaphysical revelation, a final and incontestable solution. In fact, preoccupation with these romantic visions actually encourages despair of existing institutions which instead require careful re-examination, building on their good points and eliminating defects.

Are we then to see Kleist as an essentially didactic author? Again, I think not. For he is too sophisticated a writer to fall into the trap of presenting us with 'ideal' figures held up for our uncritical admiration. Indeed it would be quite against his ideas on education were he to do so[33] and thus it comes as no surprise that his plays often end on a tantalisingly ambiguous note, epitomised by Alkmene's final pregnant 'Ach!' at the end of *Amphitryon.* Likewise, even in those plays which appear to end with the structures of the existing order intact, for example *Das Käthchen von Heilbronn*, *Amphitryon* and *Prinz Friedrich von Homburg*, we are left to wonder whether everything will carry on as it did before. Will Amphitryon and Alkmene simply excise all memory of Jupiter's visitation from their minds? Will the Prince and the Elector forget how close they came to the point of disaster? At this juncture, it may be helpful to draw a comparison between Kleist's stage-craft and his manipulation of narrative perspective in his prose fiction. Like the characters in his novellas, his stage-characters are presented from a variety of different perspectives, with the result that we are continually obliged to revise our impressions of them. In what follows, I shall be concerned to suggest that we should view the plays with the same degree of ironic detachment we bring to his *contes moraux* ('Moralische Erzählungen'; *SW* II, 835). But whilst Kleist never tires of playing with his audience, he does, of course, do far more than simply question structures of meaning and interpretation. As we shall see in the next chapter, he had very clear views on what was wrong with the society of his time and how it might be improved. Nor did he think that it was beyond the capacity of his fellow human beings to implement such changes. And by showing how, despite their best intentions, human beings are all too often led to behave in ways they subsequently regret, his plays hint – albeit subtly – at ways in which disaster might have been avoided.

PART I

The young Kleist

CHAPTER 2

The quest for 'Glück'

Although Kleist was to meet with all manner of personal misfortune during his own lifetime, his writing consistently bears witness to his firm belief in the capacity of human beings for self-improvement and in the vital role of art and literature in assisting them towards this goal. He persistently sought to establish the conditions under which the individual might enjoy the greatest degree of personal autonomy, and both the exhilaration of this quest, and the realisation of the limited extent to which this goal could be achieved are clearly reflected in his personal correspondence and in his work as a whole.[1] Whilst his writings can at times seem unremittingly gloomy, this is not because he despaired of his fellow human beings, but rather because he was so acutely aware of the nearly insuperable obstacles society placed in the way of individual self-fulfilment. The insistence with which he explores the tension between the aspirations of the individual and the demands of society shows how profoundly he was engaged in the philosophical and literary debates of his age, a fact further confirmed by the numerous allusions in his writing to the ideals and values of his eighteenth-century upbringing and, above all, to the works of Goethe and Schiller. Unwilling to accept the uncertainty that is an unavoidable part of everyday human existence, the young Kleist continually looked to the ideal models put forward in the works of his literary forebears in an attempt to shore up his own life against the caprices of fate and chance. Time and again, however, he was forced to recognise the discrepancy between the world as it is in fiction and the world as it is in fact.

Kleist's overwhelming desire to remove the element of uncertainty from his own life is apparent even in the title of his earliest essay, *Aufsatz, den sichern Weg des Glücks zu finden und ungestört – auch unter den größten Drangsalen des Lebens – ihn zu genießen!* (*An essay on the means whereby Man can be certain to attain and enjoy a state of lasting happiness under even the most adverse of circumstances!*).[2] In this essay – in which the influence of his upbringing in the tradition of the Enlightenment is very obvious[3] – he attempts to establish the conditions which he believes must of necessity lead to an enduring state of human happiness ('Glück'). Starting from the premise that happiness is something to which all human beings have an equal claim, he argues that in a world created by a just God, happiness must lie equally within the grasp of every individual. Accordingly, happiness cannot be contingent upon our material well-being, since not all human beings enjoy the same standards of material comfort and, furthermore, these are always liable to change without warning. In the light of this, Kleist arrives at the conclusion that the only secure basis for lasting human happiness is that of knowing that we have acted in accordance with the dictates of our moral will: 'in virtue and virtue alone' he says, 'lies the source of human happiness and thus the most virtuous man is also the happiest' ('die Tugend, und einzig allein nur die Tugend ist die Mutter des Glücks, und *der Beste ist der Glücklichste*'; *SW* II, 303).

Despite the at times extravagant conclusions which he draws from his metaphysical speculations on the nature of human happiness, Kleist never loses sight of the limitations of finite human nature. Indeed he openly admits that in advocating the practice of virtue as a means to happiness, he is falling short of the highest ideal which should be, surely, the practice of virtue for its own sake. However, he seeks to justify this (not without a passing sense of regret) on the grounds that such exceptional moral athleticism is 'a quality possessed by only a few beautiful souls' ('das Eigentum einiger wenigen schönern Seelen'; *SW* II, 303) and as such, beyond the capabilities of most ordinary individuals. In the light of this, he offers his programme for the attainment of happiness as a realistic compromise:

Aber mein Herz sagt mir, daß die Erwartung und Hoffnung auf ein menschliches Glück, und die Aussicht auf tugendhafte, wenn freilich nicht mehr ganz so reine Freuden, dennoch nicht strafbar und verbrecherisch sei. (*SW* II, 303)

(But my heart tells me that to expect and hope for a sentient happiness along with the prospect of virtuous joys, though this be no longer so pure, is still not culpable and criminal.)

Indeed, it was this tension between, on the one hand, his desire for absolute certainty, and on the other, his awareness of the limitations of human nature that was to exercise so profound an influence on him during the early years of his aesthetic and philosophical development. Even so, the apparent 'realism' of his discourse on the nature of happiness also serves to disguise its essentially speculative character, since although it is perfectly plausible to suggest that an individual who consistently tries to act virtuously may, in a world of like-minded individuals, be more likely to enjoy the feeling of happiness that derives from having a clear conscience, it is an altogether different proposition to claim that such moral behaviour will of necessity lead to happiness. Kleist himself seems to have had some sense of the flawed nature of his argument when he anticipates an imaginary objection on the part of his reader[4] saying:

Ich weiß es, Sie halten diese Art zu denken für ein künstliches aber wohl glückliches Hülfsmittel, sich die trüben Wolken des Schicksals hinweg zu philosophieren, und mitten unter Sturm und Donner sich Sonnenschein zu erträumen. (*SW* II, 305)

(I know that you regard this way of thinking as a crutch, albeit a comforting one, as simply a way of philosophising away the dark clouds of fate and of conjuring up a little ray of sunshine in the midst of the storm.)

For although he admires the ability of human beings to construct such metaphysical arguments, he is fully aware that the truth or falsity of such *a priori* accounts of the relationship between happiness and morality cannot be validated either empirically or metaphysically, but is, in the final analysis, solely dependent upon an act of faith. Unable to put forward any logical arguments that would counter his friend's scepticism, Kleist is left with no option other than to emphasise the pleasurable benefits that the latter would reap, could he but find such faith within himself:

Das ist nun freilich doppelt übel, daß Sie so schlecht von dieser himmlischen Kraft der Seele denken, einmal, weil Sie unendlich viel dadurch entbehren, und zweitens, weil es schwer, ja unmöglich ist, Sie besser davon denken zu machen. (*SW* II, 305)

(It is doubly unfortunate that you think so ill of this divine power of the human spirit, firstly, because you are denying yourself so much and secondly, because it is hard, indeed quite impossible, to convince you to adopt a more favourable view of the matter.)

However, as we shall see, it is the failure to recognise that the attainment of happiness is only a possible, and indeed far from necessary, consequence of virtuous behaviour that stands in the way of human beings achieving either.

In the second part of the essay, Kleist explores the problems that arise when individuals are held too tightly in the grip of idealised descriptions of human achievement found in certain forms of art and literature. Here he notes that the restricted and often mundane circumstances in which the majority of people are compelled to live their lives can lead to their becoming too preoccupied with such mythical accounts of superlative virtue of the sort that is rarely, if indeed ever, encountered in fact. As a result they fail to appreciate the more modest achievements of real persons in everyday life. For when these real, but modest, achievements are measured against the extravagant deeds of fictional characters, the result is bound to be disappointment. This in turn can lead to a pessimistic view of human nature[5] and a rejection of, and even withdrawal from, society altogether. Yet it is important to note that the root cause of our disappointment is not in fact the shortcomings of others, but rather the unrealistic expectations of our inflamed imaginations. For as Kleist writes:

Wie oft gründet sich das Unglück eines Menschen bloß darin, daß er den Dingen unmögliche Wirkungen zuschrieb, oder aus Verhältnissen falsche Resultate zog, und sich darinnen in seinen Erwartungen betrog. (*SW* II, 310)

(How often is it not the case that our disappointments are simply due to our attributing impossible qualities to things, or drawing quite erroneous inferences from situations with the result that we are guilty of the most unrealistic expectations.)

For as Kleist points out, his friend's misanthropic view of human nature flies in the face of their own first-hand experiences during their travels together in the Harz mountains, where on numerous occasions, the local inhabitants offered them all manner of assistance without any thought of reward. Accordingly, Kleist advocates a policy of moderation and advises us to be realistic in our expectations: 'we cannot, and indeed should not, demand huge sacrifices on the part of others' ('große Opfer darf und soll man auch nicht verlangen'; *SW* II, 315).

THE INDIVIDUAL AND SOCIETY

In his essay on happiness, Kleist advocates the practice of morality as the only sure means by which the individual could protect himself against the caprices of fate and chance. In so doing, he offers a 'solution' to what he sees as the prevailing malaise of his time, for as he wrote to his sister, Ulrike, in May 1799:

> Tausend Menschen höre ich reden und sehe ich handeln, und es fällt mir nicht ein, nach dem Warum? zu fragen. Sie selbst wissen es nicht, dunkle Neigungen leiten sie, der Augenblick bestimmt ihre Handlungen. Sie bleiben für immer unmündig und ihr Schicksal ein Spiel des Zufalls. (*SW* II, 488)[6]

> (I hear the words and observe the deeds of thousands of people, and never does it occur to me to ask: to what end? They themselves do not know; dark impulses lead them, the moment decides their actions. They are forever dependent and their destinies remain a game of chance.)

Through the use of reason ('Vernunft') and the construction of a rational plan for his life ('Lebensplan'), the individual could take control of his or her own destiny and live a life free from internal contradictions. By contrast the individual who abjures the use of reason was destined to remain nothing more than 'a puppet whose strings are operated by fate' ('eine Puppe am Drahte des Schicksals'; *SW* II, 490). Yet before the individual could scale the exhilarating heights of such total metaphysical emancipation, there was a rather more prosaic obstacle to be overcome, namely the rigidly hierarchical structure of institutionalised Prussian life, and above all, of the Prussian army in which Kleist served as an officer from 1792–1799. Indeed, it is tempting to speculate just how far his desire for such absolute freedom was prompted by the relative lack of personal autonomy (in a more concrete sense) that a man of his age and status would have enjoyed in the society in which he lived. For in his eyes, the army – 'a living monument to tyranny' ('ein lebendiges Monument der Tyrannei'; *SW* II, 479) – was a perfect example of the disastrous consequences of instrumental reason when applied to the design and maintenance of a vital human institution. For in submitting to the rational organisation of the whole, each individual was reduced to a purely functional role and thereby deprived of any sense of his own moral autonomy. Not only did Kleist see that the ordinary soldiers were reduced to the level of obedient slaves ('Sklaven'), but that in acting against his own inner convictions, he himself, *qua* officer, was little more than the blind instrument of the military hierarchy:

Ich war oft gezwungen, zu strafen, wo ich gern verziehen hätte, oder verzieh, wo ich hätte strafen sollen . . . In solchen Augenblicken mußte natürlich der Wunsch in mir entstehen, einen Stand zu verlassen, in welchem ich von zwei durchaus entgegengesetzten Prinzipien unaufhörlich gemartert wurde, immer zweifelhaft war, ob ich als Mensch oder als Offizier handeln mußte; denn die Pflichten beider zu vereinen, halte ich bei dem jetzigen Zustande der Armeen für unmöglich. (*SW* II, 479)

(I was often compelled to punish when I would gladly have pardoned, or I pardoned when I should really have punished . . . At such moments, the wish to leave such a profession began to grow within me as a matter of course, constantly martyred as I was between two completely incompatible principles, and always in doubt whether to act as an officer or as a human being, for I consider it an impossibility to combine the obligations of both under present conditions in the military.) [M, 22]

However, it is important to note that by adding 'under *present* conditions in the military' (my emphasis), Kleist makes it clear that he believes that even the army is not beyond reform and his subsequent experience of Parisian society was sufficient to convince him that, however imperfect they might be, the institutions of his native Prussia were infinitely preferable to their French counterparts.

It was not just in the army, however, that Kleist saw that the individual was deprived of his sense of moral autonomy. For having made up his mind to resign his commission, he was equally determined not to suffer a similar fate within the Prussian civil service, and in his letter to his fiancée, Wilhelmine von Zenge, of 13 November 1800, he sets out his reasons for declining such a position: 'I am expected to do what the State asks of me, and yet may not inquire whether what it asks is good . . . I cannot' [M, 73] ('Ich soll tun was der Staat von mir verlangt, und doch soll ich nicht untersuchen, ob das, was er von mir verlangt, gut ist . . . ich kann es nicht'; *SW* II, 584). He had decided, therefore, to take up the study of mathematics and philosophy at the university in Frankfurt an der Oder, but had quickly become disenchanted with the aridity of his studies and their near total neglect of the emotional side of human life, as his letter of 12 November 1799 to his sister, Ulrike, shows: 'While one is eternally proving this and deducing that, the heart almost forgets how to feel; and yet happiness dwells only in the heart, in the feelings, and not in the head and its understanding' [M, 30] ('Bei dem ewigen Beweisen und Folgern verlernt das Herz fast zu fühlen; und doch wohnt das Glück nur im Herzen, nur im Gefühl, nicht im Kopfe, nicht im Verstande'; *SW* II, 494). For Kleist, as for so many of his contemporaries, the dualistic anthropology of the radical Enlightenment and in particular, its objectification of human nature, was seen as something that had destroyed the unity of Man. Thus in the same letter, he goes on – in terms that, as is the case with so many of his early writings, are clearly indebted to his reading of Goethe's *Wilhelm Meister*[7] – to emphasise the complementary roles of reason ('Verstand') and feeling ('Gefühl') in the development of the complete human personality:

> man müßte wenigstens täglich *ein* gutes Gedicht lesen, *ein* schönes Gemälde sehen, *ein* sanftes Lied hören – oder ein herzliches Wort mit einem Freunde reden, um auch den schönern, ich möchte sagen den menschlicheren Teil unseres Wesen zu bilden. (*SW* II, 494)

> (one should read at least *one* good poem daily, see *one* beautiful painting, hear *one* sweet melody, or exchange heart to heart words with a friend, and thus educate the more beautiful, I might say the more human, side of our nature as well.) [M, 30]

Kleist's critical response to the dualistic categories of the radical Enlightenment is reflected most clearly, however, in his attitude towards Nature. Far from being merely a collection of objective facts to be 'mastered' by the rational individual, he regarded the natural world as an organic unity, an idealised model of perfection, against which Man could measure himself. For as he wrote to Wilhelmine on 5 September 1800:

Einsamkeit in der offnen Natur, das ist der Prüfstein des Gewissens. In Gesellschaften, auf den Straßen, in dem Schauspiele mag es schweigen, denn da wirken die Gegenstände nur auf den Verstand und bei ihnen braucht man kein Herz. Aber wenn man die weite, edlere, erhabenere Schöpfung vor sich sieht, – ja da braucht man ein Herz, da regt es sich unter der Brust und klopft an das Gewissen. (*SW* II, 547–8)[8]

(Solitude in nature's great openness: that is the touchstone of one's true moral worth. In the salons, on the street, in the theatre, our moral judgement is silent, there things appeal only to the intellect, and one has no need of the heart. But when we see the spacious, more noble, more sublime Creation before us, why, then one has need of a heart. Astir in our breast, its beating awakens the conscience.)

Only in aspiring to emulate the perfection of Nature, could the individual hope to escape from the corrupting influence of conventional society.

At the same time, Kleist's correspondence also reflects the extent to which he had begun to ask himself whether there were not in fact limits to the speculative powers of human reason. For when he writes to Wilhelmine on 15 September 1800, he suggests that:

Über den Zweck unseres ganzen *ewigen* Daseins nachzudenken, auszuforschen, ob der Genuß der Glückseligkeit, wie *Epikur* meinte, oder die Erreichung der Vollkommenheit, wie *Leibniz* glaubte, oder die Erfüllung der trocknen Pflicht, wie *Kant* versicherte, der letzte Zweck des Menschen sei, das ist selbst für Männer unfruchtbar und oft verderblich. (*SW* II, 565)

(To reflect on the goal of our existence for all eternity, probing whether mankind's ultimate purpose is the highest happiness, as *Epicurus* believed, or the achievement of perfection, as *Leibniz* believed, or the fulfilment of dry Duty, as *Kant* assures us – such speculation is unfruitful even for men, often even destructive.) [M, 63]

Since, as Kant had shown, Man could observe the totality of Nature only from his own restricted viewpoint, the ultimate purpose of Nature itself was inscrutable, and accordingly Kleist concludes that only the purpose ('Bestimmung') of the individual's earthly life can be a proper object of rational inquiry:

Also wage Dich mit Deinem Verstande nie über die Grenzen Deines Lebens hinaus . . . Was Du für dieses Erdenleben tun sollst, das kannst Du begreifen, was Du für die Ewigkeit tun sollst, nicht; (*SW* II, 565)

(Do not venture, then, beyond the limits of your own life . . . You may comprehend what to do for your earthly life, but not for all eternity.) [M, 63]

In setting such limits to the powers of human reason, Kleist comes very close to embracing the same line of argument that Kant had put forward in the *Critique of pure reason* in an attempt to show that the speculative ambitions of deductive metaphysics were, in principle, unrealisable. In the light of this, it is perhaps strange that he should take so disparaging a view of the Kantian concept of 'duty' that forms the central pillar of the latter's ethical theory.[9] For Kleist, however, the radical separation of duty and inclination was quite at odds with his own conception of Man as an organic unity. But whilst he rejects the 'dry duty' ('trockne Pflicht') of Kantian ethics, he does not dispense with the notion of 'Pflicht' altogether. In his view the duty of each human being consisted in striving towards the fullest possible expression of his authentic individuality, and thus the ultimate aim of such self-cultivation ('Bildung') consisted in each individual making, *via* his own self-realisation, the only contribution to the grand design of Nature as a whole that he can properly make. For as he notes in a short essay, *Über die Aufklärung des Weibes (On the enlightenment of woman)* that he sent to his fiancée together with the letter above:

Dabei bin ich überzeugt, gewiß in den großen ewigen Plan der Natur einzugreifen, wenn ich nur den Platz ganz erfülle, auf den sie mich in dieser Erde setzte. (*SW* II, 318)

(Accordingly I am convinced that I shall be sure to partake in the grand, eternal plan of Nature if I merely confine myself to making the most out of the situation here on earth into which I have been placed.)

It was not long, however, before Kleist was to feel only too keenly the obstacles that conventional society placed in the way of the quest for personal authenticity. For in advocating that Man should mirror the perfection of Nature, he was continually forced to recognise the extent to which those around him – and indeed he himself – fell short of this ideal. Nonetheless, he still believed that it was possible for the individual to free himself from the distorting influence of social convention, and this is clearly shown by his enthusiastic endorsement of his fiancée's analogy of the mirror. For as he wrote to her on 29 November 1800:

Ganz vortrefflich . . . ist der Gedanke, daß es bei dem Menschen, wie bei dem Spiegel, auf seine eigne Beschaffenheit ankommt, wie fremde Gegenstände auf ihn einwirken sollen. Aber nun . . . müssen wir auch die Lehre nutzen, und fleißig an dem Spiegel unserer Seele schleifen, damit er glatt und klar werde, und treu das Bild der schönen Natur zurückwerfe. (*SW* II, 605)

(What a splendid notion, the idea that people are like mirrors, insofar as it is their own particular qualities that determine what sort of an impression others make upon them. But now . . . we must profit from this lesson and work on improving our soul's mirror so that it becomes smooth and clear and perfectly reflects Nature's beauty.)

The motif of reflection is one that persistently recurs throughout his correspondence and one that offers us a number of insights into the nature of Kleist's views not only on social convention, but also on language itself. In an earlier letter of 18 November 1800, he draws his fiancée's attention to the fact that the image we see in the mirror is always subject to a two-fold distortion. For in addition to the unavoidable distortion caused by the external surface of the mirror ('die vordere Seite'), there is the far more serious distortion caused by its internal surface ('die hintere Seite'). Accordingly, he writes that:

die *äußere* (vordere) Seite des Spiegels nicht eigentlich bei dem Spiegel die Hauptsache sei, ja, daß diese eigentlich weiter nichts ist, als ein notwendiges Übel, indem sie das eigentliche Bild nur verwirrt, daß es aber hingegen vorzüglich auf die Glätte und Politur der *inneren* (hinteren) Seite ankomme, wenn das Bild recht rein und treu sein soll. (*SW* II, 596)

(the *external* (the nearer) side of the mirror is really not its most important part, and indeed is really nothing more than a necessary evil, in that the reflected image is merely disarranged in it, but that contrariwise the smoothness and polish of the *inner* (the further) side is what counts most if the reflection is to be pure and true.) [M, 77]

The blemishes on the *internal* surface of the mirror correspond to those left on the self by the pernicious effects of social convention, blemishes which the individual could, and should, strive to remove in the attempt to realise an ever more authentic expression of his or her true self, and to perceive other selves as they really are.

Essentially the same arguments can be advanced in respect of the relationship between language and individual self-expression. For when Kleist suggests that the slight blurring caused by the exterior surface of the mirror is 'a necessary evil' ('ein notwendiges Übel') his words call to mind a similar observation in a much later essay, *Brief eines Dichters an einen anderen (Letter from one poet to another)* in which he suggests that language, rhythm and melody are also 'a veritable, if also natural and necessary, evil' [M, 236] ('ein wahrer, obschon natürlicher und notwendiger Übelstand'; *SW* II, 348) insofar as they too result in a certain inevitable distortion of the idea they are used to convey. Seen only from this angle, Kleist's view on language amounts to little more than the relatively common-place notion that *any* idea, once expressed in language, is inevitably subject to some degree of distortion. But it is in his insistence on the need to work at refining the *internal* surface of the mirror ('die hintere Seite') that he alerts us to the possibility of a second-order distortion that in his view is far more serious. For if the imperfections of the external surface of the mirror ('die vordere Seite') are to be equated with the pitfalls of language itself and are, as such, to a large extent unavoidable, then the defects on the internal surface ('die hintere Seite') correspond to the much more serious distortions caused by ideology and other conventional structures of discourse. Even so, whilst such ideological modes of discourse constituted a considerable obstacle to genuine knowledge of the self and of the external world, it was, he maintained, an obstacle that could be overcome through human endeavour.

The extent to which he felt the conventions of society stood in the way of authentic self-expression can be seen most clearly in his observations on the salon culture of literary Berlin. For as he wrote to Ulrike on 5 February 1801:

> Indessen wenn ich mich in Gesellschaften nicht wohl befinde, so geschieht dies weniger, weil andere, als vielmehr weil ich mich selbst nicht zeige, wie ich es wünsche. Die Notwendigkeit, eine Rolle zu spielen, und ein innerer Widerwillen dagegen machen mir jede Gesellschaft lästig, und froh kann

ich nur in meiner eignen Gesellschaft sein, weil ich da ganz wahr sein darf. (*SW* II, 628)

(Thus it may be that, if I am ill at ease in the salons, it is less because of others than because I myself do not appear as I would like. The need to play a role, and an inner repugnance for it, make social gatherings burdensome for me, and I can only be happy in my own company, because there I can be what I really am.) [M, 92]

Not only was Kleist well aware that those around him were merely acting in accordance with what was expected of them, but, in addition, he is filled with despair at the degree to which he himself is implicated in such conventional role-playing. Nonetheless, however painful this process of self-scrutiny may be, it is important to recognise that it is precisely this capacity for critical introspection that enables us to recognise the conventional character of human existence for what it is and thereby to avoid falling into the same trap ourselves. There are even moments when Kleist draws considerable comfort from this consideration and suggests that the apparent immorality that we see around us is not in fact due to the inherently 'evil nature' of individual human beings, but is, on the contrary, a reflection of the extent to which our view of the world and of human behaviour has been distorted by ideology and social convention. For as he writes:

Ich weiß wohl, daß . . . mancher würde aufhören über die Verderbtheit der Sitten zu schelten, wenn ihm der Gedanke einfiele, ob nicht vielleicht bloß der Spiegel, in welchen das Bild der Welt fällt, schief und schmutzig ist. (*SW* II, 628)

(I know very well that . . . many would stop decrying the decline of morals if the thought once occurred to them that perhaps it is really the mirror in which the world that they see is reflected that is so dirty and distorted.) [M, 92]

Accordingly, we should be less hasty to condemn individuals for holding opinions which, strictly speaking, are not actually their own, and more sanguine about the prospects of improving the prevailing structures of society so as to make it easier for individuals to enjoy a greater degree of personal autonomy and a correspondingly more authentic existence.

THE 'UTOPIA' OF LOVE

Throughout his early correspondence, Kleist looks upon love as a relationship that makes possible an infallibly honest communication between lovers that is proof against the pernicious effects of social convention. In conventional society, considerations of self-interest and the fear of rejection put pressure upon the individual to present a distorted image of his or herself that is acceptable to others. By contrast, love, in the ideal sense in which Kleist conceives it, is a relation that is devoid of all such considerations and one in which the individual can, accordingly, reveal his or her true self to the other. It was this quality of altruism ('Uneigennützigkeit') that he so admired in his travelling companion, Ludwig von Brockes, and above all in his sister, Ulrike, to whom he wrote on 5 February 1801:

Nie denke ich anders an Dich, als mit Stolz und Freude, denn Du bist . . . der einzige Mensch, von dem ich sagen kann, daß er mich ganz ohne ein eignes Interesse, ganz ohne eigne Absichten, kurz, daß er nur *mich selbst* liebt. (*SW* II, 625)

(I never think of you but with pride and joy, for . . . of no other fellow being, could I find it within me to say: he loves me without any self-interest, with no self-serving intentions whatsoever; in short, he loves me *for myself alone.*) [M, 89–90]

Nonetheless, his enthusiastic endorsement of her qualities is tempered by the painful awareness that, as yet, he had no experience of such selfless behaviour on his own part that would convince him that he too was capable of reciprocating such altruistic love:

Recht schmerzhaft ist es mir, daß ich nicht ein Gleiches von mir sagen kann, obgleich Du es gewiß weit mehr verdienst, als ich; denn Du hast zu viel für mich getan, als daß meine Freundschaft, in welche sich schon die Dankbarkeit mischt, ganz rein sein könnte. (*SW* II, 625)

(It is truly painful to be unable to say the same for myself in regard to you, although you are certainly far more deserving than I, for you have already done so much for me that my feelings of friendship, mixed with those of gratitude, are no longer pure.) [M, 90]

In drawing attention to his own 'short-comings', however, he is guilty of idolising both Brockes and his sister to the extent of crediting them with a wholly 'infallible' capacity for altruistic behaviour. In addition, his correspondence betrays the fact that – at this stage of his development – he is quite unaware just how self-contradictory this notion of 'infallible' virtue is. Thus when he writes to Wilhelmine on 31 January 1801, declaring his intention to emulate the 'perfect' virtue of Brockes,[10] he falls into the trap of striving for an 'ideal' that is wholly illusory, and in fact a contradiction in terms. That is to say, he fails to appreciate that it is never possible for human beings to act in the certain knowledge that they are doing so from wholly altruistic motives. More importantly, however, he fails to understand that it is precisely this element of uncertainty, together with the capacity to reflect on the motivation underlying our actions, that makes such altruistic acts possible in the first place. For if there were human beings who were in fact 'incapable' of acting from anything other than 'altruistic' motives, then this would not only render the concept of 'altruism' meaningless, but with it the notion of moral freedom itself. Had Kleist been able to look into the minds of his idols, Ulrike and Brockes, he would have seen that they were no less subject to doubts than he. This in turn might have prompted him to scrutinise his own motives rather more closely, thereby increasing the likelihood of genuinely selfless behaviour on his part.

It was this same desire for absolute certainty in human affairs – together with his failure to realise that it is the very impossibility of such certainty that is the essence of love – that was to poison Kleist's relationship with his fiancée, Wilhelmine von Zenge. Nowhere is this clearer than in one of his earliest letters to her, in which he begs her: 'lead me into the inner sanctuary of your heart, whose feelings I am still uncertain of' ('Führen Sie mich einmal in das Heiligtum Ihres Herzens das ich noch nicht mit Gewißheit kenne; *SW* II, 502). This letter bears witness to the almost continual agony Kleist experienced in his attempt to elicit an affirmation of love that would, once and for all, remove every vestige of doubt from his mind. Despite the emphatic tone of his declaration: 'I am *completely convinced* that you love me' [M, 34] ('eigentlich bin ich es *fest überzeugt*, daß Sie mich lieben'; *SW* II, 502), he still feels compelled to ask her for a written declaration of her love:

Ich glaube, daß . . . Sie mir einen Augenblick, voll der üppigsten und innigsten Freude bereiten werden, wenn Ihre Hand sich entschließen könnte, diese drei Worte niederzuschreiben: *ich liebe Dich.* (*SW* II, 502)

(I believe . . . that you would vouchsafe me a moment of the innermost, the *fullest* joy, if your hand could resolve itself to the writing down of these three words: *I love you* .) [M, 34]

And whilst recognising, quite correctly, that 'the fact that I love you does not necessarily mean that you are obliged to love me' ('Ich will nicht sagen, daß Sie mich lieben müßten, weil ich Sie liebe'; *SW* II, 502), the tone of the letter strongly suggests that he would prefer to believe the opposite. The letter reveals how inadequate his understanding of love was at this stage of his life. He simply fails to grasp that love is not a 'contractual arrangement', not something that can be 'possessed' once and for all, but on the contrary, a gift given by the lover to the beloved which can be withdrawn at any time. From this it is clear that the mere fact that one human being loves another does not entail that the converse relation holds. Nor is it possible for one human being to persuade, let alone force, another to fall in love with him. No assurance, however firm and solemn, could have removed all the doubts from his mind. For the source of these doubts lay not in Wilhelmine, nor indeed in his own mind, but in the nature of the love relation itself.

Kleist sought to escape from this impasse by educating his fiancée in such a way that she 'could not but love him', and he 'could not but love her', evidently unaware of the wholly self-contradictory nature of such a project. His correspondence shows the extent to which his own feelings for Wilhelmine fell short of his ideal of 'unconditional love'. It becomes increasingly clear that Kleist's aim is to 'transform' his fiancée into little more than a highly conventional masculine fantasy of 'ideal' femininity. Thus on 15 September 1800, he writes to her, imploringly:

wenn Du es mir gelingen lassen könntest, mir an Dir eine Gattin zu formen, wie ich sie für mich, eine Mutter, wie ich sie für meine Kinder wünsche, erleuchtet, aufgeklärt, vorurteillos, immer der Vernunft gehorchend, gern dem Herzen sich hingebend . . . (*SW* II, 564–5)

(If you would just allow me to succeed in moulding you into a wife and mother such as I should wish for myself and my children: enlightened, instructed, unprejudiced, ever obeisant to Reason and gladly following the dictates of her heart . . .)

Kleist is just generous enough to stop short of suggesting that she lacks the desired qualities altogether, and in a subsequent letter, he reassures her that the aim of his programme of education ('Bildung') is simply to refine and develop those qualities with which Nature has already endowed her:

Ich kenne die Masse, die ich vor mir habe, und weiß, wozu sie taugt. Es ist ein Erz mit gediegenem Golde und mir bleibt nichts übrig, als das Metall von dem Gestein zu scheiden. Klang und Gewicht und Unverletzbarkeit in der Feuerprobe hat es von der Natur erhalten, die Sonne der Liebe wird ihm Schimmer und Glanz geben. (*SW* II, 576)[11]

(I have taken the measure of the material before me and know its value. It is an ore that holds pure gold, and what I must do is separate the metal from the rock. As to tone and weight and invulnerability in the trial by fire, these it has from nature, while the sun of love lends it glitter and brightness.) [M, 67]

In other words, she is to be 'designed' in such a way as will both enable her 'creator' to see in her only those qualities that he wishes to see, qualities which will 'compel' him to love her unconditionally, and will reinforce his image of himself as a man whom Wilhelmine 'cannot help' but love. For as he continues:

Ich habe nach der metallurgischen Scheidung nichts weiter zu tun, als mich zu wärmen und zu sonnen in den Strahlen, die seine Spiegelfläche auf mich zurückwirft. (*SW* II, 576)

(the metallurgical refining once accomplished, I shall have nothing further to do but to warm and sun myself in the rays reflected upon me by its mirrored surface.) [M, 67]

Clearly, however, an inevitable effect of this process of 'refinement' – though one which Kleist fails to anticipate – will be to deprive Wilhelmine of her status as an autonomous individual, and thus of the ability to love at all. For 'love' which cannot be revoked is no love, and in his Pygmalion-like desire to transform his fiancée into the 'perfect wife', Kleist failed to see that he was destroying the very possibility of love itself.

For the details of this programme of education ('Bildung') we need look no further than book v of Jean-Jacques Rousseau's *Emile*. Kleist himself was well-acquainted with several of Rousseau's works and he tells his fiancée quite explicitly that: 'Given that I myself can no longer be on hand to see to your education personally, I can think of no better substitute than the works of Rousseau' ('Rousseau ist mir der liebste durch den ich Dich bilden mag, da ich es selbst nicht mehr unmittelbar, wie sonst, kann'; *SW* II, 655). In *Emile*, Rousseau proposes that the sexes live together in a relationship of mutual complementarity. To justify his belief that men and women should perform disparate, but complementary tasks, he refers the reader to what seemed to him the most natural situation of all, the act of love, and notes that 'in the union of the sexes each alike contributes to the common end, but in different ways. From this diversity springs the first difference which may be observed between man and woman in their moral relations. The man should be strong and active; the woman should be weak and passive' (*E*, 322). On the basis of this pseudo-biological explanation, he goes on to claim that the social hierarchy in which men and women are allotted different tasks is not arbitrary, but derived from a consideration of the 'nature' of the sexes. In line with Rousseau, Kleist assigns men and women to the public and private spheres of activity respectively. In his letter of 30 May 1800, he tells Wilhelmine:

Da findet nun die Urteilskraft zuerst, daß der Mann nicht bloß der Mann seiner Frau, sondern auch noch ein Bürger des Staates, die Frau hingegen nichts als die Frau ihres Mannes ist; daß der Mann nicht bloß Verpflichtungen gegen seine Frau, sondern auch Verpflichtungen gegen sein Vaterland, die Frau hingegen keine andern Verpflichtungen hat, als Verpflichtungen gegen ihren Mann; (*SW* II, 506)

(Then our Judgement finds, first, that the man is not only husband to his wife but a citizen of the state, while the woman is only a wife; that the man has obligations not only to his wife but to his country, while the wife has no obligations to anyone but her husband.) [M, 36]

That this is an arrangement heavily weighted in favour of the male is clearly revealed when he concludes:

daß folglich das Glück des Weibes zwar ein wichtiger und unerlaßlicher, aber nicht der *einzige* Gegenstand des Mannes, das Glück des Mannes hingegen der *alleinige* Gegenstand der Frau ist; (*SW* II, 506) (that therefore a wife's happiness, though indeed an important and irremissible concern for the man, is not his *only* one, while the husband's happiness, contrariwise, is the *sole* concern of his wife;) [M, 36]

At times the echoes of Rousseau's work in Kleist's correspondence can be very precise indeed. Thus just as Rousseau defines the 'nature' of 'ideal woman' by explaining that 'she endures patiently the wrong-doing of others' (*E*, 359), so too Kleist writes to Wilhelmine advising her that 'no virtue is more womanly than patience with the faults of others' [M, 86] ('keine Tugend ist weiblicher, als Duldsamkeit bei den Fehlern andrer'; *SW* II, 617). At this stage, Kleist would obviously be happy to endorse Rousseau's abominable conclusion: 'What is most wanted in a woman is gentleness; formed to obey a creature so imperfect as man . . . she should early learn to submit to injustice and to suffer the wrongs inflicted on her by her husband without complaint' (*E*, 333). But in his uncritical acceptance of Rousseau's programme of education, the young Kleist merely demonstrates the extent to which he was a product of his age, an age in which the early Enlightenment's more emancipated concept of femininity had been superseded by the sentimental fictions of Samuel Richardson and of Rousseau himself.[12] The fact that at this stage of his development he refrains from subjecting this conventional picture of 'woman' to closer critical scrutiny merely underlines how strong was his desire to believe that it corresponded to the way women are. Unwilling to accept the element of uncertainty that is intrinsic to the love relation itself, he seeks refuge in the illusory 'certainty' that is available only in a fictional world created by the male imagination and populated by equally fictitious 'women'. But as he was to discover, it is precisely the uncritical acceptance of such conventional fictions that makes the formation of genuinely loving relationships so difficult. This is the problem that he was to explore in so challenging a fashion in the two plays, *Penthesilea* and *Das Käthchen von Heilbronn*.

KLEIST AND KANT

Although Kleist believed that individual human beings could avail themselves of reason in order to transcend the conventional constraints of social existence, his encounter with the philosophy of

Kant was to call into question that very possibility and with it, his faith in the ideal of self-cultivation ('Bildung'). It should be said right at the outset that it is not likely that Kant himself would have endorsed Kleist's interpretation of his philosophy. In drawing so radical a distinction between the noumenal and phenomenal world, between the 'world-as-it-is-in-fact' and the 'world-as-it-is-in-appearance', Kant appeared – at least in Kleist's reading of his work[13] – to have demonstrated the impossibility of knowledge that was both absolute and objective. It is this that Kleist attempts to convey to his fiancée *via* the analogy of the 'green glasses' ('grüne Gläser') in his despairing letter of 22 March 1801:

Wenn alle Menschen statt der Augen grüne Gläser hätten, so würden sie urteilen müssen, die Gegenstände, welche sie dadurch erblicken, *sind* grün – und nie würden sie entscheiden können, ob ihr Auge ihnen, die Dinge zeigt, wie sie sind, oder ob es nicht etwas zu ihnen hinzutut, was nicht ihnen, sondern dem Auge gehört. So ist es mit dem Verstande. Wir können nicht entscheiden, ob das, was wir Wahrheit nennen, wahrhaft Wahrheit ist, oder ob es uns nur so scheint. (*SW* II, 634)

(If everyone saw the world through green glasses, they would be forced to judge that everything they saw *was* green, and could never be sure whether their eyes saw things as they really are, or did not add something of their own to what they saw. And so it is with our intellect. We can never be certain that that which we call Truth is really Truth, or whether it does not merely appear so to us.) [M, 95]

In Kleist's view, Kant's categories of space, time, cause and effect (the 'green glasses' referred to above) constituted a third, and this time insurmountable, barrier to the understanding of the noumenal world in addition to the already considerable barriers of language and social convention.[14] Now he had to come to terms with the consideration that if the self is a proper constituent of the noumenal world (and clearly he believed that it was) then Kant appeared to have removed all possibility of genuine self-knowledge which, as we have already seen, is so central to Kleist's ideal of self-cultivation ('Bildung'). This meant that in advocating the pursuit of genuine self-knowledge, he was exhorting both himself and those around him to seek knowledge of an object which Kant – at least in Kleist's interpretation of his epistemology – had shown to be excluded from the domain of rational inquiry.

If Kleist had looked to reason as a means of surmounting the obstacles to truth constituted by social conventions, it now seemed as though he was inescapably trapped within them, and it is this impasse that is reflected in his letter to his sister of 23 March 1801:

Es scheint, als ob ich eines von den Opfern der Torheit werden würde, deren die Kantische Philosophie so viele auf das Gewissen hat. Mich ekelt vor dieser Gesellschaft, und doch kann ich mich nicht losringen aus ihren Banden. (*SW* II, 636)

It seems I am to become another one of those victims of folly of which the Kantian philosophy already has so many on its conscience. I loathe the people here and yet cannot wrestle free of the bonds that tie me to them.) [M, 97]

Given the acute epistemological crisis in which he now found himself, it is perhaps all the more surprising that he appears not to have been aware of the one (and indeed only) window that Kant had opened upon the noumenal world, namely the assertion that each individual has genuine knowledge of the Categorical Imperative. Yet this seems to have been the case, for Kleist continues to write as though he had failed to recognise (or perhaps did not *wish* to recognise) the vital role of Kant's notion of duty ('Pflicht') in preserving the autonomy of the individual moral will. For in the very first paragraph of his letter of 22 March 1801 to his fiancée, Wilhelmine, he persists in rejecting the Kantian dichotomy of duty and inclination:

Schmerzhaft würde es mir sein, wenn ich Dir jemals aus bloßer Pflicht treu sein müßte. Gern möchte ich meine Treue immer nur der Neigung verdanken. (*SW* II, 631)

(How painful it would be to me if my loyalty to you was due solely to my sense of duty and had nothing to do with inclination. I would rather it was exclusively due to the latter.)

Had Kleist had a better understanding of the moral component of Kant's philosophy, he would have realised that in separating out duty from inclination, Kant's over-riding concern was to preserve the notion of morality itself. For in contrast to animals, who are wholly at the mercy of their (natural) inclinations, human beings possess the capacity to reflect on whether or not to comply with the Categorical Imperative. Indeed it is precisely the fact that human beings can choose to act in accordance with the dictates of their moral will – but are not necessarily bound to do so – that makes the concept of morality possible in the first place. It is therefore all the more ironic that Kleist should regard Kant's philosophy not as an affirmation of human freedom, but on the contrary, as a final, and indeed insurmountable, obstacle to its assertion. This misunderstanding on his part is perhaps most clearly reflected in the way in which he seizes once again upon the image of the helpless puppet, wholly at the mercy of forces outside of itself, when he writes in his letter of 9 April 1801 to Wilhelmine, 'we think that we are free and yet in reality we are wholly at the mercy of chance that leads us along by a thousand finely spun threads' ('wir dünken uns frei, und der Zufall führt uns allgewaltig an tausend feingesponnenen Fäden fort'; *SW* II, 642).[15]

PARIS AND ROUSSEAU

Depressed by the conventional character of Prussian society and unable to concentrate on his scientific studies, Kleist proposed to embark on a trip to Paris. No doubt he was glad of an excuse to abandon his work with the *Technische Deputation* in Berlin, since he had developed a profound distaste for the arid technical reports which he was required to summarise for the other members of the commission.[16] But there was another, more important, reason behind his decision to leave Berlin: some months earlier, he had begun to think seriously about the possibility of becoming a writer, as his letter of 13 November 1800 to Wilhelmine clearly shows:

> Ich bilde mir ein, daß ich Fähigkeiten habe, seltnere Fähigkeiten, meine ich . . . Da stünde mir nun für die Zukunft das ganze schrifstellerische Fach offen. (*SW* II, 587)

> (I am inclined to regard myself as being blessed with certain unusual talents . . . And I am convinced that I could have a future as a writer.)

And in setting off for post-revolutionary Paris on a journey that was to take in the art treasures of Dresden *en route*, he was heading for the same artistic and cultural centres to which many aspiring artists of his generation were making their pilgrimage at this time.[17]

Dresden provided Kleist with a welcome relief and his letter to Wilhelmine of 21 May 1801 is filled with his enthusiastic appreciation.[18] But when he arrived in Paris on 6 July 1801, the contrast between the serenity of Dresden, with its rich cultivation of the arts, and the scenes of urban depravity he encountered in post-Revolutionary Paris could hardly have been greater. Here he was confronted with the alleged triumph of reason, the French technological 'miracle'. But behind this façade of modern progress, he saw only universal moral decay, an impression which served to reinforce his belief that there was an inherent contradiction between Man's original healthy urge to pursue knowledge for essentially humanitarian and moral ends and the corruption of these objectives in the use of technology in the service of Man's baser appetites of sensuality and greed. What Kleist saw amounted to an almost inverse relationship between technological and moral progress and as he wrote to Wilhelmine in a letter of 15 August 1801:

> Ohne Wissenschaft zittern wir vor jeder Lufterscheinung, unser Leben ist jedem Raubtier ausgesetzt . . . und sobald wir in das Reich des Wissens treten, sobald wir unsre Kenntnisse anwenden, uns zu sichern und zu schützen, gleich ist der erste Schritt zu dem Luxus und mit ihm zu allen Lastern der Sinnlichkeit getan. (*SW* II, 682)

> (Lacking science, we tremble at every comet, our life is exposed to every predator . . . and when we enter the realm of knowledge, when we seek to implement our learning in order to secure and protect ourselves, we have already taken the first step toward luxury, and thus to all the other vices of sensuality.) [M, 124]

It was precisely this contradiction that Kleist saw reflected in the financial support given by the French government to scientific research. He believed that the pursuit of truth and knowledge ought to be regarded as ends in their own right,[19] whereas for the French government, they were simply means to the baser ends of increased wealth and power:

> Warum verschwendet der Staat Millionen an alle diese Anstalten zur Ausbreitung der Gelehrsamkeit? Ist es ihm um *Wahrheit* zu tun? Dem *Staate*? Ein Staat kennt keinen andern Vorteil, als den er nach Prozenten berechnen kann. Er will die Wahrheit *anwenden* – (*SW* II, 681)

(Why does the state squander millions on all these institutions for the dissemination of learning? Does *it* care about *Truth*? The *state*? A state knows no advantage that it cannot reckon in percentages. It wants only to *implement* Truth –) [M, 124]

Worse still, in Kleist's view, was the way in which even Nature had been reduced to an artificial version of herself, an amusement park created by the 'enlightened' French authorities for the entertainment of their bewildered citizens, who paid twenty sous to wander 'as naturally as possible, through meadows, by the shores of lakes, beneath the shadows of the alders, one hundred paces as far as the walls beyond which Unnature once again begins' [M, 129] ('so natürlich wie möglich, über Wiesen, an dem Ufer der Seen, unter dem Schatten der Erlen, hundert Schritte lang, bis an die Mauer, wo die Unnatur wiederanfängt'; *SW* II, 689–90).

His dissatisfaction with Prussian society now compounded by his experiences of the French Enlightenment in Paris, Kleist began to despair of ever finding a social milieu in which he could lead a worthwhile existence. For, as he writes to Wilhelmine on 10 October 1801, the conventional forms of employment that he had had experience of hitherto are 'so unsuitable to my thoughts, it would be impossible for me to join in working for their continuance or furtherance' [M, 130–1] ('so wenig meinem Sinn gemäß, daß es mir unmöglich wäre, zu ihrer Erhaltung oder Ausbildung mitzuwirken'; *SW* II, 692). Accordingly, he decided to embark on his next ill-starred project, a complete Rousseauesque withdrawal from society. His original plan to buy a small-holding in Switzerland having been thwarted, much to his disgust, by the relentless advance of Napoleon and his forces, he found an alternative refuge on the Aarinsel in Thun. Yet even on his idyllic island retreat, Kleist found it considerably more difficult than he had imagined to escape from the pressures of conventional society. On 1 May 1802, he wrote to his sister, saying 'I would be quite without any feeling of distress except that it has always been my habit in life to invent something of the kind for myself' [M, 146] ('Ich würde ganz ohne alle widrigen Gefühle sein, wenn ich nicht, durch mein ganzes Leben daran gewöhnt, sie mir selbst erschaffen müßte'; *SW* II, 724). What was preying on Kleist's mind? His embittered letter of 20 May 1802, to Wilhelmine – who had turned down his invitation to join him in Switzerland – offers an important clue, for in it he makes any return to conventional society conditional upon the recognition of his success:

Es ist nur ein einziger Fall in welchem ich zurückkehre, wenn ich der Erwartung der Menschen, die ich törichter Weise durch eine Menge von prahlerischen Schritten gereizt habe, entsprechen kann . . . Kurz, kann ich nicht mit Ruhm im Vaterlande erscheinen, geschieht es nie. (*SW* II, 726)

(There is only one condition under which I would return and that is when I can fulfil the expectations that I so foolishly aroused in people by so many boastful actions . . . In short, either I return to my Fatherland as a famous man or not at all.) [M, 147]

What Kleist craved, above all else, was the recognition of his literary talents. For although illness was to put a premature end to his Rousseauesque idyll, his sojourn in Thun coincided with the beginning of his career as a writer, for it was there that he completed the draft versions of *Die Familie Schroffenstein* and embarked on the ill-fated *Robert Guiskard.*

LITERATURE AND THE CONVENTIONS OF FICTION

Throughout his life, Kleist deplored the way in which human beings' perception of the world around them had been distorted by what he, along with many others, regarded as the pernicious influence of popular sentimental fiction. The latter half of the eighteenth century had seen the rise of the novel as a literary genre together with the rapid development of a predilection amongst the contemporary reading public for escapist fiction of a highly exotic and sentimental kind.[20] Kleist's contempt for this type of work is clearly revealed in his account of a visit to the public library in Würzburg. Noting the absence of any works by Wieland, Goethe or Schiller, he quotes, with undisguised cynicism, the librarian's description of his stock:

Rittergeschichten, lauter Rittergeschichten, rechts die Rittergeschichten mit Gespenstern, links ohne Gespenster, nach Belieben. (*SW* II, 563)

(Tales of chivalry, and nothing but; the ones with ghosts are on the right, the ones without ghosts on the left, just as you prefer.)[21]

But whilst Kleist could smile at the stereotypical forms of this genre, he was also aware that the reading of such novels distracted human beings from tackling real-life problems by diverting their attention to a fantasy realm of banal wish-fulfilment. Thus in his letter of 10 October 1801 in which he attempts to persuade Wilhelmine to accompany him to his island retreat in Thun, he apologises for its dry tone, saying:

Ich habe Dir das so trocken hingeschrieben, weil ich Dich durch Deine Phantasie nicht bestechen wollte. Denn sonst gibt es wohl keine Lage, die für ein reines Herz so unüberschwenglich reich an Genüssen wäre, als diese. – Die Romane haben unsern Sinn verdorben. Denn durch sie hat das Heilige aufgehört, heilig zu sein, und das reinste, menschlichste, einfältigste Glück ist zu einer bloßen Träumerei herabgewürdigt worden. (*SW* II, 695)

(I have put it to you very colourlessly, because I would not wish to bribe you by way of your fantasy. For there is in fact no other situation so unassumingly rich in its enjoyments for the pure of heart. We have been corrupted by novels. For through them the sacred has ceased to be sacred, while the purest, most human, most innocent happiness is degraded to a daydream.) [M, 132]

However, whilst he was in little doubt as to the degrading effect of such novels, this did not deter him from subjecting them to considerable scrutiny to discover how they achieved their effects. In consequence, Kleist, perhaps more than any of his literary contemporaries, not only understood the conventions of popular literature, but knew how to deploy – and subvert – them in his own work, most obviously in the play *Das Käthchen von Heilbronn*. Indeed it was this understanding, together with his acute perception of the expectations and desires of the contemporary reading-public, that were to be combined so successfully in his short-lived career as editor of the *Berliner Abendblätter*.[22]

Although Kleist readily understood the pernicious influence of the cruder varieties of this type of literature, it is clear that his own view of the world was, at this stage at least, to a considerable extent mediated *via* the categories of literary fiction, albeit those of a rather more sophisticated variety. Perhaps the most blatant example of this tendency on his part is to be found in his letter to Wilhelmine of 16 August 1800, in which he exhorts her to read

Schiller's *Wallenstein* and casts himself and his fiancée in the roles of Max and Thekla respectively:

Lies ihn, liebes Mädchen, ich werde ihn auch lesen . . . Alles was *Max Piccolomini* sagt, möge . . . für mich gelten, alles was *Thekla* sagt, soll . . . für Dich gelten. (*SW* II, 517–8)

(Read it, my dear girl, and I will read it too. Read everything that Max Piccolomini says . . . as though it were spoken by me, and I shall read everything that Thekla says . . . as though it were spoken by you.)

A less obvious use of the literary conventions of his eighteenth-century upbringing is to be found in his descriptions of Nature in the letters written on the journey to Würzburg and in his descriptions of Parisian life in the latter part of 1801. Not only does his account of the depravity of urban life call to mind similar observations made by St. Preux in the second part of Rousseau's *La nouvelle Héloïse,*[23] but at the same time, in painting so negative a picture of the French metropolis in a series of letters, Kleist was writing within a well-established epistolary genre, the origins of which, in German literature, go back at least as far as Herder.[24] Similarly, his observations on Parisian life clearly reveal the influence of Montesquieu.[25] There is even a sense in which his trip to Paris in the company of Ulrike can be seen as a literal re-enactment of the fictional journey undertaken by Uzbek and Rica in the *Lettres Persanes.* For this reason we must be wary of accepting uncritically the 'observations' he makes in these letters, which in many instances are themselves highly self-conscious literary artefacts.

At this stage of Kleist's development, his letters seem almost like a series of literary 'experiments', attempts to imitate the forms and styles of the authors he admired. Perhaps, like the young artists in the Dresden art gallery busily copying the works of the Old Masters to familiarise themselves with the techniques of painting,[26] he regarded himself as involved in a corresponding process in the sphere of literature. As he was to discover, imitating great works of art could easily fail to provide inspiration, and might even prove a hindrance to the artist's own creative impulses. For in the years to come the stranglehold of tradition was to bring Kleist close to despair. But by 1805–6, years which coincide with the conception of a number of his most successful works, his essays and personal correspondence show that he had turned his attention to the complexities of this relationship between the forces of tradition and originality.

The extent to which conventional discursive forms hinder the pursuit of originality is the subject of the essay *Über die allmähliche Verfertigung der Gedanken beim Reden (On the gradual construction of thoughts whilst speaking)*, an essay written almost certainly in either 1805 or 1806. In it, Kleist draws attention to the way in which human beings are often unable to articulate their ideas because they become self-conscious and too preoccupied with the form of their expression. Taking as his example, the 'thunderbolt' ('Donnerkeil') with which Mirabeau dismissed the King's Master of Ceremonies on 23 June 1789, Kleist suggests that on this historic occasion, Mirabeau had no clear idea of what he was going to say when he embarked upon his momentous speech. That he delivered such an effective oration was – in Kleist's view – due to the desperate circumstances in which he found himself, circumstances that gave him little or no chance to monitor his own performance and forced him to speak in a wholly unselfconscious manner. In the light of this example, Kleist concludes that the emergence of fresh ideas is often due less to the originality of a particular individual than to the fact that the circumstances in which the individual is called upon to act rule out any opportunity for the usually stultifying effects of deliberation to occur. As he writes, 'it is not *we* who "know"; it is rather a certain condition, in which we happen to be, that "knows"' [M, 222] ('Denn nicht *wir* wissen, es ist allererst ein gewisser *Zustand* unsrer, welcher weiß'; *SW* II, 323). For when human beings are given time to 'think', instead of putting forward their own answer to a problem, very often they try to recall and reproduce one that already exists. Preoccupied with the past achievements of others, they end up producing something that is not as good as their model and, more importantly, probably inferior to that which they would have produced of their own accord, had they not, Orpheus-like, 'looked back' at the crucial moment. As an example of this, Kleist cites the situation of the examinee in the presence of his examiners. Answering from 'cold', as it were, he is unable to generate in himself the necessary state of mental involvement with the question, and as a result, either dries up completely or simply reproduces 'stock' answers to the no less 'stock' questions put to him by his examiners. This process, which consists in little more than a perpetual reiteration of received views, not only constitutes a serious obstacle to revealing the student's grasp of the matter in hand, but at the same time, robs the received view of such force as it may once have had by reducing it to an empty formula. Accordingly, when we are groping towards a particular idea, Kleist advises us to seek out a suitable interlocutor (even a silent one) in order to engineer a situation in which we will experience an appropriate degree of 'mental agitation' ('Erregung des Gemüts'), a condition that is essential if we are to avoid lapsing into the paralysis self-consciousness so often induces.

In its analysis of the difficulties that arise when human beings try to imitate (uncritically) the achievements of the past in an attempt to attain the same standards of excellence, this essay throws considerable light on Kleist's own way of working. For, like his essays and letters, Kleist's more overtly literary works are packed with allusions to the literary and philosophical ideals of the eighteenth century. But there is a marked difference between the reception of these ideals in Kleist's early writings (roughly speaking, the letters and essays written during the period 1799–1802) and their reception in his subsequent work (the bulk of which was written in the period 1805–1811). Thus whereas in his early correspondence these ideals are, for the most part, reproduced in a relatively uncritical light, when they are re-worked in the plays and stories, they are often ironised, parodied and subverted in their new aesthetic context. Kleist seems to hint at this process of 'critical assimilation' in a letter written to his friend Rühle von Lilienstern on 31 August 1806:

Ich höre, Du, mein lieber Junge, beschäftigst Dich auch mit der Kunst? Es gibt nichts Göttlicheres, als sie! Und nichts Leichteres zugleich; und doch, warum ist es so schwer? Jede erste Bewegung, alles Unwillkürliche, ist schön; und schief und verschroben alles, sobald es sich selbst begreift. O der Verstand! Der unglückselige Verstand! (*SW* II, 769)

(Am I right in thinking that you too are devoting yourself to artistic pursuits? There is nothing more divine, nothing more simple; and yet why is it so hard? Every initial gesture, everything that is done spontaneously is beautiful; but once conscious of itself, it becomes twisted and distorted. The intellect. What a wretched thing it is.)

For although, in his later works, the ideals and values of Kleist's eighteenth-century upbringing appear to be promoted as primary impulses ('erste Bewegungen') that are spontaneous and beautiful ('unwillkürlich und schön'), these same ideals appear distorted when subjected to the critical analysis ('Verstand') of the mature writer. In this way, the formal organisation of the later texts both reflects and re-enacts Kleist's initial enthusiasm for, and subsequent disenchantment with, the 'transcendent' ideals of his youth. But this changed attitude is not to be interpreted as despair of the human condition. Here it is necessary to draw a clear distinction between, on the one hand, genuine ideals that are, in principle, realisable by human beings (although often not without considerable effort) and on the other hand, empty 'transcendent' versions of these ideals that are not. Although Kleist criticises the latter, exposing their bogus status and revealing their purely conventional character, he never suggests that human beings should abandon the pursuit of genuine (i.e. potentially realisable) ideals, but shows how this preoccupation with spurious 'transcendent' fictions stands in the way of individual and social improvement. For when finite minds aspire to model temporal norms of behaviour on such (unknowable) 'transcendent' ideals, they blunder and fail for lack of genuine guidance, and treat as infallible criteria of excellence what are merely the social devices necessary to maintain the power of a dominant class and preserve the *status quo* from the healthy reforming influence of men and women of good will and experience. By drawing attention to the spurious character of such 'solutions', as well as to the hypocrisy of the characters who avail themselves of them, Kleist seeks to provoke his audience into an active, critical consideration of the central themes of his plays, a response that is further enhanced by their dissonant endings.

It is important not to confuse the opposition in Kleist's aesthetics between 'spontaneity' and 'self-consciousness' with the deceptively similar oppositions of the Early German Romantics, such as Friedrich Schlegel, who sets 'instinct' ('Instinkt') against 'intention' ('Absicht') in the *Kritische Fragmente* (*Critical Fragments*):[27]

In jedem guten Gedicht muß alles Absicht, und alles Instinkt sein. Dadurch wird es idealisch. (*KA* II, 149, §23)

(Every good poem must be wholly intentional and wholly instinctive. That is how it becomes ideal.) [*PF*, 23; §23]

For in the juxtaposition of 'instinct' and 'intention', Schlegel puts forward a programme to compensate for what he and his contemporaries saw as the lost ideal of 'Hellenic naïveté'. In this way, the Romantic artist can (Schlegel claims) create or reveal as by successive amplification in a series of 'magic mirrors', a Transcendent Reality. Thus in the *Fragmente* (*Athenäum Fragments*) he writes:

Nur sie [die romantische Poesie] kann gleich dem Epos ein Spiegel der ganzen umgebenden Welt, ein Bild des Zeitalters werden. Und doch kann auch sie am meisten zwischen dem Dargestellten und dem Darstellenden, frei von allem realen und idealen Interesse auf den Flügeln der poetischen Reflexion in der Mitte schweben, diese Reflexion immer wieder potenzieren und wie in einer endlosen Reihe von Spiegeln vervielfachen. (*KA* II, 182–3, §116)

(It [Romantic poetry] alone can become, like the epic, a mirror of the whole circumambient world, an image of the age. And it can also – more than any other form – hover at the midpoint between the portrayed and the portrayer, free of all real and ideal self-interest, on the wings of poetic reflection, and can raise that reflection again and again to a higher power, can multiply it in an endless succession of mirrors.) [*PF*, 31–2; §116]

On the way to this goal, the poet is said to pass through a satiric period in which the ideal and the 'real' are not related, to an elegiac phase where we perceive only the disparity between the ideal furnishings of the poet's world and their 'real' equivalents, and then on to an idyllic phase in which we see the allegedly 'superior', 'transcendent' nature of these subsistent entities in their own right, and come to appreciate that, generation by generation, the poet can and should reveal this nature to us more and more fully, and point ahead to an inexhaustible quest towards an altogether 'higher order of reality'. For as Schlegel writes:

Es gibt eine Poesie, deren eins und alles das Verhältnis des Idealen und des Realen ist, und die also nach der Analogie der philosophischen Kunstsprache Transzendentalpoesie heißen müßte. Sie beginnt als Satire mit der absoluten Verschiedenheit des Idealen und Realen, schwebt als Elegie in der Mitte, und endigt als Idylle mit der absoluten Identität beider. (*KA* II, 204, §238)

(There is a kind of poetry whose essence lies in the relation between ideal and real, and which therefore, by analogy to philosophical jargon, should be called transcendental poetry. It begins as satire in the absolute difference of ideal and real, hovers in between as elegy, and ends as idyll with the absolute identity of the two.) [*PF*, 50; §238]

It is specifically in respect of this concept of 'transcendental poetry' ('Transzendentalpoesie') that the disparity between the aesthetics of Kleist and Schlegel can be seen most clearly. Whereas for Schlegel, the categories of 'instinct' and 'intention' are not seen as incompatibles, but as polarities to be reconciled into a 'higher unity' within the domain of 'transcendental poetry', for Kleist, the fact that the artistic product always seems to fall short of the 'transcendent vision' that allegedly lies behind it, serves to undermine the belief that there is such a 'transcendent world' in the first place. For this reason Kleist rejects the notion that the function of art is to mirror the 'contents' of a 'transcendent realm'.[28] Since this 'transcendent world' is not in fact a reality that finite human beings can know, the adverse comparison between the artistic product and its supposed 'original' is in fact a pseudo-comparison that is of no value as a guide to further action on the part of the artist. Thus in Kleist's view, the way to better works of art does not lie in the fruitless contemplation of an inaccessible Platonic realm in search of an, in principle, unknowable reality, but on the contrary, in the realistic, hopeful and, above all, analytical scrutiny of one's own artistic products. Only thus will the artist arrive at a realistic appraisal of his work and come to see that it is neither unimprovably perfect nor hopelessly flawed, but an amalgam of better and inferior elements, an insight which will enable him to build upon the former and eradicate the latter. What is encouraging in this very human tendency to believe in the existence of a 'transcendent realm' is the fact that human beings seem to set no limits to the degree of improvement that can be made upon their previous best efforts, and it is this constant desire to do better that constitutes the psychological basis for the dedication – and enthusiasm – of the true artist.

Viewed from this perspective, the extract from Kleist's letter of 31 August 1806 to Rühle von Lilienstern is to be seen as a piece of positive encouragement and, at the same time, as a warning of the difficulties with which he will be confronted as an artist. For to give way to despair at the impossibility of ever realising that which is, in principle, unattainable is to lapse into a pathological condition; but to experience disappointment at a failure to realise that which is, at least in principle, within one's grasp is simply to be human and this insight, when correctly assimilated, may become a spur to greater and better achievements. It is in this latter sense that we are to understand Kleist's remark: 'the truth is that the contents of my imagination always seem more beautiful to me than the results of my literary endeavour' ('Die Wahrheit ist, daß ich das, was ich mir vorstelle, schön finde, nicht das, was ich leiste'; *SW* II, 769). While he was working on *Robert Guiskard* – a project that he never succeeded in completing – Kleist had already experienced the crippling sense of despair that inevitably resulted, as Christoph Martin Wieland noted, from 'his fruitless pursuit of an unattainable ideal of perfection' ('sein *fruchtloses Streben* nach einem unerreichbaren Zauberbild von Vollkommenheit'; *Lebensspuren* no. 125a). Nonetheless, when we compare Kleist's letter of 1806 to Rühle von Lilienstern with a letter written to his sister at the height of his difficulties over *Robert Guiskard* in 1803, there is a striking difference of tone. In the earlier letter he writes: 'It was hell that gave me this half-talent of mine: heaven grants a whole one or none at all' [M, 152] ('Die Hölle gab mir meine halben Talente, der Himmel schenkt dem Menschen ein ganzes, oder gar keins'; *SW* II, 736); by contrast, his letter of 1806 bears scant trace of such extravagant despairing rhetoric, and shows him to have a far more realistic attitude towards both his own talents and the creative process itself, when he writes, 'my estimation of my ability is but a pale shadow of what it used to be during the time I spent in Dresden' ('meine Vorstellung von meiner Fähigkeit ist nur noch der Schatten von jener ehemaligen in Dresden'; *SW* II, 769). In short, his earlier tendency to conceive of artistic ability purely in 'transcendent' terms – as a gift that one either wholly possesses or wholly lacks – has been replaced by a more realistic notion of artistic ability as a skill that can be developed and improved. Significantly, towards the end of the letter, he affirms his intention to work even harder at honing his 'half-talents' ('Halbtalente'), saying: 'I also have to improve my technical skills as a writer, practise more, and learn how to produce better quality material in a shorter space of time'

('Auch muß ich mich im Mechanischen verbessern, an Übung zunehmen und in kürzern Zeiten, Besseres liefern lernen'; *SW* II, 769). Given that he goes to some lengths to emphasise the importance for the writer of developing his writing skills and the need for yet more practice ('Übung'), it may seem paradoxical that he warns his friend of the corrupting influence of the rational intellect ('der Verstand'), adding that he should simply 'follow his inclinations' ('Folge Deinem Gefühl'; *SW* II, 770). Here Kleist is not drawing a straightforward distinction between instinct and the intellect, whereby the former is privileged at the expense of the latter. What he is emphasising is that human beings have the capacity to evaluate and criticise their own performances and that since these are the performances of finite beings, this process of critical scrutiny is almost certain to give rise to disappointments. At the same time, he points out that any performance is liable to be disturbed and made more difficult when the performer is simultaneously engaged in evaluating and giving the performance, simply because now he is engaged in executing two tasks at once. That would be sufficient to disturb a performer even in private. But since, in addition, the human performer has the capacity – and indeed is very liable – to reflect upon the figure he is cutting in the eyes of his fellow human beings, this increases the likelihood that the performance will be disturbed still further when an audience, real or imaginary, is involved. To perform the action itself, no evaluating process is necessary, but to improve upon this action for future performances, a detailed reflection on its precise nature is essential; to modify the action so as to alter the public's response to it, requires yet a third order of reflection. The results of these various processes of critical scrutiny, when appropriately directed towards their proper ends, are often painful, but sometimes pleasurable, and it is important not to overlook the fact that the latter is a perfectly possible (if less common) outcome. Nonetheless, whether painful or pleasurable, this process of self-scrutiny is essential – but only *after* the work of art has been executed – if progress is to be made.[29] Thus Kleist's advice to his friend is to limit the process of reflection to that which is strictly necessary for the purpose in hand. And since, as he points out, no artist can know with absolute certainty whether or not a work of art will succeed or fail, he goes on to offer a further piece of advice: 'If something seems beautiful to you, then show it to us and hope for the best. It's little better than a throw of the dice, but that's all there is' ('Was Dir schön dünkt, das gib uns, auf gut Glück. Es ist ein Wurf, wie mit dem Würfel; aber es gibt nichts anderes'; *SW* II, 770).

The real import of all this advice is to warn his friend against giving in to the temptation of simply reproducing the conventions of great works of art in the (forlorn) hope that this will necessarily result in the emergence of new and equally successful works. For art, like love and morality, cannot simply be reduced to a system of 'conventions' or 'rules' which, when followed, inevitably guarantee success.[30] On the contrary, when the artist deliberately tries to ape the past achievements of his predecessors, the result is very likely to be 'mannered' work which lacks the qualities of the original on which it is 'based'. In sum, Kleist suggests that the artist should seek to *emulate* – not *imitate* – the past achievements of great writers and artists. This view is perhaps most clearly articulated in the essay *Brief eines jungen Dichters an einen jungen Maler* (*Letter from a young writer to a young painter*) in which he formulates his views on the 'appropriate' uses of tradition as follows:

Wenigstens dünkt uns, läßt sich ein doppelter Gebrauch von einem Bilde machen; einmal der, den ihr davon macht, nämlich die Züge desselben nachzuschreiben, um euch die Fertigkeit der malerischen Schrift einzulernen; und dann in seinem Geist, gleich vom Anfang herein, nachzuerfinden. Und auch diese Fertigkeit müßte, sobald als nur irgend möglich, gegen die Kunst selbst, *deren wesentliches Stück die Erfindung nach eigentümlichen Gesetzen ist*, an den Nagel gehängt werden. (*SW* II, 336, my emphasis.)

(For it seems to us that there are two uses to be made of a picture: first, as you now overdo, to imitate its features, with the object of acquiring skill in the letter of your art; and secondly, progressing from letter to spirit, to imitate its creative impulse, which was its own sine qua non. But even this second and deeper skill, as soon as at all possible, should be stored somewhere out of the way of Art herself, *whose primary dictate is creation according to the unique and inherent principles of each individual sensibility*.) [M, 238; my emphasis]

It is essential here to distinguish between, on the one hand, specific techniques used in painting ('die Fertigkeit der malerischen Schrift') and on the other, certain stylistic conventions ('die Gesetze der Kunst'). Having studied the works of the Old Masters to learn the former, the artist must put them out of his mind in order to develop his own version of the latter, for as Kleist goes on to say, 'the objective . . . is not to become someone else, but to be yourself' [M, 238] ('die Aufgabe . . . ist ja nicht, ein anderer, sondern ihr selbst zu sein'; *SW* II, 336). In addition, he warns that the study of great works of art can be a double-edged sword. For whilst there is much that a prospective artist can learn from the works of the Old Masters (on account of their superior quality) there is also the danger that he will fall into the trap of idolising these artists to such an extent that he comes to regard their paintings as ideal embodiments of 'artistic perfection' which are quite beyond the reach of ordinary men, let alone capable of being surpassed. This can result in the artist's losing faith in his own ability and lapsing into a state of self-deception, whereby he merely reproduces the painterly conventions of his idols in the misguided belief that this will, *of necessity*, result in the emergence of new great works. Idolatry of this kind exalts the rules personally hammered out by the great artist into 'infallible principles' guaranteeing success to other men.

Although Kleist's discussion refers to painting, it is clear that the same arguments apply to the production and critical reception of literary works. Thus in the essay *Ein Satz aus der höheren Kritik* (*A passage from the higher criticism*) he notes paradoxically that often 'it requires more genius to evaluate properly the second-rate than the first-rate work of art' [M, 241] ('Es gehört mehr Genie dazu, ein mittelmäßiges Kunstwerk zu würdigen, als ein vortreffliches'; *SW* II, 346). The works which Kleist regards as outstanding are those in which beauty is 'so purely contained, that every intelligence, as such, responds to it instantly' [M, 241] ('so rein enthalten, daß es jedem gesunden Auffassungsvermögen . . . in die Sinne springt'; *SW* II, 346). By contrast, inferior works are those in which beauty is alloyed 'with so much that is fortuitous or even contradictory' [M, 241] ('mit soviel Zufälligem oder wohl gar Widersprechenden'; *SW* II, 346). Of course, the point of his essay is not to deny the particular merits of great works of art, but to draw attention to the way in which the reader, when confronted with such artistic excellence, is liable to be reduced to an almost exclusively passive role in which he can do little more than gasp in awe at the author's achievements.

Inferior works, on the other hand, can offer the reader much needed encouragement to engage in active and educative debate upon the nature of artistic merit. They are therefore often of greater value for the development of the critical sense than their more perfect counterparts. This is why he suggests that:

Wer also Schiller und Goethe lobt, der gibt mir dadurch noch gar nicht, wie er glaubt, den Beweis eines vorzüglichen und außerordentlichen Schönheitssinnes; wer aber mit Gellert und Cronegk hie und da zufrieden ist, der läßt mich . . . vermuten, daß er Verstand und Empfindungen, und zwar beide in einem seltenen Grade besitzt. (*SW* II, 347)

(Whoever praises Schiller and Goethe, therefore, hardly, as he may think, provides proof of an extraordinary and superior aesthetic sense; but whoever finds something good here and there in Gellert and Cronegk causes me to suspect . . . that understanding and sensitivity, and both in rare measure, are indeed creditable to him.) [M, 241]

Naturally Kleist is not denying the achievements of Goethe and Schiller, but simply pointing out that the true test of aesthetic appreciation lies in an ability to recognise the relative strengths and weaknesses of works whose status is in doubt. This suggests a commitment to the more Aristotelian view that beauty is not an abstract quality waiting to be discovered in some Platonic heaven, but comes into existence only insofar as it is embodied in actual works of art. Indeed it is typical of his profoundly realistic attitude to the pursuit of aesthetic excellence that he should look for – and find – qualities to admire even in works of art that, for the most part, he held in only modest esteem.

Kleist's reflections on art and literature show that he believed he was living in an age in which, as he puts it, 'the majority of human beings have lost any sense of the wonders of poetry and literature' ('die Wunder der Poesie der großen Mehrzahl der Menschen auf Erden fremd geworden sind'; *SW* II, 423). In his view, the reason for this 'decline' lay in the fact that those around him had lost the capacity to distinguish between the conventions of 'good taste' and beauty itself. Also, he seems to have believed that this process of decline had been encouraged by those artists who, having lost confidence in their own ability as a result of an over-valuation of the works of their predecessors, sought refuge from failure by placing their trust in a supposedly infallible aesthetic theory. In this respect the attitude of such artists recalls that of the young man in Kleist's essay *Über das Marionettentheater* (*On the puppet theatre*), who, when removing a thorn from his foot becomes aware that his pose resembles that of a well-known classical statue. For like the young man, these artists have become caught in the grip of 'an invisible and incomprehensible force' [M, 215] ('eine unsichtbare und unbegreifliche Macht'; *SW* II, 344) as they seek, in vain, to reinstate the 'perfect' posture of the past, instead of using it as a source of inspiration for further fresh achievements of grace and beauty of their own. Nonetheless, as Kleist reminds us in the *Gebet des Zoroaster* (*Prayer of Zarathustra*) we should not ignore the great achievements of the past, since:

> wenn die Vorwelt nicht wäre und die göttlichen Lieder, die von ihr Kunde geben, so würden wir gar nicht mehr ahnden, von welchen Gipfeln, o Herr! der Mensch um sich schauen kann. (*SW* II, 325)

> (if not for the ages long past and the sacred song that remains to tell of them, we should have no glimmer of those heights, O Lord, whence man may look all around him.) [M, 242]

But having reminded ourselves of the heights to which Man can aspire, we should, in the words of the young poet writing to the painter, turn our backs on the great works of our predecessors and 'set off in a totally different direction to seek out and scale the summits of art' ('in diametral entgegengesetzter Richtung, den Gipfel der Kunst, . . . auffinden und ersteigen.'; *SW* II, 337).

CHAPTER 3

Die Familie Schroffenstein

When Kleist's first play, *Die Familie Schroffenstein* was published (anonymously) in February 1803, it was welcomed enthusiastically by a number of reviewers as the work of a promising, though as yet inexperienced, author.[1] Soon after it appeared, however, Kleist distanced himself from the play and wrote to his sister, Ulrike, on 13 March 1803, begging her not to read it, on the grounds that it was 'a wretched piece of rubbish' ('eine elende Scharteke'; *SW* II, 731). Nevertheless, it was one of only three plays by Kleist to be performed during his own lifetime – the others being *Der zerbrochne Krug* and *Das Käthchen von Heilbronn*[2] – and though lacking some of the sophistication of his later work, it contains, *in nuce*, almost all the themes that he was to explore in greater depth in the subsequent years.

Unlike Kleist's later works, the majority of which often provoked bitter and uncompromising debates, *Die Familie Schroffenstein* has been relatively free from critical controversy.[3] What critical debate there has been has tended to focus on the role of the lovers, Ottokar and Agnes, who die at the hands of their respective fathers, Rupert and Sylvester, thereby ending the line of both branches of the Schroffenstein family. At first sight, the denouement of the play appears to confirm the widely-held view that Kleist's work is characterised by a profoundly pessimistic view of the human condition. Certainly, it was the violence of the denouement that attracted the attention of Kleist's near contemporaries, who, whilst acknowledging the play's merits, believed that it would benefit from certain revisions. One critic, writing some years after Kleist's death, suggested that, if the ending were revised, it would be quite possible to have the play performed.[4] His suggestions did not fall on deaf ears, for in 1822, Franz von Holbein produced an adaptation of the play under the new title of *Die Waffenbrüder* (*Brothers in arms*) in which the violent denouement of the original was replaced by a new ending in which the young lovers get married, thereby healing the rift between the rival factions, an ending more in keeping with the taste of nineteenth-century theatre audiences. Whilst recent commentators on the play have been more tolerant of its violent ending than were the nineteenth-century theatre managers, there is almost universal agreement amongst contemporary critics that the figures of Ottokar and Agnes represent an emancipatory tendency within the play that is tragically cut short by the misplaced intervention of the fathers.[5] Nonetheless, it is striking that the basic positions of twentieth-century critics, who see the destruction of the 'idyll' in act v as an unequivocally pessimistic commentary on the human predicament, and those nineteenth-century theatre managers who wished to substitute the allegedly 'tragic' denouement of the play with a more 'optimistic' ending involving marriage and a 'harmonious reconciliation', are perhaps rather closer to each other than they seem at first sight. In each case, there is a tacit assumption that were the love of the children to triumph, then the conflict between the rival houses of Rossitz and Warwand could be resolved. However, to endorse this reading of the play is to endorse a 'solution' that is both anticipated and subverted in the play itself, when the elderly Jeronimus tells Eustache of the children's love for one another, saying:

> Denn fast kein Minnesänger
> Könnt etwas Besseres ersinnen, leicht
> Das Wildverworrene euch aufzulösen,
> Das Blutig-angefangne lachend zu
> Beenden, und der Stämme Zwietracht ewig
> Mit seiner Wurzel auszurotten, als
> – Als eine Heirat. (*SW* 1, 111; 1663–9)

(For even a poet of courtly-love could hardly have devised a better scheme to end so simply all this wild confusion; to end with laughter that which began with bloodshed; and to remove for all eternity, all trace of discord between the rival houses. What better way for this to come about than through such a marriage?)

By placing these words in the mouth of the more sentimentally-inclined Jeronimus, Kleist invites the audience to take a sceptical view of what is shown to be an essentially sentimental 'solution'. The very fact that it is described as a solution, the like of which 'even a poet of courtly-love' could hardly have improved upon serves to underline just how far this love affair is itself both constructed from, and viewed through, a variety of literary conventions.[6] Accordingly, the fact that Kleist implicitly rejects the notion that the love of Ottokar and Agnes could herald a fresh start in human affairs should not be regarded as symptomatic of a pessimistic cast of mind on his part, but rather as evidence of his clear-sightedness as to the (strictly limited) emancipatory potential of this relationship. Unlike Jeronimus, Kleist is too much of a realist to take seriously the possibility that this sentimental affair could provide a genuine solution to the very real difficulties with which the rival branches of the family are confronted. Were the relationship of Ottokar and Agnes to offer a genuine solution to that conflict, the depth of their love would have to be of the same order as the grief of Sylvester and the self-disgust of Rupert at the end of the play. If there is an emancipatory tendency in the play – and it is my view that there is – then it is not to be found in the false 'utopia' of the children's love, but in the very real change of heart that takes place in both Rupert and Sylvester.

THE ADULT WORLD

In *Die Familie Schroffenstein*, the rival houses of Rossitz and Warwand reflect two views of human nature that are diametrically opposed to one another. In Rossitz, Rupert enjoys the support of a highly authoritarian and autocratic society and believes that human beings act solely from considerations of self-interest and can be controlled only by the use of force. By contrast, in Warwand, Sylvester enjoys the support of an essentially benevolent Christian society and believes fervently in the perfectibility of Man and the possibility of human progress through the application of reason and moral enlightenment. But whilst the structures of social organisation in Warwand represent a considerable advance over those in Rossitz, neither system offers a wholly correct account of human nature. For, as we shall see, whilst Sylvester's ideology fails to allow for a residual streak of evil in Man, Rupert's ideology overlooks a real capacity in Man for good.[7]

In the opening scene of the play, we are shown the extent to which the social and cultural institutions in Rossitz reflect the ideology that underpins it. During the perverted version of the Eucharist it becomes clear that the 'divinity' Rupert worships is the god of his own malign autocracy, a god who demands violent retribution whenever his authority is challenged and requires unquestioning obedience from his subjects. The abhorrent use of the Christian sacrament to confirm and celebrate a monstrous oath of revenge emphasises Rupert's malevolent, despotic nature. However, by portraying Rupert as the only sincere participant in the ritual, Kleist shows that he alone, unlike the other members of his entourage, is totally convinced that the world he inhabits is one in which 'the last stirrings of humanity for the infant lying in the crib have been extinguished' ('die letzte Menschenregung für | Das Wesen in der Wiege ist erloschen'; *SW* I, 53; 51–2) and that the only way to act effectively in such a world is to resort to the rule of force. As the scene unfolds, Rupert's wife, Eustache, openly challenges the ideological basis of his conception of human society when she appeals to the 'natural benevolence' of her sex in order to absolve herself from the oath, exclaiming: 'Oh God! How should a woman exact revenge?' ('O Gott! Wie soll ein Weib sich rächen?'; *SW* I, 52; 38). Confronted with an alternative account of human nature that calls into question the pseudo-objectivity of his own, Rupert is unable to advance any rational arguments in defence of his position, and simply chooses to disregard his wife's more benevolent (though equally ideological) view of humanity on the grounds that it is nothing more than a 'childish fiction', merely a 'distortion' of the way the world is 'in reality':

> Ich weiß, Eustache, Männer sind die Rächer –
> Ihr seid die Klageweiber der Natur.
> Doch nichts mehr von Natur.
> Ein hold ergötzend Märchen ists der Kindheit,
> Der Menschheit von den Dichtern, ihren Ammen,
> Erzählt. Vertrauen, Unschuld, Treue, Liebe,
> Religion, der Götter Furcht sind wie
> Die Tiere, welche reden. (*SW* I, 52; 40–7)

(I know, Eustache, that Nature has assigned the task of revenge to men and that it is woman's lot to mourn. But enough of Nature. It is nothing more than a pleasant, childish fairy-tale told to humanity by its nursemaids, the poets. Trust, innocence, loyalty, love, religion, and the fear of the gods are qualities as rare as animals that speak.)

Although Rupert's position of absolute authority is such that he can force the members of his court to accept his own unrealistic and self-justifying account of human nature, he does not have the power to re-fashion the world in such a way as to make it correspond to the categories of his pessimistic view of human nature. Indeed, as he (like his rival, Sylvester) will discover to his cost, it is the uncritical acceptance of such ideological systems in which human beings are said to be either 'infallibly' benevolent or 'irredeemably' wicked, that frustrates human enterprises, be they directed towards good, as in Sylvester's case, or towards evil, as in his own.

As the play progresses, Rupert resorts to increasingly absurd feats of self-deception as he attempts to deny responsibility for his monstrous crimes. Nowhere is this more clearly demonstrated than in act III, scene 2, when Jeronimus, a long-standing friend of both Rupert and Sylvester, is lynched by the crowd in Rossitz. The significance of the episode lies not so much in the question of Rupert's guilt; what shocks us are his reactions and those of his entourage to the event. For when his henchman, Santing, returns and announces: 'It's all been seen to, Sir' ('’s ist abgetan, Herr'; *SW* I, 116; 1805), Eustache realises that, by means of his henchman, her husband has incited the crowd to kill Jeronimus. Knowing that his wife considers him to be a murderer, Rupert cannot meet her censorious gaze and assigns the blame to a third party: 'Whoever it was who struck the first blow, his life is forfeit' ('Wer zuerst ihn tödlich | Getroffen hat, der ist des Todes!'; *SW* I, 116; 1818–9). Yet his reactions here constitute clear evidence that even this 'perfect' villain does not wholly lack the ability to make moral judgements, and it is from this point on that the cracks in his ideological system become ever more apparent. For Rupert's belief that every human being acts solely out of self-interest, no matter how violent the means involved, is manifestly contradicted by his recognition that the murder of Jeronimus is an act so despicable that even he does not wish to accept responsibility for it. And, as we shall see, it is because he does not altogether lack this capacity for self-scrutiny that he undergoes a profound change of heart in the final scene of the play.

The question of Rupert's moral culpability is explored more fully in the first scene of act IV, in which he reflects on the nature of the social institution over which he presides. As he observes, quite correctly, the structures of power that underlie the social organisation of Rossitz do indeed facilitate the execution of violent and immoral acts:

> Das eben ist der Fluch der Macht, daß sich
> Dem Willen, dem leicht widerruflichen,
> Ein Arm gleich beut, der fest unwiderruflich
> Die Tat ankettet. (*SW* I, 117; 1824–7)

(That is the curse of power: that there is always a willing hand to turn a whim, that can be unthought, into a deed that cannot be undone.)

Moreover, in the previous scene we see Rupert surrounded by servants who, like obedient dogs, are only too willing to carry out the instructions of their leader without question. And as he himself points out, it is precisely this reduction of human beings to unreflecting automata that renders the execution of evil deeds so straightforward:

> Nicht ein Zehnteil würd
> Ein Herr des Bösen tun, müßt er es selbst
> Mit eignen Händen tun. (*SW* I, 117; 1827–9)

(No master would commit even a fraction of the evil that he does had he to do it with his own hands.)

It is particularly striking that these lines – which bear witness to Kleist's realistic and optimistic view of human behaviour – are placed in the mouth of the arch-villain of the play. At this point, however, rather than follow up the implications of his own insights, Rupert reverts once more to self-deception and continues to deny any responsibility for the evil consequences of his actions on the grounds that he is 'compelled' by 'sheer necessity' to act as he does:

> seiner Knechte
> Geringster hat den Vorteil über ihn,
> Daß er das Böse wollen darf. (*SW* I, 117; 1830–2)

(Even the lowliest of his servants has this advantage over him, that he is free to choose whether or not to commit an evil act.)

Clearly, he is guilty of another grotesque act of *mauvaise foi*, in that he imagines himself to occupy a position far lower on the social hierarchy than he does in fact. The structure of society in Rossitz may facilitate the execution of violent and immoral acts, but it does not actually bring them about without human instigation. Thus although Rupert's position at the pinnacle of this despotic society enables him to commit any outrage he chooses, its autocratic structure is such that it isolates the leader in a position of exclusive responsibility for such acts; and it is this inescapable truth that lies behind Santing's remark:

Ich kann
Das Herrschen dir nicht lehren, du nicht das
Gehorchen mir. Was Dienen ist, das weiß
Ich auf ein Haar. Befiehl, daß ich dir künftig
Nicht mehr gehorche, wohl, so will ich dir
Gehorchen. (*SW* I, 117; 1832–7)

(I cannot teach you how to give orders, nor can you teach me how to obey them. I know all there is to know about subservience. If you order me to disobey you in future, so be it, I will do as you command.)

During this exchange with Santing, Rupert comes very close to accepting responsibility for the death of Jeronimus, but stops just short of actually doing so, and resorts to yet another act of self-deception: pinning the blame on Santing, he portrays himself as the 'victim' of an over-zealous servant:

Es ist
Mir widerlich, ich wills getan nicht haben.
Auf deine Kappe nimms – (*SW* I, 117; 1842–4)

(It is a deed that fills me with disgust; I wish it could be undone. You must take responsibility for it –)

Rupert is offered a number of opportunities to redeem himself well before the fateful events of the last act. For when he reflects on the vileness of the murder of Jeronimus, confessing to Eustache that: 'I have become repugnant even in my own eyes' ('Denn selbst ein Ekel bin ich mir'; *SW* I, 120; 1918), his wife, whose ethical system closely resembles that of Sylvester, reminds him that no human being is beyond redemption:

Den soll
Kein Mensch verdammen, der sein Urteil selbst
Sich spricht. O hebe dich! Du bist so tief
Bei weitem nicht gesunken, als du hoch
Dich heben kannst. (*SW* I, 120; 1918–22)

(No one should condemn a man who thus condemns himself. Rise up, for the depths to which you have sunk are as nothing compared to the heights to which you can aspire.)

Her words not only act as a warning to those critics who would dismiss Rupert as simply an 'incorrigible' villain,[8] but also offer us an insight into the essentially Christian system of ethics which Kleist is at pains to promote in the play. Eustache points out that since all human beings have the capacity to subject their behaviour to moral scrutiny, they can also repent and seek forgiveness. Her doctrine of forgiveness is based on the argument that since we can never know with certainty the precise nature of the circumstances under which a particular individual chose to act as he did, we must resist all temptation to pass judgement on that individual ourselves. However, Rupert has not yet advanced to the point at which he can accept this concept of redemption, and seeks 'salvation' in a further of act of *mauvaise foi*, this time maintaining that he has been 'tricked' into murdering Jeronimus by the 'cunning' of Sylvester:

Gewendet, listig, haben sie das ganze
Verhältnis, mich, den Kläger, zum Verklagten
Gemacht. (*SW* I, 121; 1953–5)

(They have been cunning, have turned the tables on me, turned me, the accuser, into the accused.)

From this point on, Rupert's attempts to deny responsibility for his actions become increasingly far-fetched, culminating in the manifestly unconvincing outburst of act v, scene I, where he stands over the body of what he (mistakenly) believes to be Sylvester's daughter, Agnes, and asks Santing:

Warum denn hätt ich sie gemordet? Sage
Mir schnell, ich bitte dich, womit sie mich

Beleidigt, sags recht hämisch – Basiliske,
Sieh mich nicht an, sprich, Teufel, sprich, und weißt
Du nichts, so lüg es! (*SW* I, 144; 2524–8)

(Why should I have murdered her, then? Quick, tell me, tell me with all the spite you can muster, what wrong did she do me – don't look at me like that, you viper, speak you devil, and if you cannot find a reason, then make one up!)

Only when he realises that the body before him is not that of Agnes but of Ottokar, and that he has, inadvertently, killed his own son, does he recognise both the full extent of his capacity for evil, and, more importantly, that he alone is responsible for the crime that has just been committed. As he contemplates the body of his son, he finally comes to recognise himself for the devil he is:

Höllisch Gesicht! Was äffst du mich?
Ein Teufel
Blöckt mir die Zung heraus. (*SW* I, 150; 2677–8)

(Hellish countenance! Why do you mock me thus? A devil is sticking out its tongue at me!)

In this act of self-recognition he demonstrates the truth of Eustache's observations on the Christian doctrine of repentance and redemption outlined above. It is only because he is not altogether devoid of a sense of morality that he is able to recognise his own behaviour as satanic and to reject it. Thus although it is tempting to view the violent denouement of the play as a profoundly pessimistic commentary on the human condition, this is to overlook the radical change of heart that takes place within Rupert in the final scene. The full depth of this transformation is confirmed by the fact that it is he – and not Sylvester – who initiates the reconciliation between the rival houses of Rossitz and Warwand when he addresses his former rival, saying:

Sylvester! Dir hab ich ein Kind genommen,
Und biete einen Freund dir zum Ersatz. (*SW* I, 151; 2712–3)

(Sylvester! I have robbed you of a child, but offer you a friend in return.)

And just as Sylvester will reflect that no man can resist the temptation to do evil with the infallibility of God, so Rupert, for his part, will reflect that no human being can resist the temptation to do good with the infallibility of the Devil.

Whilst Kleist goes to considerable lengths to suggest a real possibility for self-improvement in a man such as Rupert, in his characterisation of Sylvester, he shows his audience how a man with essentially benevolent aspirations is nonetheless capable of descending to Rupert's level of wickedness. Of course it would be foolish to conclude from the catastrophic ending of the play that Kleist did not wish to draw a distinction between the social systems of Rossitz and Warwand, for it is clear that Sylvester's society represents a considerable advance on that of Rupert. But just as Rupert fails to understand the nature of the autocratic institution over which he presides, so too Sylvester, for his part, fails to appreciate that whilst the more benevolent structures of social organisation in Warwand constitute a considerable barrier to arbitrary acts of violence, they cannot prevent such acts from occurring altogether. In his desire to believe in the essential goodness of Man, he attributes to Rupert a far greater capacity for good than the latter possesses and, as a result, exposes various members of his entourage – including himself and Jeronimus – to unnecessary risks. However, his most serious error is to regard himself as a man who is, quite literally, 'incapable' of the kind of monstrous behaviour exhibited by Rupert. Thus in act I, scene 2, when the herald arrives from Rossitz and accuses Sylvester of the murder of Rupert's youngest son, Peter, to begin with Sylvester simply dismisses the matter on the grounds that the messenger has made a mistake. But when it becomes apparent that even the loyal Jeronimus believes him capable of such a monstrous crime, Sylvester is so affronted that he faints on the spot. When he regains consciousness (in act II, scene 2), the extent of both his hubris and his capacity for self-deception are made clear to the audience. Fearing that Jeronimus may have interpreted his faint as a sign of guilt, he explains that, on the contrary, it should be regarded as evidence of his absolute moral integrity and, by extension, as a sign of his sheer 'inability' to commit such a crime. And in likening himself to the 'healthy oak' ('die gesunde Eiche'), he implies that a man of lesser integrity would have simply brushed off Jeronimus's suggestion:

Freilich mag
Wohl mancher sinken, weil er stark ist. Denn
Die kranke abgestorbne Eiche steht

Dem Sturm, doch die gesunde stürzt er nieder,
Weil er in ihre Krone greifen kann. (*SW* I, 84; 959–63)

(Often it is the strength of a man that may cause his downfall. For whilst the diseased oak withstands the storm, its healthy counterpart is sent crashing to the ground because the wind can seize it by the crown.)

Sylvester's downfall in the play is, in part, a reflection of his failure to grasp the full significance of his own metaphor: the fact that the *healthy* tree is toppled by the storm should have warned him that it is those who strive for absolute moral perfection (and, above all, those like himself, who believe they have achieved it), who are most at risk of lapsing into sin. Believing themselves to be 'infallibly' virtuous (and thereby 'proof' against all risk of committing immoral actions), they become proudly complacent and fail to take due account of their residual capacity for evil. Of course in this particular instance, Sylvester is quite justified in protesting his innocence. But his fatal error is to believe – quite mistakenly – that he, the virtuous Sylvester, is literally 'incapable' of murdering another human being. As we shall see, the false sense of security that he derives from this erroneous belief results in his being caught off guard in act IV, when he yields to the temptation to take revenge on Rupert.

Just as some members of Rupert's entourage are not wholly committed to the brutal ideology of Rossitz, so too there are those in Warwand who do not fully endorse Sylvester's more benevolent conception of human nature. The symmetrical structure of the play is further reinforced by the conduct of Sylvester's wife, Gertrude. She continually reminds her husband of the suspicious circumstances surrounding the death of their own child in an attempt to convince him of Rupert's involvement in the matter. This prompts Sylvester to exclaim:

Das Mißtraun ist die schwarze Sucht der Seele,
Und alles, auch das Schuldlos-Reine, zieht
Fürs kranke Aug die Tracht der Hölle an. (*SW* I, 69; 515–7)

(Mistrust is an evil cancer of the soul and to a mind thus infected, even that which is pure and innocent appears in a hellish garb.)

In short: Eustache sees the world from Sylvester's perspective; Gertrude sees it through the eyes of Rupert. Of course there is a serious flaw even in the more benevolent view of human nature to which Sylvester (and Eustache) subscribe. Throughout the play, Sylvester is confronted with a series of suspicious incidents, all of which appear, to the members of his entourage, to have been orchestrated by Rupert. But despite his advisors' demands for violent retribution, Sylvester stubbornly refuses, believing wilfully that an alternative explanation will emerge exonerating Rupert and thereby rendering the use of force unnecessary. However when it seems that his daughter, Agnes, has been attacked by Johann in act III, scene 2, he comes perilously close to specifying the circumstances in which he would be prepared to take violent revenge, when he says:

> ja hätten sie
> Im Krieg mein Haus verbrannt, mein Weib und Kind
> Im Krieg erschlagen, noch wollt ichs entschuldgen.
> Doch daß sie mir den Meuchelmörder senden,
> – Wenns so ist – (*SW* I, 91; 1138–42)

(If war had been openly declared and they had burned down my house or killed my wife and child, why even then I could forgive them; but to send secret assassins – if that is the case –)

But although he stops just short of naming the necessary and sufficient conditions that, in his opinion, would justify an act of revenge, the tacit admission that such conditions do exist, reveals the presence of a crucial flaw in the particular version of the Christian ethic that he espouses. For what Sylvester fails to understand is that no matter how damning the evidence against Rupert may appear, there can never be circumstances in which revenge would be justified, since such acts of vengeance are wholly contrary to the system of ethics that underpins the form of society towards which Warwand is progressing.[9] His failure to appreciate the full implications of the ethical system he purports to embrace shows just how flawed is his concept of human nature. Seduced by his doctrine of the perfectibility of Man into disregarding his own human limitations, he fails to give due consideration to the possibility that circumstances may arise when even he will be sorely tempted to take revenge and that he is – as the ending of play underlines – quite capable of giving in to such temptation.

Sylvester may hope that the lack of clear-cut evidence against Rupert will always protect him from having to take action, but in adopting this approach, Sylvester is deceiving himself. He would do better to remind himself that, no matter how damning the evidence against Rupert appears, no matter how great the temptation to take revenge, he must always do his utmost to resist and that even so, there is no guarantee that he will succeed in this. This element of *mauvaise foi* in Sylvester's system of ethics has even been incorporated into the very structure of Warwand society itself in the form of a modest military force (for the purposes of 'deterrence', we may assume). And thus when, in act IV, scene 2, Sylvester finally decides that the moment for retaliation has come, he discovers, almost to his surprise, that the necessary military machinery – Theistiner's band of thirty men – is already in place, just waiting for him to give his authorisation.

On hearing of the death of Jeronimus in Rossitz, Sylvester loses faith in the ethical system that he has hitherto espoused and succumbs to the temptation to take revenge. 'Have no fear', he reassures his wife, 'From now on I will harbour no other feeling in my heart than revenge' ('Beruhge dich – fortan kein anderes | Gefühl als nur der Rache will ich kennen'; *SW* I, 125; 2055–6). Mistakenly, he believes that he has seen through the error of his previous ways, when all he has done is to exchange his own flawed view of human nature ('Man essentially good') for another that is equally flawed ('Man essentially evil'). And it is his uncritical acceptance of such simplistic accounts of human nature that blinds him to the true nature of Rupert's behaviour. For the fact is that Rupert was neither the fundamentally benevolent man that Sylvester would have liked to believe he was up to act IV, scene 2, but nor has he turned into a monster.

At this point in the play, Sylvester imagines he has learned his lesson, whereas a much harder one awaits him in the cave-scene of act V. There the prophetic quality of his words in act I, scene 2: 'I must throw some light on the matter, even if that means descending into hell itself' ('Ich muß mir Licht verschaffen, | Und sollt ichs mir auch aus der Hölle holen'; *SW* I, 74; 655–6) is most cruelly revealed. Only in the final act when he enters the 'hell' of the cave[10] does he become truly enlightened, for it is there that he discovers that he is in fact capable of committing an act no less evil than that performed by Rupert. And when Rupert addresses him at the end of the play saying:

> Sylvester! Selbst bin ich ein Kinderloser!
> *Pause*
> Sylvester! Deines Kindes Blut komm über
> Mich – kannst du besser nicht verzeihn, als ich?
> (*SW* 1, 152; 2714–16)

(Sylvester, I too have lost my child. *(Pause)* Sylvester! My hands shall be stained with the blood of your child. Can you not find it in you to forgive me as I forgive you.)

the fact that Sylvester cannot bear to look him in the face – the stage directions indicate that Sylvester offers his hand, averting his gaze as he does so – is not, as some critics have suggested,[11] an indication of the 'dubiousness' of this reconciliation, but on the contrary, an indication of the depth of Sylvester's grief and self-disgust. For having earlier expressed his desire to be 'a figure one can always look up to' ('stets des Anschauns würdig'; *SW* 1, 84; 969) he now cannot bear to see his own satanic nature reflected in the gaze of his rival, Rupert.

THE WORLD OF CHILDHOOD

In addition to these two 'veterans' of their respective social systems, we are presented with three children, two of whom, Agnes and Ottokar, have been brought up in the conventions of Warwand and Rossitz respectively, and a third, Johann, the *enfant sauvage* who has, for the most part, been excluded from the influence of either system. In his portrayal of the love affair between Agnes and Ottokar, Kleist explores the possibility of a utopian realm where lovers communicate with complete honesty and in which the conflicts of the adult world may be transcended.[12] But just as Rupert and Sylvester are thwarted in their endeavours by an uncritical acceptance of their two disparate, but flawed, concepts of human nature, so too the children, despite their excellent intentions, are misled by a misconception of love as an amalgam of eroticism, contractuality and insincere posturing, a misconception that effectively blocks all feeling at source. Both can be seen to cull the elements of their amorous exchanges – however inexpertly – from their respective upbringings in 'polite society'. Agnes has been taught to deny the reality of female eroticism in the interests of preserving a mythical notion of 'feminine modesty'; Ottokar has been brought up to suppress the affectionate aspects of erotic love in a display of macho sexual conquest.

The essentially conventional character of their affair is highlighted by Johann's (unrequited) passion for Agnes which results in true madness.[13] Curiously enough, however, critics have largely ignored the significance of Johann's role in the play's structure. Unlike Ottokar, Johann, Rupert's illegitimate son, is a figure who inhabits the margins of Rossitz society: he is not on stage during the opening scene in which the oath of revenge is sworn, and has almost no inside knowledge of the family feud. The qualitative difference between him and the other members of the Rossitz clan is intimated in an incident which calls to mind another well-known illegitimate child of German literature, namely Goethe's Eugenie in *Die natürliche Tochter* (*The natural daughter*).[14] When Johann attempts to take part in the hunt – the activity that most typically encapsulates the Rossitzers' relationship to the world around them – he loses his seat ('Sitz') on his horse ('Roß') and as he explains to Ottokar:

> eh ich, was ich sehe, wahr
> Kann nehmen, stürz ich, Roß und Reiter, schon
> Hinab in einen Strom. (*SW* I, 60; 281–3)

(before I could grasp what was happening, we tumbled, my horse and I, together into a stream.)

The conflated image of 'horse and rider' ('Roß und Reiter') – an image which recurs in Kleist's work, most notably in the play *Penthesilea* – hints at the fact that his relationship to the natural world is not the same relationship of mastery and control that characterises the other Rossitzer. Likewise, Johann's relative lack of social sophistication is in marked contrast to the more devious cunning of Ottokar; not only is he quite unable to conceal his passion for Agnes, arriving on stage tear-stained and distraught,[15] but he is equally unable to conceal the identity of his beloved from Ottokar:

Ottokar – Ich muß
Ein schreckliches Bekenntnis dir vollenden –
Es muß heraus aus dieser Brust . . . (*SW* I, 62; 335–7)

(Ottokar! There is something I must confess to you – something I can no longer hide . . .)

But whilst Johann, as Rupert's illegitimate son has little to lose by confessing his love of Agnes, for Ottokar, there is much more at stake. Given his father's distrust of Sylvester, not to mention the oath of revenge that he has just sworn, Ottokar cannot make his feelings for Agnes known without incurring the wrath of his father. Thus when Johann intimates that Ottokar knows the identity of the woman in question, saying, 'Your suspicions were correct' ('Du hasts geahndet'; *SW* I, 63; 352), Ottokar immediately denies this in the most emphatic terms. Both here and elsewhere, his sense of discretion is such that he never wittingly allows his feelings for Agnes to place his own future in Rossitz at risk.

In contrast, Johann's feelings for Agnes are much closer to Kleist's ideal of love as a relationship wholly devoid of self-interest and worldly discretion. Unlike Ottokar, for whom love is predominantly a matter of sexual conquest and possession, Johann understands that love – in the true sense of the term – is always a gift freely given by the lover to the beloved, and something quite distinct from exclusive sexual ownership. The difference between his genuine feelings of love and the possessive desire of Ottokar is most clearly reflected in their contrasting attitudes to the veil that Agnes has given to Johann. When Ottokar recognises it, he attempts to barter for it with his rival, offering a ring in exchange. But Johann is unwilling to part with the veil even on pain of death: 'Take anything – even my life if you so desire – but not that' ('O Nicht – o nimm mir alles, | Mein Leben, wenn du willst'; *SW* I, 60; 256–7). The contrast between Johann's genuine passion and Ottokar's shallow eroticism is further underlined in the opening scene of act II. Filled with despair when he realises that Agnes loves Ottokar and not him, Johann is quite unable to conform to the standards of 'decency' advocated by his more successful rival. Ottokar offers to excuse his friend's 'ungentlemanly' behaviour on the grounds that he is acting quite out of character, but Johann merely draws his attention to the operations of cunning self-interest that lie behind this appeal to 'maintain one's dignity' even in defeat:

> Weil ich mich edel nicht erweise, nicht
> Erweisen will, machst du mir weis, ich seis,
> Damit die unverdiente Ehre mich
> Bewegen soll, in ihrem Sinn zu handeln? (*SW* I, 80; 836–9)

(Since I cannot behave decently, since I *refuse* to, you tell me that I am a decent fellow really in the hope that this ill-deserved compliment will compel me to behave in a manner that suits your purposes.)

This leads to an almost comic incident when Ottokar mistakenly assumes that Johann has drawn his sword in order to fight a duel over Agnes, and we see the extent to which Ottokar has been conditioned by his education in the Rossitz tradition. As Johann is obliged to explain to his convention-bound rival, it is not Ottokar's death but his own that he desires.[16] For unlike Ottokar, Johann understands that love is not a question of ownership; he cannot take possession of Agnes's love by killing his rival, and that since love is a feeling that resides solely within the lover, the only death that can rid him of his passion is his own.[17] And when Ottokar refuses to kill him, he turns to Agnes herself in act II, scene 3, saying, 'Take this dagger, I beg you – for have you not already plunged one into my heart?' ('Nimm diesen Dolch, sag ich. – Hast du nicht einen | Mir schon ins Herz gedrückt?'; *SW* I, 87; 1052–3). For Johann, hyperbole is no longer hyperbole, metaphor is no longer metaphor: for him the metaphorical 'dagger' of unrequited love is no less deadly than the literal dagger he holds in his hands.[18]

The wild, untutored behaviour of Johann throws into relief the extent to which Agnes – like Ottokar – is a product of the repressive and conformist society in which she is growing up. For when Johann declares his love for her (in act II, scene 3), she, with her limited understanding of passion, imagines that he has in mind to kill her. Tempting though it is, at least at first sight, to see Agnes as an artless embodiment of feminine innocence, this is forestalled by Kleist's frequent portrayal of her self-conscious attempts to conform to the highly conventional image of femininity current in her society. Her grasp and acceptance of these conventions is apparent in the exchange with her grandfather, Sylvius, in act I, scene 2, when he remarks that, despite being old enough for marriage, she has not yet been confirmed, and goes as far as to suggest that she would quite welcome such an amorous interest. At first she denies this coyly, saying: 'Those are your words, not mine' ('Das sag ich nicht'; *SW* I, 66; 421), but only a few lines later, she cannily asks Sylvius to approach her mother on her behalf and organise her confirmation on the grounds that were she herself to do it, her mother 'might think untoward of her' ('möchte ungleich von | Mir denken'; *SW* I, 66; 425–6). Far from being a straightforward protestation of 'naïve innocence', her earlier denial betrays her awareness that the articulation of female sexual desire is incompatible with the idealised image of femininity that she has been brought up to project. A further instance of her social sophistication is to be found in act II, scene 1. Fully aware of the presence of Ottokar watching her, she continues to deliver her monologue 'as though she had not seen him' ('als hätte sie ihn nicht gesehen'; *SW* I, 75) and with the same assurance projects an image of femininity that perfectly reflects the interests of her male observer:

> Nun wär mirs recht, er hätte was er sucht,
> Bei mir gefunden, und die Eifersucht,
> Der Liebe Jugendstachel, hätte, selbst,
> Sich stumpfend, ihn hinaus gejagt ins Feld,
> Gleich einem jungen Rosse, das zuletzt
> Doch heimgekehrt zu dem Stall, der ihn ernährt.
> Statt dessen ist kein andrer Nebenbuhler
> Jetzt grade um mich, als sein Geist. (*SW* I, 75; 704–11)

(How happy I would be if he were to find in me everything he seeks; how happy I would be if the thorn of jealousy, that thorn in the side of young love that drove him out into the open field, had blunted itself, so that, like a young stallion, he might return to the manger where his food lies waiting. For now, his only rival is my memory of him.)

At this point, not only does she reassure him that he is the sole object of her affection (perhaps mindful of her earlier encounter with Johann), but, in likening herself to the manger to which the exhausted stallion eventually returns, she re-affirms her willingness to assume the conventional role of woman, catering for the needs and moods of her male partner in the domestic sphere in order that he may function all the more effectively in the public domain. This image of femininity which she presents to the watching Ottokar, is no less artificial than the garland she weaves as she speaks her 'monologue', of which she says:

> Der Kranz ist ein vollendet Weib. Da, nimm
> Ihn hin. Sprich: er gefällt mir; so ist er
> Bezahlt. (*SW* I, 76; 724–6)

(The garland is a woman in her prime. Take it. Tell me that you like it and it is yours to keep)

Clearly we must be wary of taking the 'idyllic' scenes of acts II, III and V at face value. Although the lovers meet in the mountains, away from their normal social contexts, Kleist intimates at a number of points in the play that this 'idyll' is little more than a romantic tableau of their own making, and one that, as we shall see, requires an increasing investment of effort on their part to sustain.[19] Their conversation may, at first sight, appear to be an 'artless' declaration of 'young love', but a closer examination of the text reveals it to be a self-conscious, though crude, attempt to imitate the rhetoric of adult coquetterie and the only genuine feelings it evokes are those of adolescent sexual excitement. They attempt to 'conceal' their identity from each other, but do this so self-consciously that neither they themselves (nor the audience) is left in any doubt that each knows exactly who the other is. In act II, scene I, Agnes denies that her family is involved in any feud, thereby implying that she is not in fact Sylvester's daughter.[20] But Ottokar's subsequent exclamation of relief: 'so I don't have to murder you after all!' ('so brauch ich dich ja nicht nicht zu morden!'; *SW* I, 77; 750), a remark so absurd as to be almost comic, cannot but remove any doubts from her mind that he is from Rossitz. The fact that he has no qualms about referring quite openly to the death-threat hanging over her makes it clear that he has no intention of harming her and, what is more, that he is confident she knows this. Thus her 'bewildered' response, 'murder me?' ('Morden?' *SW* I, 77; 751) and all her subsequent remarks suggesting that she is at risk from Ottokar, are not expressions of fear, but are increasingly artful projections of herself as an innocent frail creature who can only throw herself on the mercy of her beloved. In effect the dramatic function of the idyll scene is to show how the lovers' exploitation of the clandestine nature of their encounter and their own fantasies of danger and violence creates a heightened sense of erotically-tinged excitement and prevents their having a realistic appreciation of the very real dangers they face.

The possibility that their relationship might assume once more the character of a utopian realm in which lovers communicate with complete honesty and in which the conflicts of the adult world might be transcended is explicitly raised by Ottokar in the opening scene of act III, when he casts his mind back nostalgically to their very first encounter:

> Wie war es damals
> Ganz anders, so ganz anders. Deine Seele
> Lag offen vor mir, wie ein schönes Buch,
> Das sanft zuerst den Geist ergreift, dann tief
> Ihn rührt, dann unzertrennlich fest ihn hält.
> Es zieht des Lebens Forderung den Leser
> Zuweilen ab, denn das Gemeine will
> Ein Opfer auch; doch immer kehrt er wieder
> Zu dem vertrauten Geist zurück, der in
> Der Göttersprache ihm die Welt erklärt,
> (*SW* I, 95–6; 1268–77)

(How very different it all was then. Your soul lay open before me like a wonderful book that at first gently draws the reader in, touches him deeply and then holds him fast. Now and then he is distracted by life's demands, for everyday matters must be attended to as well; but he always returns to the familiar text in which the mysteries of life are revealed to him in language divine.)

His choice of imagery, however, reveals how convention-bound his perception of even this initial encounter is. In likening Agnes to a passive object, 'a wonderful book', that is displayed for the enjoyment of its (male) reader and to which that reader returns when he has dealt with the demands of everyday life, he is describing this original moment of innocent love wholly in terms of his inherited notions of male-female relations. The fact that this image of femininity corresponds perfectly to that articulated earlier by Agnes in act II, scene I – where she likens herself to the 'manger' to which the exhausted 'stallion' returns – underlines the extent to which both these young people share essentially the same stilted, conventional notion of love. This original state of innocence in which perfect communication between lovers was possible, if ever it existed, now lies in the distant past as is made clear by Ottokar's remark: 'But now you are a closed book' ('Nun bist | Du ein verschloßner Brief'; *SW* 1, 96; 1280–1). Later, when Agnes announces that she feels faint and Ottokar offers to fetch her water from the spring, Ottokar's artful exploitation of the situation to revive images of their first encounter seems neither spontaneous nor sincere. For as Ottokar reminds her, on that occasion:

> Ich fragte dich nach deinem Namen;
> Du seist noch nicht getauft, sprachst du. – Da schöpfte
> Ich eine Hand voll Wasser aus dem Quell,
> Benetzte dir die Stirn, die Brust, und sprach:
> Weil du ein Ebenbild der Mutter Gottes,
> Maria tauf ich dich. (*SW* 1, 95; 1263–8)

(I asked you what your name was. You said you had not been christened. So I took a handful of water from the spring, and pouring it on your head and breast said: Since you are made in the image of the Mother of God, I name you Maria.)

But now his behaviour appears a deliberate attempt to replay a series of well-rehearsed gestures, plainly inviting the audience to take a more sceptical view of all the subsequent action revolving around his attempt to 'poison' her, and to regard the whole episode as an example of elaborate self-dramatisation: a self-indulgent charade designed as much for each individual's own gratification as for that of his partner – the familiar pattern of adolescent egotism.

And as we suspect, although Ottokar and Agnes tell themselves that they have succeeded in restoring their relationship's former state of perfect openness, it is not long before both of them retire behind the security of their respective social and cultural programming with the result that fresh disagreements break out between them. When Ottokar asks Agnes:

> Und wäre der Verdacht auch noch so groß,
> Dem Vater nicht, der Mutter nicht so traun,
> Als mir? (*SW* 1, 99; 1343–5)

(And would you, no matter how great your suspicions, trust me more than your own father and mother?)

his question is the first of a series which, in recalling the reality of the family feud, threatens the precarious 'harmony', so recently recaptured. Nonetheless, his question shows he knows that if this affair is to have a future, it will be not he, but Agnes, the female partner (and her family) who will have to compromise. Unlike Johann, who genuinely loves Agnes, and for whom the feud is of no relevance, Ottokar is constitutionally incapable of knowingly risking his future position at the head of Rossitz society for the sake of a woman. However, as the remainder of the scene unfolds, he is forced to recognise that whilst Sylvester might be persuaded to compromise, the main obstacle to his relationship with Agnes is not her father but his own. He realises that Rupert will have to be convinced of Sylvester's innocence, and that this cannot be achieved through persuasion, but only through the production of incontrovertible empirical evidence. For as he says, 'it will all be in vain, unless the error that plagues us can be resolved' ('Denn fruchtlos ist doch alles, kommt der Irrtum | Ans Licht nicht, der uns neckt'; *SW* I, 103; 1457–8). At the same time, his remarks reveal that, as far as his own father and the realities of power in Rossitz are concerned, he himself has a better grasp of such realities than the more sentimental Jeronimus.[21] For whilst Jeronimus seriously regards the love affair as a means of ending the feud, Ottokar knows that the families will have to be reconciled by entirely other means before even the existence of the love affair can be revealed.

Ottokar's thoroughly realistic attitude at this point is in stark contrast to the way he behaves in the cave scene of act v. For just as the erotic tension of the lovers' previous encounters was heightened by a false appraisal of the elements of risk and adventure involved, here too it feeds off an equally unrealistic assessment of the very real danger in which they are placed. So concerned is Ottokar to exploit the situation and convince Agnes that now the irresistible moment of consummation of their 'love' has arrived, that he fails to see that he has placed her life in grave danger by asking her to come to the cave in the first place. Moreover, whilst the heroic defence of his beloved may appeal to his wilder, chivalrous fantasies, we feel certain that he has no real expectation that he will be required to sacrifice his life for Agnes.

The allegedly 'utopian' character of the scene is undermined before it even begins, when we remember that in seducing his bride-to-be on the eve of their projected 'wedding', Ottokar is, quite literally, following in his father's footsteps. For in act IV, scene I, Eustache draws the audience's attention to the corresponding night in her relationship with Rupert when she pleads with him to spare Agnes's life, saying:

> auf meinen Knien beschwöre
> Ich dich, bei jener ersten Nacht, die ich
> Am Tage vor des Priesters Spruch dir schenkte,
> (*SW* I, 122; 1979–81)

(On my knees, I implore you now, by that one night which I did grant you before the priest pronounced our wedding vows)

This renders Kleist's presentation of the 'idyll' in act V no less ambiguous than his presentation of the 'idylls' in acts II and III, and as the scene unfolds, it becomes apparent that what we are witnessing is little short of sentimentality run riot. The fictional wedding that Ottokar describes belongs to the world of chivalrous romance, a tale designed to suit the taste of a well brought-up young lady, who might just agree to surrender her virtue for the charm of the moment in the picaresque setting of a secret rendezvous. In typical Kleistian fashion, pathos is relentlessly juxtaposed with bathos. Thus when Ottokar says to Agnes:

> Denn wozu noch
> Das Unergründliche geheimnisvoll
> Verschleiern? Alles Schöne, liebe Agnes
> Braucht keinen andern Schleier, als den eignen,
> Denn der ist freilich selbst die Schönheit.
> (*SW* I, 142; 2487–91)

(Why cast a veil over that which is secret and unfathomable? Oh Agnes, beauty needs no other veil than its own and that is beauty's self.)

the extravagant rhetoric of these lines is crucially undercut by the stage directions which show Ottokar struggling to remove Agnes's clothes before his father arrives.[22] At the same time, Agnes does not fail to play her part as the 'innocent victim' of her devotion; 'bewildered' by it all, she murmurs coyly, 'Oh Ottokar, what are you doing?' ('O Ottokar, | Was machst du?' *SW* I, 142; 2485–6).

CONCLUSION

It was with good reason that Kleist condemned Ottokar and Agnes to a premature death, even if this lay beyond the understanding of nineteenth-century theatre-managers. For it is clear that the emancipatory potential of a marriage between Ottokar and Agnes is strictly limited, and indeed quite trivial, when compared to the genuine reconciliation that takes place between Rupert and Sylvester. Indeed were this love affair to survive into marriage, we feel it would almost certainly result in the perpetuation of precisely those conventional modes of behaviour which were responsible for the tragedy in the first place. In time, Ottokar would reveal himself to be a true son of his father, Rupert, and Agnes would turn out to be little more than the faithful wife of her husband. And when compared with Johann, they appear too deeply steeped in the conventions of their world to constitute a real force for change.

The reconciliation between Rupert and Sylvester at the end of the play is of far greater significance, based as it is on a tragedy which both will remember to the end of their lives. However, the fact that this tragedy strikes equally powerfully at both branches of the family should not obscure the fact that Kleist views the institutions of Warwand in a far more favourable light than those of Rossitz. Despite Sylvester's misguided faith in the unimprovable perfection of the institutions of Warwand, those institutions are based on the essentially Christian precepts of love and forgiveness, and are close to Kleist's ideal of a society designed for the benefit of all its members rather than simply for that of the few. As we shall see, several years later, in his portrayal of the Amazon State in *Penthesilea*, Kleist was to present his readers with a similarly advanced society, only to show that it too was cursed by the same flaws of the perfectionist's philosophy.

PART II

Virtue assailed

CHAPTER 4

Der zerbrochne Krug

When Kleist first declaimed his tragedy, *Die Familie Schroffenstein*, before a group of friends on his island retreat in Thun, the reaction of those present was recorded by Heinrich Zschokke, a former colleague of the author from his army days as follows:

> Als uns Kleist eines Tages sein Trauerspiel *Die Familie Schroffenstein* vorlas, ward im letzten Akt das allseitige Gelächter der Zuhörerschaft, wie auch des Dichters, so stürmisch und endlos, daß, bis zu seiner letzten Mordszene zu gelangen, Unmöglichkeit wurde. (*Lebensspuren*, no. 67a)

> (One day when Kleist declaimed his tragedy *Die Familie Schroffenstein*, not only the assembled listeners, but the author himself, were so convulsed with laughter during the last act that it was quite impossible to get to the final murder scene.)

No doubt the laughter was, in part, a reaction to the melodramatic aspects of the play. However, there are a number of genuinely comic moments in *Die Familie Schroffenstein*, not least the way in which the exalted pathos of the characters' rhetoric is deflated by the bathos of the situation in which they find themselves. Time and again, the characters adopt conventional, ritualistic poses yet, because of their youth and inexperience, do so in a manner that makes their behaviour appear ridiculous. Indeed, it is striking how often the dividing line between tragedy and comedy is blurred in Kleist's work. This is true even of those works not explicitly referred to as comedies, such as *Die Hermannsschlacht* and *Prinz Friedrich von Homburg*, all of which contain genuinely comic moments.[1] Of course, often a second viewing or reading of these works is required for the reader or spectator to appreciate the subtleties of Kleist's irony. It may well be that the novella was a genre more suited to Kleist's ironic style than drama, for the reader of prose fiction can always turn back and re-read sections of a story. Not surprisingly, perhaps, critics have been more receptive to the ironic dimension of his stories than they have to that of his plays.[2]

Given the extent to which literary critics and theatre directors have focused on what they regard as the inherently 'tragic' dimension of each play, it is easy to overlook the fact that both *Der zerbrochne Krug (The broken jug)* and *Amphitryon*, were written as comedies.[3] In *Der zerbrochne Krug* we laugh at the lengths to which both Walter and Adam are obliged to go to preserve the façade of an allegedly 'ideal' system of 'justice' which, by the end of the play, has been exposed as nothing more than a precarious structure, cobbled together by time and seriously biased in favour of the interests of the ruling classes. In *Amphitryon*, we laugh at the way in which Alkmene's belief that she is constitutionally 'incapable' of being unfaithful to her husband, Amphitryon, propels her from the arms of one lover, Amphitryon, into the arms of another, Jupiter. Although very different in style – Kleist described *Der zerbrochne Krug* as written in the rustic style of a painting by the Flemish landscape painter David Teniers,[4] whilst *Amphitryon* is closely modelled on Molière's classical comedy of the same name – both plays have one very important feature in common. In each, a major source of comedy lies in the juxtaposition of the exotic refinements of the members of the dominant class in their struggle to maintain the various mythologies with which history has burdened them, and the down-to-earth realism of the lower orders, whose more mundane preoccupations enable them to see through the absurdities of their 'superiors' and to present solutions to their problems obvious to the mind of anyone not blinded by the absurd conventions of upper-class manners.

The play *Der zerbrochne Krug* is perhaps best known for the violent quarrel that it provoked between Kleist and Goethe over the latter's disastrous production of the play at the Weimar theatre in March 1808. From the start Goethe had misgivings about the play. He wrote to Adam Müller on 28 August 1807, acknowledging its considerable merits, but went on to add: 'it is a pity that it is yet another play written for a theatre that does not as yet exist' ('nur schade, daß das Stück auch wieder dem unsichtbaren Theater angehört'; *Lebensspuren*, no. 185). Goethe's belief that the play was not well-suited to the requirements of the contemporary stage, at least as far as Weimar was concerned, proved correct, though perhaps not for the reasons he puts forward. Writing some three years later to Johann Daniel Falk, he explains that the play's lack of success was due not so much to his direction, but rather to the fact 'that the plot . . . lacked pace' ('daß es dem . . . Stoffe an einer rasch durchgeführten Handlung fehlt'; *Lebensspuren*, no. 252).[5] Given that the play was divided up (by Goethe) into three acts and, by all accounts, poorly acted, it is perhaps not surprising that it failed to please the Weimar audience. Almost all the contemporary reviewers commented unfavourably on the length of the 'final act' (which included the longer *Variant* to scene 12). For example, one critic, writing in the *Zeitung für die elegante Welt* on 14 March 1808, attributed the play's failure to the fact that 'especially in the last act, everything becomes so drawn-out and tedious' ('besonders wird im letzten Akte so entsetzlich viel und alles so breit erzählt'; *Lebensspuren*, no. 248a). Yet the impatient tone of this and other critics' reports suggests that they failed to see the real significance of the final scene, in which Walter is challenged and required to defend the integrity of those he represents. As a result, they overlooked the elements of social criticism in the play, and regarded it as little more than a comic 'detective story' in which the main point of interest is whether or not Adam's corruption will be revealed.[6] As we shall see, however, it is in the longer, (original) version of scene 12, that the target of Kleist's social criticism is most clearly revealed.[7] For although he heeded the critics' advice and subsequently produced a radically shortened version of scene 12 (the version that is now regarded as the standard text), the fact that he included both versions in the later published edition of the text (the 'Buchfassung') suggests that he remained reluctant to abandon his original conception of the play.

ADAM AND EVE

As is so often the case with Kleist's work, literary critics remain sharply divided, in this instance over the role of Walter in *Der zer-*

brochne Krug.[8] Is it really the case that his intervention results in order being restored and justice being done? Are they one and the same thing? Does his offer to buy Rupert out of the army[9] result in Eve's overcoming her 'crisis of faith' or is she merely the dupe of his superior authority and adroitness?[10] It is, however, striking that whilst critics seem unable to make up their minds on the question of Walter's integrity, there is a fairly general consensus that Eve's role in the play is that of the 'victim', a figure whose 'naïve innocence' exposes her to the machinations of the unscrupulous Adam (and possibly of Walter as well). As we shall see, however, a closer examination of the text, and above all of the longer *Variant* to scene 12, reveals that she is considerably more shrewd than many critics have been willing to concede. And far from being the 'victim' of her own 'innocence', at the end of the *Variant*, it is she, rather than Walter, who is in control of the situation. Thus although the play ostensibly depicts the struggle of the 'weak' against the 'strong', through his characterisation of Eve, Kleist gently reminds his audience that often, the 'weak' have rather more weapons up their sleeves than might, at first sight, appear to be the case.[11]

It was with good reason that Kleist named the central protagonists of his play after the original occupants of the Garden of Eden. For just as the biblical Eve brought about the Fall of Adam by offering him an apple plucked from the Tree of Knowledge, so too Kleist's Eve tempts her 'Adam' by offering him 'forbidden fruit' (albeit of a rather different kind) thereby bringing about his downfall. For in *Der zerbrochne Krug*, it is woman, as represented by Eve, who is in control, and this is further underlined by the essentially weak character of her two 'husbands', Adam and Ruprecht, each of whom manifestly lacks her shrewd understanding of human affairs and her steadfast resolve. In the later, shortened version of the play, this aspect of Eve's character does not emerge nearly as clearly as in the original version,[12] and so it is to the *Variant* of scene 12 that we must turn, if we are to appreciate the full import of this thought-provoking comedy.

The cause of Adam's downfall and the defeat of the system of justice that he represents can be attributed to his mistaken belief that Eve will adhere to the same unrealistic notion of the absolute value of 'feminine virtue' as her mother, and that as a result, she will want to conceal the details of their nocturnal rendezvous. In this he is, of course, sadly deluded. The fact is, that when the life of her fiancé, Ruprecht, is at stake, Eve has scant regard for such conventional notions of 'honour', and it is this that emerges so clearly from an examination of the original *Variant* to scene 12. Thus when Ruprecht (who likewise believes that she has hitherto concealed the truth from the court out of a concern for her 'reputation') apologises to Walter on her behalf, saying 'She was ashamed, you see. Please forgive her, your Honour' ('Sie schämte sich. Verzeiht ihr, gnädger Herr'; *SW* 1, 839; 1928), the scornful tone of Eve's aside, 'Oh yes, that's right. Ashamed!' ('Ja, schämen!'; *SW* 1, 839; 1931) underlines just how little her fiancé has understood of what has been going on. What he is unable to see is that Eve has single-handedly taken on the authorities (and won) thereby saving his life.

Whilst the rather slow-witted Ruprecht believes that, once conscripted into the army, he will remain in the comparative safety of Utrecht, Eve knows full well what the future has in store for him. Thus in the *Variant* to scene 12 she tells Walter that Adam has revealed to her:

> Daß die Miliz sich einschifft nach Batavia,
> Den eingebornen Kön'gen dort, von Bantam,
> Von Java, Jakatra, was weiß ich? Raub
> Zum Heil der Haager Krämer abzujagen.
>
> (*SW* 1, 843; 2058–61)

(That the militia is to be sent to Batavia in order to rob the local rulers of Bantam, Java, Jakarta and goodness knows where else of their wealth in order to fill the coffers of the Hague merchants.)

Not only has she found out that Ruprecht is to be sent to the East Indies to fight in a colonial war, but she is well informed as to the odds on his returning from Batavia, an island where, as she puts it 'out of every company that disembarks there, one half buries the other' ('von | Jedweden Schiffes Mannschaft, das ihm naht, | Die eine Hälfte stets die andere begräbt'; *SW* 1, 844; 2083–5). Although the source of her information is a letter read out to her by Adam, it is important to note that she has no doubts as to the reliability of this information and considers it perfectly plausible that the authorities would deliberately attempt to mislead the ordinary citizen in this way. Thus when Walter attempts to deny all knowledge of the matter, Eve wastes no time in challenging his posture of ignorance and says, 'Your Honour, I know that you are obliged to say that' ('Gestrenger Herr, | Ich weiß, Ihr seid verbunden so zu reden'; *SW* I, 843; 2063–4). Moreover, when he continues to protest his innocence, appealing to his sense of 'duty' in so doing, she debunks this too, saying, 'That's right, duty compels you. And your duty is to conceal the truth from us' ('Gut, gut. Auf Eure Pflicht. | Und die ist, uns, was wahr ist, zu verbergen'; *SW* I, 844; 2065–6). We shall return to the question of whether the alleged contents of Adam's letter can be quite as easily dismissed as Walter and Licht claim. For the time being, it is sufficient to note that she is under no illusions as to the state's capacity for double-dealing and clearly understands that it is the duty of civil servants, such as Walter, to preserve the public image of the state authorities at all costs. In this, she demonstrates a far more sophisticated understanding of the way the state works than her naïve fiancé, who exclaims incredulously, 'What? Sent to Asia? Me?' ('Ich, nach Asien?'; *SW* I, 843; 2062). Moreover, she also considers it quite feasible to oppose this deliberate act of deception by the state, with an equally subversive act on her own part, or as she puts it, 'to fight cunning with cunning' ('List gegen List'; *SW* I, 844; 2093).

In the light of this remark, and of her clear-sightedness regarding the machinations of state politics, it is not possible to regard Eve as a straightforward embodiment of 'naïve innocence'. For it is hard to take seriously the possibility that a young woman possessed of so shrewd an understanding of human nature does not appreciate that, like everything else in the world she inhabits, the medical certificate excusing Ruprecht from military service (the 'Attest') has its price. Of course, to claim that Eve does not attach the same exaggerated importance to the concept of 'feminine virtue' as her mother is not to say that she does not understand the significance of such conventions in her society. Accordingly, when she describes how Adam called by on the night in question, she says:

> Drauf ich: Ei, was Herr Richter,
> Was will er auch so spät zu Nacht bei mir?
> 'Je, Närrchen', spricht er – Dreist heraus, sag ich:

Was hat Er hier Glock zehn bei mir zu suchen?
'Was ich Glock zehn bei dir zu suchen habe?' –
Ich sag, laß Er die Hand mir weg! Was will Er? –
(*SW* 1, 845–6; 2122–7)

(So I said to him, 'Well I never, your Honour, what can you be wanting from me at this late hour?' whereupon he said, 'You saucy little goose'. So I says, boldly, 'It's gone ten, what on earth do you want from me?' 'What on earth do I want from you?' he says. Then I says, 'Take your hands off me. What do you think you're doing?')

That is, she is sufficiently circumspect to include her own protestations of 'shocked outrage' for the benefit of those present and, above all, for the benefit of her mother and fiancé. That this is merely a feigned posture of 'innocence' is revealed a few lines later on when she reports Adam's indignant retort:

'Ich glaube wohl, du bist verrückt', spricht er.
'Warst du nicht heut Glock eilf im Amt bei mir,
Und wolltest ein Attest für Ruprecht haben?'
(*SW* 1, 846; 2128–30)

('Have you lost your wits', he says. 'I thought you came to my office at eleven o'clock today to ask me for a medical certificate for Ruprecht?')

Adam's words make it clear that he is in no doubt that she knows what favours will be required if she is to obtain the medical certificate. Although Eve knows full well what is expected of her, she has, of course, no choice in the matter if she is to save Ruprecht from being sent to near certain death in the East Indies. In addition, she realises that the cost of obtaining this certificate is fairly high, since it seems reasonable to assume that a night spent with Adam is not without some social risk. However, she is, above all, a realist who sees that she is faced with a stark choice: either she can preserve her 'honour' and risk her fiancé's life; or she can risk her 'honour' and save him. Not surprisingly, she chooses the latter option, since she cares considerably more about the real-life Ruprecht than she does about a spurious notion of 'priceless' feminine virtue.

In the event, Eve is saved by a stroke of good fortune: her nocturnal rendezvous with Adam is interrupted by the unexpected arrival of Ruprecht. However, this also poses a problem since she does not, as yet, have the certificate in her possession. Thus the reason for her silence in court is not, as Ruprecht believes, her sense of 'shame', but rather her understanding that if she is to get what she wants, she must keep quiet about Adam's involvement in the affair. This demonstrates the workings of calm, resourceful intelligence, and although Adam may appear to be in control of the situation, the matter is not as straightforward as it seems. For whilst Adam's position of authority allows him to exploit the situation, paradoxically it also renders him vulnerable, especially when his superior, Walter, unexpectedly arrives. Of course Eve is no less aware of this than Adam, and significantly it is he – not Eve – who desperately wants the facts of their rendezvous to remain secret. Thus when the plaintiffs appear in scene 7, he asks imploringly: 'Tell me . . . the reason why you've come to court' [G, 108] ('Was ists, das ihr mir bringt?'; *SW* I, 195; 522). However, her dismissive 'You'll soon hear why' [G, 108] ('Er wirds schon hören'; *SW* I, 195; 522) confirms that she is clear about who has the upper hand at this point. For if Adam fulfils his part of the bargain, Eve will fulfil hers, thereby rescuing the judge's reputation.

Of course, the whole business could be quite simply and satisfactorily resolved if only the slow-witted Ruprecht would accept the responsibility for breaking the jug, and it is with good reason that his fiancée exclaims in exasperation, 'Shame, shame on you! . . . You couldn't say: *I* broke the jug, could you?' [G, 129] ('. . . Pfui, schäme dich, | Daß du nicht sagst, gut, ich zerschlug den Krug!' *SW* I, 216; 1162–3) and only a few lines later she spells out to him how he should have behaved: 'you should have thought: Eve's an honest girl and I am confident there is an explanation for all this which honours her' [G, 129] ('Du hättest denken sollen: Ev ist brav, | Es wird sich alles ihr zum Ruhme lösen'; *SW* I, 216; 1171–2). Given Ruprecht's inability to grasp what is required of him and his failure to appreciate what his fiancée is going through for his sake, we sympathise with her when she cries, 'You odious, ungrateful man! Yes, I should spare myself the stocks, for you deserve it' [G, 130] ('O du Abscheulicher! Du Undankbarer! | Wert, daß ich mir die Fiedel spare!'; *SW* I, 217; 1187–8). Eve is under no illusions about her fiancé's fundamental lack of intelligence, and it is a sign of the genuineness of her affection for him that she is prepared to go to so much trouble to save this simpleton who, if left to his own devices, would rush blindly to his doom.

Eve is confronted with a further problem when it becomes clear that Adam, thrown into a panic by the arrival of Walter, is incapable of concealing his involvement in the affair. Unlike Eve, who keeps a perfectly cool head throughout, Adam is unable to master his emotions. She fulfils her side of the bargain and does not, at least to begin with, name him as the culprit, but he fails to fulfil his and, in one last ditch attempt to save his own skin, orders Ruprecht to be thrown in jail:

> Den Hals erkenn ich
> Ins Eisen ihm, und weil er ungebührlich
> Sich gegen seinen Richter hat betragen,
> Schmeiß ich ihn ins vergitterte Gefängnis.
> Wie lange, werd ich noch bestimmen. (*SW* 1, 241; 1876–80)

(Our judgement is, that he must wear the iron collar – and by reason of his contempt of court I'm sticking him behind bars, too. How long his term shall run, we will determine later.) [G, 154]

At this point Eve's bold use of her trump card leaves Adam thunderstruck, and delivers him – with his authority in tatters – to the mercy of his superior. For suddenly, and quite against all his expectations, she names him as the guilty party.[13] The very fact that she, 'a mere peasant lass', is prepared to take the risk of accusing him before the higher authority, is sufficient to convince all present that Adam must be guilty, and there ensues a mass pursuit of the hapless philanderer who has taken to his heels in blind panic. Several scenes earlier, just prior to the start of the trial, Adam has been overheard to say, 'I'll be damned. There are two cases here – no more, no less' ('Ei! Hols der Henker auch! Zwei Fälle gibts, | Mein Seel, nicht mehr'; *SW* 1, 197; 553–4) and it is at this point, with the courtroom plunged into chaos, that the first trial ends and the second begins. The first, was concerned with the relatively insignificant questions of broken vows and broken jugs, but in the second, it is the integrity of the state vis-à-vis its citizens that is on trial. Strictly speaking, of course, the second 'trial' is not really a trial, but a settlement out of court.

Though the stakes involved are now that much higher, Eve's task in the *Variant* to scene 12, is more manageable than that in the earlier scenes of the play. For she can now, at least temporarily, dispense with the services of the slow-witted Ruprecht, and she sees in Walter a negotiator far superior to Adam and far more amenable to realistic suggestions for compromise in a case such as this. She understands that, to a very considerable extent, Walter's hands are tied: his first duty is to maintain the public image of the state – a task that has been rendered all the more difficult in view of the recent, highly embarrassing, uncovering of a blatant case of corrupt officialdom. In addition, Eve claims to have been shown a letter which implicates the government in misleading the public. Can she perhaps, be persuaded to disregard this evidence on the grounds of 'unreliability'? As we shall see, the cost of her so doing will be an assurance from Walter that Ruprecht will not be transported to the East Indies. However, Eve is shrewd enough to guess that if these negotiations are to reach a successful conclusion she must not challenge Walter's authority too openly, and that any concession she may obtain must not appear to have been extracted under duress. With consummate artlessness, she begins her 'performance' by throwing herself on his 'mercy': 'Your Honour, if you won't come to our aid, we are lost!' ('Herr, wenn Ihr jetzt nicht helft, sind wir verloren!' *SW* 1, 840; 1950). In truth, of course, Walter is no less at her mercy, and both know this. Eve goes on to proclaim her unquestioning allegiance to the state authorities, maintaining that she has no objection to Ruprecht's being called up for military service. What she does object to, is the possibility that he will be sent to an almost certain death in a colonial war intended to fill the coffers of the Hague merchants:

> Das ist ja keine offen ehrliche
> Konskription, das ist Betrug, Herr Richter,
> Gestohlen ist dem Land die schöne Jugend,
> Um Pfeffer und Muskaten einzuhandeln. (*SW* 1, 844; 2086–9)

(That's hardly a fair and honest form of conscription. That's deception, Your Honour. The nation is being robbed of its youth in order to further the trade in pepper and spice.)

Needless to say, for Walter, this is a revelation of the greatest professional import. The only way out of this difficult situation is to prove that Adam's letter is a forgery, thereby making Eve's evidence inadmissible. Thus having first denied all knowledge of the matter, he then asks her if she has actually read the letter herself, to which she replies: 'No. I didn't read the letter. I can't read. But the judge, he read it out to me' ('Ich nicht. Ich las es nicht. Ich kann nicht lesen. | Doch er, der Richter, las den Brief mir vor'; *SW* I, 844; 2078–9). We can imagine Walter's relief on hearing this. It only remains to check with the clerk – 'Do you know anything about such an order?' ('Wißt Ihr was von der Order?'; *SW* I, 846; 2147) – to which the obsequious Licht obligingly replies, 'Not a thing' ('Nicht ein Wort'; *SW* I, 846; 2147). At this point, the terms of a possible compromise have been established: the 'integrity' of the state will be preserved and in return, Ruprecht will remain in Utrecht. For Walter is about to propose that, in view of the obvious corruption of the local judge, the letter 'must surely' have been a fake and should, therefore, be disregarded. However, he does not get a chance to make his offer, since the prescient Eve anticipates his train of thought and makes it for him:

> Gut, gut, gut. Denn der Richter log, nicht wahr?
> So oft: und *also* log er gestern mir.
> Der Brief, den ich gesehen, war verfälscht; (*SW* I, 851; 2311–3)

(Oh yes, I see what you're getting at. The judge can't have been telling the truth, can he? Because he was always lying, he must have been lying yesterday too. And so naturally the letter I saw must have been a forgery.)

In so doing, Eve intimates that whilst there is much to commend this proposal, it is not good enough and that, as the subsequent episode with the bag of guilders makes clear, Walter will be required to 'put his money where his mouth is'. She therefore rejects his proposition and communicates her scepticism of even Walter's integrity, exclaiming to Ruprecht, 'You hear all that, my friend, even now they would still deceive us!' ('Du hörst es, alles, alles, | Auch dies, daß sie uns täuschen sollen, Freund'; *SW* I, 852; 2324–5) and although her words are ostensibly addressed to her fiancé, we can be sure that their true significance will not be lost on the district magistrate.

At this point, we might pause to consider whether or not Adam's letter is really the forgery that Walter (with Licht's support) wishes to maintain. For there is considerable evidence that, in the past, soldiers have been improperly diverted to serve in the East Indies. Even the dull-witted Ruprecht appears to have registered as much, for as he says, 'It wouldn't be the first time' ('es wär das erstemal wohl nicht') adding, one line later, 'Something similar is supposed to have happened about seven years ago' ('Vor sieben Jahren soll was Ähnliches | Im Land geschehen sein'; *SW* 1, 852; 2329–30). But each time he is cut short, first by Eve, and then by Walter, both of whom now have an interest in concealing those 'troublesome' facts. For these shrewd negotiators realise that what appears to be the case is considerably more important than what is the case. What matters, is that the record will show – and the general public believe – that the letter was forged. Ruprecht's ill-timed interventions merely oblige Walter to rush to the defence of the disintegrating reputation of the government he represents:

> Wenn die Regierung
> Ihn hinterginge, wärs das erstemal.
> So oft sie Truppen noch nach Asien schickte,
> Hat sies den Truppen noch gewagt, zu sagen.
> (*SW* 1, 852; 2330–3)

(If the government were to deceive you, then that would be the first occasion on which anything like that has happened. Each time they've sent troops to the East Indies, they been perfectly open about it.)

This may satisfy the likes of Ruprecht, but it will not do for someone of Eve's intelligence and Walter knows it; accordingly, he offers her enough money to buy Ruprecht out of the army, should he be destined for Batavia. So important is it to him that this matter be hushed up that he is prepared to part with hard cash if need be. And in offering to do as much, he acknowledges the strength of Eve's position, for the money is nothing less than his guarantee that she will indeed receive the favours that she was promised by Adam. Eve is now close to 'settling', but she stretches Walter's nerves a little further still, weighing up the offer he has just made as she repeats the terms of the contract, before handing back the money. In returning the twenty guilders, she is agreeing, at least for the time being, to 'trust' him, whilst at the same time underlining the inherent weakness of Walter's position. For in so doing, Eve makes it clear that she knows not that he *will* not, but that he *cannot* in fact go back on his promise. And when Walter attempts to elicit a more straightforward public affirmation of her 'trust', asking her, 'so now you really do believe I was telling you the truth?' ('So glaubst du jetzt, daß ich dir Wahrheit gab?'; *SW* I, 854; 2374), Eve is unmoved and offers what is, at best, a highly ambiguous reply – 'So you want to know if I really do believe that you were telling me the truth? ('Ob Ihr mir Wahrheit gabt?' *SW* I, 854; 2375) – a reply calculated to remind Walter that she can always go back on the arrangement should she feel compelled to. She is not for sale and when she subsequently refers to the twenty guilders, saying:

O scharfgeprägte,
Und Gottes leuchtend Antlitz drauf. O Jesus!
Daß ich nicht solche Münze mehr erkenne.
(*SW* I, 854; 2375–7)

(Oh those freshly-minted coins glinting in the sun-light. Oh Lord! May I never see such coins as these again.)

her rejection of this royal 'currency' shows she understands that her own 'weapons' offer more protection than those of her enemies and so long as she relies upon her own, highly effective, 'weapon' – her powers of sexual attraction – she will almost always emerge victorious. Accordingly when Walter asks her fiancé if he may kiss the bride-to-be,[14] his gesture is, in effect, an act of submission, an acknowledgement that any man who marries this woman – even Ruprecht – deserves a measure of respect and will obtain it, as happens only a few lines later when Walter promises to recommend him to his brother:

Und ich empfehle meinem Bruder ihn
Dem Hauptmann von der Landmiliz, der ihn
Aufnimmt, wollt ihr, in seine Kompanie? (*SW* I, 854; 2386–8)

(And I shall recommend him to my brother who is a captain in the army and who will have him assigned to his battalion, if you both agree?)

Likewise, his wish to be invited to the wedding can be seen almost as an 'act of homage': for Walter has had to acknowledge that, in Eve, he has met an equal and he has a sneaking admiration for this woman who has taken on the system and won.[15]

ADAM

Although the full extent of Adam's corruption is exposed at the end of the play, he is not portrayed as a seriously evil man, but rather as a weak-willed opportunist whose control over his appetites is less than adequate for a man in his position. At the beginning of the play, he is confronted with two alternatives: whether to 'come clean' and confess his involvement to Walter, in the (not unrealistic) hope that his superior will have to bail him out in order to uphold the court's honour; or whether to try to conceal his guilt from Walter altogether, in the hope of avoiding all disgrace, public or private. In the event, his cowardice and stupidity prompt him to attempt the impossible: he tries to do both and, of course, succeeds in doing neither. Perhaps the clearest example of Adam's attempt to pursue both courses of action simultaneously is to be found at the beginning of scene 9, when Walter orders him to hurry up and get to the bottom of the case, to which Adam replies: 'If the truth gets out then I'm a villain' ('Doch wenn Ihrs herausbekommt, bin ich ein Schuft'; *SW* I, 214; 1092). For like the audience, Adam is left wondering how Walter will interpret his remark. Will he understand it as a rhetorical outburst, a comment on the sheer intractability of the case, or will he interpret it as a covert admission of guilt on Adam's part, as a warning that a thorough investigation of the facts will expose the judge as 'a villain' ('ein Schuft')? Adam's panic results in his pursuing neither course of action successfully; it also provides much of the play's comedy. A further factor in Adam's downfall is that in his past dealings with the local inhabitants, he has never before encountered a woman of Eve's intelligence and determination. As the trial unfolds and the strength of Eve's resolve becomes increasingly clear, Adam comes to realise just how impossible a task he has set himself and begins to wish he had taken Walter into his confidence from the beginning. As his indecision mounts, his attempts to conceal his guilt from Walter become increasingly half-hearted until he ends up making what amounts to a pathetic, covert confession, in the hope that the latter will realise what has happened and be drawn into arranging a cover-up. Indeed, his ludicrous handling of the case prompts Walter, as early as scene 7, to utter the chilling remark:

Von Eurer Aufführung, Herr Richter Adam,
Weiß ich nicht, was ich denken soll. Wenn Ihr selbst
Den Krug zerschlagen hättet, könntet Ihr
Von Euch ab den Verdacht nicht eifriger
Hinwälzen auf den jungen Mann, als jetzt.

(*SW* I, 205; 820–4)

(Judge Adam, I'm baffled by your conduct of this case. If you yourself had been the one to break the jug, you couldn't exert yourself more eagerly to shift suspicion from yourself onto the youth.) [G, 118]

Although Adam seriously under-estimates the strength of Eve's hold over him, he does not lack an understanding of the workings of 'justice' and, above all, of the idiosyncratic procedures of the local courts. Most importantly, he appreciates that what really matters is not that justice in fact be done, but that justice be seen to be done. When Licht informs him of Walter's impending arrival, he at first dismisses the whole matter as idle rumour: a man of Walter's 'integrity' would not want to dirty his hands by getting involved with the corrupt judicial procedures in Huisum:

Heut noch, er, der Gerichtsrat, her, aus Utrecht!
Zur Revision, der wackre Mann, der selbst
Sein Schäfchen schiert, dergleichen Fratzen haßt.
Nach Huisum kommen, und uns kujonieren.

(*SW* I, 179; 77–80)

(The district magistrate! From Utrecht! Coming here today for an inspection! But he's the best of fellows who shaves his own sheep close and hates silly tricks. No, I don't believe it – that he'd come here to Huisum just to annoy us!) [G, 92]

During the course of the scene, Adam makes it clear that he does not really take Walter's alleged 'integrity' too seriously and finds some solace in the fact that his own (relaxed) view of the legal system and that of his superior are not fundamentally at odds. For, as he says to Licht:

Wenngleich Rat Walter! Geht, laßt mich zufrieden.
Der Mann hat seinen Amtseid ja geschworen,
Und praktisiert, wie wir, nach den
Bestehenden Edikten und Gebräuchen. (*SW* I, 180; 97–100)

(So let it be Judge Walter, I don't care! The fellow's sworn his oath of office and must conduct himself, as we do, in the time-honoured way.) [G, 92]

Moreover, although Walter, as the district magistrate ('Gerichtsrat'), is subject to somewhat different constraints from those that bind a local judge ('Dorfrichter'), Adam's assessment of the situation is fundamentally correct. For as the trial proceeds, it becomes ever more apparent that Walter is more concerned with preserving the villagers' confidence in the state judiciary than he is in seeing that justice is done in the case before him. Similarly, when Adam learns of the fate of the judge in Holla, his analysis of the latter's situation is no less accurate. He shows that he understands that what really counts in such cases of fraud is not whether or not the judge is corrupt, but rather how successfully (or unsuccessfully) he conceals his corruption. For as he says of his unfortunate colleague in Holla:

> Ein liederlicher Hund wars –
> Sonst eine ehrliche Haut, so wahr ich lebe,
> Ein Kerl, mit dem sichs gut zusammen war;
> Doch grausam liederlich, das muß ich sagen.
> (*SW* I, 181; 119–22)

(The rascal did things in a slipshod way – but otherwise an honest beast, so help me, a fellow it was easy to get on with; but no administrator, if you make me say so: too slipshod.) [G, 93]

No doubt Adam would regard himself also as 'a fellow easy to get on with', but by the end of the play, he will be forced to recognise just how 'slipshod' he, in his own way, has become. As the catastrophic events of the trial demonstrate, to take on a woman such as Eve and at the same time succeed in concealing his misdemeanours requires a far greater degree of skill than Adam in fact possesses: if there is a lesson to be learned from his experiences here, it will be that he must, in future, steer well clear of those women whom he has been accustomed to designate (patronisingly) as 'silly little geese' ('Närrchen'). He may casually dismiss the events of the previous night as nothing more than 'a night-time romp that need not see the light of day' ('Ein Schwank . . ., der zur Nacht geboren, | Des Tags vorwitzgen Lichtstrahl scheut'; *SW* I, 182; 154–5), but for Eve – and this is what he fails to realise – the whole affair is far more serious. Nonetheless, though Walter may advise Adam to be a little more circumspect regarding any subsequent 'romps', it does not escape his notice that Adam has many qualities as a representative of 'justice' that equip him particularly well to settle minor disputes in the local court in Huisum. Indeed, it is precisely because Adam, in his saner moments, possesses these qualities (the most important of which is an understanding that the appearance of 'justice' must be preserved at all costs) that Walter has little hesitation in reinstating him at the end of the play.

WALTER

In contrast to Adam, Walter is an altogether more impressive figure. Although it must be supposed that, like the rest of his profession, he would claim to serve an earthly system of near-perfect justice modelled on an allegedly 'transcendent' idea to which his elitist class has exclusive and privileged access, in practice, his main function is to shore up the existing system against the largely legitimate complaints of its unfortunate victims. By showing him in this role, acting shrewdly and sensibly, with a proper regard for the strengths and weaknesses of the system, Kleist highlights the absurdity of its metaphysical pretensions compared with the common sense understanding of human nature possessed by the likes of Walter.

Walter is a man who has a realist's view of the practical problems of administering justice. For example, he says in scene 4: 'if I find everything is not just as it should be, still, I'll be content to find it passable' [G, 101] ('Und find ich gleich nicht alles, wie es soll, | Ich freue mich, wenn es erträglich ist'; *SW* 1, 188; 303–4). As soon as he arrives, he advises Adam not to panic and, above all, not to follow the example of the judge in Holla, who, in attempting to hang himself, 'made a bad thing worse' [G, 102] ('machte Übel ärger'; *SW* 1, 189; 341). And he goes on to explain that:

> Was nur Unordnung schien, Verworrenheit,
> Nimmt jetzt den Schein an der Veruntreuung,
> Die das Gesetz, Ihr wißts, nicht mehr verschont.
>
> (*SW* 1, 189; 342–4)

(What seemed no more than muddled records and mismanagement now looks like misappropriation of funds, which the law, as you know very well, can scarcely tolerate.) [G, 102]

Adam is being given to understand that, providing he does nothing as rash as his colleague in Holla, there is no form of corruption so serious that it cannot be covered-up as 'mismanagement' or 'muddled records'. And as the district magistrate assures him, 'my own object on this tour is a milder one, to observe and not to punish' [G, 100–1] ('Doch *mein* Geschäft auf dieser Reis ist noch | Ein strenges nicht, sehn soll ich bloß, nicht strafen'; *SW* I, 188; 301–2). In short, Walter holds the view that a certain degree of corruption does not of itself prevent a judge from carrying out his official function in a perfectly satisfactory manner; and this is borne out at the end of the play, when he orders Licht to go and find Adam, saying, 'Go after him, Clerk, and fetch him back, lest in running away he make a bad thing worse' ('Geschwind, Herr Schreiber, fort! Holt ihn zurück! | Daß er nicht Übel rettend ärger mache'; *SW* I, 855; 2415–16).[16] From this, both the Clerk and the audience must infer that, in time, the judge will be found an alternative district to administer. For as Walter says:

> Doch sind die Kassen richtig, wie ich hoffe,
> So wird er wohl auf irgend einem Platze
> Noch zu erhalten sein. (*SW* I, 855; 2420–2)

(But if the accounts are in order, as I hope they are, I am sure we will find somewhere where we can make use of him.)

Indeed, throughout the play, Adam can draw some comfort from the knowledge that the only way Walter can save the face of 'justice' is by saving him; Walter's outburst in scene 11 makes this much clear: 'The only thing that saves you is my concern for the honour of the court' [G, 152] ('Was Euch schützt, | Ist einzig nur die Ehre des Gerichts'; *SW* I, 239; 1840–1). Here Kleist draws our attention, once again, to the way in which the 'weak (in this instance, Adam) often have more of a hold on the 'strong' (Walter) than is apparent at first sight. If only Adam could have exploited this advantage to the same degree as Eve exploits her advantage over him, how different the outcome might have been!

At the beginning of the trial, Walter has no inkling of Adam's involvement in the case. However, quite early on in the action, the discrepancy between the obvious simplicity of the case and the incompetence displayed by the judge leads him to suspect that

Adam is himself involved in some way. Of course, it is not possible for the audience to determine the precise moment at which the district magistrate's suspicions are confirmed, and this leaves open the possibility that when he says, 'Judge Adam, I feel a great desire in myself to get to the bottom of this case' [G, 131] ('Ich spüre große Lust in mir, Herr Richter, | Der Sache völlig auf den Grund zu kommen'; *SW* I, 219; 1250–1) he is deliberately teasing Adam before finally bailing him out at the end of the play. Thus as the trial proceeds, the audience – together with Adam – is left unsure as to just how much Walter does in fact suspect. Kleist deftly exploits this ambiguity in scene 10 in which we witness a struggle between the false *bonhomie* of Adam, who attempts to bribe the district magistrate with the delicacies of his well-stocked larder, and the feigned 'asceticism' of Walter. For when Adam plays for time by sending out for Frau Brigitte at the end of scene 9, Walter starts to question the judge on the details of the case, pointing out that:

> Wenn hier die Sache,
> Wie ich fast fürchte, unentworren bleibt,
> So werdet Ihr, in Eurem Ort, den Täter
> Leicht noch aus seiner Wund entdecken können.
>
> (*SW* I, 227; 1505–8)

(And if there's no getting to the bottom of things here in court, which I almost think will be the case, it shouldn't be hard for you, in your small village, to recognise the guilty party by his wounds.) [G, 140]

What is Adam to make of this remark? Is it to be taken naïvely at face value, or is it a veiled suggestion that Walter is in little doubt that the judge's wounds betray his complicity in the affair? The ambiguity of the situation is further compounded when Walter rounds off his remarks by asking him whether the wine they are drinking is a Niersteiner.[17] Adam, whose mind is still mulling over the real import of his superior's previous remarks, can only splutter, 'What?'. Adam is panic-stricken at the thought that Walter has indeed seen through him, whilst Walter (mischievously?) interprets this 'What?' as a question relating to the provenance of the wine, and plunges him into further uncertainty by going on to ask: 'Or just a good Oppenheimer?'.

By this stage, the audience probably believes that Walter

suspects more than he is admitting and is getting ready to arrange a cover-up in order to preserve the 'honour' of the court. Despite not knowing all the details of the case, Walter is, of course, confident that he can arrange such a cover-up if called upon to do so, for this is, as it were, his speciality. It comes as no surprise, therefore, that he sets about interrogating the other parties, so as to be in full possession of the facts, should his particular skills be called upon. His cross-examination of Ruprecht, during which he asks: 'But you couldn't recognise him in the dark?' [G, 142] ('Konnt Er ihn denn im Dunkeln nicht erkennen?' *SW* 1, 229; 1549) throws up the first vital piece of information: one of the key witnesses in the case will be unable to confirm the identity of the culprit. Walter then proceeds to establish a list of the regular visitors to Frau Marthe's house, and asks the widow whether Judge Adam was not amongst their number. His surprise when she denies this merely underlines how nearly certain he is of Adam's guilt. And any doubts lingering in his mind are finally dispelled when Frau Brigitte appears with the judge's wig in the following scene. Clearly, the discovery of the wig on Frau Marthe's trellis is a damning piece of evidence, and Walter shrewdly declines to ascertain – at least in public – to whom it belongs. Although the scheming clerk, Licht, begs him to find out, Walter says, emphatically, 'I don't want to know who owns it' [G, 145] ('Ich will nicht wissen, wem sie angehört'; *SW* 1, 232; 1623). The situation has now become critical and the district magistrate offers Adam one last chance to demonstrate his 'maturity' and make a clean breast of the matter:

Herr Richter Adam,
Habt Ihr mir etwas zu vertraun,
So bitt ich, um die Ehre des Gerichtes,
Ihr seid so gut, und sagt mirs an. (*SW* 1, 232; 1629–32)

(Judge Adam, if you have anything you would like to impart to me in confidence, I beg you, do so now, for the sake of our court's good name.) [G, 145]

But Adam, to his lasting regret, we feel, fails to avail himself of the opportunity. For Walter has not asked Adam to confess his guilt in public (indeed that is the very last thing he wants) as is shown by the fact that he addresses the judge in an aside. On the contrary, he is hoping his subordinate will have the presence of mind to fill him in on the facts of the matter, thereby to supply him with some scraps of information that he can use to cobble together a cover-up. Adam's panic and confusion render him incapable of a coherent response and prompt Walter to ask impatiently: 'Nothing to say? Nothing at all?' [G, 145] ('Nicht? Habt Ihr nicht – ?' *SW* 1, 232; 1633). Walter then makes one final effort to rescue his floundering subordinate, hinting (very strongly) at the importance of denying the ownership of the wig, when he all but puts the words into Adam's mouth, saying: 'This wig's not yours, then?' [G, 145] ('Hier die Perücke ist die Eure nicht?'; *SW* 1, 232; 1634). Even this suggestion fails, since Adam, believing that he cannot deny the wig is his, decides (in a stroke of panic-stricken improvisation) that a bold assertion of the truth might be more likely to succeed than a lie and exclaims: 'This wig, by God, is mine, sirs!' [G, 145] ('Hier die Perück ihr Herren, ist die meine!'; *SW* 1, 232; 1635). Adam is now pinning his hopes on Eve's not having the courage to accuse him directly in public and reverts once more to the strategy of attempting to conceal his guilt from the court and, more importantly, from his superior. But in doing so, he has chosen disastrously, and from this point on, his fate is all but sealed.

Adam has demonstrated his inability to conceal his guilt; at the same time, he is equally unable to accept the life-line thrown to him by Walter and leaves the district magistrate no choice but to abandon him completely and take matters into his own hands in order to preserve the 'good reputation' of the court. As a result he is compelled to make it obvious to anyone who cares to look closely enough that Adam is the guilty party. When Frau Brigitte has finished giving her evidence, Walter asks Adam to walk across the courtroom and pass him a snuff-box, thereby making it plain to all present that he knows that the mysterious 'devil' with the club-foot ('Pferdehuf') is the judge. However, whilst he is prepared to offer the villagers the satisfaction of seeing Adam's guilt ruthlessly exposed, and the delicious spectacle of their judge wholly at his mercy, he is not prepared to go so far as to condemn the judge formally in the name of the state authorities. For when Adam reveals his misshapen foot, Walter (in a remark that is too ironic to be taken at face value) 'officially' (and quite brazenly) declares: 'Upon my honour! That foot's fine' [G, 152] ('Auf meine Ehr. Der Fuß ist gut'; *SW* I, 239; 1821) and then, in a further aside to his incompetent subordinate, tells him: 'Wind the session up at once!' [G, 152] ('Macht jetzt mit der Session sogleich ein Ende'; *SW* I, 239; 1822). For the only way that Walter can preserve the reputation of 'justice' is to expose Adam's guilt now and let him off on a 'technicality' when the matter has blown over; and this is precisely what he does. Of course, the fact that Adam will henceforth bear the stigma of having had to be 'bailed out' by the authorities is part of the 'punishment' for his incompetence. Walter is particularly anxious that the case should not drag on a moment longer than necessary. Thus when Adam makes one last misguided attempt to protest his innocence by denying the ownership of the wig (which only a few moments previously he had so vigorously asserted was his), Walter brushes this aside impatiently, demanding, 'Once again: you end the sitting or I will!' [G, 153] ('Noch einmal, wollt *Ihr* gleich, soll *ich* die Sache enden?'; *SW* I, 240; 1865). Moreover, when the hot-headed Ruprecht blurts out the question, the answer to which is patently obvious to everyone – 'Eve! Was he the one?', [G, 153] ('Eve, sprich, ist ers?'; *SW* I, 240; 1866) – Walter pulls rank and rebukes him for daring to venture an opinion: 'How dare you, you young lout!' [G, 153] ('Was untersteht der Unverschämte sich?'; *SW* I, 240; 1867). For whilst Walter is prepared to concede that there is a limit to the degree of corruption that the authorities will accept, he wishes to make it very clear that it is he, not Ruprecht, who will determine what that limit is. Indeed Walter's stern rebuke is echoed by Ruprecht's father, Veit, who warns his son to keep quiet (*SW* I, 240; 1868). For Veit understands that no matter how obvious Adam's guilt, the district magistrate need not, and will not, tolerate such blatant insubordination from Ruprecht, and that accusing Adam directly is only likely to land his son in further trouble. For the canny peasant knows, no doubt from bitter experience, that those in Adam's position are answerable only to their superiors and that although the state's representatives may from time to time be caught out – as indeed Adam has been here – the authorities will not tolerate the likes of Veit and Ruprecht getting even with them by means of *formal* legal redress.

At last Adam grasps the seriousness of the situation and quickly declares Ruprecht to be the guilty party, a judgement which, it will be recalled had enraged Walter earlier in scene 7, but which is now perfectly acceptable to him: 'Fine, fine. What else?' [G, 154] ('Auch gut das. Weiter'; *SW* 1, 240; 1876). For by pinning the blame, albeit temporarily, on Ruprecht, Walter believes – mistakenly as it turns out – that he can preserve the 'good reputation' of the court. He goes on to declare: 'The sitting's over. And Ruprecht may appeal the verdict at the Superior Court in Utrecht' [G, 154] ('Geschlossen ist die Session. | Und Ruprecht appelliert an die Instanz zu Utrecht'; *SW* 1, 241; 1884–5), thus making it clear that Ruprecht's sentence will be repealed in due course, which he thinks will be the end of the matter – but he has underestimated Eve's resolve. She is far from content with this 'solution', which would deprive her of her fiancé for the immediate future; she is the key-witness in the case and so, to Walter's consternation, she accuses the judge directly in front of all: 'Judge Adam broke the jug' [G, 155] ('Der Richter Adam hat den Krug zerbrochen!'; *SW* 1, 241; 1893). Her naming Adam as the guilty party deprives Walter of a key element in his strategy, *viz.* the inability of anyone so far to identify the culprit. The court dissolves into anarchy and Walter is confronted with a situation which can be resolved only on Eve's terms. Even so, with his back to the wall, Walter shows his superior mettle: unlike Adam, he does not panic but contests the truth of Eve's accusation:

> Ein Wort keck hingeworfen, macht den Richter
> In meinem Aug der Sünd noch gar nicht schuldig.
>
> (*SW* 1, 840; 1940–1)

(So glib an accusation, brazenly tossed off like that isn't enough to convince me of the judge's guilt.)

But, alas for Walter, Eve is not so easily put down. Her straightforward account of the events of the past few days is so convincing that it rules out any possibility of smothering the scandal in the way that Walter had in mind. To conceal the now firmly established fact of the state's corruption, he will have to meet Eve's demands and provide a personal guarantee that Ruprecht will not be drafted to the East Indies. Once this bargain has been struck, however, and Eve agrees to 'trust' him, Walter can put the last part of his planned cover-up into action, including the rehabilitation of Adam.

Walter knows that Adam will continue to dispense justice in his corrupt fashion (and although he would not actually say as much, he recognises that a certain degree of dishonesty is simply a perk of the job) but he can be confident that Adam will take greater care in future not to risk disclosing important secrets of state, such as the illegal recruitment of troops for a colonial war being fought in the East Indies.

FRAU MARTHE AND THE JUG

Throughout the play, Kleist makes it clear that Frau Marthe's jug, like her belief in the over-riding importance of 'perfect' feminine virtue (which the jug symbolises), is both irrelevant to, and a distraction from, the real business in hand. As Ruprecht points out to his father in scene 6, 'It's the wedding not the pot she's mad about' [G, 105] (''s ist der zerbrochne Krug nicht, der sie wurmt, | Die Hochzeit ist es'; *SW* 1, 193; 440–2) and Frau Marthe herself endorses Ruprecht's remark, when she says to Eve, 'What was in that pot, would you like to know? Your good reputation' [G, 107] ('Dein guter Name lag in diesem Topfe'; *SW* 1, 194; 490). Frau Marthe's main concern is to find a husband for Eve and she is convinced that, in her world, the preservation of her daughter's 'virtue' is an essential pre-requisite of this. At first sight, she appears to be more concerned with this fictitious notion of feminine virtue than with her daughter's happiness, even to the extent of declaring that if it could be shown that she had spent the night with someone other than her fiancé, she would be branded a 'whore' ('Metze') and thrown out of her home:

> Den Stuhl setzt ich, zur ersten Einrichtung,
> Ihr vor die Tür, und sagte, geh, mein Kind,
> Die Welt ist weit, da zahlst du keine Miete,
> Und lange Haare hast du auch geerbt,
> Woran du dich, kommt Zeit, kommt Rat, kannst hängen.
>
> (*SW* 1, 220; 1293–7)

(I would have stood a chair outside the door for her dowry, so she could start housekeeping under the sky, and said: Go, my child, the world is wide, and for the open spaces no one charges rent, and long hair too, you have inherited, to hang yourself with when the time comes.) [G, 133]

The truth is that it is the infatuation felt by Frau Marthe and her like with such unrealistic norms of feminine virtue that has put Eve's prospects of marriage at risk and forced her mother to adopt such an extreme stance which she would almost certainly not maintain in her private dealings with her daughter, whose excellent qualities she is well aware of. And the more down-to-earth Walter, who understands that in everyday life, such 'principles' must give way to more realistic and conciliatory attitudes, advises her against adopting a stance from which she will almost certainly wish to back down: 'Frau Marthe, gently, gently' [G, 133] ('Ruhig, ruhig, Frau Marthe'; *SW* 1, 220; 1298). For Walter (like Eve) understands that such allegedly 'transcendent' principles, whether of 'feminine virtue' or of 'justice', only get in the way of finding genuine solutions to real human problems.

In contrast to Frau Marthe, all the more insightful characters in the play, Veit, Eve and Walter, point out that the jug, though a beautiful antique, is not irreplaceable. In scene 6, Veit offers to make amends: 'If one of us broke your jug, we'll make amends for it' [G, 105] ('Wenn einer Ihr von uns den Krug zerbrochen, | Soll Sie entschädigt werden'; *SW* 1, 192; 431–2). Eve offers to have it repaired or replaced at her own cost:

> Laßt doch den Krug! Laßt mich doch in der Stadt versuchen,
> Ob ein geschickter Handwerksmann die Scherben
> Nicht wieder Euch zur Lust zusammenfügt,
> Und wärs um ihn geschehn, nehmt meine ganze
> Sparbüchse hin, und kauft Euch einen neuen.
>
> (*SW* 1, 194; 479–83)

(Enough about the jug! I'll see in town if there's a master craftsman who can put the pieces back together to your satisfaction. If not, I'll buy a new one for you with what I've saved.) [G, 107]

And in the last scene of the play, when Walter is confronted by Frau Marthe's demand for 'justice' for her jug, he advises her to apply to the 'higher court' in the market-place: 'Excuse me ma'am! You're right, you're right. In the marketplace. The Superior Court meets there on Tuesdays and on Fridays' [G, 158] ('Verzeiht mir!

Allerdings. Am großen Markt, | Und Dienstag ist und Freitag Session'; *SW* I, 244; 1972–3). Thus it is made clear to the audience – if not to Frau Marthe – that the matter of the jug is wholly irrelevant, and but for her misplaced preoccupations the whole matter would have been forgotten. In the same way, it has been made clear that, for Walter, the dispensation of 'justice' is not a question of slavish adhering to a set of 'transcendent' principles, but a matter of reaching acceptable real-life compromises and of keeping up the appearance that all is well with the legal system.

LICHT

Would the cause of justice be served any better if Licht were to succeed Adam? It seems unlikely, since the court clerk is little more than a devious and cunning sycophant, whose desire to reveal the truth is not motivated by any concern for justice itself, but purely by self-advancement;[18] he is loyal neither to his profession nor to Adam. As a judge – if he ever attains such a position – we can be sure that he will be more successful than Adam in avoiding scandal, for unlike his superior, he entertains no romantic interests of the kind that, as we have just seen, put those in authority at risk. Throughout the play, he keeps his emotions firmly under control, and this is his strongest, though least appealing, asset. Indeed, his treacherous behaviour towards his dissolute superior plays a crucial role in eliciting the audience's sympathy for the latter. For whilst Walter, as a representative of the state authorities, is obliged to punish the judge for his corruption, Licht has no such brief. Adam is under no illusions as to the slippery character of his clerk when, in scene I, he attempts to secure Licht's loyalty by holding out the only prospect the latter's pedestrian soul can appreciate, namely promotion:

> Jetzt gilts Freundschaft.
> Ihr wißt, wie sich zwei Hände waschen können.
> Ihr wollt auch gern, ich weiß, Dorfrichter werden,
> Und Ihr verdients, bei Gott, so gut wie einer.
> (*SW* I, 181; 128–31)

(All right, my friend, what counts now, as I'm sure you understand, is friendship. One hand must wash the other. I know you'd like to be a judge some day; by God, if anyone deserves it, you do.) [G, 93]

His ruse, however, is unsuccessful; Licht's steady stream of inopportune remarks shows him that the clerk has abandoned his more immediate superior and is pinning his hopes on the district magistrate instead. But the more experienced Walter is not taken in by Licht's grovelling behaviour; he recognises that Adam's occasional blunders present far less of a threat than would the ambitious scheming of the sharp-witted Licht. In fact Walter (and those he represents) have no intention of allowing their system to be infiltrated by ambitious upstart meritocrats like Licht. Perhaps it is for this reason that Licht has remained a clerk for the past nine years[19] and that even with the suspension of Adam, his prospects do not appear to be greatly enhanced. Thus when Walter says to him at the end of the play:

> Von seinem Amt zwar ist er suspendiert,
> Und Euch bestell ich, bis auf weitere
> Verfügung, hier im Ort es zu verwalten;
> Doch sind die Kassen richtig, wie ich hoffe,
> Zur Desertion ihn zwingen will ich nicht.
> (*SW* I, 244; 1962–6)

(Of course I must suspend him from his judgeship, and I appoint yourself to perform his duties here in Huisum until further notice; but if the accounts are in good order, as I trust they are, I have no wish to compel him to desert this place.) [G, 157]

it is not hard for the audience to imagine – and indeed take pleasure in – the galling sense of frustration that Licht must experience when he discovers that his 'promotion' will not only be temporary, but that he will probably have to give way, once more, to Adam. Thus Kleist subtly suggests that in pinning his hopes on Walter and the establishment, the clerk is making a grave mistake, and would do better to join forces with the faction of society represented by the resourceful Eve instead of servilely following the carrot of promotion held out by the powers that be.

CONCLUSION

In *Der zerbrochne Krug*, Kleist shows how human beings, in their quest for glib, incontrovertible solutions to the problems that arise in their dealings with one another, invent spurious notions of 'perfect' justice, 'perfect' purity and the like. The truth is that such notions constitute little more than an upgrading of the conventional arrangements designed to favour the ruling hierarchy and to absolve them from having to consider genuine root and branch reforms even when these are clearly overdue. Incidentally, this causes at least as many problems for the dominant group as for their victims. For since the system of justice thus created by the dominant class is manifestly flawed (by bias in their favour, if nothing else) there is always a serious risk that the flaws within it will be revealed whenever an attempt is made to compare it with the allegedly 'perfect' concept of justice on which it is said to be based. Therefore there is a constant need to go to extraordinary lengths to conceal its more obvious imperfections from the ordinary citizens and even from the rulers themselves. But however hard the representatives of the system (here Walter and Adam) may strive to preserve appearances, the inherent contradictions make failure inevitable. For every such 'solution' on their part can be at best only temporary, as is hinted at in the last scene of the play when Frau Marthe declares her intention to take her case to a 'higher court', thereby raising the spectre of the whole procedure being set in motion all over again. In place of this hopeless task, Kleist's comedy hints at the need for us to turn our attention to the more down-to-earth business of removing some of the many obvious unfair elements in the existing system of justice and building up from there towards a better state of affairs. Thus Kleist's debunking of this notion of allegedly 'perfect justice' should not be seen as a cause for despair, but on the contrary, as an essential prerequisite if genuine human progress is to be made.[20] And the prospects for this are not hopeless.

CHAPTER 5
Amphitryon

The origins of the critical debate surrounding *Amphitryon* can be traced back to a letter written by Adam Müller on 25 May 1807 to Friedrich Gentz in which he explains that, 'the play is as much concerned with the Virgin Birth as it is with the mystery of love itself' ('Der Amphitryon handelt ja wohl ebensogut von der unbefleckten Empfängnis der heiligen Jungfrau, als von dem Geheimnis der Liebe überhaupt'; *Lebensspuren*, no. 173). It is perhaps one of the more unfortunate ironies of literary history, that in his efforts to promote the play by bringing it to the attention of the literary establishment, Müller, who at that stage had not met Kleist, was partly responsible for its being subjected to an interpretation quite contrary to the intentions of its author. There can be little doubt that Müller's view of the play as an essentially Christian drama was coloured by his recent conversion to Catholicism, and it was to have a profound effect on the play's critical reception, not least because Müller, in his preface to the first published edition,[1] drew attention to what he saw as its religious dimension.[2] Thus it comes as no surprise to find Goethe, in a remark to F. W. Riemer recorded on 14 July 1807, describing the play as simply 'a reinterpretation of the myth in Christian terms' ('eine Deutung der Fabel ins Christliche'; *Lebensspuren*, no. 182a). However, he was far closer to the spirit of Kleist's intentions than he perhaps realised, when he went on to add that, 'the ending is unconvincing. The real Amphitryon has no choice but to accept the honour of Zeus's visitation. Otherwise Alkmene's situation appears highly embarrassing and that of Amphitryon downright cruel' ('Das Ende ist aber klatrig. Der wahre Amphitryon muß es sich gefallen lassen, daß ihm Zeus diese Ehre angetan hat. Sonst ist die Situation der Alkmene peinlich und die des Amphitryon zuletzt grausam'; *ibid.*). Like almost all those who saw the play as a straight-faced testimony to the 'purity' of Jupiter's love for Alkmene, he too was inclined to regard the ambiguous aspects of the denouement as indicative of the play's 'shortcomings' rather than as evidence of an ironic attitude on Kleist's part.

The central issues of Kleist's 'comedy in the manner of Molière' ('Lustspiel nach Molière') have often been obscured by the polemical character of the critical debates it has provoked.[3] In the twentieth century, literary critics have remained divided over the question of who emerges triumphant at the end of the play.[4] Is it the god or is it Alkmene? Is Jupiter a benevolent deity who guides Alkmene to a fuller understanding of the love relation?[5] Or is Alkmene a 'Promethean' figure questing for ethical autonomy against the structures of institutionalised religion?[6] Finally, does all end on a happy note of reconciliation or is the play really a 'tragedy in disguise'? As we shall see, however, none of these views does full justice to the complexities of Kleist's play and a closer examination of the text will reveal that in the end, neither Jupiter nor Alkmene is vindicated.

In *Amphitryon*, Kleist presents us with the dilemmas encountered by a high-born married couple, on the one hand, and an adulterous all-too-human 'Casanova-type' god on the other. In this way, Kleist demonstrates the difficulties that arise from an uncritical acceptance of two contrasting, allegedly perfect concepts of 'love', which are in fact only man-made caricatures of reality serving the interests of a male ruling elite. Jupiter embodies a version of romantic love as an all-consuming passion that provokes an immediate and involuntary response from those it engulfs. For their part, Amphitryon and Alkmene subscribe to a correspondingly romantic version of married love which they see as a flawless bonding of souls that excludes infidelity, almost 'by definition'.

AMPHITRYON

Kleist presents Amphitryon as a despotic ruler, a sadistic master and patriarchal husband. His position of absolute authority gives him the power to determine what is to be regarded as truth and falsehood, and in this he enjoys the support of an autocratic society with all that that implies.[7] He projects an image of himself that he sees perfectly reflected in the admiring gaze of the members of his obedient entourage. Although he has long since ceased to be aware of it, the conventional character of the world he inhabits is obvious to any external observer and, above all, to his servant, Sosias. We shall see, however, that an inevitable consequence of his autocratic position is that he cannot actually find out the truth about anything, even when he most needs to. For example, when he asks Sosias for an explanation of what has happened in his absence, the latter prefaces his remarks with a pert enquiry, 'Do I speak the truth straight out to you, or do as well-bred people do?' [G, 24] ('Sag ich Euch dreist die Wahrheit, oder soll ich | Mich wie ein wohlgezogner Mensch betragen?'; *SW* 1, 266; 626–7). It is clear that before the arrival of Jupiter, Amphitryon has never had much need for objective truth. Whenever he is confronted with an account of the world that threatens to contradict his own, he does not seek to disprove it by reasoned argument (for to do so would merely expose the precariousness of his own position) but simply denies it and expects his subjects to do likewise. Thus when he dismisses Sosias's account of events on the grounds that it is 'irrational':

> Schweig. Was ermüd ich mein Gehirn? Ich bin
> Verrückt selbst, solchen Wischwasch anzuhören.
> Unnützes, marklos-albernes Gewäsch,
> In dem kein Menschensinn ist, und Verstand.
>
> (*SW* 1, 270; 762–5)

(Silence! That's enough! Why should I tire out my brain? I'm mad myself to listen to such stuff – useless, senseless, childish gabble, devoid of any trace of reason or intelligence.) [G, 29]

he is guilty, as indeed he is throughout the play, of self-deception. That this is the privilege of his position is not lost on Sosias, who comments:

> So ists. Weil es aus meinem Munde kommt,
> Ists albern Zeug, nicht wert, daß man es höre.
> Doch hätte sich ein Großer selbst zerwalkt,
> So würde man Mirakel schrein. (*SW* 1, 270; 766–9)

(That's the way it is. If it's my mouth it comes out of, it's childish nonsense, pay it no attention. But if it'd been a great one flogged himself himself, you'd hear the whole world crying miracle.) [G, 29]

– a remark which anticipates with no little irony the ending of the play where such 'foolish rubbish' does indeed have to be assigned to the realm of the 'miraculous' to preserve Amphitryon's 'honour' and with it the prevailing power structures.

Since 'truth' for Amphitryon is simply the opinion of 'the high-ranking man' ('ein Großer'), it is entirely fitting that the only 'truth' he is capable of recognising is that which the more powerful Jupiter 'imposes' upon him. Throughout the play, he ignores the claims of reason and looks instead to power and authority to 'prove' his case. Indeed he dare not examine the facts too closely, for if he did, the wholly conventional and arbitrary nature of his position in the world would be revealed – as he comes very close to acknowledging in act III, scene 4, when he says: 'Oh, how I am on fire to know the truth, and how I fear to know it – equally' [G, 66] ('O! hier im Busen brennts, mich aufzuklären, | Und ach! ich fürcht es, wie den Tod'; *SW* I, 303; 1835–6). The sort of person Amphitryon likes to have by him is the First Officer ('Erster Oberster'), Argatiphontidas, who says:

ich, für mein Teil,
Bin für die kürzesten Prozesse stets;
In solchen Fällen fängt man damit an,
Dem Widersacher, ohne Federlesens,
Den Degen querhin durch den Leib zu jagen.
(*SW* I, 313; 2139–43)

(but as for me, I'm for the shortest way of doing things; in cases such as these, you run your man through with your sword right off and never mind formalities.) [G, 76]

But although Amphitryon can, like Argatiphontidas, impose his version of the 'truth' on those who serve him, as the drama of act III unfolds, he is gradually forced to acknowledge that there is a reality 'out there' which he is powerless to alter. His attempts to silence Mercury in act III, scene 2,[8] and Jupiter in act III, scene 5,[9] are to no avail, and his impotence is cruelly signalled in the stage directions by the broken plume ('der eingeknickte Feder') on his helmet.

Amphitryon's 'love' for Alkmene is subject to essentially the same image-preserving conventions as his convenient conception of truth. For his relationship with his wife is, as Jupiter suggests in act I, scene 4, primarily, if not exclusively, a matter of virtue ('Tugend') and has little to do with love ('Liebe'). Thus when he returns to the palace in act II, scene 2, his primary concern is not that he may have lost Alkmene's affection, but rather that, as a cuckolded husband, his standing in the eyes of the world may have diminished. For as he says:

> Ich habe sonst von Wundern schon gehört,
> Von unnatürlichen Erscheinungen, die sich
> Aus einer andern Welt hieher verlieren;
> Doch heute knüpft der Faden sich von jenseits
> An meine Ehre und erdrosselt sie. (*SW* I, 275; 907–11)

(How many tales of wonder I have listened to, about unnatural phenomena, appearances in this world from another – but now it's me, my honour, that a thread spun from the skies has wound itself around and chokes to death.) [G, 34]

Moreover, when Alkmene recounts the events leading up to her seduction, Amphitryon, the man on whose public image his very existence depends, perceives these events, quite literally, as body-blows of increasing intensity, culminating in a final fatal thrust: 'It strikes right to my heart, this dagger does!' [G, 36] ('O dieser Dolch, er trifft das Leben mir!'; *SW* I, 277; 970). For in his mind, love is not a gift given freely by lover to beloved, but is a matter of exclusive sexual ownership. For him cuckoldry equates with loss of love, and loss of love with loss of the exclusive possession of Alkmene, and with this, loss of honour ('Ehre'); and thus he rejects 'love' altogether:

> Fahr hin jetzt Mäßigung, und du, die mir
> Bisher der Ehre Fordrung lähmtest, Liebe,
> Erinnrung fahrt, und Glück und Hoffnung hin,
> Fortan in Wut und Rache will ich schwelgen.
> (*SW* I, 277; 976–9)

(Restraint, farewell! And that which only injured me in what regards my honour, love, farewell to you! Farewell to memories, and hope, and happiness – and welcome bitter hatred and revenge!) [G, 37]

His misconception of the nature of love is total: for even if he were able to destroy his rival – which he is not – this would not result in the restoration of his wife's affection, unless she were to renew her gift.

There are moments in the play when it is tempting to believe as indeed a number of critics have done[10] – that Amphitryon is undergoing a profound change of heart. For at the beginning of act III, he appears to reaffirm his faith in Alkmene when he reflects that:

> Zu argen Trug ist sie so fähig just,
> Wie ihre Turteltaub; eh will ich an
> Die Redlichkeit dem Strick entlaufner Schelme,
> Als an die Tücke dieses Weibes glauben. (*SW* I, 298; 1690–3)

(She is as capable of base deception as her turtle dove: I'll sooner trust the honesty of rogue escaped the noose than think her false.) [G, 60]

However, he is guilty of an act of *mauvaise foi*. For he does not take comfort from some 'inner conviction' that Alkmene still loves him, but rather from his belief that whatever has happened, she could not wittingly have committed adultery: in his scheme of things, royal wives are 'incapable' of such betrayal. The standard explanation comes immediately to his lips: 'she has lost her wits; tomorrow when it dawns, the doctors must be sent for' [G, 60] ('Verrückt ist sie, und morgen, wenn der Tag graut, | Werd ich gewiß nach Ärzten schicken müssen'; *SW* I, 298; 1694–5). Likewise, we must avoid the temptation to see Amphitryon as 'rediscovering' his 'love' for Alkmene in the final scene of the play,[11] when, unable to conceal the disgrace that has come over his house, unable to dispose of his 'rival' by force, and rejected by his wife in front of the assembled Thebans, he exclaims:

> O ihrer Worte jedes ist wahrhaftig,
> Zehnfach geläutert Gold ist nicht so wahr.
> [. . .]
> Jetzt einen Eid selbst auf den Altar schwör ich,
> Und sterbe siebenfachen Todes gleich,
> Des unerschütterlich erfaßten Glaubens,
> Daß er Amphitryon ihr ist. (*SW* I, 317–8; 2281–90)

(Every word she utters is the truth – not gold ten times refined is truer [. . .] I'll swear an oath upon the altar here and now, die ten times over if I'm not unshakeably persuaded: to her he is Amphitryon.) [G, 81–2]

For Amphitryon, his wife's fidelity has always been of greater significance than her love for him; and even her fidelity is an issue only insofar as it threatens to compromise his public standing. He has already considered the possibility of a 'cover up' earlier in act III, scene 3, when he reflects whether he should 'make a public explanation of the shame my house has suffered, or keep silent?' [G, 64] ('Soll ich die Schande, die mein Haus getroffen, | Der Welt erklären, soll ich sie verschweigen?'; *SW* I, 301; 1784–5). After all this, Amphitryon's 'performance' in the final scene is simply a 'face-saving' exercise, a last-ditch attempt to save his position by convincing the assembled public that his wife's adultery was committed unwittingly. Since this apparent disgrace ('Schande') can no longer be concealed, he has little choice but to make a grand proclamation of faith in his wife's 'innocence' (which all of his subjects will appreciate it is their duty to endorse), and to hope desperately that some mitigating consideration will emerge, as indeed happens.[12]

JUPITER

Jupiter is clearly not modelled on the Christian conception of a wholly benevolent and omniscient deity – but is cast in the mould of a typical Greek god, endowed with all-too-human characteristics, albeit on a larger-than-life scale. Accordingly, when he seduces Alkmene, he is not motivated – as some critics would have it[13] – by 'pedagogical zeal', but by jealousy and lust for Amphitryon's recently-acquired, beautiful, young and above all, 'innocent' bride. His greatness – such as it is – lies primarily in the extravagance of his passion and when he alludes to his previous encounters with Kallisto, Europa and Leda,[14] it is made clear to us that Alkmene is not his first conquest nor, we may safely assume, will she be his last. He is a sophisticated, but essentially egocentric, 'Don Juan' figure, confident in his ability to outwit both Amphitryon and Alkmene, but at the same time gloriously unaware of the logical trap that he has set for himself. For in attempting to win possession of an impeccably faithful woman, he must – if he is to succeed – destroy the very quality which attracted him to her in the first place, namely her impeccable faithfulness.

Behind this paradoxical quest lies an equally self-contradictory notion of love, the nature of which is revealed by the semantics of the term 'conquest' ('siegen'),[15] when Jupiter declares:

> *Ich* möchte dir, mein süßes Licht,
> Dies Wesen eigner Art erschienen sein,
> Besieger dein, weil über dich zu siegen,
> Die Kunst, die großen Götter mich gelehrt.
>
> (*SW* I, 261; 474–7)

(But I should like, my angel light, to have seemed to you a being of a nature all his own, your conqueror because the gods themselves instructed him in that fine art, the way to conquer you.) [G, 19]

Although Jupiter, by virtue of his 'divine skill' ('Götterkunst'), has little difficulty in seducing Alkmene, he is forced to recognise that love (as opposed to sex) is rather more difficult to obtain: for unlike sex, love cannot be obtained by force, deceit or even persuasion but is only a gift that is voluntarily bestowed by the lover upon the beloved. And as we observe with amusement, it is precisely this 'gift' that Alkmene continuously withholds from him. It is the god himself who offers the most fitting image of his predicament when he casts himself in the role of a 'Pygmalion-like' figure, who in creating Alkmene has created the 'perfect woman':

> Mein süßes, angebetetes Geschöpf!
> In dem so selig ich mich, selig preise!
> So urgemäß, dem göttlichen Gedanken,
> In Form und Maß, und Sait und Klang,
> Wie's meiner Hand Äonen nicht entschlüpfte!
>
> (*SW* I, 294; 1569–73)

(My creature whom I worship! In whom I am so blessed – in blessing, blessed! So perfectly concordant with the great original divine conception, in shape and substance, string and sound! Such a one has not issued from my hand in eons!) [G, 56]

However, at the same time, he has created the ineradicable source of his own discomfiture:

> O einen Stachel trägt er, glaub es mir,
> Den aus dem liebeglühnden Busen ihm
> Die ganze Götterkunst nicht reißen kann.
>
> (*SW* I, 286; 1295–7)

(Oh, he has got a sting, let me assure you, planted in his fevered bosom all the skill the gods possess can't pull out.) [G, 47]

For Alkmene is the 'perfect' woman only in the sense that she corresponds perfectly to an 'ideal' model of femininity constructed from the sexual and patriarchal fantasies of the men of Thebes. The product of this (inevitably self-contradictory) fantasy is the perfectly loving wife who is, quite literally, incapable of infidelity. But what the creators of such 'fantasy wives' forget, is that such an absolute guarantee of perfect fidelity can be obtained only at the cost of the individual woman's humanity, that is, at the cost of her free will. For if the notion of fidelity is to have any meaning, it must presuppose the possibility of infidelity, and the gift of fidelity from a being that has no choice but to be faithful is no gift at all. In short, an individual who is incapable of infidelity is, by the same token, incapable of fidelity.[16] Jupiter's frustration, therefore, is a direct reflection of the self-contradictory nature of this fantasy image of 'perfect womanhood'. For whilst this Don Juan figure cannot resist the challenge that Alkmene's 'perfect innocence' poses to his talents as a seducer, what he 'forgets' – although strictly speaking he never actually knows it – is that he cannot enjoy the corruption of this 'innocence' and at the same time preserve its integrity.

Although Jupiter never succeeds in grasping the paradoxical nature of his predicament, there are moments when he comes close to doing so, such as in act II, scene 5, where he mutters in an aside: 'Damn the deluded hope that tempted me down here!' [G, 54] ('Verflucht der Wahn, der mich hieher gelockt!'; *SW* I, 292; 1512). The delusion to which he refers is that which has arisen from his unquestioning belief in his own (macho) conception of romantic love as an irresistible and all-conquering force. For although he tells Alkmene that:

> Du sahst noch sein unsterblich Antlitz nicht,
> Alkmene. Ach, es wird das Herz vor ihm
> In tausendfacher Seligkeit dir aufgehn.
> Was du ihm fühlen wirst, wird Glut dir dünken,
> Und Eis, was du Amphitryon empfindest
>
> (*SW* I, 292; 1497–501)

(You've still not seen, Alkmene, his immortal countenance. In his presence, how it would dissolve with bliss unspeakable, your heart, your feeling for him seem like fire, like ice your feeling for Amphitryon.) [G, 54]

the fact is that, as a human being possessed of free will, she is not bound by any necessity to fall in love with him, whatever he may believe to the contrary. And she will always be able to claim that she was tricked and never succumbed to his advances wittingly: indeed she does this so effectively that the great god is left dumbfounded. In addition, however, by invoking the conventional image of royal marital fidelity, Alkmene forces the god to provide an 'excuse' for her infidelity, that is precisely equal to the terms she sets for him: he must have presented such an overwhelming force that even a 'perfectly faithful wife' could not have been expected to resist. In other words, what she requires of him is that he 'compel' her to fall in love with him 'of her own free will', a blatant contradiction in terms. This would indeed be a miracle: but it is one which is not within the (strictly limited) powers of this god.

In the light of the above, it is impossible to regard Jupiter as a would-be educator of Alkmene who leads her to a true understanding of love. For Jupiter the whole affair is – as Mercury points out – merely another amorous 'adventure' [G, 60] ('verliebte[s] Erdenabenteuer'; *SW* I, 298; 1697) and one which is not altogether successful. If Jupiter were capable of learning from experience (which he is not), he might come to see the need to reassess his faith in his own (self-contradictory) account of romantic love as a totally irresistible force. However, the fact is, that he is not given to such self-scrutiny. For as a Greek god, his attributes may not be infinite, but they are nonetheless immutably frozen in time by the constraints of myth and literary tradition and he will remain a larger-than-life Don Juan figure to the end. As far as Alkmene's understanding of the nature of love is concerned, he provides nothing more than a historic opportunity for her to alter her views on love and even then if, and only if, she chooses to do so. He, as the artificial construction of a poetic tradition cannot change; she, as a real living woman, is free to choose.

ALKMENE

Kleist's characterisation of Jupiter and Amphitryon is not fundamentally different from Molière's, but in his presentation of Alkmene and her predicament, he introduces a new dimension into the material. In Molière's play, the central conflict is between Amphitryon and Jupiter, whereas in Kleist's version of the myth, our attention is focused on the struggle between Jupiter and Alkmene. When Alkmene is confronted with the possibility that she may have been seduced by someone other than her husband, she resorts to a series of responses which, though different from those of her husband, are no less conventional and indeed equally fragile when tested against the hard facts of reality. Nonetheless, Kleist goes to some lengths to distinguish between her youthful and, above all, feminine involvement with the conventions of her society and Amphitryon's masculine and autocratic manipulation of them.

Although Alkmene selects the 'wrong' Amphitryon in the final scene of the play, it is tempting to see her as an idealised figure of feminine innocence who is cruelly deceived by Jupiter, and whose adultery is excused by the fact that it was unwitting. Time and again, however, we are left wondering whether her self-image as a woman 'incapable' of infidelity is not so much a reflection of her 'innermost feelings' ('innerstes Gefühl'), as an attempt on her part – though one that is never openly acknowledged – to comply with the demands of the social and moral codes of her upbringing. For although her steadfast resolve in the face of Jupiter's relentless pursuit of her appears, at least at first sight, to be a heroic gesture founded in an unshakeable conviction of her own 'unassailable' fidelity, on closer analysis, this gesture is undermined by her contradictory behaviour at several points in the play. This is most clearly the case in the final scene, where Jupiter is on the point of revealing his true identity and she cries out in desperation: 'Let me stay deceived forever, if your light is going to plunge my soul into eternal night' [G, 82] ('Laß ewig in dem Irrtum mich, soll mir | Dein Licht die Seele ewig nicht umnachten'; *SW* 1, 318; 2305–6). These words prompt us to ask whether Alkmene's condition is not so much one of genuine ignorance, but rather a state of culpable 'innocence', carefully sustained by self-deception.

Kleist makes it abundantly clear that this 'rich princess' [G, 19] ('reiche Fürstentochter'; *SW* I, 261; 480), although young and inexperienced, is a true product of her society. The genteel character of her upbringing is emphasised in act I, scene I, when Sosias rehearses both her questions and his replies in respect of the recent victory: '"Oh dearest Sosias, I entreat you, tell me the whole story, do, omitting nothing!"' [G, 5] ('"O teuerster Sosias! Sieh, das mußt du | Umständlich mir, auf jeden Zug, erzählen"'; *SW* I, 249; 73–4). As he tells his clichéd story of the battle it becomes clear that what Alkmene wants is not an accurate account of the battle, but a glorified and, if necessary, wholly fictitious account, of her famous husband's heroic deeds. Just how far Alkmene has succumbed to this process of cultural indoctrination is made clear when she appears on stage for the first time in act I, scene 4:

Ach, wie
So lästig ist so vieler Ruhm, Geliebter!
Wie gern gäb ich das Diadem, das du
Erkämpft, für einen Strauß von Veilchen hin,
Um eine niedre Hütte eingesammelt.
Was brauchen wir, als nur uns selbst? Warum
Wird so viel Fremdes noch dir aufgedrungen,
Dir eine Krone und der Feldherrnstab?
(*SW* I, 260; 423–30)

(Oh, what a burden so much fame is, love! How gladly I'd give up the diadem you won for me, for a bunch of violets picked outside a cottage door. What do we need, we two, except ourselves? Why should so much which is really alien to you, royal crowns and marshal's maces, be imposed upon you still?) [G, 18]

At first sight, this may seem like a Rosseauesque declaration of pure love, that transcends the world of luxury and sophistication that she inhabits. But a few lines later, this 'simple country maid' collects herself: perhaps her husband will think that she is denying the worth of the things he holds most dear, his power and wealth? So she quickly reassures him that she values his standing in the public eye:

Zwar wenn das Volk dir jauchzt, und sein Entzücken
In jedem großen Namen sich verschwendet,
Ist der Gedanke süß, daß du mir angehörst;
(*SW* I, 260; 431–3)

(It's true that when the people cheer you to the skies and give expression to their rapturous feelings by heaping every glorious title on your head they can invent, the thought that you belong to me is sweet –) [G, 18]

The self-contradictory nature of her behaviour here and elsewhere in the play alerts us to the fact that she is considerably more sophisticated than some critics have been prepared to admit.[17] As we shall see, the image of 'unconditional love' to which she subscribes is based upon an elaborately artificial conception of 'perfect' womanhood. We should, therefore, not be surprised to discover that, despite her claim to be 'incapable' of distinguishing between lover ('Geliebter') and husband ('Gemahl') she is well aware of the significance of such a distinction. For when Jupiter asks her whether it was her husband or her lover whom she received into her arms that night, she replies:

> Geliebter und Gemahl! Was sprichst du da?
> Ist es dies heilige Verhältnis nicht,
> Das mich allein, dich zu empfahn, berechtigt?
> (*SW* I, 261; 458–60)

(My husband *and* my lover! What a thing to say! It's only our state of lawful matrimony, isn't it, that justifies me in receiving you?) [G, 19]

At the same time, we begin to wonder at the vehemence of this display of moral indignation. For is not Jupiter speaking to a woman whose understanding of mature sexual passion has been transformed – as she makes clear both in this scene and subsequently, in act II, scene 4 – during the night they have just spent together? Any inability to distinguish between her lover and her husband would appear to require an adroit suppression of her new-found knowledge of the realities of erotic experience in favour of a more pious pronouncement of the conventional moral clichés of her upbringing. But this is something she does with little or no difficulty. She pertly repudiates any suggestion of her husband's inferiority and (shrewdly?) reminds him of the dangers to his reputation if such talk were to go beyond the confines of the bedroom:

> Amphitryon! Du scherzest. Wenn das Volk hier
> Auf den Amphitryon dich schmähen hörte,
> Es müßte doch dich einen andern wähnen.
> (*SW* I, 262; 484–6)

(Amphitryon, you must be joking! If people here could hear you going on so in that way against Amphitryon, they couldn't but think you were somebody else.) [G, 19]

adding (coyly?), 'I don't know who' [G, 19] ('Ich weiß nicht wen?'; *SW* I, 262; 487), a remark, which leaves Jupiter (and the audience) wondering just what kind of a woman she is. Is she really as innocent as she claims to be? Or is this innocence merely a façade designed to conceal the workings of a sophisticated intelligence? This is the dilemma which the god tries – unsuccessfully – to resolve in act II, scene 5.

When the real Amphitryon arrives in act II, scene 2, Alkmene is forced to take seriously both the accusation that she has been unfaithful to her husband and the threat that this poses to her marriage. She responds by exchanging her earlier role of the 'innocent young bride' for the new, but equally conventional, role of 'Penelope', the dutiful and eternally faithful wife, which she invokes as she recounts the details of her amorous encounter of the previous night:

> Ich saß in meiner Klaus und spann, und träumte
> Bei dem Geräusch der Spindel mich ins Feld,
> Mich unter Krieger, Waffen hin, als ich
> Ein Jauchzen an der fernen Pforte hörte. (*SW* I, 275; 931–4)

(I sat inside my closet at the wheel, the humming of the spindle lulled me off into the field, among armed warriors, when I heard a loud exulting shout from the direction of the farther gate.) [G, 35]

During the course of the scene, the behaviour of both Alkmene and Amphitryon becomes increasingly stilted as they strive to preserve their conventional images of themselves. The prospect of losing Alkmene's love hardly seems to worry Amphitryon; what concerns him is the preservation of his honour. Similarly, Alkmene is ready to sacrifice her relationship with Amphitryon in order to preserve an image of herself as an impeccably faithful wife. Accordingly, she denounces his accusation as a cunning ploy to conceal his own 'infidelity':

> Wenn du dich einer andern zugewendet,
> Bezwungen durch der Liebe Pfeil, es hätte
> Dein Wunsch, mir würdig selbst vertraut, so schnell dich
> Als diese feige List zum Ziel geführt. (*SW* I, 277; 983–6)

(If all your longing now looks elsewhere, to another, if love has smitten you resistlessly, by honestly avowing it to me the goal of your desire would have been attained as fast as by your coward's trick.) [G, 37]

Here Kleist suggests that her behaviour is motivated more by the desire for respectability than by sincere feelings. As a result, her position in this scene is almost identical to that of the boorish Amphitryon and at the end of the scene, their joint refrain – 'Silence, not a word' [G, 37 and 38] ('Schweig, ich will nichts wissen'; *SW* I, 278; 1004 and 1006) – seems peculiarly apposite: the desire for respectability outweighs the desire for honesty.

In act II, scene 4, Alkmene reinforces her conviction that she is literally 'incapable' of being unfaithful to her husband by declaring it to derive from the promptings of her 'innermost feeling'.[18] As such, it becomes part of 'human nature' in the classic way in which time and again throughout history, human conventions acquire the status of incontrovertible insights into the nature of Man and the world: it is the uncovering of this error that lies at the heart of Kleist's critique of society. Alkmene, in her extravagant exchanges with her maid, Charis, seems to be determined, above all, to place an unassailable image of wifely devotion between herself and the hard evidence of the diadem. However, she reveals that her conscience is not perhaps as clear as she would have her maid believe, when the two of them discuss how it can be that the diadem clearly has a 'J' inscribed on it, when Alkmene has all along insisted that it was an 'A' (for Amphitryon). The down-to-earth Charis[19] tries to be helpful and asks: 'Is it possible you were mistaken, then?' [G, 42] ('solltet Ihr getäuscht Euch haben?'; *SW* I, 282; 1149), but her mistress dismisses the idea out of hand: 'Mistaken!' [G, 42] ('Ich mich getäuscht!'; *SW* I, 282; 1150). Her words betray – almost in the manner of a 'Freudian slip' – her erroneous assumption that she has been accused of having mistaken, not the initial on the diadem, but the identity of her nocturnal visitor. And when Charis clears up any possible misunderstanding with the words: 'No, I mean about the letter' [G, 42] ('Hier in dem Zuge, mein ich'; *SW* I, 282; 1150), it is made explicit that the source of this 'accusation' lies not in her mind, but in the mind of her mistress. Alkmene, in her confusion, is driven to a further unnecessary protestation of innocence: 'Oh – about the letter: so it seems, I fear' [G, 43] ('Ja in dem Zug meinst du – so scheint es fast'; *SW* I, 282; 1151). Now the expression of outrage prompted by her discovery of the 'J' on the diadem must be construed as the first of a series of increasingly grandiloquent protestations of outraged innocence made in the face of the clearest possible evidence that she has in fact been unfaithful to her husband. As a result, it becomes impossible to take her exclamation, 'Oh Charis, As soon mistake myself, I would!' [G, 43] ('Oh Charis! – Eh will ich irren in mir selbst!'; *SW* I, 282; 1154) as a sincere expression of genuine bewilderment. Likewise, the impossibly naïve tone of her observation:

> Wenn ich zwei solche Namen, liebste Charis,
> Nicht unterscheiden kann, sprich, können sie
> Zwei Führern, ist es möglich, eigen sein,
> Die leichter nicht zu unterscheiden wären?
>
> (*SW* I, 283; 1181–4)

(If I can't tell two such names apart, dear Charis, might they not, just possibly, belong to two commanders no easier to tell apart?) [G, 43]

makes it clear that this is a purely rhetorical question, or at any rate one not requiring a considered answer. Kleist mercilessly exploits the comic potential of the situation by making Charis take this question at face value and ask: 'But you are absolutely certain, are you?' [G, 44] ('Ihr seid doch sicher, hoff ich, beste Fürstin?'; *SW* I, 283; 1185). And once again, Alkmene's response – 'Certain as I am my soul is pure, my soul is innocent!' [G, 44] ('Wie meiner reinen Seele! Meiner Unschuld!'; *SW* I, 283; 1186) – jars. In keeping with her self-image as a woman who is, by her very nature, 'incapable' of infidelity, Alkmene steadfastly maintains that her ability to distinguish between Amphitryon and any would-be impostor is based, not on empirical experience, but on a sublime, intuitive rapport:

> Nimm Aug und Ohr, Gefühl mir und Geruch,
> Mir alle Sinn und gönne mir das Herz:
> So läßt du mir die Glocke, die ich brauche,
> Aus einer Welt noch find ich ihn heraus. (*SW* I, 282; 1164–7)

(Put out my eye; still I would hear him; stop my ear and I would feel him; take touch away I'd breathe his presence in; take all my senses, every one, but only leave my heart, that bell – its note is all I need to find him out, wherever, in the world.) [G, 43]

However, for one who 'doth protest' her innocence so loudly, Alkmene's behaviour is disturbingly self-contradictory. For no sublime 'bell' ('Glocke') is required to distinguish between the love-making of Jupiter and Amphitryon, only a sufficient experience of the pedestrian performances of the latter. And without any prompting on Charis's part, Alkmene launches into a speech that explicitly highlights the difference between the previous night's encounter and all the other nights of her marriage:

> Du müßtest denn die Regung mir mißdeuten,
> Daß ich ihn schöner niemals fand, als heut.
> Ich hätte für sein Bild ihn halten können,
> Für sein Gemälde, sieh, von Künstlershand,
> Dem Leben treu, ins Göttliche verzeichnet.
> Er stand, ich weiß nicht, vor mir, wie im Traum,
> Und ein unsägliches Gefühl ergriff
> Mich meines Glücks, wie ich es nie empfunden,
> Als er mir strahlend, wie in Glorie, gestern
> Der hohe Sieger von Pharissa nahte.
> Er wars, Amphitryon, der Göttersohn! (*SW* I, 283; 1187–97)

(You mustn't put a wrong construction on the fact that I never felt he was so handsome as last night. I might have thought he was a portrait of himself, a painting by a master's hand showing him exactly as he is, and yet transfigured, like a god! Standing there he seemed, I don't know what, a dream; unspeakable the bliss I felt, whose like I'd never known before, when he, Pharissa's conqueror, radiant as if with Heaven's glory, appeared to me. Amphitryon it was, the son of the gods!) [G, 44]

Here Alkmene's speech epitomises her habitual recourse to the vagaries of conventional rhetoric to account for the magnificence of her 'husband's' love-making on the previous night, by creating an exaggerated 'portrait' of him as 'god-like' and 'divine'. In short, she asserts the reality of an unreal husband in order to deny the existence of a real god. In so doing, she avails herself of a rhetorical strategy for which Kleist had nothing but contempt, namely that process by which unsustainable metaphysical speculations become encapsulated in social stereotypes and are handed down from one generation to the next thereby constituting a further obstacle to knowledge of reality. Thus in typical fashion, Kleist ensures that the transcendent flight of Alkmene's rhetoric is brought smartly down to earth by the common-sense observation of her maid: 'It was imagination, dear – love's way of seeing things' [G, 44] ('Einbildung, Fürstin, das Gesicht der Liebe'; *SW* I, 283; 1201).

In act II, scene 5, Alkmene's behaviour demonstrates the same inconsistencies. Having rejected the evidence of 'all her senses' ('alle Sinn') in favour of her 'intuition' ('innerstes Gefühl') in the previous scene, she now falls to her knees, shows her 'husband' the diadem with the mysterious 'J' and begs him to pass judgement on her, all of which points to the fact that her intuition may not be as trustworthy as she would like to maintain. The exaggerated rhetoric with which she repeatedly rejects the god's affirmations of her innocence together with her equally extravagant protestations that she would rather die than be unfaithful to her husband[20] casts serious doubts on her sincerity. This is 'high melodrama' played out before Jupiter, Charis and Sosias: Jupiter aiding and abetting her protestations of innocence; Charis and Sosias soaking up the intoxicating rhetoric of the 'stage'.[21]

As the scene unfolds, it becomes increasingly apparent that the aim of Alkmene's 'performance' is to force her 'male lead' to offer the only 'solution' that is compatible with the conventional image of marital fidelity to which she subscribes: the man who deceived her must have been a god, nothing less will do. As a result, Jupiter is driven on remorselessly into making ever more definitive affirmations of her innocence, starting from the premise that she could never have committed adultery wittingly:

> Wie könnte dir ein anderer erscheinen?
> Wer nahet dir, o du, vor deren Seele
> Nur stets des Ein- und Ein'gen Züge stehn?
> (*SW* I, 285; 1256–8)

(How should another man appear to you, to you whose soul has eyes for one face only, only one?) [G, 46]

and culminating in his 'promise' that even if she had been unfaithful, he, her 'husband', would never abandon her nor allow her to abandon 'him':

> Bis an den Strand des Meeres folgt ich dir,
> Ereilte dich, und küßte dich, und weinte,

Und höbe dich in Armen auf, und trüge
Dich im Triumph zu meinem Bett zurück.
(*SW* I, 287; 1324–7)

(As far as to the edge of Ocean, I'd race and overtake you, kiss you, cry, and lifting you in my arms, carry you in triumph to my bed.) [G, 48]

When even this proves unacceptable to her, he changes tack altogether and moves to exploit her acute sense of social standing; she should consider that she has been found worthy of the love of no less a being than the king of the gods himself:

Es war kein Sterblicher, der dir erschienen,
Zeus selbst, der Donnergott, hat dich besucht.
(*SW* I, 287; 1335–6)

(It was no mortal man appeared to you, but Zeus himself, the Thunder God!) [G, 48]

In the face of such a social triumph, Alkmene registers a becoming modesty; in fact it has to be asserted 'thrice' that it is indeed 'the holy spirit' who has visited her.[22] With appropriate humility she professes to be aghast at the blasphemous suggestion that the great god could have been involved in so heinous a crime, but Jupiter hastens to reassure her that, far from being a crime, it is an honour to be the object of the god's love:

Wenn du empfindlich für den Ruhm nicht bist,
Zu den Unsterblichen die Staffel zu ersteigen,
Bin ichs: (*SW* I, 288; 1349–51)

(If mounting up to the ranks of the immortals is an honour you don't feel – well, I do.) [G, 49]

The real Amphitryon might have been content to stop here: in the final scene of the play, he shows himself to be perfectly capable of recognising the 'honour' of such a divine visitation. As it is, however, Alkmene's appetite for this kind of flattery is not yet satisfied, and under the guise of 'humility' she goes on to ask disarmingly:

Darf ich auch den Gedanken nur mir gönnen?
Würd ich vor solchem Glanze nicht versinken?
(*SW* I, 288; 1364–5)

(Do I dare even to think of such a thing? How would I fail to be submerged and drowned in such radiance?) [G, 49]

This is Jupiter's cue to spell out in detail why she has been singled out from all other women for preferential treatment. Now even she is almost satisfied, for has she not succeeded in eliciting a total confirmation of her image of herself as an utterly faithful wife, as a woman whose intuition could only be deceived by a divine visitation? As Jupiter says:

> Wer könnte dir die augenblickliche
> Goldwaage der Empfindung so betrügen?
> Wer so die Seele dir, die weibliche,
> Die so vielgliedrig fühlend um sich greift,
> So wie das Glockenspiel der Brust umgehn,
> Das von dem Atem lispelnd schon erklingt?
> (*SW* I, 289; 1395–1400)

(Who else, I'd like to know, could ever have deceived the finely poised gold-balance of your feeling, eluded the antennae your woman's soul puts out toward all around it, failed to jar the bells the whisper of a breath sets ringing in your bosom?) [G, 50]

This is an endorsement she welcomes enthusiastically: 'He himself' [G, 50] ('Er selber! Er!'; *SW* I, 289; 1401). At a stroke she has managed to contrive a solution that – as the final scene demonstrates – will be wholly in accord with the real Amphitryon's conception of honour and this is implied by Jupiter's smug remark:

> Nur die Allmächtgen mögen
> So dreist, wie dieser Fremdling, dich besuchen,
> Und solcher Nebenbuhler triumphier ich!
> (*SW* I, 289; 1401–3)

(Only the All-powerful dare to visit you as boldly as that stranger did – and see how I defeat such rivals!) [G, 50]

For Alkmene this is the perfect solution, maintaining as it does the stability of the *status quo*. She throws her arms around him, kisses him and exclaims:

> Wie glücklich bin ich!
> Und o wie gern, wie gern noch bin ich glücklich!
> Wie gern will ich den Schmerz empfunden haben,

Den Jupiter mir zugefügt,
Bleibt mir nur alles freundlich wie es war. (*SW* 1, 289; 1410–14)

(I'm so happy now! And oh how glad, how very glad that I'm so happy. I'll be glad to have suffered all the pain that Jupiter has caused me, if only everything is nice again between us.) [G, 51]

At the same time, neither the audience – nor indeed Jupiter himself – can overlook the ambiguous character of Alkmene's remarks in the first half of the scene. The scene is contrived in such a way that the audience can never be quite sure whether Alkmene knows whether the person currently embracing her is her husband or her seducer and, in a deliciously languid enjoyment of the situation, Kleist has his heroine 'manage' her remarks to suit either contingency. Thus when Jupiter reminds Alkmene of the passionate extravagances of a night in which her image of herself as a woman of impeccable virtue has been called into question, we, like the god, are left wondering whether her response, 'if only Zeus would strike him down, here at my feet' [G, 47] ('Daß ihn Zeus mir zu Füßen niederstürzte!'; *SW* 1, 286; 1298) does not in fact betray her sneaking suspicion that the 'Amphitryon' to whom she is speaking is not her husband, but the lover. This presents Jupiter with a dilemma because her remarks can always be interpreted in two ways. If Jupiter (and the audience) assume that Alkmene believes she is speaking with her husband, Amphitryon, then it would appear that she is seized by remorse and wishes she could return to that point in time when her virtue was still intact, an interpretation which would compel her lover, Jupiter, to interpret a remark such as, 'Now you and I must separate, oh god, forever!' [G. 47] ('O Gott! Wir müssen uns auf ewig trennen'; *SW* 1, 286; 1299) as the words of a married woman determined to break off an affair.[23] However, if Jupiter (and the audience) assume that Alkmene believes she is speaking to her lover, the god, then it would appear that she is inviting him to invent a better 'solution' to her predicament, namely one which would allow the affair to continue whilst preserving her self-image as an 'impeccably' faithful wife. Under that assumption, Jupiter has no choice but to interpret the remark cited above – 'Now you and I must separate, oh god, forever' – as a warning that the affair will be terminated if he fails in his appointed task. This reading of the situation would then imply that the kiss administered at line 1410 (G, 51; *SW* I, 289) is both a reward for his cunning – his 'explanation' that her virtue is so unassailable that only a god could have deceived her – and a promise of what is to come.

Hardly has Alkmene had time to savour Jupiter's affirmations of her 'perfect' virtue, before he (in the persona of her husband) embarks on a new line of attack. For, he suggests, perhaps Jupiter is not so much enamoured of her, as displeased with her unholy preoccupation with him (Amphitryon). He has little difficulty in convincing her that she is often thinking of her husband – the 'divine' Amphitryon – when she is praying to the god, and points out that she has been exaggerating the magnificence of her earthly lord and master (Amphitryon) until it bears comparison with that of the lord and master of the gods (Jupiter) himself:

> Wenn hoch die Sonn in seinen Tempel strahlt
> Und von der Freude Pulsschlag eingeläutet,
> Ihn alle Gattungen Erschaffner preisen,
> Steigst du nicht in des Herzens Schacht hinab
> Und betest deinen Götzen an? (*SW* I, 290; 1429–33)

(When the sun aloft in his great temple sends his beams abroad, when through Creation beats a pulse of joy and all things hymn his praise, don't you descend into the mine shaft of your heart to adore your idol?) [G, 51]

Having taken this 'reproach' suitably to heart, Alkmene (coyly?) assures him, that she will not confuse her husband and the god (her lover) in future:

> Wohlan! Ich schwörs dir heilig zu! Ich weiß
> Auf jede Miene, wie er ausgesehn,
> Und werd ihn nicht mit dir verwechseln. (*SW* I, 291; 1471–3)

(Oh yes! I swear it, by the sacred gods! I recollect the way he looked, every feature of him, perfectly, and shan't mix up the two of you.) [G, 53]

Moreover she assures her 'husband' that she will even set aside an hour each day for communing solely with the god (her lover) and we cannot help but smile at the satisfaction that Jupiter must derive from such an arrangement. Suitably encouraged, Jupiter resumes his cross-examination of Alkmene, but she, having recovered her composure, successfully evades every attempt on his part to elicit a confession of genuine infidelity by hiding behind the trusty shield of her image as the 'perfectly' faithful wife. And when he ends his interrogation by asking:

> Wenn ich, der Gott, dich hier umschlungen hielte,
> Und jetzo dein Amphitryon sich zeigte,
> Wie würd dein Herz sich wohl erklären? (*SW* I, 294; 1561–3)

(But now suppose *I* am the god embracing you, and lo, Amphitryon appears – your heart, what would it say to that?) [G, 56]

to which she replies:

> Ja – dann so traurig würd ich sein, und wünschen,
> Daß er der Gott mir wäre, und daß du
> Amphitryon mir bliebst, wie du es bist. (*SW* I, 294; 1566–8)

(I'd be so very sad, oh so dejected, and wish that he could be the god and you would go on being my Amphitryon forever, as you are.) [G, 56]

Alkmene makes it perfectly clear that she will never, of her own free will, acknowledge that she has been unfaithful to her husband and that if the fact of her adultery is indeed to be exposed then it will only be because Jupiter chooses to do so. Here we witness both the victory and the defeat of Alkmene. With her use of the conditional 'would' ('würde') she makes one final attempt to avoid openly confessing her infidelity, one final attempt to ensure that 'everything is nice again'. At the same time, however, she reveals that Jupiter has identified the only circumstances in which she would have no choice but to acknowledge the fact of her adultery, and these are precisely the circumstances which the god engineers at the end of the play. Her lover is thunderstruck and he can only gasp in amazement at the strength of her resolve: 'My creature whom I worship! In whom I am so blessed – in blessing, blessed' [G, 56] ('Mein süßes, angebetetes Geschöpf! | In dem so selig ich mich, selig preise!'; *SW* I, 294; 1569–70). He has been hoist by his own petard: defeated by a creature of his own making, defeated by a woman who so perfectly reflects the masculine fantasy of the 'infallibly' faithful wife that without actually being faithful to Amphitryon, can never be unfaithful with Jupiter.

THE DENOUEMENT

From Amphitryon's perspective, the play ends in triumph: his wife's 'honour' (and consequently his own) has been vindicated before all the citizens of Thebes, for as Jupiter announces:

> Die ganze Welt, Geliebte, muß erfahren,
> Daß *niemand* deiner Seele nahte,
> Als nur dein Gatte, als Amphitryon. (*SW* I, 314: 2170–2)

(Your husband, Lord Amphitryon, and *no one else* has ever been allowed within the precincts of your soul – and I wish the world to know it.) [G, 77]

What greater honour could there be for a man like Amphitryon than for his wife to receive a divine visitation? Nonetheless, he maintains sufficient presence of mind to hold out for an even more 'honourable' solution: he requires a (demi-god) son as proof positive of the god's involvement in his family affairs. Amphitryon's 'love' for Alkmene cannot be jeopardised by the events that have taken place because he is, as we have seen, incapable of loving her in any genuine sense of the word. Indeed the true nature of his 'love' is revealed when he says to Jupiter, 'all I have is thine' [G, 83] ('dein ist alles, was ich habe'; *SW* I, 319; 2314) and the brutal reality of this offer is borne out by the image of Amphitryon discussing with his 'superior' the use to which his wife's body should be put, whilst she lies prostrate before them. At the end of the play, Amphitryon can feel that his authority in Thebes is more secure than ever before, and this is confirmed by the reactions of the watching generals ('Feldherrn'), who applaud in admiration: 'My goodness, such a triumph!' [G, 84] ('Fürwahr! Solch ein Triumph'; *SW* I, 320; 2361). And we can be sure that Amphitryon will never change, except perhaps to become even more firmly entrenched in the brutish conventional world he inhabits.

For Jupiter, the ending of the play is more ambivalent. Just prior to revealing his true identity to the onlookers, he says to Alkmene, 'Why, I would curse the bliss you've brought me if I couldn't be a living presence to you, dear, eternally' [G, 82] ('O Fluch der Seligkeit, die du mir schenktest, | Müßt ich dir ewig nicht vorhanden sein'; *SW* I, 318; 2307–8). These lines refer back to his earlier remark in act II, scene 5, where he said to Alkmene, 'You've still not seen . . . his immortal countenance' [G, 54] ('Du sahst noch sein unsterblich Antlitz nicht'; *SW* 1, 292; 1497). Here Jupiter is still clinging to that conventional concept of love in which the victim does not give her 'love' freely, but is compelled to submit to a force greater than human will can oppose. And thus, risking everything on one last throw of the dice he reveals his true identity to Alkmene, in the hope that once she has 'seen his immortal countenance', she will succumb and be unable to forget him to the end of her days. But what if this macho view of love is mistaken? What if there is no 'beatific vision' that can swamp Alkmene's free choice of whom to love and whom to deny? What if, like Lucifer before her, she can reject the god?

The question remains: will Jupiter learn anything from his latest amorous escapade? If he had been a man like Amphitryon, he might have learned something, though probably very little. But since he is a god, an immutable metaphysical being, he cannot learn anything at all. For just as the Christian god cannot change without losing his perfection, so Jupiter, as the imaginary creation of Homer, is a literary fiction frozen in time. Like Alkmene, the 'perfect' wife, Jupiter, the 'perfect' lover, is an artificial construction and just as her 'virtue' remains 'intact', so do his 'vices' and thus he can say to Amphitryon:

> Was du, in mir, dir selbst getan, wird dir
> Bei mir, dem, was ich ewig bin, nicht schaden.
>
> (*SW* 1, 319; 2321–2)

(The injury that you, in me, inflicted on yourself, no injury is, in my eternal Allness.) [G, 83]

Alkmene's predicament at the end of the play is considerably more open to speculation. In choosing Jupiter instead of Amphitryon, she chooses prudently – in that she takes the only course of action that holds out any possibility of her maintaining her image as the faithful wife – but wrongly. In making her choice she follows less the dictates of her intuition than the demands of social correctness. Kleist emphasises this (with no little irony) by showing her act according to the dictates of the boorish Argatiphontidas, who, just prior to the decision, tells everyone: 'She recognises him she came out of the house with, him' [G, 78]

('Ihn erkennt sie, | Ihn an, mit dem sie aus dem Hause trat'; *SW* I, 315; 2194–5). Having chosen, Alkmene resorts once more to the same rhetoric we heard in act II, scene 5, attempting to attribute her 'fall from grace' to the malicious cunning of an 'outsider', rather than confronting her own human fallibility:

> Was tat ich dir, daß du mir nahen mußtest,
> Von einer Höllennacht bedeckt,
> Dein Gift mir auf den Fittich hinzugeifern?
> (*SW* I, 316; 2242–4)

(What harm did I do you that you should creep up on me under cover of a night engendered out of Hell and dribble your disgusting venom on my wings?) [G, 80]

Although she begs to be 'left in the dark' so that her image of herself may be unharmed: 'Let me stay deceived forever, if your light is going to plunge my soul into eternal night' [G, 82] ('Laß ewig in dem Irrtum mich, soll mir | Dein Licht die Seele ewig nicht umnachten'; *SW* I, 318; 2305–6) she realises she cannot keep up the pretence any longer. If we now ask what Alkmene might salvage from her part in this affair, we should, perhaps, remind ourselves that she is young and, as a woman, a marginalised member of Theban society. As we have seen, it would not be in keeping with Kleist's optimistic attitude to the possibility of human progress were she to be left with no hope of self-improvement. Of course it is perfectly possible that she may try to forget the whole incident and share in her husband's 'triumph'; but it is equally possible that she will come to see both her husband and, more importantly, herself in a more realistic light and each of these possibilities lies concealed behind her final enigmatic 'Oh!' ('Ach!'). It seems, however, at least probable that she will henceforth put less trust in the conventional paraphernalia of her society; having eaten of the Tree of Knowledge, she will never again rest easy in the bed of metaphysics.

THE SERVANTS: SOSIAS

Amphitryon and Alkmene are not the only ones to have their world turned upside down by the arrival of the gods; the servants, Sosias and Charis, are affected too. Sosias, with his native cunning is Jupiter's counterpart, just as Amphitryon, with his reliance on brute force, is the counterpart of Mercury. Jupiter, by virtue of his superior standing, is able to exploit his rhetorical cunning in the furtherance of his own aims, namely the seduction of Alkmene, whereas Sosias deploys his chiefly to save his own skin and avoid disaster.

Sosias sees the loss of his personal identity as offering the possibility of emancipation and, as he points out to Mercury, he would gladly swap his own identity for that of his master, but cannot do so:

> Und das aus dem gerechten Grunde, weil es
> Die großen Götter wollen; weil es nicht
> In meiner Macht steht, gegen sie zu kämpfen,
> Ein andrer sein zu wollen als ich bin;
> Weil ich muß Ich, Amphitryons Diener sein,
> Wenn ich auch zehenmal Amphitryon,
> Sein Vetter lieber, oder Schwager wäre. (*SW* I, 253; 205–11)

(And for the best of reasons, too: because the gods would have it so; because it's quite beyond my power to quarrel with them over who I am and try to be somebody else; because it is my fate to be myself, the servant of Amphitryon, though I would like it ten times better if I could have been Amphitryon himself, his brother-in-law or cousin.) [G, 10]

Sosias's response could not be more different from that of Amphitryon when he too is deprived of his identity during his confrontation with Mercury in act III, scene 2. Sosias, who regards himself as firmly anchored at the bottom rung of the Theban social hierarchy sees in Mercury a glimpse of what he might become; whereas Amphitryon, the king, knows that any change must entail a catastrophic loss of status. He is perfectly satisfied in being 'just' Amphitryon, and whilst even the 'de-Sosiased' ('entsosiatisierte') Sosias remains 'something',[24] for Amphitryon, loss of identity is tantamount to death. Amphitryon sees in Jupiter only a more powerful version of himself; the intervention of Mercury in Sosias's life, however, contains the very seeds of revolution. What might he not achieve were he to adopt the assertive model of himself that Mercury has revealed to him? And at a number of points in the play we catch a glimpse of his covert admiration for his divine *Doppelgänger*, for example, in act II, scene 6, where he says to himself:

> Mein Seel, er war nicht schlecht bedient.
> Ein Kerl, der seinen Mann stund, und sich
> Für seinen Herrn schlug, wie ein Panthertier.
> (*SW* I, 295; 1592–4)

(He wasn't badly served – stood up to his man, the fellow did, and hit out like a tiger for his master.) [G, 57]

Indeed, Sosias himself gets a taste of the sort of treatment an 'improved' Sosias could expect when Charis, mistaking him to be a god, prostrates herself before him and promising 'bratwurst and cabbage' [G, 59] ('gebratne Wurst mit Kohlköpf'; *SW* I, 297; 1650). And thus Mercury's intrusion into his life – however painful – may perhaps render Sosias capable of shrugging off what is in fact the only instance of conventionally dictated behaviour he manifests in the play, namely his belief in the 'natural inevitability' of servitude, especially his own at the very bottom of society.

For the most part, Sosias never loses his grip on reality; he is the one character who is not firmly in thrall to social convention, as is shown in act II, scene 6, where despite being mistaken for a god, he says:

> Apollon, ich? bist du des Teufels? – Der eine
> Macht mich zum Hund, der andre mich zum Gott? –
> Ich bin der alte, wohlbekannte Esel,
> Sosias! (*SW* I, 297; 1660–3)

(I, Apollo? You're possessed, I think. I'm cur to one, and to another god. But what I am's the old familiar donkey, Sosias!) [G, 59]

Nonetheless, were he to put into practice the lessons he should have learned from Mercury and succeed in raising himself in the social hierarchy, even he would be at risk of becoming a convention-bound individual like the others. Indeed, we are offered a glimpse of the dangers that lie in store for such an 'improved Sosias' when he lapses into the grandiose rhetoric of 'Sosias, the faithful servant', a 'Sosias' who has at last managed to break into the 'moral' chain by owing a debt of loyalty to his master, a debt which the old Sosias, the 'old familiar donkey', would infallibly have recognised as one he had never incurred. For in act III, scene 9, we see Sosias 'the man of honour', who would 'even' refrain from eating his sausages rather than betray his master:

> Und hätt ich Würst in jeder Hand hier eine,
> Ich wollte sie in meinen Mund nicht stecken.
> So seinen armen, wackern Herrn verlassen,
> Den Übermacht aus seinem Hause stieß. (*SW* I, 311; 2073–6)

(If I had a wurst in both hands now, I'd not allow myself a single bite. To desert your master that's so good to you, poor man, when he was driven from his house by superior force!) [G, 74]

We almost feel a sense of relief, when, in the final scene, the 'old' (and more realistic) Sosias is back once more, cursing his departing tormentor:

> Daß du für immer unbesungen mich
> Gelassen hättst! Mein Lebtag sah ich noch
> Solch einen Teufelskerl, mit Prügeln, nicht.
> (*SW* I, 320; 2358–60)

(If only you had left me obscure still, no theme for song! In all my life I never encountered one like him for beating up on fellows.) [G, 84]

Unlike Amphitryon, Sosias can see nothing honourable in being thrashed by a god, no matter how expertly, and his words draw attention (with no little irony) to the spuriousness of his master's 'triumph'. Furthermore, when he wishes that none of this had happened, he is not, like Alkmene, referring to some fictional notion of respectability which he has had to dispense with, but to the real stripes on his back, and we must hope that if he does make some headway in society, he will not lose sight of the difference between being respectable and being respected.

THE SERVANTS: CHARIS

Charis is a woman whose unquestioning acceptance of the conventions of feminine respectability has barred her from all sexual adventure just like the woman of Kleist's ironic epigram, *Die Reuige* (*A woman with regrets*):

> HIMMEL, welch eine Pein sie fühlt! Sie hat so viel Tugend
> Immer gesprochen, daß ihr nun kein Verführer mehr naht.
> (*SW* I, 23)

(Heavens above! See how she suffers. She's talked so much about her virtue that now no one even bothers trying to seduce her.)

She may profess to be dissatisfied with Sosias as a lover, but she is not really interested in anything other than the outward signs of affection from a husband, who fails – quite lamentably – to live up to her idea of what a proper husband should be. Similarly, when she expresses her frustration at the way in which her reputation for respectability now stands in the way of her taking a lover (and getting back at her husband) and exclaims: 'how I regret it now, my reputation for respectability!' [G, 23] ('Wie ich es jetzt bereue, daß die Welt | Für eine ordentliche Frau mich hält!'; *SW* I, 265; 598–9) the truth of the matter is that it is of little consequence to Sosias whether or not she takes a lover. For a man in his position, the implications of his wife's infidelity would not be the far-reaching implications that would attend the same event in the case of his superiors. Unlike Amphitryon and Alkmene, who cannot bear to confront the facts of the matter, Sosias can hardly be bothered, and shrugs it all off, saying: 'It's all one in the end so long as you don't look too closely into things' [G, 38] ('Zuletzt ists doch so lang wie breit, | Wenn mans nur mit dem Licht nicht untersucht'; *SW* I, 278; 1020–1).

Despite her penchant for the conventions of feminine respectability, Charis, like Sosias, represents the voice of common sense, as can be seen in act II, scene 4, where her down-to-earth interjections persistently undermine the exalted rhetoric of Alkmene. She is not, however, without a sentimental streak herself and so impressed is she by her mistress's 'performance' during the exchange with Jupiter that, in act II, scene 6, she starts to take seriously the very same explanation – divine intervention – that she had scoffed at only two scenes previously: 'Unlucky woman, what was that you heard? They may have been Olympians?' [G, 56] ('Was hast du da gehört, Unselige? | Olympsche Götter wären es gewesen?'; *SW* I, 295; 1585–6). And just as in the very first scene of the play, Sosias adopts the conventional rhetoric of his superiors when 'describing' the battle, so Charis adopts the correct 'Olympian' form of address 'dear husband' when conversing with her 'divine' Sosias: 'Can I have a word with you, dear husband, first?' [G, 57] ('Vergönne mir ein Wort vorher, mein Gatte'; *SW* I, 295; 1599). She is, of course, not exaggerating when she remarks that, 'Thebes never has enjoyed, in all its years, a triumph such as this' ('Solch ein Triumph, wie über uns gekommen, | Ward noch in Theben nicht erhört'; *SW* I, 295; 1614–15), for it would indeed have been a quite unheard of 'triumph' for her to have succeeded in attracting the 'attentions' of the gods. Her sentimentalising tendency is comic and serves to undermine any attempt on the part of the audience to take seriously Alkmene's excuse of divine visitation; but it could pose a threat to a man like Sosias, if ever he succeeded in moving up in the social hierarchy, for Charis is perfectly capable of giving herself airs and graces – and graces cost money.

CONCLUSION

In Molière's version of *Amphitryon*, Alcmène is a wholly idealised figure, whose innocence is never in question and who is never allowed to discover that she has been seduced by Jupiter. To achieve this, he does not allow her to be present at the denouement. Although in Molière's characterisation of her, she is presented as a woman possessed of a peerless understanding of the true nature of love, from the point of view of empirical reality, she remains a dupe. Kleist's Alkmene is very different; she has been educated to an acceptance of a conventional conception of love that has itself been shaped by the fantasies of a male ruling elite. And it is her preoccupation with the distorted products of such an education that prevents her from examining the true nature of her predicament and places serious obstacles in the way of a more mature understanding of the true nature of love. Unlike Molière's Alcmène, she has a great deal to learn. And thus in the final scene of Kleist's play, Alkmene has to be on stage so that she may have the opportunity to realise that she does not really know herself: to recognise that the image she has had of herself is fundamentally false and that the 'ideals' of love ('Liebe') and fidelity ('Treue') – as she has been taught them – have let her down in the face of reality.

Nonetheless, it is far from being Kleist's intention to suggest that human beings should abandon the quest for better and truer living. On the contrary, by showing that Alkmene's downfall is the result of misguided education, he hints at the need for – and the possibility of – a more realistic kind of education in society: one that takes account of the limitations of human knowledge whilst respecting the positive capacity for self-improvement of ordinary men and women when they think aright.

PART III

Fictions of femininity

CHAPTER 6

Penthesilea

Even the most cursory examination of Kleist's correspondence will reveal the important role women played in his life, for the vast bulk of his correspondence is addressed either to his sister, Ulrike von Kleist, or to his fiancée, Wilhelmine von Zenge. In addition, his letters to his cousin, Marie von Kleist, most of which were written towards the end of his life, bear witness to the closeness of their relationship. It should come as no surprise, therefore, that women feature so prominently in his literary works. Kleist realised that women, by virtue of their marginalised position in the predominantly patriarchal culture of his day, were, for the most part, shielded from some of the more pernicious effects of social ideology. And although few of Kleist's characters display no trace of their upbringing in conventional society, more often than not, his female characters have a surer grip on reality than their men folk. For example, Eve, in *Der zerbrochne Krug*, is able to see beyond the prevailing conventions of her society and grasp the reality of her situation precisely because she is marginalised by that culture for being 'just a woman', young, and coming from a lowly peasant family. Alkmene, on the other hand, although she has the 'advantages' of youth and gender, is of noble birth and, as a result, is more thoroughly marked by the conventions of her male-oriented society than Eve is by hers. But despite the difficulties that result from her uncritical acceptance of the misguided notion of 'feminine virtue' enshrined in the conventions of Theban society, she is far more likely to recognise her mistake than her 'suitors', Jupiter and Amphitryon, are to recognise theirs.

As we saw in chapter 2, Kleist himself espoused a notion of 'ideal' femininity very similar to that current in the society in which he places Alkmene. However, it was only a matter of time before he revised these opinions[1] and came to understand that such conventional descriptions of 'perfect' femininity did not correspond to reality and were merely devices for ensuring that women would force their true natures into the distorted caricatures of life designed to satisfy the erotic fantasies of their patriarchal masters. A major component of these fantasies was the idea that the love of a woman could be owed as a duty or paid as a debt to the man who gave her his 'protection', without which her life was not really viable. Kleist came to see that these ideas were quite inimical to a proper conception of love. In addition he saw that these mistaken norms had been put in place not simply by the sexual fantasies of the dominant male class, but by an even more potent force – fear, and above all, fear of the unknown. For if 'woman' is not as she is portrayed in these comforting man-made fictions, the highly uncomfortable question remains: what *is* the nature of woman? This was the question that Kleist set out to answer in so radical a fashion in his next two plays, *Penthesilea* and *Das Käthchen von Heilbronn*.

Kleist was never optimistic about the chances of seeing his tragedy, *Penthesilea* performed on stage, as he explains to his cousin, Marie von Kleist, in a letter written in the late autumn of 1807:

Ob es, bei den Forderungen, die das Publikum an die Bühne macht, gegeben werden wird, ist eine Frage, die die Zeit entscheiden muß. Ich glaube es nicht, und wünsche es auch nicht, so lange die Kräfte unsrer Schauspieler auf nichts geübt, als Naturen, wie die Kotzebueschen und Ifflandschen sind, nachzuahmen. (*SW* II, 796)[2]

(Whether it can be played, considering the public's expectations from the stage these days, time alone must decide. I rather think not, nor do I wish it, while the talents of our actors are practised only in aping the characters of a Kotzebue or Iffland.) [M, 175]

In the light of these remarks, it is ironic that one critic should dismiss the play precisely on the grounds that it pandered to the contemporary vogue for 'sensationalist dramas' ('Spektakelstücke').[3] Given the way in which the play challenged not only the prevailing norms of feminine behaviour in Kleist's society, but also the idealised picture of classical antiquity handed down *via* the work of Winckelmann and others, it is hardly surprising that there was no room for it in the repertoires of the contemporary theatres. Kleist himself understood that his uncompromising exploration of the nature of love was unlikely to appeal to audiences brought up on the sentimental clichés of the popular theatre, its farces and chivalrous romances ('Ritterstücke'), and he deplored the way in which the realities of human behaviour had been 'tailored' to conform to conventional models of 'feminine respectability', conventions which he had exposed in his previous play, *Amphitryon*. For as he continues in his letter to Marie:

> Wenn man es recht untersucht, so sind zuletzt die Frauen an dem ganzen Verfall unsrer Bühne schuld . . . Ihre Anforderungen an Sittlichkeit und Moral vernichten das ganze Wesen des Drama, und niemals hätte sich das Wesen des griechischen Theaters entwickelt, wenn sie nicht ganz davon ausgeschlossen gewesen wären. (*SW* II, 796)

> (Rightly inquired into, it is the women who are guilty of the total decline of our stage . . . Their demand for manners and morals destroys the very nature of the drama, and the Greek conception of theatre could never have developed if women had not been excluded from it.) [M, 175]

Of course, the apparently derogatory tone of Kleist's remarks is not intended as an attack on women *per se*, but rather on the conventional make-believe role created for them by society.

Although properly sceptical about the chances of having his play put on in the popular theatre, Kleist did hope for a more sympathetic response from the literary establishment, and above all from Goethe. Encouraged perhaps, by the latter's decision to stage *Der zerbrochne Krug*, he sent him an excerpt from the play (the 'Organisches Fragment') he had published in his own literary journal, *Phöbus*, in the hope that it might grace the stage of the Weimar Court Theatre, for as he explains, 'no other theatre of ours would seem so provided, on either side of the curtain, that I might expect such an honour of it' [M, 179] ('unsre übrigen Bühnen sind weder vor noch hinter dem Vorhang so beschaffen, daß ich auf diese Auszeichnung rechnen dürfte'; *SW* II, 805–6). He was, of course, to be cruelly disappointed, and Goethe's bewilderment upon reading the play is all too discernible in his letter of 1 February 1808: 'To Penthesilea I have as yet been unable to warm.

She is of so singular a race, and inhabits so alien a region, that I shall need time to find my way in both' [M, 179] ('Mit der Penthesilea kann ich mich noch nicht befreunden. Sie ist aus einem so wunderbaren Geschlecht und bewegt sich in einer so fremden Region, daß ich mir Zeit nehmen muß, mich in beide zu finden'; *Lebensspuren*, no. 224).[4] That Kleist firmly believed his work had been rejected because it failed to conform to the harmonising aesthetics of Goethe's theatre is expressed in the bitterly ironic epigram,[5] *Der Theater-Bearbeiter der Penthesilea (The producer of Penthesilea)* in which the elliptical W . . . stands for Weimar:

> NUR die Meute, fürcht ich, die wird in W . . . mit Glück nicht
> Heulen, Lieber; den Lärm setz ich, vergönn, in Musik. (*SW* I, 21)

(My dear fellow, I just wanted to say that with any luck there won't be any howling dogs in W. . . .; If you please, I shall be having the cacophony set to music.)

Kleist may have been disappointed but he can hardly have been surprised, for his essentially negative presentation of the Greeks in *Penthesilea* was intended to draw the audience's attention to the highly idealistic picture of antiquity to which the aesthetics of Weimar Classicism were committed. As Adam Müller was to explain in response to an objection raised by Friedrich Gentz:

> Sie werden in der Penthesilea wahrnehmen, wie er . . . den antiken Schein vorsätzlich beiseite wirft, Anachronismen herbeizieht, um . . . nicht darin verkannt zu werden, daß von keiner Nachahmung, von keinem Affektieren der Griechheit die Rede sei. Demnach ist Kleist sehr mit Ihnen zufrieden, wenn Sie von der Penthesilea sagen, daß sie *nicht* antik sei. (*Lebensspuren*, no. 226)

(You will note how, in *Penthesilea*, he makes a particular point of rejecting any appearance of antiquity and uses anachronisms so as to avoid any accusation of having attempted to produce an imitation or affectation of Hellenism. Accordingly, Kleist would be very happy to hear you say that his play is *not* in the classical mode.)

In fact, Kleist's unflattering depiction of Achilles and the other members of the Greek camp is not only quite unlike Goethe's portrayal of the heroes of Troy in his *Achilleis* fragment, but is far closer in spirit to Homer[6] than many critics have been willing to acknowledge.[7]

ACHILLES AND THE GREEKS

In *Penthesilea,* Kleist presents two contrasting notions of love – the Greek and the Amazon – and shows that these notions are not simply part of a fixed and unchanging 'human nature', but reflect a crucial difference in the structures of the societies in which they appear.[8] The Greek army is portrayed as an authoritarian institution, an aggressive military machine designed to establish Greek domination throughout the world. When the play opens, the Greek commanders, who are incapable of understanding any form of military action that is not directly related to an increase of territory or of power, are in a state of total bewilderment because they have become involved in a battle apparently lacking these objectives. In Odysseus' words:

> Du siehst auf diesen Feldern,
> Der Griechen und der Amazonen Heer,
> Wie zwei erboste Wölfe sich umkämpfen:
> Beim Jupiter! sie wissen nicht warum? (*SW* I, 323; 3–6)

(Look there: the Greek and Amazonian armies fighting like two wolves – and can't say why, by god!) [G, 161]

In an attempt to escape from this state of bewilderment, both the Greeks and the Trojans seek some vantage point from which to obtain an 'objective' understanding of the nature of the Amazon tactics. And they feel sure that, when viewed from the correct standpoint, it will be apparent that the Amazons, like themselves, are simply fighting for territory and power. Both Greeks and Trojans have assumed (mistakenly) that the Amazons are their allies, simply because, for them, fighting outside the terms of their Greek-Trojan conflict is meaningless. Hence Odysseus' remark about Penthesilea: 'She . . . *must* fight on one side or the other;' [G, 162] ('Sie muß zu einer der Partein sich schlagen'; *SW* I, 324; 53) and Antilochus' rejoinder: 'What other course of action could there be, by god!' ('Was sonst, beim Styx! Nichts anders gibts'; *SW* I, 324; 56). But as both Greeks and Trojans will shortly discover, the Amazons do not fight for territorial domination; they are interested only in taking captives for the purposes of their mating ritual.

The inability of the Greeks to understand why the Amazons fight is a reflection of – and indeed may even be caused by – the position of women in Greek society, excluded as they are from positions of authority and reduced to the status of mere objects of male desire. For unlike the Amazons, the Greeks see love in terms of exclusive sexual ownership as is borne out by the stated aim of their expedition, *viz.* the return of Helen to her rightful 'owner'. This Greek view of male-female relations has arisen not from an empirically-based attempt to produce a workable form of society, but from the mistaken assumption that this arrangement is final and immutable because it corresponds to the 'natural order of things'. In this respect, Odysseus' view of Greek society parallels the High Priestess's ('Oberpriesterin') belief – or professed belief – in the 'infallible correctness' of the Amazon way of life. Despite the generally preferable attitudes underpinning the latter, essentially the same type of delusion underlies both forms of society, namely the belief that each is founded upon incontrovertibly true principles.

ACHILLES

Achilles is not actually on stage at the start of the play, but the dramatic action of its opening scenes is dominated by the absent hero to such an extent that in scene 3, his 'presence' seems quite to overshadow all else. Kleist uses teichoscopia and reported scenes to show the audience this young 'warrior god' ('Kriegsgott') from a variety of different perspectives, Amazonian and Greek. In this way, he calls into question the validity of yet another element of Greek ideology – 'the hero' (as exemplified here by Achilles) – whose conduct throughout the play falls well short of the norm.

The play starts in typically Kleistian fashion with the hero off stage, and his 'glorious' return in scenes 3 and 4 is undermined by the discussion that takes place between the Greek commanders during scene 1, from which we learn that Achilles has already suffered defeat at the hands of Penthesilea. Diomedes tells an incredulous Antillochus:

> Doch jüngst, in einem Augenblick, da schon
> Sein Leben war in ihre Macht gegeben,
> Gab sie es lächelnd, ein Geschenk, ihm wieder:
> Er stieg zum Orkus, wenn sie ihn nicht hielt.
>
> (*SW* I, 327; 167–70)

(Yet yesterday, when for a moment only his life lay in her hands, back she gave it to him with a laugh, her gift – down he'd gone to Orcus, that's for sure, except for her.) [G, 165]

Thus even before he appears, Achilles' reputation as an invincible champion has been called into question: he owes his life to the timely intervention of the queen who has rescued him from the unwelcome attentions of the Trojan, Deiphobus.[9] And as the scene unfolds, it becomes increasingly clear that Odysseus and the other Greek commanders view the exploits of Achilles from an essentially pragmatic perspective. They see his recklessness as jeopardising the success of their military objectives, and this almost wholly negative picture of the young hero is further emphasised by Diomedes' unflattering description of him as 'a senseless blockhead' ('einem Klotz gleich, weil der Sinn ihm fehlt'; *SW* I, 329; 236). But in contrast to the Greek commanders' realistic assessment of their hot-headed colleague's probable contribution to the success of their operation, the ordinary citizen-soldiers, holding to the official 'war-office' image, believe that their idol must play an active part in the campaign, if they are to defeat the Trojans. This is certainly the view of the captain ('Hauptmann') when, in scene 2, he reports: 'Achilles – captured by the Amazons! And now Troy's walls are sure to stand for ever' [G, 167] ('Achill – ist in der Amazonen Händen, | Und Pergams Mauern fallen jetzt nicht um'; *SW* I, 330; 242–3). Both here and in the following two scenes, it becomes increasingly clear that Achilles' main contribution to the Greek cause is as a morale boosting cult figure rather than as a soldier. Thus although they are aware that, at least in strategic terms, Achilles is a liability, Odysseus and the other commanders (perhaps mindful of Calchas' prophecy)[10] appreciate his importance in maintaining the fighting spirit of their troops, and immediately propose a rescue mission.

Achilles' largely symbolic role in the Argive camp becomes clear in the next scene. Now the 'blockhead' of scene I is portrayed as a larger-than-life figure whose reappearance is likened to the sun-rise itself:

> Jetzt, auf dem Horizonte, steht das ganze
> Kriegsfahrzeug da! So geht die Sonne prachtvoll
> An einem heitern Frühlingstage auf! (*SW* I, 333; 367–9)

(Now on the skyline car and horses show entire! Just so the glorious sun car climbs the sky on a bright day in spring!) [G, 171]

Of course, this is hardly an impartial description, coming, as it does from the mouths of Achilles' devoted Myrmidonians;[11] but it draws attention to the fact that, in the eyes of the ordinary soldier, he is the perfect embodiment of Greek masculinity. In particular his chariot-driving is 'something marvellous':

O, wie er mit der Linken
Vor über seiner Rosse Rücken geht!
Wie er die Geißel umschwingt über sie! (*SW* 1, 334; 377–9)

(His left hand, how far out it's stretched above his horses' backs, how he swings the whip above the four of them!) [G, 171]

Once again, however, the extravagant rhetoric of the scene is relentlessly undermined: for Achilles is not displaying his driving skills chasing his opponent, but desperately fleeing from her! And in the next scene, where Diomedes adds:

Man könnte fragen,
Ob du bei Tagesanbruch, da wir zum
Gefecht noch allererst uns rüsteten,
Den Feldstein schon gedacht dir, über welchen
Die Königin zusammenstürzen sollte:
So sichern Schrittes, bei den ewigen Göttern,
Hast du zu diesem Stein sie hingeführt. (*SW* 1, 339; 513–9)

(At daybreak, when all of us were arming for the fight, I do believe, unless I'm much mistaken, that you had figured out already, in your head, which stone you'd have the Queen go tripping over – so sure each step seemed, by the deathless gods, by which you lead her around to it.) [G, 176]

he feeds our doubts about Achilles' heroism by pointing out – perhaps inadvertently – that his escape from the queen was due more to her ill-fortune than to his superhuman abilities. After this assessment, Odysseus' welcome to the returning 'hero' at the beginning of scene 4 seems decidedly ambiguous: 'I welcome you, Aegina's hero-prince, with swelling heart! Winner just as much in running from as to!' [G, 175] ('Sei mir, Äginerheld, aus heißer Brust | Gegrüßt! Du Sieger auch noch in der Flucht!'; *SW* 1, 338; 486–7). The irony of this false praise will, of course, be lost on the troops, and the remark can be interpreted by Achilles and his fellow officers as a loyal attempt to restore (and even enhance) Achilles' mythical status in the eyes of his adoring followers. Similarly, when the cunning Odysseus goes on to add:

> Beim Jupiter! Wenn hinter deinem Rücken,
> Durch deines Geistes Obmacht über ihren,
> In Staub die Feindin stürzt, was wird geschehn,
> Wenns dir gelingt, du Göttlicher, sie einst
> Von Angesicht zu Angesicht zu fassen. (*SW* I, 338; 488–92)

(By Jupiter, if you behind your back, by your superior wits, can make the enemy go sprawling in the dust, think what will happen when you make her meet you, man-god, face to face!) [G, 175]

we hear only an attempt to flatter the younger man, so that he can be persuaded to abandon his pursuit of Penthesilea without loss of face. Odysseus knows that Achilles has had the narrowest of escapes and the captain's remarks in scene 2 have left him in no doubt that the champion's demise would have a catastrophic effect on the troops' morale. At the same time, the presence on stage of the two surgeons attending to his wounds reminds us that this supposedly invincible, larger-than-life character, this god-like being ('Göttersohn') is, nonetheless, a man of flesh and blood. More importantly, however, his impatience in the face of their efforts to bind his wounds – 'Stop bothering me, I say' [G, 176] ('Was neckt ihr'; *SW* I, 338; 503) – shows that Achilles, like his admirers, is in serious danger of succumbing to the myth of his own 'indestructibility'; a danger further underlined in scene 15, when Penthesilea apologises for having hurt him. His reply, 'If you love me, not another word about it' [G, 221] ('Wenn du mich liebst, so sprichst du nicht davon'; *SW* I, 383; 1763) makes it clear that his concern is not so much the risk of physical injury as the preservation of the mythical image of himself as an indestructible warrior-god.

As the play proceeds, this image of the hero prepared to risk all in the cause of love, is constantly eroded. Occasionally his youth and lack of experience place him – accidentally – in quite dangerous situations, but he never knowingly risks his life for the sake of his beloved. When he approaches the queen in scene 11, describing himself as 'one who has been disarmed – in every sense of the word – and who kneels before your tiny feet' ('ein Entwaffneter, in jedem Sinne, | Leg ich zu euren kleinen Füßen mich'; *SW* I, 370; 1417–8), he comes close to believing, in his vanity, that no Amazon could bring herself to harm him. Even so, we note that he has the presence of mind to bring along his personal bodyguards who have instructions to shoot down any Amazon who appears to threaten his life. No wonder the Second Amazon ('Zweite Amazone') comments dryly, 'Unarmed, he says!' [G, 208] ('Entwaffnet nennt er sich'; *SW* I, 370; 1420). Further evidence of his insincerity is provided in scene 21, when he is preparing for the final confrontation with Penthesilea. Diomedes at first believes that he really intends to fight her, but Achilles makes it clear that this 'fight to the death' is only a charade and that he is prepared to indulge in such 'heroics' only because he is sure that there is no real risk, when he says (albeit mistakenly):

> Sie *tut* mir nichts, sag ich! Eh wird ihr Arm,
> Im Zweikampf gegen ihren Busen wüten,
> Und rufen: 'Sieg!' wenn er von Herzblut trieft,
> Als wider mich! (*SW* I, 407; 2471–4)

(there's nothing she will do to me, I tell you. Her arm would sooner launch a mad attack against her own self, her own bosom, hurrahing wildly when it saw the heart's-blood streaming from it, than strike me!) [G, 246]

Perhaps the clearest example of this discrepancy between the image and the man can be appreciated in two scenes involving Odysseus. First when Odysseus attempts to prevent the 'duel' and Achilles responds with yet another piece of braggadocio:

> Ich bitte dich,
> Halt deine Oberlippe fest, Ulyß!
> Es steckt mich an, bei den gerechten Göttern,
> Und bis zur Faust gleich zuckt es mir herab.
> (*SW* I, 408; 2496–9)

(Let me beg you not to clench your jaws like that, Ulysses. It is catching, don't you know, and I start clenching too – my fists!) [G, 247]

But this display when there is no risk to his person contrasts sharply with the terror he shows when he is, for the first time, forced to confront the fact that he is going to die.[12] There we see this 'warrior god' attempt – like Pentheus – to hide behind a tree, screaming for help from the same man he had scorned only two scenes before. Meroe describes it all:

> Er ruft: Odysseus! mit beklemmter Stimme,
> Und sieht sich schüchtern um, und ruft: Tydide!
> Und will zurück noch zu den Freunden fliehn;
> Und steht, von einer Schar schon abgeschnitten,
> Und hebt die Händ empor, und duckt und birgt
> In eine Fichte sich, der Unglücksel'ge,
> Die schwer mit dunkeln Zweigen niederhangt.
> (*SW* I, 412–3; 2633–9)

(He cries 'Odysseus!' so anxiously, looks timidly around and cries 'Tydides!' too, and turns to run back where his comrades are; and stops, the line of his retreat already cut, lifts up his hands dismayed and ducks and looks for cover, the unlucky man, beneath a pine tree's dark and drooping boughs.) [G, 251–2]

In like manner, Kleist invites us to examine Achilles' ideas on love. Far from regarding it as an altruistic relationship between equals, for him, love is a matter of sexual conquest and 'taking prisoner'. The knowing glances exchanged by Odysseus and Achilles when they first meet Penthesilea[13] strongly suggest that she is not the first to have been overwhelmed by the young warrior's radiant form and our hero will not allow us to forget it. For as he reminds the assembled generals in scene 4:

> Im Leben keiner Schönen war ich spröd;
> Seit mir der Bart gekeimt, ihr lieben Freunde,
> Ihr wißts, zu Willen jeder war ich gern: (*SW* I, 342; 599–601)

(Since my beard first sprouted, as you know, good friends, I've gladly done what all the ladies wished.) [G, 179]

Central to this notion of love is the belief that a woman is not a person, but an object to be won and possessed by her male conqueror, and in scene 12, Achilles is quite prepared to use force to protect his newly-won 'booty':

> Der weicht ein Schatten
> Vom Platz, der mir die Königin berührt! –
> Mein ist sie! Fort! Was habt ihr hier zu suchen –
> (*SW* I, 372; 1460–2)

(Whoever lays a finger on the Queen will leave this place a ghost! She's mine! Move, will you, you've no business here.) [G, 210]

And when Diomedes challenges him:

> So! Dein! Ei sieh, bei Zeus', des Donnrers, Locken,
> Aus welchen Gründen auch? Mit welchem Rechte?
> (*SW* I, 372; 1463–4)

(Oh, so she's yours! Well, look here, man, by Zeus the Thunderer's beard, on what grounds, by what right – ?) [G, 210]

he crudely invokes the right of conquest, shouting: 'on two grounds, first, this right, and secondly, this left' [G, 210] ('Aus einem Grund, der rechts, und einer links'; *SW* I, 372; 1465). Given his restricted outlook, it comes as no surprise to find him talking of his 'love' for Penthesilea in terms of total subjugation, and in scene 4 declaring that he will not break off his pursuit of the queen:

> Als bis ich sie zu meiner Braut gemacht,
> Und sie, die Stirn bekränzt mit Todeswunden,
> Kann durch die Straßen häuptlings mit mir schleifen.
> (*SW* I, 342; 613–15)

(till she's my bride and with her forehead wreathed in deadly wounds parades beside me through the streets of Troy, feet first!) [G, 179]

Worse still, in scene 13, his declaration of love for Penthesilea includes a ferocious allusion to his desecration of Hector's corpse:

> Mein Will ist, ihr zu tun, muß ich dir sagen,
> Wie ich dem stolzen Sohn des Priam tat.
> (*SW* I, 374; 1513–14)

(My will, I have to tell you, is, to do with her just as I did with Priam's haughty son.) [G, 212]

We can imagine the bewilderment of the innocent, civilised Prothoe when he goes on to explain that this is merely his way of announcing his amorous intentions, and in so doing exposes the profoundly flawed, self-contradictory nature of his mode of 'loving':

> Beim Himmel, wie! Wie Männer Weiber lieben;
> Keusch und das Herz voll Sehnsucht doch, in Unschuld,
> Und mit der Lust doch, sie darum zu bringen.
> (*SW* I, 375; 1521–3)

(How, do you ask? I'll tell you *how!* Like men love women: respectfully but full of longing too – in innocence, and yet desiring to take hers from her.) [G, 213]

It is, of course, self-contradictory because the realisation of such 'love' brings with it its own destruction. Like Jupiter in *Amphitryon*, Achilles fails to understand that it is impossible to enjoy the corruption of innocence and at the same time preserve that innocence. Likewise, he fails to see that love, in the true sense of the word, can only be a gift freely given from the lover to the beloved and, worse still, he is too insensitive to realise that Penthesilea is prepared to offer him this very gift. Moreover, although we are invited to see the Amazons' random selection of sexual partners in the same terms as Achilles, when he asks in scene 15:

> Und woher quillt, von wannen ein Gesetz,
> Unweiblich, du vergibst mir, unnatürlich,
> Dem übrigen Geschlecht der Menschen fremd?
> (*SW* 1, 387; 1902–4)

(Out of where did your law come, and how, a law – if you'll forgive my saying so – unwomanly, unnatural, and quite unknown to all the rest of humankind?) [G, 226]

Kleist soon makes it clear that Achilles' allegedly 'natural' mode of 'loving', whereby women are simply random objects of masculine desire, is at least equally, if not more, inhuman than anything in the Amazons' courtship rites.

In conclusion then, we cannot regard Achilles' attitude to this 'love' affair as something that sets him apart from the other members of the Greek camp: Odysseus and the other generals have all been through it. Their only concern is that an officer in love is a threat to efficiency and needs all the management they can provide. It is not his desire for Penthesilea that causes friction between Achilles and his fellow officers, but their fear that his erotic liaison with the queen may lead him to engage in operations which conflict with their overall military strategy. At the same time, we should be wary of regarding Achilles as the 'helpless' victim of a truly insuperable, 'magnanimous' passion, for like so many of Kleist's young male protagonists, he is too well-schooled in the conventional ways of his society to be taken seriously as the representative of a genuinely emancipatory tendency within it. Although he may claim in scene 11 that he feels 'pierced to his innermost' [G, 208] ('im Innersten getroffen'; *SW* I, 370; 1416), the hollowness of his rhetoric is exposed in scene 21, where he offers an alternative (and more realistic) account of his feelings:[14]

> Auf einen Mond bloß will ich ihr,
> In dem, was sie begehrt, zu Willen sein;
> Auf einen oder zwei, mehr nicht . . . (*SW* I, 407; 2474–6)

(I'll suit her wishes for a month, that's all, a month or two, no more . . .) [G, 246]

THE AMAZON STATE

In contrast to the Greeks, for whom love is predominantly a matter of sexual conquest and 'ownership', the Amazons take as their model the altogether more worthy ideal of the selfless love of mother for child. This type of love – which we see in the mother-daughter relationship of Otrere and Penthesilea and in the 'sisterly' love of Prothoe for Penthesilea – excludes all self-interest, possessiveness and compulsion; it also accounts for the fact that Amazon society represents a very real advance over its highly authoritarian and aggressively-oriented Greek counterpart. Yet this strength is, paradoxically, a weakness because the altruistic nature of the Amazons' concept of love leaves them particularly vulnerable to exploitation by more ruthless natures, especially by men brought up within a predominantly patriarchal culture. To defend themselves and their superior ideal of love, the Amazons have devised a ritual – the 'Festival of the Roses' ('Rosenfest') – which permits the consummation of heterosexual relations only with males who have been captured in the hunt by their respective Amazonian 'warrior-brides' ('Marsbräute'). However, the very nature of Amazon love renders them peculiarly unsuited to the kind of heterosexual relations – 'love-as-conquest' – their law requires. For, as the 'case' of Penthesilea demonstrates, although 'Tanaïs's Law' ('Das Gesetz der Tanaïs') is intended to reduce heterosexual relations to the bare sexual act, it cannot, of its own accord, prevent the development of genuinely loving (i.e.

'Amazonian-type') relationships between the women and their captives.

The Amazon state is a society in which the complete autonomy of women is guaranteed through the deliberate exclusion of men. No man may set eyes on Themiscyra, the mating ritual ('Rosenfest') does not take place within the boundaries of the state, and all male children are killed at birth. It is a state with a long tradition[15] and the respect for 'Tanaïs's Law' shown by its members is on a par with that shown by the Greeks for their ancestral customs. As Penthesilea says to Achilles in scene 15:

> Der ersten Mütter Wort entschied es also,
> Und dem verstummen wir, Neridensohn,
> Wie deiner ersten Väter Worten du. (*SW* 1, 387; 1909–11)

(Our first mothers' words decreed it, son of Thetis, and dumbly we receive them, as you do your first fathers' words.) [G, 226]

Accordingly we must be wary of seeing Penthesilea's society through the eyes of Achilles as 'unfeminine' ('unweiblich') and unnatural ('unnatürlich'), for to do so is to accept uncritically precisely those categories which are called into question so persistently in this play. Kleist presents the Amazon state as a viable form of social organisation: we are meant to take it seriously. For the most part, the Amazons are much more sympathetically depicted than the Greeks, who fight solely for personal gain and territorial domination, whereas the Amazons are involved not in a war of vengeful destruction, but in capturing alive enough men to ensure the continuation of their preferred form of society.[16] Once captured, their Greek prisoners, far from being harmed, are looked after in lavish style, and when they have fulfilled their function in the mating ritual, their Amazon 'brides' 'load them down with gifts, each one, like kings, and at the Feast of Fertile Mothers send them home again in shining cars' [G, 231] ('Beschenken sie, wie Könige zusamt; | Und schicken sie, am Fest der reifen Mütter, | Auf stolzen Prachtgeschirren wieder heim'; *SW* 1, 392; 2080–2). In particular, Kleist emphasises that Amazon law does not require Penthesilea to kill Achilles, let alone desecrate his corpse as she does at the end of the play. Thus when the High Priestess ('Oberpriesterin') is presented with Achilles' mangled corpse in scene 24, she explicitly (and correctly) rejects any responsibility for what has happened: 'Goddess, hear me: I am not to blame for this horrific act' [G, 254] ('Diana ruf ich an: | Ich bin an dieser Greueltat nicht schuldig!'; *SW* I, 415; 2711–12). Furthermore, both the stage directions: 'horror-stricken pause' [G, 253] ('Pause voll Entsetzen'; *SW* I, 414) during Meroe's report on the action in scene 23, and Prothoe's remark in scene 24: 'The thing she did's too awful' [G, 255] ('Die Tat, die sie | Vollbracht hat, ist zu scheußlich'; *SW* I, 416; 2741–2) make it abundantly clear that the Amazons view the defilement of the corpse with no less horror than have theatre audiences from Kleist's day onwards. In this way Kleist invites us to compare the Amazons' horrified reactions to Penthesilea's treatment of Achilles with the Greeks' ecstatic viewing of his desecration of Hector's body; the deed that makes Achilles a hero in his society, makes Penthesilea an abomination in hers.[17] This is central to an understanding of the play.

We learn from Penthesilea's account in scene 15, that the Amazon state was set up by the Scythian women in response to an act of gross barbarism on the part of Vexoris and the invading Ethiopians. Like the other possessions of their husbands, the Scythian women were regarded by the invaders as only so much 'booty' which, by right of conquest, was now theirs to do with as they pleased. Stripped of their identity as autonomous individuals and reduced to the status of anonymous objects of male desire, the Scythian women, inspired by the example of their queen, Tanaïs, murdered Vexoris and all his followers. Amazonian history has judged this massacre a just response to unendurable oppression. For as Penthesilea says:

> Doch alles schüttelt, was ihm unerträglich,
> Der Mensch von seinen Schultern sträubend ab;
> Den Druck nur mäßger Leiden duldet er.
>
> (*SW* I, 388; 1934–6)

(What's more than can be borne, man struggles every way to shake off from his shoulders.) [G, 227]

And to prevent a repetition of such horrors, the leaders of this 'revolution' declared:

> Ein Staat, ein mündiger, sei aufgestellt,
> Ein Frauenstaat, den fürder keine andre

Herrschsüchtge Männerstimme mehr durchtrotzt.
(*SW* I, 389; 1957–9)

(Let a state, a women's one, complete in all respects, be instituted where men's boastful, over-bearing voices shall never be allowed to clamour noisily again.) [G, 227]

The one exception to this is the 'Festival of Roses', a ritual permitting temporary sexual relations with randomly selected males captured in raids.

It is, of course, one of the ironies of the play that the Amazons, who have experienced the degradation that results from enforced sexual relations, should retain the notion of 'conquest' in their dealings with the opposite sex. But there is, quite literally, a world of difference between the mating ritual of the Festival of Roses and the violent mass-rape carried out by the murderous hordes ('Mordgeschlecht') of the Ethiopians. The latter is portrayed as an act of barbarism that is 'intolerable' ('unerträglich') to the Scythian women, whereas for the Greek captives, the idea of being 'raped' by their female captors is downright appealing and quite exceeds their wildest fantasies. Indeed in scene 6, one incredulous Greek whispers to his comrades, 'Was ever there a dream as mad as what's the truth here?' [G, 191] ('War je ein Traum so bunt, als was hier wahr ist?'; *SW* I, 354; 986). However, unlike the original situation where the (male) Ethiopian invaders attempted to 'legitimise' their outrage through the institution of marriage, thereby taking permanent possession of their Scythian 'brides', in Amazon society, Tanaïs's Law rules out the possibility of such permanent 'ownership' by decreeing that heterosexual relations shall take place only on a temporary and arbitrary basis. Nonetheless, it is important to note that, despite the alleged 'inhumanity' of Amazon law, genuinely loving relations between the Amazon women and their male captives can, and do, develop and – as Penthesilea's account of the unhappy scenes that occur when the time comes for the men to depart reveals – this often happens:

Dies Fest dann freilich ist das frohste nicht,
Neridensohn – denn viele Tränen fließen,
Und manches Herz, von düsterm Gram ergriffen,
Begreift nicht, wie die große Tanaïs
In jedem ersten Wort zu preisen sei. (*SW* I, 392; 2083–7)

(This feast, let me assure you, son of Thetis, it's not our jolliest one – for tears aplenty flow and many a heart that now heaves dismally can't see why we should praise great Tanaïs in every other breath.) [G, 231]

To understand why this should be so, it is necessary to look a little more closely at the structure of Amazon society. The relations between the members of this society are, for the most part, of a much more altruistic, nurturing kind than the corresponding relations in Greek society. The model for the prevailing concept of love in Amazon society is the unconditional love of a mother for her child and, as we shall see, Penthesilea's relationship to her own mother crucially informs her subsequent behaviour towards Achilles.[18] Kleist, however, does not present this 'motherly love' ('Mutterliebe') in terms of a crude biological bond: there is nothing that 'compels' an Amazon mother to love the child she has given birth to and, significantly, the disposal of the (unwanted) male off-spring appears to cause little distress to the members of this society. The unforced nature of the mother's love for her child is a reflection of the general way of life in this particular community. In Amazon society the central feature of the mother-child relationship is that whilst the child is almost wholly dependent on the mother for its every need, it is almost impossible for the mother to derive any advantage from loving her child.[19] There is no necessity for a mother in Amazon society to love her child: if she does choose to do so that is the end of the matter: she has given the child the gift of her love. Of course it is quite possible for an Amazon mother to decide to provide for the child's needs out of a sense of 'moral obligation', but this form of 'dutiful love' is not to be confused with the true Amazonian concept of love that we have been discussing above.

Thus if the Amazons appear more appealing in their dealings with one another than their Greek counterparts, this is not because they are women, but rather because they have been brought up in a society which takes as its basic model for human relationships, the freely-given selfless love of the mother for her child. By prohibiting any heterosexual relations within Themiscyra itself, the Amazon state ensures that its members are not distracted from their genuinely altruistic concept of love by the false picture of 'love', so central to patriarchal cultures; for the latter, far from being 'selfless', is merely a social contrivance designed to conceal male needs and desires – even from the eyes of its inventors – so that they may be all the more effectively satisfied by the women who are its dupes. Thus in the patriarchal world of the Greeks, the true nature of love is obscured by the twin notions of property and the preservation of the male lineage as is demonstrated in scene 15, when Achilles tells Penthesilea: 'by war's fortune you belong to me' [G, 236] ('durch der Waffen Glück gehörst du mir'; *SW* I, 397; 2246), having expressed, only a few lines earlier, the (very masculine) desire: 'you'll mother me the new god of our Earth!' [G, 235] ('Du sollst den Gott der Erde mir gebären!'; *SW* I, 397; 2230). Of course it is perfectly possible (although it is not stated unambiguously as such in the text) that, once removed from the structures of patriarchal power and taken to the temple of Diana where the notions of sexual 'ownership' and patrilinear descent are meaningless, even the male captives may be converted to the gentler notions of their Amazonian 'brides'.

PROTHOE

The superior quality of the Amazons' concept of love can be seen clearly in the relationship between Prothoe and Penthesilea. Throughout the play Prothoe always tries to act in the queen's best interests, even though this brings her into conflict with her beloved on a number of occasions. In this respect, her behaviour contrasts sharply with that of Asteria, in scene 5, whose sole motive for encouraging the queen's pursuit of Achilles is to prolong the fighting so that she and her troops – whose arrival has been delayed – may also have an opportunity to capture their Greek mates.[20] Prothoe censures Asteria for her fawning behaviour, and is herself prepared to risk provoking the queen's anger by telling her the uncomfortable truth:

> So wag ich meiner Königin Zorn!
> Eh will ich nie dein Antlitz wiedersehen,
> Als feig, in diesem Augenblick, dir eine
> Verräterin schmeichlerisch zur Seite stehn.
> Du bist, in Flammen wie du loderst, nicht
> Geschickt, den Krieg der Jungfraun fortzuführen;
>
> (*SW* I, 347; 792–7)

(I'll dare her anger! Let me never see your face again if I stand here, a coward, at your side, and play you false by speaking flatteries. The fire burning hotly in you now, undermines your fitness to conduct a war of virgins;) [G, 185]

Although Prothoe is cruelly taunted for her alleged 'cowardice' and subsequently banished from the presence of the enraged queen, her love remains undiminished, and when she is asked by a repentant Penthesilea at the end of the scene 'Will you follow me?' [G, 187] ('Willst du mir folgen?'; *SW* 1, 350; 874), she pledges her devotion with the words: 'All the way to Orcus!' [G, 187] ('In den Orkus dir!'; *SW* 1, 350; 874).

Prothoe's understanding of the Amazon concept of love is superior to that of Penthesilea, for she never loses sight of the truth that love is not a matter of possessing but of giving. More importantly, however, Prothoe understands that the gift of love cannot be made conditional upon reciprocation: it is not a contractual arrangement. It is, therefore, highly appropriate that it should be she who 'stage-manages' the 'idyll' of scene 15, in a desperate attempt to save her beloved: for the selfless character of her love is such that she does not perceive Achilles' 'love' for the queen as a threat to her own. In a society in which possessiveness and love are mutually exclusive, notions of jealousy and rivalry have no meaning. In the very last scene of the play, her love for the queen is tested yet more severely, for she is called upon to demonstrate her love for a being whose unspeakable actions have turned her into a monster in the eyes of her own people. For as the Amazon women exclaim:

> O jammervoller Anblick! O so öde
> Wie die Sandwüste, die kein Gras gebiert!
> Lustgärten, die der Feuerstrom verwüstet,
> Gekocht im Schoß der Erd und ausgespieen,
> Auf alle Blüten ihres Busens hin,
> Sind anmutsvoller als ihr Angesicht. (*SW* 1, 417; 2762–7)

(A look of woe, dear gods, as desolate as empty wastes without a blade of grass! Gardens devastated by the lava spilling from the burning bowels of the earth and spewed out over all the flowers on its breast, look sweeter than her face.) [G, 256]

Throughout this scene, Kleist goes out of his way to underline the revulsion with which all the Amazons – and especially Prothoe – react to the mutilation of Achilles. Prothoe's exclamation: 'I never want to lay my eyes on her again!' [G, 255] ('Ich will sie nie mit Augen wiedersehn!'; *SW* I, 416; 2745) leaves the audience in no doubt as to how inhuman and loathsome Penthesilea has become in her eyes. Nevertheless, when the High Priestess declares: 'if Prothoe refuses her help, she'll die here in her misery, for sure' [G, 257] ('wenn Prothoe ihr nicht helfen will, | So muß sie hier in ihrer Not vergehn'; *SW* I, 418; 2790–1), Prothoe demonstrates the supremely selfless nature of her love: she does indeed go – albeit reluctantly – to the aid of the queen. Here it is important to note that Kleist does not present Prothoe as a woman endowed with supra-human qualities, for her remarks above, together with the stage direction: 'her face expressing the violent struggle going on inside her' [G, 257] ('Prothoe drückt den heftigsten Kampf aus'; *SW* I, 418) make it clear that she has the greatest difficulty in overcoming her feelings of revulsion. The fact that she is able, despite the vileness of the queen's deed, to offer both forgiveness and love marks her as a person of heroic selflessness and at the same time, illustrates the special quality of love as an Amazon conceives it.

PENTHESILEA AND AMAZON SOCIETY

In the play, Kleist suggests that the Amazons' isolation in Themiscyra has resulted in their having an inadequate grasp of the realities of male-dominated societies; in particular, they have a highly sentimental picture of Greek society. Thus when, in scene 15, Penthesilea describes the reactions of her people to the news that their next opponents are to be the Greeks, it becomes clear that the Amazons' perception of this race is heavily indebted to the mythical categories of epic poetry.

> An allen Ecken hörte man erjauchzend,
> Auf allen Märkten, hohe Lieder schallen,
> Die des Hero'nkriegs Taten feierten:
> Vom Paris-Apfel, dem Helenenraub,
> Von den geschwaderführenden Atriden,

Vom Streit um Briseïs, der Schiffe Brand,
Auch von Patroklus' Tod, und welche Pracht
Du des Triumphes rächend ihm gefeiert;
Und jedem großen Auftritt dieser Zeit. (*SW* I, 393; 2118–26)

(At every corner you heard exclamations of delight, the marketplaces rang with epic songs rehearsing deeds done in the war of heroes: Paris' apple, Helen's rape, the squadron-marshalling Atrides, the quarrel over Briseïs, the setting fire to the ships, and Patroclus' death and with what pomp of triumph of revenge you did the last rites for him; and all the episodes of that great time.) [G, 232]

In contrast, by depicting the Greeks as a collection of boorish, violent, insensitive individuals on their worst behaviour (at war), Kleist draws attention to the discrepancy between their extravagantly 'heroic' image in myth and legend and the reality of their day-to-day behaviour.[21] Indeed, Penthesilea's predicament is largely brought about by her failure to distinguish between the real-life Achilles and the wish-fulfilling image of him that exists in her imagination. Thus in the slaying of Hector, she sees only the 'glorious' avenging of a dead comrade, not the foul violation of a hero's body. She herself recounts how, as the time for battle drew nearer, her thoughts became increasingly dominated by the larger-than-life image of her hero's spectacular exploits:

O Pelide!
Mein ewiger Gedanke, wenn ich wachte,
Mein ewger Traum warst du! Die ganze Welt
Lag wie ein ausgespanntes Musternetz
Vor mir; in jeder Masche, weit und groß,
War deiner Taten eine eingeschürzt,
Und in mein Herz, wie Seide weiß und rein,
Mit Flammenfarben jede brannt ich ein.
(*SW* I, 395; 2186–93)

(Pelides! My one thought waking, one dream sleeping, was of you! The whole world lay spread out before me like some piece of woven stuff into whose every giant square a deed of yours was worked, and I, I burnt each one into my heart, so white and pure, like silk, with fire dyes.) [G, 234]

The result is that when she meets him for the first time, it is not the real-life Achilles she sees, but Achilles 'the legend'. Part of her idolisation of Achilles can be put down to her provinciality and lack of experience and this is suggested at the beginning of the play, when Odysseus describes her as being 'like a girl of sixteen who's run home from watching the Olympic Games' [G, 163] ('gleich einem sechzehnjährgen Mädchen . . .,| Das von olympschen Spielen wiederkehrt'; *SW* 1, 325; 86–7).

The relationship between Penthesilea and her mother, Otrere, is crucial to an understanding of Kleist's play. The selflessness of Penthesilea's love for Achilles is a reflection of her upbringing in a society in which the model for love is that of mother for child and during scene 15, she alludes to her mother's influence on her in this respect. The depth of her feelings is underlined in Penthesilea's account of her mother's death:

> In Tränen schwamm ich, Jammervolle, hörte
> Mit halbem Ohr nur, was die Botschaft mir,
> In der Otrere Todesstunde, brachte; (*SW* 1, 394; 2127–9)

(I in my distress, I swam in tears and only half-heard, as Otrere lay dying, the message of the god.) [G, 232–3]

So great was her desire to remain with her mother in her final hour that she begged to be excused from having to participate in the Festival of Roses:

> 'Laß mich dir bleiben, rief ich, meine Mutter,
> Dein Ansehn, brauch es heut zum letztenmal,
> Und heiße diese Frauen wieder gehn.' (*SW* 1, 394; 2130–2)

('Mother, let me stay with you,' I cried; 'make use, this last time, of the respect that's yours and send these women back.') [G, 233]

and was unwilling, after her death to take up a position of authority within Amazon society:

> Lange weint ich,
> Durch einen ganzen kummervollen Mond,
> An der Verblichnen Grab, die Krone selbst,
> Die herrenlos am Rande lag, nicht greifend,
> (*SW* 1, 394; 2150–3)

(I cried a whole month through, grief-stricken, on my mother's grave, not touching once the crown that lay unclaimed alongside it) [G, 233]

Most importantly, however, Penthesilea's account suggests a link between her feelings for her mother and her love for Achilles. For when she tells him of her despair when Otrere died, he comments: 'Your sorrow for the dead crippled for a while that strength which otherwise so graces your young self' [G, 234] ('Wehmut um die Verblichne lähmte flüchtig | Die Kraft, die deine junge Brust sonst ziert'; *SW* I, 395; 2170–1), a remark which echoes Penthesilea's sentiments in scene 5, where she likewise describes herself as 'crippled' ('gelähmt') in the gaze of Achilles.[22] Clearly, then, her feelings for Achilles are fundamentally similar to those she had for Otrere and Otrere had for her. Her fatal, though natural, mistake is to assume that Achilles has the same capacity for selfless devotion as her mother. For the love affair between Achilles and Penthesilea to constitute a genuinely emancipatory tendency within the play, the depth of Achilles' love for Penthesilea would have to be of the same order as Otrere's love for Penthesilea. Tragically, this is not the case.

A closer examination of Penthesilea's upbringing at the hands of Otrere throws further light on the central dilemma of Kleist's play. When she singles out Achilles as her personal quarry, the queen is not acting in strict accordance with Amazon law, and for this her mother is partly to blame. Like her Amazon sisters, Penthesilea has acquired a proper respect for physical courage, strength and skill in the use of arms, and Otrere has played on her daughter's fascination with Achilles as a supreme master of these skills, to persuade her to overcome her reluctance to take part in the sexual chase, holding out the prospect that the illustrious Greek warrior will be her prize:

> Sie sagte: 'geh, mein süßes Kind! Mars ruft dich!
> Du wirst den Peleïden dir bekränzen:
> Werd eine Mutter, stolz und froh, wie ich –'
> (*SW* I, 394; 2137–9)

(She said: 'Dear child, Mars summons you, now go! You'll catch and crown Pelides, I am sure. Become a mother, proud and happy like myself – ') [G, 233]

But Penthesilea's obsessive desire to win Achilles as her prize in the Festival of the Roses exposes her to the one great flaw in the otherwise consistent institutions of Themiscyra, a flaw which those in authority ignore at their peril. Although designed to restrict heterosexual relations purely to physical sex between randomly selected partners, Tanaïs's law is, of course, not a law of nature, but only a rule of conduct and cannot prevent genuine (i.e. Amazonian) love occurring across the sexes. For as Prothoe correctly observes: 'a riddle every bosom is that feels' [G, 202] ('jeder Busen ist, der fühlt, ein Rätsel'; *SW* I, 365; 1286). No doubt the leaders of Amazon society would be most reassured were such heterosexual love literally impossible and they have a vested interest in promoting this belief. Thus when the High Priestess hears that Penthesilea's 'youthful heart' ('jugendliches Herz') has been struck by 'the most poisonous of Cupid's arrows' ('vom giftigsten der Pfeile Amors'; *SW* I, 357; 1075), she exclaims incredulously:

> Die Königin, sagst du? Unmöglich, Freundin!
> Von Amors Pfeil getroffen – wann? Und wo?
> Die Führerin des Diamantengürtels?
> Die Tochter Mars', der selbst der Busen fehlt,
> Das Ziel der giftgefiederten Geschosse? (*SW* I, 357; 1081–5)

(The Queen, you say? But that's impossible, my friend! By the Love God's arrow – when? And where? She who wears the diamond girdle? Mars's daughter's self, who's lacking just that thing which is the target of the poison-feathered darts, a bosom?) [G, 194–5]

Here, we must at least consider the possibility that she is feigning disbelief in order to lend support to her own and her sister Amazons' wish to believe the convenient doctrine (symbolised by the absence of the breast) that Amazons are incapable of loving men in the true sense of the term. The Amazons' capacity for self-deception of this kind can be seen again in scene 5. This time it is Penthesilea who invokes the same 'deterministic' account of Amazon 'nature', when she exclaims histrionically: 'I have no bosom – then tell me where this feeling's lodged within me by which I'm beaten down?' [G, 181] ('Wo ist der Sitz mir, der kein Busen ward, | Auch des Gefühls, das mich zu Boden wirft?'; *SW* I, 343; 651–2). Later, however, in scene 15, she betrays the artificiality of the notion that to cut off a breast is to excise feelings of tenderness, when she reassures Achilles that mutilated women are still capable of falling in love with men. In short, the queen vehemently denies that which her earlier remark had quite clearly implied:

Sei ganz ruhig.
Sie retteten in diese Linke sich,
Wo sie dem Herzen um so näher wohnen.
Du wirst mir, hoff ich, deren keins vermissen.
(*SW* I, 390; 2014–17)

(No need for you to take on so. These feelings all escaped from right to left and there they live the nearer to my heart. You won't, I trust, find I am lacking any.) [G, 229]

In this way Kleist reminds the audience that the Amazons' ritual self-mutilation is primarily a symbolic act. Indeed these lines, which were to attract Goethe's scorn,[23] contain a profound truth about human psychology and one which is continually reasserted throughout Kleist's work. They remind us that whilst society tries to regard the conventions it promotes as prescriptive rules, read off, as it were, from an allegedly 'transcendent' blueprint of 'human nature', the truth is that these purely social norms do not have the power to rule out alternative undesirable behaviour. Although Amazon society may encourage its members to regard men simply as sexual objects necessary for the purposes of reproduction, it cannot prevent them from falling in love with their male captives. Likewise, it might be argued – though Kleist does not actually do so in the play – that whilst Greek society encourages its members to regard women simply as objects of sexual conquest, it too cannot prevent the development of genuinely loving relationships between Greek men and the women to whom they are attracted. It is vital, nonetheless, not to fall into the trap of regarding Greek and Amazon society as simply mirror images of one another. For as the contrast between Penthesilea's love for Achilles, and Achilles' 'love' for Penthesilea shows, the concept of love promoted in Amazon society is far closer to the ideal of love (as Kleist conceives it) than that of the Greeks and indeed represents a considerable advance over the latter. In short neither the Amazonian nor the Greek concept of love amounts to an *a priori* intuition into the true nature of love or the discovery of a deterministic 'law' of human nature.

Penthesilea's dilemma is two-fold: not only has she fallen in love with a man (which theoretically should be impossible for a true Amazon), but she has fallen in love with a fantasy image of a man that is the product of her inexperienced imagination and the 'hype' that has surrounded this Greek hero. This 'Achilles' does not, and could not, correspond to any real person. In addition, Penthesilea's inexperience leads her to believe that Achilles can reciprocate the pure selfless passion that she and her sister Amazons call love. The tragic effect of this delusion is increased when we remember the essentially maternal basis of Amazon love. For a mother's selfless devotion seeks only to satisfy, at no matter what personal cost, each and every desire of the child she loves and such one-sided devotion is clearly at risk of being ruthlessly exploited should its beneficiaries feel inclined to do so.[24] This is a serious flaw in the Amazon concept of love and the risk of such exploitation is at its most threatening whenever an Amazon becomes entangled with a man from an alien culture (such as that of the Greeks). Nothing could be more different than Penthesilea's tender feelings for Achilles than his heartless lust for the possession of his (latest) 'conquest'. For despite the ferocity of their early clashes, it soon becomes obvious that the queen is not driven by any genuinely sadistic impulse. As she says in scene 9:

> Was will ich denn, wenn ich das Schwert ihm zücke?
> Will ich ihn denn zum Orkus niederschleudern?
> Ich will ihn ja, ihr ewgen Götter, nur
> An diese Brust will ich ihn niederziehn! (*SW* 1, 361; 1189–92)

(What is it that I want, when I draw my sword on him? To send him flying headfirst down to Orcus? No – the thing I want so much, eternal gods above, the only thing, is to draw him down on this breast of mine!) [G, 198]

By contrast, she is cast into deep despair by his violent treatment of her and says to Prothoe:

> Mir diesen Busen zu zerschmettern, Prothoe!
> – Ists nicht, als ob ich eine Leier zürnend
> Zertreten wollte, weil sie still für sich,
> Im Zug des Nachtwinds, meinen Namen flüstert?
> (*SW* 1, 361; 1177–80)

(To smash me in the breast the way he did, Prothoe! – Isn't it as if I stamped upon a lyre, in a rage because the night wind stirred its strings so that it whispered my name to itself?) [G, 198]

But although his violent treatment of her makes her conclude – quite correctly – that his 'love' for her is not of the same

(Amazonian) order as her love for him, she is wrong in assuming that he is primarily interested in harming her physically. In scene 8, the Amazon colonel's ('Die Oberste') description of Achilles' behaviour makes it plain – at least to the audience – that Achilles regrets any physical injury he may have caused her:

> Penthesilea! ruft er,
> In seinen Armen hebt er sie empor,
> Und laut die Tat, die er vollbracht, verfluchend,
> Lockt er ins Leben jammernd sie zurück!
> (*SW* 1, 359; 1139–42)

(He . . . calls out Penthesilea! lifts her in his arms, and inveighing loudly against what he himself has done, with his repeated cries of grief woos her back to life.) [G, 196–7]

But whilst he does not mean her any actual physical harm, his sadistic desire to humiliate her is obvious: to treat her as an object that is his, by right of conquest, an inferior to use as he sees fit. Such is his 'love', the only kind he knows.

Confronted with what she interprets as the rejection of her suit, Penthesilea declares her intention to break off her pursuit of Achilles:

> Ich will mich fassen.
> Dies Herz, weil es sein muß, bezwingen will ichs,
> Und tun mit Grazie, was die Not erheischt.
> (*SW* 1, 361; 1196–8)

(I will control myself. It can't be otherwise: I promise to subdue my heart and do with good grace what necessity requires.) [G, 199]

But both here and when she goes on to dismiss her passion for her beloved as merely a 'childish whim':

> Recht habt ihr auch. Warum auch wie ein Kind gleich,
> Weil sich ein flüchtger Wunsch mir nicht gewährt,
> Mit meinen Göttern brechen? (*SW* 1, 361; 1199–201)

(And you are right, too. Why should I, like a child, because I couldn't please a passing fancy that I had, break with all my gods?) [G, 199]

she shows not only her lack of experience, but also how far she has moved away from the Amazon concept of love as a gift (for which requital cannot be expected) and towards the inferior Greek concept of 'love' espoused by her 'hero'. Once in the grip of this baser passion, the power of which she crucially underestimates, the mere sight of the garlands of roses ('Rosenkränze') is enough to rekindle her memories of him. She remains rooted to the spot, crippled ('gelähmt') by her passion and willing to submit to whatever Achilles has in mind for her, however humiliating:

> Laßt ihn mit Pferden häuptlings heim mich schleifen,
> Und diesen Leib hier, frischen Lebens voll,
> Auf offnem Felde schmachvoll hingeworfen,
> Den Hunden mag er ihn zur Morgenspeise,
> Dem scheußlichen Geschlecht der Vögel, bieten.
> Staub lieber, als ein Weib sein, das nicht reizt.
>
> (*SW* I, 363; 1248–53)

(Let him drag me home headfirst behind his horses, fling this woman's body here, so full of life, ignominiously into the open field to be a breakfast for his dogs, for abominable birds. Be dust, rather than a woman who lacks all interest for a man.) [G, 201]

But whilst her desperate resolve bears witness to the strength of her feelings, the violence of the images she conjures up anticipate the potentially dire consequences that lie in store for an Amazon in love with a man incapable of responding with a similar pure devotion. In short, Penthesilea's desire to be loved by Achilles has become so overwhelming that she is prepared to abandon her own high ideal of love in favour of the baser eroticism of these half-savage Greeks. Ceasing to regard herself as an autonomous (Amazon) individual, she lowers herself to the status of a Greek woman, an object designed to comply unthinkingly with the needs and desires of the man who owns her. And, as the High-Priestess points out, it is her own longing to be loved by Achilles, rather than any direct intervention on his part, that brings about this act of self-abasement:

> O sie geht steil-bergab den Pfad zum Orkus!
> Und nicht dem Gegner, wenn sie auf ihn trifft,
> Dem Feind in ihrem Busen wird sie sinken.
>
> (*SW* I, 358; 1106–8)

(She's racing headlong down the road to Orcus! And it's not the foeman, when they meet, who'll make her stoop, but the enemy that lives in her own breast.) [G, 195]

In order to make this transition, Penthesilea is obliged to resort to a grotesque act of self-deception. She decides that, like a mother, she must give her lover (child) everything he asks for, and imagines that by so doing, she can cause genuine feelings of love to replace the selfishness to which she is pandering. Kleist explores this act of self-deception from two perspectives: in scenes 8–10, Penthesilea casts herself in the role of victim and, as we shall see, in the 'idyll' of scenes 13–15 that take place under the oak-tree ('Eiche') she assumes the role of victor.

The so-called 'idyll' of scene 15 is a wholly artificial construct, hastily engineered by Prothoe in an attempt to soften the blow to Penthesilea when she is forced to acknowledge that it is she who has been taken prisoner by Achilles. Prothoe does this in good faith since she is labouring under the illusion that Achilles genuinely loves Penthesilea – witness her extravagant outburst:

> O so laß
> Mich deine Füße küssen, Göttlicher!
> O jetzt, wärst du nicht hier, jetzt sucht ich dich,
> Und müßts an Herkuls Säulen sein, Pelide!
> (*SW* I, 375; 1526–9)

(Man-god, let me kiss your feet! My feelings now are such that if you were not here in front of me, I'd go in search of you myself, as far as Hercules' Pillars if need be.) [G, 213]

Prothoe succeeds in convincing Penthesilea that it is she who has won the contest, but as scene 14 proceeds, it becomes less and less clear who is deceiving whom. And when Penthesilea tells Prothoe how she had dreamed that Achilles had defeated her on the battle-field and then goes on, melodramatically: 'I told you, it was just a dream, it's not – Or is it! Did I – ? Was it true? Speak, will you?' [G, 215] ('Du hörsts, es war ja nur ein Traum, es ist nicht – | Wie! Oder ist es? Ists? Wärs wirklich? Rede!'; *SW* I, 377; 1596–7) we are left wondering whether Penthesilea genuinely wants to know the truth or whether she is trying to persuade Prothoe to connive at concealing it, until we gradually realise that it is the latter. For when Prothoe feels compelled to draw her attention to the reality of her situation, 'Just look around you, you deluded girl, and tell me where you think you are? Where are our people? Our priestesses?' [G,

217] ('Blick um dich her, Betrogene, wo bist du? | Wo ist das Volk? Wo sind die Priesterinnen?'; *SW* 1, 379: 1671–2), Penthesilea's plea for indulgence:

> O laß mich, Prothoe! O laß dies Herz
> Zwei Augenblick in diesem Strom der Lust,
> Wie ein besudelt Kind, sich untertauchen; (*SW* 1, 379; 1674–6)

(Allow me it, Prothoe! I'm a little grubby child that's dived into this stream of pure delight, for two seconds only;) [G, 218]

emphasises the fact that in assuming the role of victor, she is indulging in a pure wish-fulfilment fantasy. And having chosen to disregard the fact that she is the defeated party, she now abandons her Amazon concept of love in favour of the abhorrent version of possessive 'love' associated with the Greeks and addresses Achilles as follows:

> Ich bins,
> Du junger Kriegsgott, der du angehörst;
> Wenn man im Volk dich fragt, so nennst du *mich*.
> (*SW* 1, 384; 1806–8)

(Young god of war, it's me whom you belong to; and when people ask you, say *my* name.) [G, 222–3]

She may, of course, hope that 'love as possession' will, in the course of time, give way to 'love as selfless devotion':

> Denn eine andre Kette denk ich noch,
> Wie Blumen leicht, und fester doch, als Erz,
> Die dich mir fest verknüpft, ums Herz zu schlagen.
> Doch bis sie zärtlich, Ring um Ring, geprägt,
> In der Gefühle Glut, und ausgeschmiedet,
> Der Zeit nicht, und dem Zufall, mehr zerstörbar,
> Kehrst du, weil es die Pflicht erheischt, mir wieder,
> Mir, junger Freund, (*SW* 1, 385; 1832–9)

(It's another kind of chain, now, I am thinking of, as light as wreaths yet more unbreakable than bronze, to wind around your heart and bind you to me with. But till its links, each one, are hammered out and shaped, with finest art, in the fire of feeling, proof against the injuries of time and chance, back to me you must return as you are duty bound – to me, you understand, my friend;) [G, 223]

However, in entertaining this hope, she fatally over-estimates Achilles' ability to cast off the influence of his upbringing and, ominously, throughout the whole of scene 15, he shows a distinct lack of interest in her account of Amazon history and it is soon obvious that what interest he does show is only a pretext to detain her longer in order to possess her sexually. Appropriately enough, the one aspect of Amazon culture in which he does show some interest is their reproductive arrangements. And whilst he is willing to allow Penthesilea to assume the role of 'victor' for as long as he can be certain that it is she who – in the most literal sense of the term – belongs to him, when the 'idyll' is disrupted by the arrival of the Greeks and Amazons, he breaks off his courtly rhetoric and leaves the queen in no doubt as to the reality of the situation:

> Dein Schicksal ist auf ewig abgeschlossen;
> Gefangen bist du mir, ein Höllenhund
> Bewacht dich minder grimmig, als ich dich.
> (*SW* 1, 398; 2255–7)

(Your destiny's complete, all's over; now you're my prisoner, a dog of hell would not keep so ferocious guard as I.) [G, 236]

The 'idyll' has now been exposed as a sham. And just as the temple which Achilles promises to erect for her in Phthia[25] could be only a pale imitation of the Amazons' temple of Diana, so too the apparent 'ideal' of 'unconditional love' with which we have been presented in this scene is based exclusively on the conventional Greek picture of love as a masculine elite requires it.

At this point, Penthesilea is rescued from the 'arms' of her lover and from the Greeks, only to be drummed out of the ranks of the Amazons and left to contemplate how she has betrayed herself and all that is best in Amazon society in exchange for the lust of a braggart and womaniser. As the High Priestess says to her in scene 19:

> Frei, in des Volkes Namen, sprech ich dich;
> Du kannst den Fuß jetzt wenden, wie du willst,
> Kannst ihn mit flatterndem Gewand ereilen,
> Der dich in Fesseln schlug, und ihm den Riß,
> Da, wo wir sie zersprengten, überreichen:
> Also ja wills das heilge Kriegsgesetz! (*SW* 1, 401; 2329–34)

(In the name of our people, I pronounce you free; turn your feet whichever way you please, go running, with your skirts aflutter, after him who hung the chains on you and point him out the breach we made in them, oh do! – for your sacred rules of warfare, they demand it!) [G, 240]

The arrival of the Greek herald bearing a fresh challenge from Achilles, reminds Penthesilea once more of the humiliation she has suffered. Forced to recognise that Achilles is simply incapable of returning her love, she cries:

> Hier, diese treue Brust, sie rührt ihn erst,
> Wenn sie sein scharfer Speer zerschmetterte?
> Was ich ihm zugeflüstert, hat sein Ohr
> Mit der Musik der Rede bloß getroffen? (*SW* I, 403; 2386–9)

(This heart of mine, it doesn't touch him till his sharp spear's torn a hole in it? Did all the things I whispered only strike his ear as pretty sounds, not sense?) [G, 242]

However, Prothoe's urgings to forget about 'the unfeeling man' [G, 242] ('den Unempfindlichen'; *SW* I, 403; 2392) prompt the queen to embark on yet another fatal course of action. She will accept Achilles' 'challenge', and by destroying him, will erase his memory from her mind. Once again, she wilfully deceives herself. Since her love for Achilles is a feeling that arises from within herself and is not something 'causally determined' by an external object (Achilles), she will not succeed in removing this feeling simply by destroying the object of her love. Nor can she destroy the memory of her beloved by mutilating his corpse, 'erasing' his features. In an earlier draft of the play, Kleist makes this last point even more explicitly. For as she kneels over her beloved's disfigured corpse, his mangled features seem to reform in her imagination until his whole face 'smiles' back at her in recognition:

> Sieh, Prothoe, sieh – der Rest von einer Lippe –
> Sprich, dünkts dich nicht als ob er lächelte?
> O beim Olymp! Er ist mir ausgesöhnt,
> Und jener andre Teil er lächelt auch. (*SW* I, 884)

(Look, Prothoe, the remains of a lip – tell me doesn't it look to you as though it's smiling. Oh, by the gods of Olympus, he is reconciled with me. And see, that other part, it's smiling too!)

It is not until the end of the play that she arrives at a proper understanding of her predicament. Only then does she recognise that love cannot exact love. This recognition brings with it the insight that only by destroying herself, the willing instigator of her love for Achilles, can she escape from her commitment, and it is for this reason – and not to 'atone' for her 'crime' – that she kills herself. Indeed, the very absence of any weapons (she hands over her bow and arrows to Prothoe) underlines the fact that it is the pain of her unrequited love for Achilles that is the 'killing feeling' ('vernichtendes Gefühl') that is ultimately responsible for her death. For as she says:

> Dies Erz, dies läutr' ich in der Glut des Jammers
> Hart mir zu Stahl; tränk es mit Gift sodann,
> Heißätzendem, der Reue, durch und durch;
> Trag es der Hoffnung ewgem Amboß zu,
> Und schärf und spitz es mir zu einem Dolch;
> Und diesem Dolch jetzt reich ich meine Brust:
> So! So! So! So! Und wieder! – Nun ists gut.
> (*SW* 1, 427; 3028–34)

(This ore, I will refine it, in the burning fire of my misery, into hard steel; then in the hot corrosive poison of remorse, steep it through and through; to hope's eternal anvil next I'll carry it, to hone and point it dagger sharp; and to this dagger now I offer up my breast: like so! and so! and so! And once again! – and now all's well.) [G, 268]

THE DENOUEMENT

Just before Penthesilea commits suicide, she says to the faithful Prothoe, 'And – something I will whisper to you privately, the others must not hear: the ashes of Queen Tanaïs, scatter them to the winds!' [G, 267] ('Und – – – im Vertraun ein Wort, das niemand höre, | Der Tanaïs Asche, streut sie in die Luft!'; *SW* 1, 426; 3008–9). Her words, however, do not represent an outright rejection of the Amazonian alternative to the brutish (Greek) conception of love as submission and ownership. However they do but bear witness to her realisation that her society's vastly superior concept of love is still flawed by the presence of an ideological component. In short, they indicate the need for a change in

Amazon society that will prevent Amazons from accepting so uncritically the self-righteous ideological conviction of the High Priestess, that if they adhere to the proscriptions relating to heterosexual relationships, they will be infallibly protected from the kind of tragedy that has just befallen Penthesilea, a tragedy which the High Priestess attempts to cover up by deliberately misrepresenting its cause. For when Penthesilea unexpectedly triumphs over Achilles, the High Priestess completely reverses her negative moral judgement of her in scene 19 and now seeks to vindicate the narrow (and unrealistic) conditions of Amazon law by portraying the queen as nothing less than a 'second Tanaïs':

> Die große Stifterin des Frauenreiches,
> Die Tanaïs, das gesteh ich jetzt, sie hat
> Den Bogen würdger nicht geführt als du.
> (*SW* I, 418; 2776–8).

(The great founder of our women's state, Tanaïs, let me say it now, never drew the bow more worthily than you.) [G, 257]

In so doing, the High Priestess (deliberately?) overlooks the vital difference, namely that Tanaïs was not in love with Vexoris, whereas Penthesilea did indeed fall in love with Achilles in the true Amazonian sense. Of course, if the High Priestess is to be believed, 'Tanaïs's Law' should have afforded Penthesilea complete protection against such an eventuality. Accordingly, her words at the end of the play:

> Ach! Wie gebrechlich ist der Mensch, ihr Götter!
> Wie stolz, die hier geknickt liegt, noch vor kurzem,
> Hoch auf des Lebens Gipfeln, rauschte sie!
> (*SW* I, 428; 3037–9)

(Oh how infirm Man is, you gods! The snapped and broken blossom lying here, how mightily she thundered, high upon the peaks of life, a little while ago!) [G, 268]

are nothing more than a clichéd commentary on 'human weakness', and one that is designed to convince the weaker and more compliant members of Amazon society to strive to conform yet more closely to the flawed system of Themiscyra. It is left to Prothoe to allude to the truth of the situation, namely that Amazon law can never prevent those of superior strength from exercising their free wills:

> Sie sank, weil sie zu stolz und kräftig blühte!
> Die abgestorbne Eiche steht im Sturm,
> Doch die gesunde stürzt er schmetternd nieder,
> Weil er in ihre Krone greifen kann. (*SW* 1, 428; 3040–3)

(She fell because she bloomed too proud and strong! The dead oak stands, defying wind and weather, the gale pulls down the good wood with a crash, for with his fingers he can fasten in its crown.) [G, 268]

CONCLUSION

It is impossible to ignore the scenes of horrific violence that are so graphically depicted in Kleist's work and, in the twentieth century at least, his reputation as a dramatist is inextricably bound up with *Penthesilea*, a play containing one of the most (in)famous scenes in the history of the German theatre. As Christa Wolf so rightly points out: 'Even though we have grown accustomed to barbarism, *Penthesilea* still strikes us as barbaric' ('Die *Penthesilea* bleibt ein entsetzliches Schauspiel, selbst uns, die wir an Entsetzliches gewöhnt sind').[26] However, whilst Kleist deliberately set out to shock his audience, he also went to some lengths to emphasise that the desecration of Achilles' corpse is regarded as a monstrous act by all the Amazons, including Penthesilea herself.[27] In this way, he underlines the fact that the queen's maniacal behaviour is not only contrary to the dictates of her society, but also quite out of character. Her barbaric treatment of Achilles is not a reflection of her desire to inflict cruelty upon another human being, but is due to her having been driven mad by frustration. Her frustration stems, firstly, from the failure of her (superior) Amazon love to elicit – as she believes it must – an equivalent response from Achilles, and secondly, from her feelings of self-disgust when she is forced to acknowledge that she has descended to his level in giving way to an (unworthy) desire to 'win' him at any price. In short, her frustration is caused by the failure of actual human behaviour to conform – as she believes it 'must' – to the transcendent categories of her imagination. Moreover, it is essentially this same sense of frustration that lies behind the monstrous acts of revenge committed by such other well-intentioned individuals as Sylvester in *Die Familie Schroffenstein* and, as we shall see in due course, Thusnelda in *Die Hermannsschlacht.* Thus the real import of *Penthesilea* is to emphasise that violence of this kind is not an 'inevitable' fact of human life, but is, to a large extent, avoidable. For if human beings would renounce their fruitless quest for monolithic certainty and stop regarding their contingent man-made conventions as infallible truths about human nature and conduct, they would avoid many of the crippling and potentially catastrophic disappointments in life with which they are repeatedly beset.[28]

CHAPTER 7

Das Käthchen von Heilbronn

Kleist's 'grand historical romance' ('großes historisches Ritterschauspiel') has never found much favour with contemporary literary critics and it is not hard to see why. Its fairy-tale plot and happy ending seem far removed from the thematic and formal complexity of his other works.[1] However, it should not be forgotten that, in the nineteenth century, what reputation Kleist enjoyed as a dramatist was largely due to the stage-success of this one play. Not only did it form part of the standard theatrical repertoire in Germany (attracting a succession of star performers in the title role) but it became sufficiently well-known to form the basis of a number of parodies.[2] When the play was first performed in Vienna on 17 March 1810, whilst critics were divided as to its particular merits, there were few, if any, who doubted that it was to be taken as a straightforward celebration of the power of unconditional love. Only when the printed edition of the text appeared, (the 'Buchausgabe' of October 1810) did contemporary critics begin to take seriously the possibility that the play was a parody. Even so, this interpretation was not really taken up. Although one critic, writing in the *Morgenblatt* of 18 December 1810, suggests precisely this: 'on reading the first few pages of this chivalrous tragedy, it seemed that what we had before us was a parody of the low-grade romantic twaddle of our day' ('Bei Lesung der ersten Blätter dieser Ritter-Tragödie glaubten wir, eine Parodie auf den romantischen Schnickschnack unsrer Zeit zu finden'), he subsequently dismisses the idea, claiming instead that 'Kleist's intentions are utterly serious' ('daß es dem Hrn v. Kleist barer, brennender Ernst sei'; *Lebensspuren*, no. 373).

But can the (utterly absurd) plot of *Das Käthchen von Heilbronn* be taken at face value? Anyone who does so, is obliged to assume that Kleist had gone back on his earlier observations on the pernicious influence of the popular sentimental novels and chivalrous romances of his day.[3] He may have boasted to his publisher, Cotta, that, 'if it proved to be a success', he 'could produce a romantic play of this sort every year' ('Ich würde, wenn es Glück macht, jährlich eins, von der romantischen Gattung, liefern können'; *SW* II, 830) but it seems improbable that he was intent on establishing himself as a writer for the commercial theatre, which was dominated by the sentimental fare of Iffland and Kotzebue, whose plays he viewed with utter contempt. It is more likely that he chose this more conventional format in response to Goethe's criticism that both *Der zerbrochne Krug* and *Penthesilea* had been written for a form of theatre that did not as yet exist.[4] Writing a play in the 'romantic style' was to enable him to explore the same questions of femininity that he had raised in *Penthesilea*, but in a form more in line with the requirements of the contemporary stage. The risk he ran was that the play would be taken only at its face value, and it is perhaps for this reason that he subsequently regretted having allowed so many changes to his original script. For as his letter to Marie von Kleist dated Summer 1811 suggests, Kleist had been attempting to do more than simply produce a commercially viable play:

> Das Urteil der Menschen hat mich bisher viel zu sehr beherrscht; besonders das Käthchen von Heilbronn ist voll Spuren davon. Es war von Anfang herein eine ganz treffliche Erfindung, und nur die Absicht, es für die Bühne passend zu machen, hat mich zu Mißgriffen verführt, die ich jetzt beweinen möchte. (*SW* II, 874)

> (The judgement of others has governed me all too often in the past; *Kate of Heilbronn* [*Das Käthchen von Heilbronn*] especially shows signs of this. It was an altogether fine conception from the beginning, and only when I tried to make it more convenient for the stage was I seduced into errors over which I might now weep.) [M, 196]

We cannot be certain exactly what changes Kleist made to the play, but a comparison of the edition published in 1810 with the extracts ('Fragmente') published two years earlier in Kleist's own literary periodical, *Phöbus*, may offer some clues. The most important of these affect act II, scene 10.[5] In the later (stage) version of the play, Kunigunde's radical deconstruction of the spurious link between external (physical) beauty and inner 'beauty of soul' (*SW* I, 901–2) is replaced by the much tamer discussion on the use of a 'lime-twig' ('Leimrute') to trap a bird (see *SW* I, 472–3; 1247–66). Interestingly enough, a comparison of the published edition of the play with the prompt copy of the 1842 production at the Detmold Hoftheater also reveals that, in addition to the changes made to the *Phöbus* version of act II, scene 10, almost all the scenes that draw attention to the artificiality of Kunigunde's appearance had been removed. But if Kleist and the subsequent re-writers of *Das Käthchen von Heilbronn* may have succeeded in making the play more acceptable to contemporary theatre audiences, their efforts weakened the play's critique of 'feminine innocence'. For it is through the juxtaposition of Kunigunde's 'artificiality' and Käthchen's 'naturalness' that the play exposes the essentially conventional character of the young heroine's 'feminine innocence'. Although Kleist was to regret these changes, it seems he could hardly have done more to try and prevent contemporary audiences from interpreting the play as a straightforward eulogy of the allegedly redemptive power of unconditional love. Despite his retaining such obviously fantastical elements as the cherub that rescues Käthchen from the fire in act III, it appears that few of his contemporaries were capable of recognising that the image of femininity embodied in Käthchen was no less artificial than the fairy-tale world in which the action of the play is set. Significantly, however, some female members of the audience were less easily taken in, and in this respect the contrast between the reactions of the twelve year-old Hedwig Staegemann (a veritable 'Käthchen' in the making) and the forty-five year-old Charlotte von Schiller is highly revealing. For as Staegemann's diary reveals, Käthchen constituted the perfect embodiment of an adolescent girl's romantic fantasies: 'I don't know what it is that I find so beautiful about Käthchen, but she appeals to me above all else' (Ich weiß auch nicht, was so Schönes in dem Käthchen liegt, aber es reizt mich mehr als alles übrige'; *Lebensspuren*, no. 388). The more mature Charlotte von Schiller, on the other hand, understood exactly what her male friends found so appealing about Kleist's heroine, as a letter to her friend, Princess Karoline of Saxe-Weimar, shows: 'Do you know the famous *Käthchen von Heilbronn*? Falk and Schulze, each in their own way, think it's marvellous, because they would be so happy if they had little Käthchens who would follow them through fire and water' ('Kennen Sie das berühmte Käthchen von Heilbronn? Falk und Schulze sind entzückt davon, jeder auf seine Weise, weil es sie wohl freuen möchte, wenn sie solche Käthchen hätten, die ihnen durch Wasser und Feuer folgen'; *Lebensspuren*, no. 387).[6]

DAS KÄTHCHEN VON HEILBRONN AND *PENTHESILEA*

In his much-quoted letter of 8 December 1808 to the Austrian dramatist, Heinrich von Collin, Kleist describes the relationship between *Penthesilea* and *Das Käthchen von Heilbronn* as follows:

> Denn wer das Käthchen liebt, dem kann die Penthesilea nicht ganz unbegreiflich sein, sie gehören ja wie das + und – der Algebra zusammen, und sind ein und dasselbe Wesen, nur unter entgegengesetzten Beziehungen gedacht. (*SW* II, 818)

> (For whoever loves Kate [Käthchen] cannot find Penthesilea utterly incomprehensible; they belong together as the + and – of algebra, and are one and the same nature, but imagined under opposite circumstances.) [M, 181–2]

Although the two female protagonists are indeed 'one and the same nature' insofar as they are both 'irresistibly' attracted to a member of the opposite sex, there is, however, an important difference between them. Penthesilea has been brought up within an alien culture that is quite self-sufficient and, if not actually superior to, at least equal to that of Achilles. When she descends to the level of Achilles and attempts to 'love' him on his terms, thereby debasing her status to that of a mere sexual object, she is behaving in a manner that is quite contrary to the rules of her society. And although a rebel, she is, nonetheless, a queen, and thus occupies a privileged position in her own – female-oriented – society. Käthchen, on the other hand, is a wholly marginalised figure, a mere woman in a feudal, predominantly male-oriented society, occupying a position in the social hierarchy far inferior to that of Strahl. Thus whilst the struggle between Achilles and Penthesilea is, to a large extent, a struggle between equals, that between Strahl and Käthchen is quite one-sided since Strahl is, in almost every sense, Käthchen's superior. Moreover, in stark contrast to Penthesilea's illicit obsession with Achilles, Käthchen's 'abject devotion' (her 'gänzliche Hingebung') to Strahl is fully endorsed by the society in which she lives; only the difference in social class between herself and Strahl prevents the consummation of this relationship from taking place as a matter of course. It is in this sense that Käthchen is to be seen as the converse of Penthesilea, as Kleist suggests in his letter to his cousin, Marie:

> Jetzt bin ich nur neugierig, was Sie zu dem Käthchen von Heilbronn sagen werden, denn das ist die Kehrseite der Penthesilea, ihr andrer Pol, ein Wesen, das ebenso mächtig ist durch gänzliche Hingebung, als jene durch Handeln. (*SW* II, 797)
>
> (Now I am curious what you will think of my Kate of Heilbronn, for she is the reverse side of Penthesilea, her opposite pole, a being quite as great in her complete submission as the other is in her self-assertion.) [M, 175]

For whereas Penthesilea, by falling in love with Achilles, genuinely rebels against her culture, Käthchen's seemingly hopeless infatuation with a man of vastly superior rank is anything but a radical gesture, and her 'abject devotion' is simply a reflection of the extent to which she functions as a superlative embodiment of the prevailing norms of femininity.[7]

KÄTHCHEN AND KUNIGUNDE

Whilst Käthchen and Penthesilea are, in every sense, the opposite of each other, the relationship of Käthchen and Kunigunde cannot be seen in these terms. Although *Das Käthchen von Heilbronn* appears, at least at first sight, to operate in terms of an archetypal opposition which one critic[8] has termed the 'fairy-tale of the good and bad bride', it is precisely the uncritical acceptance of such archetypal notions of femininity that is Kleist's target in the play.[9] He draws the audience's attention to the artificiality of the idealised notion of 'feminine innocence' with which the male characters in the play are so obsessed by juxtaposing the two female protagonists. In fact, in *Das Käthchen von Heilbronn* he presents us not with two diametrically opposed images of femininity, but with the same image viewed at two different points in time. From the start,

Käthchen embodies all the self-indulgent longings of the men in whose world she moves: in act II, scene I, Strahl describes her as possessing a 'beauty, more charming than I can sing' [P, 271] ('Du Schönere, als ich singen kann'; *SW* I, 454; 695–6). She is a puppet-like figure, a picture of innocence whose perfect devotion will be thoroughly tested in the 'Test of Fire' ('Feuerprobe') to which she is subjected in act III, scenes 12–14. Kunigunde embodies essentially the same image of 'feminine innocence' and beguiling 'helplessness', but at a stage when natural beauty is fading rapidly and in constant need of repair. But, as she shows, this is no great handicap, for the image of ideal womanhood that the men find so beguiling can be (re)constructed in a morning's work in front of her 'dressing table and mirror' ('Putztisch und Spiegel'). Borrowing an image from Kleist, it might be said that if Käthchen functions as a marionette-like figure in the play, Kunigunde adopts the role of a self-repairing 'Käthchen-like' marionette.

KUNIGUNDE

Through the character of Kunigunde,[10] Kleist exposes the wholly conventional character of the notion of 'natural' femininity which operates throughout the play. And as is so often the case with Kleist's work, a more radical statement of his position is to be found in the earlier version of the play, in this instance in the *Variant* to act II, scene 10, published in *Phöbus*.[11] In this version of the scene, Kunigunde demonstrates how much better she understands the society in which she lives than do her male admirers. While they claim to love only 'the natural', she knows how artificial this 'naturalness' is. Despite their constantly repeated horror of anything unnatural, the men never direct their longings towards real, flesh-and-blood women, but always towards imaginary beings, whose stereotypical attributes can be read off monotonously from a catalogue of their creators' unrealistic requirements.[12] For although they go to extraordinary lengths to conceal the fact, what the men want in *Das Käthchen von Heilbronn* is not nature *per se*, but rather an (agreeable) illusion of 'nature', a 'nature' purged of its less unpleasant (i.e. real) elements.[13] Needless to say, since nothing can be at once natural and artificial, both sexes have to wrestle with an ineluctable contradiction. And as the scene unfolds, Kunigunde demonstrates her considerable expertise in the routine construction of just such an image of 'artificial-natural' beauty. When, in the *Variant* to act II, scene 10, she says to her maid:

> Mich dünkt, Rosalie, diese Locken sind
> Zu zierlich hier. Was meinst du? Es ist nicht
> Mein Wille, was die Kunst kann, zu erschöpfen,
> Vielmehr, wo die Bedeutung minder ist,
> Möcht ich dich gern nachlässiger, damit
> Das Ganze so vollendeter erschiene. (*SW* I, 900–1)

(Rosalie, I think these curls here are too dainty. What do you think? It's not my wish to exhaust the possibilities of art, but rather to be a little more casual where things matter less, so as to render the overall impression that much more perfect.)

her remarks draw attention the fact that a little deliberate 'casualness' ('Nachlässigkeit') can create an illusion of unadorned 'innocence' that will blind the viewer to the massive artificiality of the whole.

Although Kunigunde directs much of her time towards producing an alluring image of physical beauty, her real strength lies in her understanding that what is of primary importance in her culture is not in fact physical beauty, but rather an 'inner beauty of soul' ('Seele') which, however, is equally artificial. The enhancement of her outward appearance is simply a means to an end, as she explains to Rosalie:

> Die Kunst, die du an meinem Putztisch übst,
> Ist mehr, als bloß ein sinnereizendes
> Verbinden von Gestalten und von Farben.
> Das unsichtbare Ding, das Seele heißt,
> Möcht ich an allem gern erscheinen machen,
> Dem Toten selbst, das mir verbunden ist. (*SW* I, 901)

(The art that you practise at my dressing table is much more than simply assembling a sensuous combination of shapes and colours. I want to ensure that everything, even the mortal part of me, displays that invisible quality called 'soul'.)

But since the men she tries to attract have no interest in, or knowledge of, what women are like in reality, but look only to external appearances as an sign of 'beauty of soul', for a practitioner as skilled as Kunigunde, the creation of such an illusion of 'inner beauty' is simply a matter of rearranging her costume:

> Ein Band, das niederhängt, der Schleif entrissen,
> Ein Strauß, – was du nur irgend willst, ein Schmuck,
> Ein Kleid, das aufgeschürzt ist, oder nicht,
> Sind Züg an mir, die reden, die versammelt
> Das Bild von einem innern Zustand geben. (*SW* I, 901)

(A ribbon dangling from an bow that has come undone, a posy, or anything you like. Some ornament, a dress that is gathered up, or not as the case may be; all these tell a story: taken together they convey an illusion of an inner state.)

When she is rescued by Strahl from the clutches of Freiburg in act II, scene 8, her aside to the audience outlining the task before her, reveals her complete understanding of the image of 'femininity' prevailing in her culture:

> Ich will nichts denken, fühlen will ich nichts,
> Als Unschuld, Ehre, Leben, Rettung – Schutz
> Vor diesem Wolf, der hier am Boden liegt,
> (*SW* I, 468; 1108–10)

(I will think nothing else, feel nothing else, but honour, innocence, life, escape, protection, before this wolf who lies here on the ground.) [P, 284]

Having selected from her repertoire the appropriate behavioural props, she turns her art upon Strahl and 'performs' – in the most literal sense of the word – her 'role':

> Euch, mein Gebieter – Euer nenn ich alles,
> Was mein ist! Sprecht! Was habt Ihr über mich beschlossen?
> In Eurer Macht bin ich; was muß geschehn?
> Muß ich nach Eurem Rittersitz Euch folgen?
> (*SW* I, 468; 1118–21)

(I call you master; everything that's mine I name as yours. Speak, what have you resolved concerning me? I'm in your power. What follows? Must I go with you to your knightly castle.) [P, 284]

These artfully selected signals of abject submission culminate in a declaration of her readiness to spend the night even in the dungeons of Schloß Wetterstrahl, should her 'saviour' think fit:

'Without complaint I'd go into your dungeon' [P, 284] ('In Eure Kerker klaglos würd ich wandern'; *SW* I, 468; 1129), an offer which, as might be expected, the chivalrous Strahl has no intention of accepting and which elicits another appropriately exaggerated gesture of gratitude on her part: 'Oh do not crush me down to the earth with magnanimity' [P, 285] ('Drückt mich mit Eurer Großmut nicht zu Boden!'; *SW* I, 468; 1130). In the ease with which she plays this part, Kleist exposes the spurious character of this pseudo-femininity and this in turn invites us to examine more critically the 'abject devotion' of Käthchen herself.

It is particularly ironic that Strahl is so easily taken in by Kunigunde's display of 'helplessness'. For only a few scenes previously, he had berated his peers for their inability to look beyond the façade of her 'beauty', saying to Flammberg, 'That accursed little face of hers is the final reason for all these wars against me' [P, 273] ('Ihr kleines verwünschtes Gesicht ist der letzte Grund aller dieser Kriege wider mich'; *SW* I, 457; 790–1). Nonetheless, as the subsequent meeting between Strahl and Kunigunde shows, what convinces the men is not so much her 'accursed little face', but the well-rehearsed image of 'helplessness' she projects. Strictly speaking, it is not she who deceives the men, but the men who deceive themselves. For although male vanity requires Strahl and his colleagues to attribute a high degree of devilish cunning to this woman, the truth of the matter is that trapping the men in this play is as simple as catching a bird with a 'limed twig' ('Leimrute'). Unwilling to relinquish their preferred image of woman as a helpless dependent creature, they studiously refuse to scrutinise it too closely lest its wholly conventional character become apparent. And it is precisely because the men have such a deep-seated desire to preserve the viability of this image of femininity that Kunigunde is given so many opportunities to redeem herself. Although Strahl knows her past history, he so longs to believe in the 'authorised' version of femininity that as soon as Kunigunde strikes the correct pose he is taken in by it. And as Kunigunde's liaisons with Freiburg and Stein demonstrate, Strahl is not the first – and will probably not be the last – to have been bewitched by her art. Interestingly enough, the only character who is not immediately impressed by Kunigunde is Strahl's mother; for she, as an experienced female member of this society, is able to offer a more detached assessment of her son's would-be fiancée: 'I haven't said that she displeased me wholly' [P, 293] ('Ich sagte nicht, daß sie mir ganz mißfällt'; *SW* I, 477; 1376) and advocates a more cautious approach.

In the final scene of the play, Strahl banishes Kunigunde from the wedding ceremony calling her a 'poisoner' [P, 344] ('Giftmischerin'; *SW* I, 531; 2683), an obvious reference to the fact that she plotted to poison his bride. But if the truth be told, her crime is not her attempted murder of Käthchen, nor for that matter, her pretending to be something she was not; her real crime is not having performed her role well enough. What the men cannot forgive, is the way in which the discovery of her fraud has exposed the spurious character of their idealised picture of 'woman'. Although, in fact, they are in love with a wholly artificial image of femininity, nothing disgusts and frightens them so much as having to recognise that fact. And in act V, scene 3, they are forced to do just this, when Freiburg explains:

Sie ist eine mosaische Arbeit, aus allen drei Reichen der Natur zusammengesetzt. Ihre Zähne gehören einem Mädchen aus München, ihre Haare sind aus Frankreich verschrieben, ihrer Wangen Gesundheit kommt aus den Bergwerken in Ungarn, und den Wuchs, den ihr an ihr bewundert, hat sie einem Hemde zu danken, das ihr der Schmied, aus schwedischem Eisen, verfertigt hat. (*SW* I, 520; 2446–52)

(She is a piece of mosaic, put together from all the three kingdoms of nature. Her teeth belong to a girl in Munich, her hair was ordered from France, the healthy glow of her cheeks comes from the mines of Hungary, and the graceful figure which you admire in her she owes to a shirt that a smith made for her out of Swedish steel.) [P, 333–4]

There is nothing in the text to suggest that Kunigunde herself is ugly; what disgusts the male characters is the discrepancy between her ageing features and the image of a young beauty that she has succeeded in presenting to the world for so long. This deception symbolises a corresponding self-deception on their part in their conventional picture of the personal qualities that constitute 'ideal' womanhood. When the artificiality of this 'ideal' can no longer be denied, each of the men is filled with rage and a desire to avenge himself by publishing the 'fraud' of Kunigunde to the world at large. Thus in act II, scene 6, Freiburg declares:

Ich bringe sie nach der Steinburg zum Rheingrafen zurück, wo ich nichts tun will, als ihr das Halstuch abnehmen: das soll meine ganze Rache sein! (*SW* 1, 461; 937–9)

(I'll carry her back to Steinburg, to the Rhinegrave, where I'll do nothing but take off her neckerchief. That shall be my whole revenge.) [P, 278]

And whilst Freiburg's threat may not seem as extreme as that of his rival the Rheingrave vom Stein:

Ich will . . . den Stachel der Rache tief eindrücken in ihre treulose Brust: töten, töten, töten, und ihr Gerippe, als das Monument einer Erzbuhlerin, in dem Gebälke der Steinburg aufbewahren! (*SW* 1, 482; 1534–9)

(I will . . . drive the sting of revenge deep, deep into her faithless breast: kill, kill, kill! and preserve her skeleton as the relic of an arch-courtesan among the rafters of the Steinburg.) [P, 297]

For a woman like Kunigunde, whose very existence depends upon the preservation of the face she presents to the world, public exposure of her artificial aids is tantamount to death. Hence her despair when she realises that Strahl has seen her *au naturel* in act v, scene 9: 'He knows, it's all in vain, there's nothing helps! He saw, my life is wrecked!' [P, 337] ('Er weiß, umsonst ists, alles hilft zu nichts, | Er hats gesehn, es ist um mich getan!'; *SW* 1, 523; 2504–5).

We cannot fail to notice that the suitors, Freiburg, Stein and Strahl, whose friendship was broken up by their rivalry over Kunigunde, are now reunited in their desire to take revenge, and – in an 'admirable' display of male solidarity – all three are on stage together when she is unmasked in the final scene. What unites them, above all, is the desire to preserve the integrity of their make-believe world. If they are to continue enjoying the illusion that the world they inhabit corresponds to reality, they have no choice but to destroy that which threatens to expose its conventional character – Kunigunde, the 'poisoner', who 'spoils' it all. Nonetheless, whilst the illusion of this fairy-tale world can be restored by Kunigunde's banishment at the end of the play, this can never be more than a temporary measure. For she, of course, is not the real problem; rather it is the idealised (and unrealistic) image of femininity that exists in the male imagination, and, in this respect, it is important to note that the rage and violent desires of the male characters are largely a reflection of their fear of the unknown. When the men realise that women are not what they think they are, they also realise that they have 'lost' that which hitherto they 'owned'. And in the play, the male characters are continually haunted by a question to which they have no answer: if 'man's companion' is not the frail innocent creature he imagined she was, what is she?

KÄTHCHEN

Unlike Kunigunde, whose 'beauty' is wholly artificial, Käthchen is blessed with a physical appearance that is not only exquisite, but also, and more importantly, wholly natural. It is tempting, then, to see Käthchen as the opposite of Kunigunde in every respect, but to do so is to make the same mistake as Strahl and the other male characters, who attribute purity of soul to her simply on the basis of her (natural) physical beauty. The truth of the matter is that this 'purity of soul' is not a quality which she possesses, but rather one which her male admirers have created and projected upon her. Unlike Kunigunde, whose age and experience have endowed her with a personality in her own right, Käthchen, by virtue of her youth and lack of experience, is little more than a beautiful – but empty – vessel waiting to receive whatever 'wish-fulfilling' qualities the men, who invent the society in which she must act out her life, choose to pour into it. Thus although the men accuse Kunigunde of being nothing more than an 'unreal image' [P, 277] ('dies wesenlose Bild'; *SW* 1, 461; 918) it is in fact Käthchen who fits that description best and whose (genuine) beauty is simply a façade behind which no solid personal identity as yet exists. Both women reflect non-natural man-made images of femininity, but whereas the wholly artificial nature of Kunigunde's beauty exposes her to the risk that it, and more importantly, the image of 'ideal' femininity that it projects, will be unmasked, the naturalness of Käthchen's beauty renders her proof against such disaster – at least for the time being. For it is quite possible that in her youth, Kunigunde may well have been blessed with a natural 'Käthchen-like' beauty and almost certain that, with the passing of time, Käthchen will herself have to resort increasingly to the tricks currently deployed by her older rival.

The extent to which Käthchen is simply a reflection of her male creators' needs and desires is made clear by her father's litany of his daughter's superlative qualities in the opening scene of the play :

Ein Wesen von zarterer, frommerer und lieberer Art müßt ihr euch nicht denken, und kämt ihr, auf Flügeln der Einbildung, zu den lieben, kleinen Engeln, die, mit hellen Augen, aus den Wolken, unter Gottes Händen und Füßen hervorgucken. (*SW* I, 433; 69–73)

(You could not imagine a creature of more tender, pious, and loving nature, even though your thoughts flew on the wings of imagination to the dear little angels who peep out with bright eyes from under God's hands and feet.) [P, 251]

For what is the audience to make of the strange catalogue of contradictory qualities that the father of this youthful paragon ascribes to his child: so circumspect and obedient, yet apparently capable of a 'self-willed' pursuit of her beloved across country in complete defiance of social convention; almost simple-minded in her ignorance of ordinary matters, but profoundly insightful and sure of both her own destiny and, more importantly, of Strahl's; knowing herself so little, but understanding Strahl almost better than he does himself; so totally the object of male adoration and yet so totally uncomprehending of the underlying erotic motivation of her suitors? As Theobald's list of his daughter's qualities grows ever longer and more extravagant, the audience is bound to suspect that what is being described is not an actual human being, but a collage of all the qualities with which the idle fantasies of men have endowed their notion of 'perfect' womanhood, and like most such day-dreamed composites, full of contradictions. By the same token, it can come as little surprise that this 'young lady' is attended by cherubs and tumbles, as it were, 'motherless' out of the head of a doting father into the arms of a marvellous man, whose only obstacle to marrying her on the spot is the inviolate prohibition of the ruling caste. However, even this obstacle is about to be 'dissolved' by the discovery that – as might have been expected – such virtuous femininity is the product of noble birth: for she is the Kaiser's daughter – no less! In this way, the play both upholds and – by virtue of the patently artificial and comic 'resolution' of this problem[14] – adroitly subverts the myth that good breeding and good manners are, in the final analysis, inseparable, another fiction produced by the hierarchical and patriarchal world in which the dramatic action is set.

The crucial element in this panoply of 'feminine virtues' is a capacity to 'will' only that which her male mentors would will on her behalf. This does, of course, rule out the possibility of Käthchen having an independent 'personality' in her own right and means that she is only a puppet manipulated by her (male) puppet-masters. Nonetheless, in a blatant display of *mauvaise foi*, the male characters and, above all, Strahl, interpret this self-lessness (*sic*) on her part as a mark of her benevolent womanly nature. By making her behave in an absurdly exaggerated manner – throwing herself out of windows in pursuit of her beloved and entering burning castles to save his portrait – Kleist sows further doubts in the mind of the audience as to the correctness of the (masculine) interpretation that is placed upon Käthchen's heroics. Indeed, when Strahl describes her devotion as 'dog-like' [P, 310] ('hündische Dienstfertigkeit'; *SW* I, 495; 1866), his assessment is far closer to the truth than he realises. For Käthchen has absorbed the norms of her masculine creators to such a degree that she is incapable of acting as an autonomous individual. She risks her life by entering the burning castle, but she does so not out of love for Strahl, but because she has been 'trained' to do whatever her 'master' demands of her, and in this, she is little more than an obedient 'pet'. If she appears to be devoted to Strahl, this is only because she has been programmed to behave like a devotee.[15] Indeed Strahl would be advised not to scrutinise her behaviour too closely or he will risk recognising the patent absurdity of his 'creation'; he will realise that a woman who lacks any sense of herself as an autonomous agent is incapable of love, since love (as opposed to the recovery of pictures from burning castles) is not a question of duty, but a question of the free personal choice of the lover. In addition, Strahl would be forced to acknowledge that no matter how many 'Tests of Fire' ('Feuerproben') he subjects her to, he can never be absolutely certain of her love for him. The fact that he can rely upon her absolute devotion is, paradoxically, the very thing which prevents him from ever being loved by her: the perfect grace of the puppet can be won only at the cost of its human freedom.

The puppet-maker may have succeeded in producing more 'grace' than the human dancers, but not a human dancer with more grace, and it is in this sense that such 'puppets' are both the reward – and the punishment – for their creators.

Kleist presents Käthchen as, quite literally, the woman of Strahl's dreams. Strahl is frustrated by the lack of a suitable female partner – 'he said; the girl who could love him, had not appeared to him. Life without love was death' [P, 286] ('das Mädchen, das fähig wäre, ihn zu lieben, sei nicht vorhanden; Leben aber ohne Liebe sei Tod'; *SW* I, 469; 1160–1) – and his dream is a reflection of his desire to believe that not only does such a woman exist, but she is 'predestined' to be won by him. He therefore 'dreams up' an ideal woman, and after act IV, scene 2, is convinced that in Käthchen he has found her. In reality, he has simply projected the elements of this wish-fulfilling fantasy onto Käthchen. And although he marvels at the way in which the two halves of 'their' dream fit together perfectly 'like the two halves of a ring' ('wie die zwei Hälften eines Ringes'; *SW* I, 516; 2321), the fact is, as we shall see, it could hardly be otherwise.

From Brigitte's account in act II, scene 9, we learn that Strahl had a dream on New Year's Eve in which he is led by an angel to the one woman whom, as he explains to his mother, 'heaven has ordained for me' [P, 287] ('mir der Himmel bestimmt hat'; *SW* I, 471; 1208). This woman, however, turns out to be a familiar, highly conventional masculine fantasy made flesh. For in Brigitte's account we are told:

> wie es dagelegen, das holde Kind, mit nichts, als dem Hemdchen angetan, und die Augen bei seinem Anblick groß aufgemacht . . .; wie sie . . . vom Purpur der Freude über und über schimmernd, aus dem Bette gestiegen, und sich auf Knieen vor ihm niedergelassen, das Haupt gesenkt, und: mein hoher Herr! gelispelt; (*SW* I, 471; 1222–9)

> (how she had lain there, the sweet child, in her night-gown, had opened her eyes wide at the sight of him . . .; how then, her face agleam all over with the flush of joy, she had risen from the bed and thrown herself on her knees before him, with bowed head, and murmured, My noble lord;) [P, 287]

What is more, the angel tells Strahl that the woman is a Kaiser's daughter, a detail which must be very reassuring for a man of his social rank. Similarly, when we turn to Käthchen's dream, we find that it too is a highly conventional fantasy, albeit one tailored to the demands of an adolescent girl of her social class: 'a tall and handsome knight would marry me' ('Ein großer, schöner Ritter würd mich heuern'; *SW* I, 506; 2092).[16] Thus whilst Strahl's dream is a classic wish-fulfilment fantasy operating at an individual level, Käthchen's dream is a similar fantasy enacted at a social level.

When the two 'halves' of this 'shared' dream are slotted together in act IV, it is hardly surprising that the fit is so good, since they are derived from the same source: the prescriptive conventions of a hierarchical and predominantly male-oriented society. Thus when, in act IV, scene 2, Käthchen tells Strahl 'her' dream, he supplies the bulk of its content. He may say, 'tell me about this dream, my Käthchen,' ('Erzähl mir doch etwas davon, mein Käthchen!'; *SW* I, 507; 2114), but it is he who fills in the details of the setting when he 'asks' (i.e. tells her) 'You were lying there on haircloth cushions, weren't you, the sheets were white, the blanket red?' ('Auf einem härnen Kissen lagst du da, | Das Bettuch weiß, die wollne Decke rot?'; *SW* I, 508; 2124–5). Käthchen's response: 'That's right! just so!' [P, 322] ('Ganz recht! so wars!'; *SW* I, 508; 2126) should not be taken – as Strahl takes it – as confirmation of any actual matters of fact, but simply as an indication that she approves of his account of 'her' dream. Similarly, the 'answers' she gives in her sleep are little more than prompts which enable Strahl to construct his own fantasy-version, as can be seen very clearly in the following exchange as the scene approaches its climax:

> DER GRAF Sahst groß, mit schwarzem Aug, mich an?
> KÄTHCHEN Ja, weil ich glaubt, es wär ein Traum.
> DER GRAF Stiegst langsam,
> An allen Gliedern zitternd, aus dem Bett,
> Und sankst zu Füßen mir – ?
> KÄTHCHEN Und flüsterte –
> DER GRAF *unterbricht sie*
> Und flüstertest, mein hochverehrter Herr!
>
> (*SW* I, 508; 2130–4)

(THE COUNT: And then you looked at me with your dark eyes, didn't you? KÄTHCHEN: Yes, because I thought it was all a dream. THE COUNT: Slowly you got out of bed, trembling in every limb, and sank down on the ground before me, didn't you? KÄTHCHEN: And then I whispered – THE COUNT (*interrupting her*) And then you whispered 'My noble lord!')

Not only, then, does Strahl provide both halves of the 'script', but he also 'directs' Käthchen in her part, and she proves to be an eager pupil. Nonetheless, we can only 'admire' her 'composure' when Strahl's narration takes an unacceptably erotic turn: 'There you were wearing only a thin nightgown, weren't you?' ('Im bloßen leichten Hemdchen?'; *SW* I, 508; 2126). Käthchen herself explicitly denies this: 'Only my nightgown? Surely not.' ('Im Hemdchen? – Nein'; *SW* I, 508; 2127). However, despite this initial reluctance to accept 'direction', she comes to terms with the 'nude scene' a few lines later, when she says: 'I was lying there on the ground wearing only my thin nightgown' ('Ich lag im Hemdchen auf der Erde da'; *SW* I, 509; 2142). Käthchen manages to master most of the role Strahl has in mind for her, but she cannot – of her own accord – turn herself into the promised 'Kaiser's daughter', a matter that is of some concern to Strahl:

> Denn wie begreif ich die Verkündigung,
> Die mir noch silbern wiederklingt im Ohr,
> Daß sie die Tochter meines Kaisers sei? (*SW* I, 509; 2161–3)

(For how shall I interpret that announcement, which through my ear yet echoes silvery, saying that she's the daughter of my emperor?) [P, 323]

However, this particular 'discrepancy' between Käthchen and the 'woman of his dreams' is not enough to make Strahl doubt the reliability of the 'evidence' of the dream. Of course we might recall that this is not the first time that he has 'matched up' a real woman with the ideal woman of his dreams; he was prepared to overlook those aspects of Kunigunde which did not conform to the dream, and now he manages to turn a blind eye – at least temporarily – to Käthchen's lowly origins.

THE DENOUEMENT

As the patent artificiality – and comedy – of the play's fairy-tale ending demonstrate, Käthchen's apparent lack of social status turns out to be of little significance. For the rulers of the world in which the play is set have the capacity to make or unmake reality as they choose in accordance with the interests of the class to which they belong. Indeed, it is precisely through the adroit manipulation of such fictions that those in power are able to conceal the extent to which the prevailing structures of social organisation are not in the least 'natural', but on the contrary, reflect their personal interests. Thus when Strahl presents his 'evidence' that Käthchen is indeed the Kaiser's daughter, the Kaiser is confronted with a set of circumstances which – if brought to light – might seriously damage the social order over which he presides, and as he (quite rightly) exclaims, 'Oh heaven! the world is out of joint!' [P, 333] ('O Himmel! Die Welt wankt aus ihren Fugen!'; *SW* 1, 519; 2424–5). Rather than admit that an aristocrat, let alone he, the Kaiser, could succumb to his sexual passion for a commoner, he opts instead for the solution 'put forward' by Strahl's 'angel of God' ('Engel Gottes'):

so werd ich die Verkündigung wahrmachen, den Theobald, unter welchem Vorwand es sei, bewegen müssen, daß er mir dies Kind abtrete, und sie mit ihm verheiraten müssen: will ich nicht wagen, daß der Cherub zum zweitenmal zur Erde steige und das ganze Geheimnis, das ich hier den vier Wänden anvertraut, ausbringe! (*SW* 1, 519–20; 2427–32)

(I will make this annunciation come true, compel Theobald, under some pretext or other, to entrust the child to me, and have her marry him. I'll not risk letting the cherub for the second time descend to earth, and reveal the whole secret that I here entrust to these four walls.) [P, 333]

For the Kaiser, a fairy-tale 'explanation' – no matter how ridiculous – is infinitely preferable to the truth, and thus Käthchen ends the play as she began it, as a being whose identity is determined wholly by the needs and desires of the masculine elite. For she who began the play as Theobald's daughter, Käthchen, is 'miraculously' transformed into a member of the Kaiser's family, Katharina von Schwaben.

CONCLUSION

In *Penthesilea* and *Das Käthchen von Heilbronn*, Kleist presents us with two diametrically opposed forms of society. One we know from history as a male-oriented feudal aristocracy, in which women are kept under the heels first of their fathers and then of their husbands. The other, the Amazon state, constitutes a radical attempt to portray a completely novel form of society, the institutions of which are designed and operated entirely by women even to the extent that men are physically excluded from them. In choosing such a setting, Kleist is able to portray a society in which the traditionally marginalised elements of gentleness and co-operation become the dominant force in what is an essentially 'nurturing society'.[17] By contrasting the Amazons with the Greeks, Kleist shows what can happen when a vicious 'transcendent' ideal of male superiority is allowed free reign in the absence of civilising feminine influences. But the contrast between the situations of the female characters in *Penthesilea* and *Das Käthchen von Heilbronn* is also very revealing. The Amazon women are considerably assisted by their benevolent society, and in his characterisation of Prothoe in particular, Kleist shows the heights to which human beings can aspire when given the right kind of support. Käthchen, on the other hand, receives no assistance from the male-oriented world she inhabits and she has little or no opportunity to develop any of the characteristics of the Amazon women, such as character, strength of will or physical competence, and, as a result, what humanity she has can be expressed only in her fawning 'dog-like devotion'. In short, she is obliged to conceal her feminine qualities behind a façade of pseudo-femininity.

PART IV

Kleist and the national question

CHAPTER 8

Die Hermannsschlacht

Given the negative tone of Kleist's earliest correspondence, his condemnation of the Prussian military hierarchy and his despair of ever finding a suitable position within the equally hierarchically-structured civil service, it might seem surprising that he should commit himself so whole-heartedly to the Prussian cause towards the end of his life. However, whilst Kleist was indeed critical of the conditions in his own country, it was Napoleonic France that he despised above all else. For it was in Paris that Kleist – like so many of his contemporaries – was confronted with the grotesque caricature of the ideals of his eighteenth-century upbringing. In his letter of 15 August 1801, we find him writing to Wilhelmine:

> Zuweilen, wenn ich in die Bibliotheken ansehe, wo in prächtigen Sälen und in prächtigen Bänden die Werke Rousseaus, Helvetius', Voltaires stehen, so denke ich, was haben sie genutzt? Hat ein einziges seinen Zweck erreicht? Haben sie das Rad aufhalten können, das unaufhaltsam stürzend seinem Abgrund entgegeneilt? (*SW* II, 681)

> (Sometimes, when I see the libraries with their magnificent halls and all the works of Rousseau, Helvetius, and Voltaire that stand there, in magnificent bindings, I think to myself: of what use have they been? Has one of these works achieved its goal? Have they been able to slow the wheel that, plunging inexorably, speeds towards the abyss?) [M, 123–4]

Kleist readily conceded that the French were – at least from a technological point of view – more advanced than the Germans, but in his view this had simply produced a wholly corrupt and materialistically-oriented society, in which individual human beings were reduced to automata. His experiences in Paris seemed to offer a glimpse of what was to come if Prussian society followed the same course and encouraged him to view conditions in his native land in a more favourable light, as we can see from his letter of 28 July 1801 to Adolfine von Werdeck:

> *Gleim* in Halberstadt nahm mir das Versprechen ab, als *ein Deutscher* zurückzukehren in mein Vaterland. Es wird mir nicht schwer werden, dieses Versprechen zu halten. (*SW* II, 675)

> (Gleim obtained my promise in Halberstadt to return to my Fatherland *a German*. It will not be difficult to keep this promise.) [M, 119]

Indeed, it is his experiences in Paris that explain the development of his patriotic fervour. And thus the vehemence of his anti-French rhetoric, both in his personal correspondence and in his political essays of 1809, should not be taken as crude chauvinism; rather it is an expression of disgust at the way the enlightened ideals of the French Revolution had been reduced to a set of bourgeois conventions under the *Système Napoléon*.

Disenchanted with what he had witnessed in Paris, Kleist left for his Rousseauesque idyll on the Swiss island of Thun. Even here, though, the ever-threatening presence of Napoleon revived his loathing of the French experiment, and the imperialistic ambitions of its hero drove him to write to Ulrike on 19 February 1802: 'it seems very likely that Switzerland and the Cisalpine Republic will fall into the hands of the French and the mere thought fills me with disgust' ('Es hatte allen Anschein, daß die Schweiz sowie Zisalpinien, französisch werden wird, und mich ekelt vor dem bloßen Gedanken'; *SW* II, 718). It was not long before his worst fears proved correct. The example of Switzerland served as a warning of the dangers that lay in store for those who might be tempted to co-operate with Napoleon and the French. Kleist understood better than so many of his contemporaries that no nation could become part of the Napoleonic empire and hope to retain its freedom. He wrote as much to his friend Rühle von Lilienstern at the end of November 1805:

> Es wird sich aus dem ganzen kultivierten Teil von Europa ein einziges, großes System von Reichen bilden, und die Throne mit neuen, von Frankreich abhängigen, Fürstendynastien besetzt werden. (*SW* II, 761)

> (From the whole of civilised Europe one single huge system of realms will emerge, each throne occupied by new dynasties in thrall to the French.) [M, 163]

And his letter to Ulrike of 24 October 1806 shows that he was under no illusions as to the real purpose of French expansionism: 'The aim is to plunder all of Europe in order to make France rich' [M, 167] ('Es ist auf eine Ausplünderung von Europa abgesehen, um Frankreich reich zu machen'; *SW* II, 771). At the same time he notes that, 'only a very few people understand what a disaster it would be to fall under his [Napoleon's] rule' [M, 167] ('Nur ein sehr kleiner Teil der Menschen begreift, was für ein Verderben es ist, unter seine Herrschaft zu kommen'; *SW* II, 771). Worse still – from Kleist's point of view – was the fact that many of his contemporaries openly admired the achievements of Napoleon[1] and believed that their own interests could be best served through some form of *entente cordiale* with the French Emperor. Indeed, it was the inability of those around him to appreciate the true nature of freedom that was to give Kleist so much cause for concern, and at the same time, to provide a source of artistic inspiration for him in the years to come.

In the *Katechismus der Deutschen* (*The German Catechism*) Kleist not only provides us with an uncompromisingly realistic picture of the Germans as a people, but at the same time offers us a glimpse of his own vision of political freedom. Patriotism, as Kleist understands it, is not a question of chauvinistic national pride, but rather the love of freedom for its own sake. And the love of freedom (like the love of one human being for another) is a relation that excludes all considerations of self-interest. Accordingly, genuine patriotism cannot be made conditional on the country in question possessing (or lacking) certain attributes, a point Kleist makes very clearly in the second section of the *Katechismus der Deutschen*. Thus when the questioner asks if the respondent loves his fatherland ('Vaterland') merely:

> weil Gott es gesegnet hat mit vielen Früchten, weil viele schöne Werke der Kunst es schmücken, weil Helden, Staatsmänner und Weise, deren Namen anzuführen kein Ende ist, es verherrlicht haben . . . (*SW* II, 351)

> (because God has blessed it with an abundance of riches, because it has given rise to many beautiful works of art, because its reputation has been glorified by the deeds and works of countless heroes, statesmen and thinkers . . .)

the respondent not only repudiates this suggestion, but goes to considerable lengths to draw attention to the cultural backwardness of the Germans as a race:

Denn Rom und das ägyptische Delta sind, wie du mich gelehrt hast, mit Früchten und schönen Werken der Kunst, und allem, was groß und herrlich sein mag, weit mehr gesegnet, als Deutschland. (*SW* II, 351)

(For as you have taught me, Rome and the Egyptian Delta have been blessed with far greater riches and far more beautiful works of art, with far more that is great and glorious than has Germany.)

The true patriot cannot offer any rational grounds for his love of his country; he simply makes a pledge of unswerving allegiance: 'QUESTION: Why do you love [your fatherland]? [. . .] RESPONSE: Because it is my fatherland' ('FRAGE: Warum liebst du [dein Vaterland]? [. . .] ANTWORT: Weil es mein Vaterland ist'; *SW* II, 351). At the same time, Kleist appreciated that, in the eyes of the culturally backward Germans, the French seemed a far more sophisticated people and that many of his fellow countrymen believed they would profit (materially and culturally) from French rule. There was every reason to believe that this would, at least in the short term, be the case, but Kleist's experiences in Paris had left him in no doubt as to the long-term effects of such 'progress'. And in the eighth section of the *Katechismus der Deutschen*, he launches an attack on the German willingness to sacrifice freedom in exchange for material comfort. In answer to the question 'What is it that [the Germans] worship in so excessive and unworthy a fashion?' ('Woran hingen [die Deutschen], mit unmäßiger und unedler Liebe?') comes the following reply:

An Geld und Gut, trieben Handel und Wandel damit, daß ihnen der Schweiß, ordentlich des Mitleidens würdig, von der Stirn triefte, und meinten, ein ruhiges, gemächliches und sorgenfreies Leben sei alles, was sich in der Welt erringen ließe. (*SW* II, 356)

(Wealth and possessions. So busy are they arranging their business transactions that you can see the sweat dripping from their brows to such an extent that one feels sorry for them. All the while, however, they maintain that the only thing worth striving for is a peaceful, leisurely existence free from worry.)

Kleist saw only too clearly that France's successful expansionism owed less to Napoleon's skills as a military strategist, than to his ability to impress the leaders of other nations and convince them of the benefits that they would reap from a 'voluntary' acceptance of French culture and technology. Accordingly, if the Germans were to succeed in preventing the advance of French imperialism, it would be vital for them not to become complicit in their own oppression.

Kleist saw the cultural backwardness of the Germans as, paradoxically, their saving grace: the very fact that the nation was at an earlier stage of development meant that it might still avoid making the same mistakes as the French. Accordingly, his patriotic fervour reflects, above all, his desire to preserve – and to a certain degree, create – a system of social organisation in which individual freedom would find its fullest expression. As he writes in the essay *Was gilt es in diesem Kriege?* (*What are we fighting for in this war?*), in taking up arms against the French, the aim was not the pursuit of 'something that can be measured in financial terms'; *SW* II, 377), but on the contrary, the preservation of:

Eine Gemeinschaft, die, unbekannt mit dem Geist der Herrschsucht und der Eroberung, des Daseins und der Duldung so würdig ist, wie irgend eine; die ihren Ruhm nicht einmal denken kann, sie müßte denn den Ruhm zugleich und das Heil aller übrigen denken, die den Erdkreis bewohnen. (*SW* II, 378)

(A form of society which, having no truck with notions of domination and conquest, deserves to exist and be tolerated by others; a state which cannot harbour thoughts of its own glory without simultaneously taking due account of the glory and well-being of all the other states in the world.)

As we shall see, when this image of an ideal confederation of autonomous states is compared with Hermann's vision of the future at the end of *Die Hermannsschlacht*, the disparity between Kleist's own views and those of the play's protagonist becomes apparent.

Despite the optimistic tone of *Was gilt es in diesem Kriege?*, Kleist never lost sight of the realities of human behaviour. He recognised that most people had little notion of the true nature of freedom and were, therefore, quite willing to throw in their lot with any leader who seemed likely to satisfy their (predominantly material) needs and desires. He also recognised the potency of false ideologies claiming to represent the 'true nature' of Man and knew how they could sway ordinary men and women – a point he makes in his analysis of French propaganda techniques in the *Lehrbuch der französischen Journalistik* (*Manual of French journalism*). He was in little doubt that the heavily-censored, pro-government *Moniteur* played a key role in preserving the *status quo* in France, and in the opening section of his treatise he writes, 'The art of French journalism is to make the masses believe whatever happens to suit the government' ('*Die französische Journalistik* ist die Kunst, das Volk glauben zu machen, was die Regierung für gut findet'; *SW* II, 361). Moreover, when he goes on to characterise the two fundamental principles underlying the successful dissemination of propaganda, saying: 'The masses do not get excited about matters they never hear of. If you tell them something three times, they will believe it to be true' ('Was das Volk nicht weiß, macht das Volk nicht heiß. Was man dem Volk dreimal sagt, hält das Volk für wahr'; *SW* II, 361), he offers a realistic, if depressing, assessment of the political awareness of the ordinary members of society. However, he can hardly have been unaware that there were factions within his own country advocating the use of similar propaganda techniques to whip up anti-French sentiment.[2] He also saw – as is clear from the critical tone of the *Lehrbuch der französischen Journalistik* as well as from his other writings – that the use of such propaganda would encourage the blind acceptance of precisely those spurious scientific and philosophical notions that threatened individual freedom. The Prussian Reformers might incite the Germans to rise up against Napoleon by using anti-French propaganda, but they should not, he argued, imagine that such resistance could be attributed to a genuine love of freedom. For whilst the leaders had a real choice between freedom and enslavement, the bulk of the population had made their choice essentially irrationally, seeing their short-term selfish interests as better served by the one regime than the other. Moreover, Kleist foresaw that once the structures of authority had been successfully restored through the use of such suspect methods, those in command would be tempted to resort to the same measures time and again to preserve the *status quo* and with it their own positions of power.[3]

On 1 January 1809, Kleist sent the manuscript of a new play, *Die Hermannsschlacht*, to the Austrian dramatist, Heinrich von Collin, together with a request that he press for a production at the earliest possible opportunity. Some four months later, impatient at the apparent lack of progress, he wrote again, asking:

Doch, wie stehts, mein teuerster Freund, mit der Hermannsschlacht? Sie können leicht denken, wie sehr mir die Aufführung dieses Stücks, das einzig und allein auf diesen Augenblick berechnet war, am Herzen liegt. (*SW* II, 824)

(Tell me, my friend, what is happening with *Die Hermannsschlacht?* I am sure you can imagine how deeply concerned I am that this play, which was written expressly for the current situation, be performed.)

In fact, the political circumstances were such that the play could not be performed even in Austria, and whilst Kleist may have been disappointed by this he can hardly have been surprised, for of all his works, none was more closely related to contemporary political events than *Die Hermannsschlacht.* When he started work on the play – almost certainly sometime in mid-1808 – the situation in Prussia had become critical. With the institution of the Rheinland Confederation in July 1806, the last vestiges of the Holy Roman Empire had disappeared and, at the battles of Jena and Auerstedt, the Prussian army suffered crushing defeats at the hands of Napoleon's forces. This in turn was followed by a massive reduction in territory coupled with the removal of the court and administration from Berlin to Königsberg. But, although French domination was now firmly in place, by 1808 the tide had started to turn against Napoleon and his imperial armies. In Spain there had been a successful uprising against the French and in Prussia itself there were moves to instigate a popular uprising that would result in the overthrow of the foreign invaders.[4] But for men like Stein, Scharnhorst and Gneisenau, all of whom were associated with the Prussian Reform Movement, the real motive for planning such a revolt was not just the removal of the French, but the implementation of an altogether new political dispensation. The similarity between the views of the Prussian Reformers and those of Kleist is very striking, not least between the latter's concept of a confederation of autonomous states outlined in the essay *Was gilt es in diesem*

Krieg? and Gneisenau's memorandum to the Prussian king, in which he writes: 'We recognise all Germans as our comrades and solemnly declare that it is not our intention to amalgamate their territory with ours; only those German peoples who wish to live with us and share the same laws will become members of our federation' ('Wir erkennen alle Deutsche als unsere Brüder und erklären feierlich, daß wir nicht die Absicht haben, ihr Gebiet mit dem unsrigen zu vereinigen; nur diejenigen . . ., welche mit uns unter gemeinschaftlichen Gesetzen leben wollen, werden in unsern Bund aufgenommen'; GN, 19). Significantly, from this point on, the talk is not of Prussia, but of Germany. But whilst the declared aims of the Prussian Reformers may have been admirable, some of the means they proposed to use to bring about their ends were more questionable. In Stein, the Prussian administration had discovered a man who, though he longed to oust the French, admired Napoleon's methods enough to resort to them himself if necessary.[5] And thus we find him urging the Prussian king to be less scrupulous in his dealings with the French on the ground that he should combat their deceit with lies and treachery of his own.[6]

Kleist was determined to make his own contribution to the contemporary upsurge of patriotic feeling in his native Prussia; the result was *Die Hermannsschlacht*.[7] As we shall see, however, although it is a patriotic play, it is not a straightforward propaganda work urging the audience to abandon all considerations of morality in the service of the 'national cause'. Rather it draws the audience's attention to the horrors of violent conflict and warns the would-be leader of any such revolution that, if successful, he will be tempted to do nothing more than replace the imperialist system he has overthrown with one of his own, no less brutal and oppressive. On closer examination, *Die Hermannsschlacht* reveals itself to be a good deal more complex than many of its detractors have been willing to admit, and forms an integral part of the Kleistian *œuvre*.[8]

HERMANN

In the opening scenes of *Die Hermannsschlacht*, we see the German chieftains, a group of solid, home-loving individuals, hopelessly divided by self-interest and, as a result, particularly vulnerable in the face of the Romans' strategy of divide-and-rule. Hermann himself has no illusions as to the weaknesses of these allies and realises that they are quite incapable of presenting a united front to the Roman invaders:

> Denn setzt einmal, ihr Herrn, ihr stündet
> (Wohin ihr es im Lauf der Ewigkeit nicht bringt)
> Dem Varus kampfverbunden gegenüber; (*SW* I, 543; 245–7)

(Supposing, my lords, that you were to put up a united front – something you would never manage, even if you had all eternity – and took on Varus and his legions.)

He is equally certain that they will be crushed if they try to tackle the well-organised Roman legions head-on.[9] The crucial difference between Hermann and the other chieftains is that he genuinely understands the meaning of freedom. They fall into the trap of equating freedom with the preservation of their personal possessions and the safety of their loved-ones, whereas he recognises that one's first duty to oneself is to be an autonomous individual and that to give up one's freedom is to give up one's selfhood, to become the chattel of another. Against this, all other duties to oneself are as nothing. And from this it follows that the individual who truly loves freedom must be prepared to sacrifice even his life in the process of asserting that freedom. As he says to the uncomprehending chieftains:

> So weit im Kreise mir der Welt
> Das Heer der munteren Gedanken reichet,
> Erstreb ich und bezweck ich nichts,
> Als jenem Römerkaiser zu erliegen.
> Das aber möcht ich gern mit Ruhm, ihr Brüder,
> Wies einem deutschen Fürsten ziemt: (*SW* I, 542; 228–33)

(As far as the future is concerned, I have only one aim: to be defeated by that Roman Emperor. But this I intend to do with glory, brothers, as befits a German chieftain.)

It is of no consequence to Hermann whether he lives or dies in asserting his right to freedom, since, for such an individual, a life of slavery is no life at all. From this it can be inferred that the individual who has such freedom must strive to continue in this state or he will cease to 'exist'. So when threatened by the imperialist ambitions of Rome, Hermann has no option but to resist enslavement: nothing ventured, everything lost. And obviously, if an individual like Hermann is 'overcome' by the Romans, he does not lose his freedom because in resisting (and continuing to resist) he is constantly reasserting it. What matters is not the success or failure of such resistance, but the act of resistance itself. Indeed it is a mark of Hermann's integrity, that at no point does he hold out the prospect of success in order to tempt the others into following his chosen course of action; if anything he is unduly pessimistic about his chances of overcoming the Romans:

> Welch ein wahnsinnger Tor
> Müßt ich doch sein, wollt ich mir und der Heeresschar,
> Die ich ins Feld des Todes führ, erlauben,
> Das Aug, von dieser finstern Wahrheit ab,
> Buntfarbgen Siegesbildern zuzuwenden,
> Und gleichwohl dann gezwungen sein,
> In dem gefährlichen Momente der Entscheidung,
> Die ungeheure Wahrheit anzuschaun? (*SW* I, 545; 342–9)

(What a fool I would be, if I allowed myself and my army in the field to be distracted from the appalling truth by dazzling images of victory, only to have to confront the monstrous truth in the danger of the decisive hour itself.)

It is Hermann's realistic appraisal of the situation that sets him apart from the well-intentioned, but essentially sentimental Wolf,[10] who recognises that the other leaders' blinkered pursuit of their own interests is playing into the hands of the Romans,[11] but who fails to appreciate the relative strengths and weaknesses of the Germans and their adversaries. For Wolf accepts the prevailing stereotype of the Romans as an 'invincible' race of 'demi-gods':

> Es ist umsonst, Thuskar, wir sind verloren!
> Rom, dieser Riese, der, das Mittelmeer beschreitend,
> Gleich dem Koloß von Rhodus, trotzig,
> Den Fuß auf Ost und Westen setzet,
> Des Parthers mutgen Nacken hier,
> Und dort den tapfern Gallier niedertretend:
> Er wirft auch jetzt uns Deutsche in den Staub.
> (*SW* I, 535; 1–7)

(It is all in vain, Thuiskomar, we are done for! Rome, this giant, who strides across the Mediterranean like the Colossus of Rhodes, defiantly stamping on East and West, here crushing the Parthians into submission, there beating down the plucky Gauls; Rome will rub our German noses into the dirt as well.)

More seriously, however, Wolf's unswerving devotion to the German cause has left him with a sentimental notion that his fellow-countrymen are a race of brave and hardy fighters. This leads him to imagine that if the Germans could marshal all their forces for one final battle, they might defeat the Romans – a view, which is not only unrealistic, but contradicts what he has said earlier. When this idea is dismissed out of hand, he is taken aback by what he perceives as Hermann's lack of patriotism:

> Es scheint, du hältst dies Volk des fruchtumblühten Latiens
> Für ein Geschlecht von höhrer Art,
> Bestimmt, uns roh're Kauze zu beherrschen?
>
> (*SW* 1, 544; 300–2)

(It would seem you regard these richly-endowed Latins as a superior race whose destiny is to rule over primitive savages like us.)

But whilst Hermann has few illusions about the current technological backwardness of the Germans, he is diplomatically sanguine about the possibility of their overcoming this:

> Hm! In gewissem Sinne sag ich: ja.
> Ich glaub, der Deutsch' erfreut sich einer größern
> Anlage, der Italier doch hat seine mindre
> In diesem Augenblicke mehr entwickelt. (*SW* 1, 544; 303–6)

(Well, there is a sense in which I would agree with you. I think the German race is endowed with superior talents; but at the present moment, these Italians have exploited their lesser talents to a greater degree.)

He goes on to outline his vision of the future: a confederation of states under some great leader (not necessarily a German) which, unlike the Roman Empire, would tolerate within its rule a wider range of cultural diversity and permit a genuine degree of national autonomy for each of the individual member-states:

> Wenn sich der Barden Lied erfüllt,
> Und, unter *einem* Königsszepter,
> Jemals die ganze Menschheit sich vereint,
> So läßt, daß es ein Deutscher führt, sich denken
> Ein Britt', ein Gallier, oder wer ihr wollt;

Doch nimmer jener Latier, beim Himmel!
Der keine andre Volksnatur
Verstehen kann und ehren, als nur seine.

(*SW* I, 544–5; 307–14)

(When the prophetic words of the bards' song come true and all mankind is united under the rule of *one* royal sceptre, it is quite conceivable that it will be wielded by a German, a Briton or a Gaul; but not by one of those Latins, by God, who have no understanding or respect for any other culture than their own.)

These remarks suggest – at least at this stage – that Hermann does not intend to replace the imperialist domination of Rome with a new and equally oppressive form of German imperialism.

THUSNELDA

Kleist uses the lovers, Thusnelda and Ventidius, to explore the possibility that their 'mutual loving trust' might offer a means of transcending the conflict between Roman and German culture. However, as the violent denouement of this relationship shows, it is precisely within this allegedly transcendent realm that such ideological conflicts are played out in all their ferocity. This affair is not simply a sub-plot and has important parallels with the main action of the play. For just as Thusnelda looks to love as a blessed sphere of human activity in which Roman and German might meet on equal terms and in total openness, so too the German leaders are tempted to believe in the existence of a 'higher' political understanding in which the apparent conflict between their interests and those of Rome could be transcended and harmoniously reconciled. At the same time, Hermann's manipulation of the Ventidius-Thusnelda affair highlights how profoundly he understands human behaviour. He recognises that human beings are all too ready to believe in the existence of a 'higher realm', wholly detached from social and political reality, and that, as a result, they are tempted to credit others with splendid qualities they do not possess, leaving themselves hopelessly exposed to exploitation by the ruthless natures they have so callowly misjudged. This is exactly the case with Thusnelda.[12] Strictly speaking, Hermann does not have to manipulate this affair, since both of the participants seem perfectly willing to act out their 'roles' without any prompting on his part. Thusnelda professes herself to be a reluctant participant in Hermann's plan to trick the Romans;[13] the truth is, however, she enjoys the image of herself she sees reflected in the gaze of her admirer.[14] She knows that she was never in any danger during the hunting episode of act I, scene 2, but she would dearly like to believe that a man with Ventidius's hard-headed sense of self-interest and with so much to lose, would see in her a woman worth risking his life for. Her unwillingness to countenance the idea that, in his eyes, she is a being of no account, fit only to provide the raw materials for Roman wig-makers and cosmetic dentists, blinds her to the facts about Ventidius that are so obvious to her husband, who does not hesitate to tell her: 'I love my dog more than he loves you' ('Ich liebe meinen Hund mehr, als er dich'; *SW* I, 557; 679). But rather than face up to the reality of her situation, she accuses him of prejudice:

> Dich macht, ich seh, dein Römerhaß ganz blind.
> Weil als dämonenartig dir
> Das Ganz' erscheint, so kannst du dir
> Als sittlich nicht den Einzelnen gedenken. (*SW* I, 557; 685–8)

(I see that your hatred of the Romans has made you blind. Because you think that all Romans are monstrous, you are unable to countenance the possibility that there may be individual Romans who are perfectly decent.)

As the drama unfolds, the extent of her self-deception is gradually brought home to Thusnelda. In act III, scene 3, Hermann sets out to shatter her illusions about the alleged humanity of the 'civilised' Romans. When she appears dressed in the fashion of a Roman lady, he points out that the 'beauty' of Roman women is routinely maintained with the aid of plaits of hair and teeth taken from the women of nations oppressed by Rome. In so doing, he brutally exposes the way in which the edifice of Roman culture, of which she is so in awe, is built upon the oppression and exploitation of people like herself.

> Für wen erschaffen ward die Welt, als Rom?
> Nimmt August nicht dem Elefanten
> Das Elfenbein, das Öl der Bisamkatze,

Dem Panthertier das Fell, dem Wurm die Seide?
Was soll der Deutsche hier zum voraus haben?
(*SW* I, 570; 1061–5)

(For whom else was the world made if not for Rome? Does not the Emperor Augustus obtain ivory from the elephant, oil from the musk, fur from the panther and silk from the worm? Why should it be any different for us Germans?)

Hermann is even more concerned by the fact that his wife subscribes to an equally unrealistic notion of a 'universal humanity' shared by Romans and Germans alike. In act IV, scene 9, for example, she enthusiastically cites a number of instances of humane behaviour on the part of the Romans, quite unable to perceive the contradiction between, on the one hand, the genuinely humane – but essentially trivial – acts of some individual Roman soldiers, and on the other, the gross inhumanity that has furthered the aims of Roman imperialism. But Hermann points out that it is the over-valuation of such individual acts of kindness carried out by their oppressors that blinds his compatriots to the true nature of the Roman threat, and at the same time leads to well-intentioned Germans (like Thusnelda) becoming accomplices to their own subjection. Thus he dismisses the benevolent behaviour of the young Roman who rescued a German family from their burning house as insignificant when viewed in its proper context:

Er sei verflucht, wenn er mir das getan!
Er hat, auf einen Augenblick,
Mein Herz veruntreut, zum Verräter
An Deutschlands großer Sache mich gemacht!
Warum setzt' er Thuiskon mir in Brand? (*SW* I, 594; 1718–22)

(I would curse him for all eternity if he had done the same for me! For he would, momentarily, have touched my heart and made me betray Germany's great cause! Why did he set Thuiskon on fire in the first place?)

Moreover, his declaration: 'I do not *want* to love this insolent demonic pack! ('Ich *will* die höhnische Dämonenbrut nicht lieben!'; *SW* I, 594; 1723) is proof that he knows that anyone (himself included) is capable of such sentimental lapses, and that hostility towards the Roman invaders, far from being natural, is something that must be consciously cultivated by the freedom-fighter.[15] Hermann does not altogether rule out the possibility that a Roman could undergo a genuine change of heart, but such a change would not be indicated by the kind of actions cited by Thusnelda; it would have to consist in actively opposing the imperialist ambitions of Rome itself.

Although it is tempting to regard *Die Hermannsschlacht* as a play in which the notion of humanity is abandoned altogether, such a reading is explicitly contradicted by the text itself. It is not mere coincidence that Thusnelda, who is the play's most passionate advocate of humane behaviour, should be the one who perpetrates the play's most barbaric act of violence. She is cast headlong out of her heaven of magnanimity into a hell of bestial revenge and remorse because she confuses the world she inhabits with the (fictitious) 'transcendent' world of her imagination in which 'naturally' benevolent men and women cannot resist the attraction of an ideal society of co-operation and compassion. Like Sylvester in *Die Familie Schroffenstein*, she exchanges one unrealistically optimistic account of human nature (Man naturally good) for another, that, in its pessimism, is equally unrealistic (Man naturally evil). And once her illusions about Ventidius are finally shattered in act IV, scene 9, she cries to her husband, 'Go away, I beg you! I hate everything, the world, you, even myself: leave me alone!' (Geh, geh, ich bitte dich! Verhaßt ist alles, | Die Welt mir, du mir, ich: laß mich allein!'; *SW* I, 598; 1818–19). How different is this extravagant reaction from the sober assessment of the more realistically-inclined Hermann in act III, scene 4:

> Die Sach ist zehnmal schlimmer, als ichs machte,
> Und doch auch, wieder so betrachtet,
> Bei weitem nicht so schlimm. (*SW* I, 571; 1098–1100)

(Everything is ten times worse than I have told you, and yet, when you look at it again, not that bad at all.)

In devising the monstrous death of Ventidius in the arms of a she-bear ('Bärin'), she fondly imagines that this grotesque act of revenge will somehow purify her and make her 'worthy of Arminius once more' ('Arminius . . . wieder würdig'; *SW* I, 616; 2322). But what else can come out of this other than an agony of remorse as forecast by her maid, Gertrud, who warns her mistress:

> Die Rache der Barbaren sei dir fern!
> Es ist Ventidius nicht, der mich mit Sorg erfüllt;
> Du selbst, wenn nun die Tat getan,
> Von Reu und Schmerz wirst du zusammenfallen!
>
> (*SW* I, 616; 2317–20)

(Do not contemplate the revenge of the barbarians! It is not Ventidius for whom I am concerned, but you yourself: for when the deed is done, you will be struck down with pain and remorse.)

Thusnelda faints at the sound of Ventidius's screams, and when she reappears in the penultimate scene, haggard and almost monosyllabic – 'It is over now. Let us not speak of it' ('Das ist geschehn. Laß sein'; *SW* I, 625; 2545) – the catastrophic effect on her of her revenge is plain for all to see. Thusnelda stands as a lesson to all who succumb to the temptation to view life through the distorting lens of comforting half-truths and wish-fulfilling platitudes; sooner or later the reality they have shunned breaks in all the more furiously upon their unprepared consciences. Had Thusnelda taken a more realistic view of her situation, she might have recognised Ventidius for the exploitative seducer he was and thereby have avoided being drawn into the awful revenge she contrived for him. Instead we can only hope that, having learned the hard way, she will come to understand that all human beings (including herself) are capable of even the most savage acts of violence. For the present she must endure the 'pain and remorse' that accompanies the memory of her own behaviour.

VENTIDIUS AND THE ROMANS

Ventidius, like Thusnelda, has a distorted view of the situation in which he finds himself and this leads to his own terrible death and the barbaric massacre of an entire Roman army. In his self-satisfied sophistication, he sees the Germans as a race of sub-human primitives from whose ranks there could never arise a leader with the cunning and sagacity of an Arminius. Likewise, he supposes their women 'must' be naïve and simple, and Thusnelda, though the wife of a chief, 'must' be another harmless sentimental creature who cannot fail to succumb to the polished charms of a 'civilised' high-ranking Roman. It is his gross misunderstanding that delivers him to the terrible rendezvous with the 'she-bear'. His blindness is all too apparent in his reply in act III, scene 6, to Varus's question whether Hermann can be trusted:

> Quintilius! Das faß ich in zwei Worten!
> Er ist ein Deutscher.
> In einem Hämmling ist, der an der Tiber graset,
> Mehr Lug und Trug, muß ich dir sagen,
> Als in dem ganzen Volk, dem er gehört. (*SW* I, 576; 1249–53)

(Quintilius! I can answer that in one sentence. He's a German. There is more cunning and deceit in a lamb grazing on the banks of the Tiber than in the entire race to which he belongs.)

Of course it is ironic that Ventidius should endorse such a sentimental picture of the Germans when it is he, of all the Romans, who sees most clearly what lies behind the offer to help Hermann in his struggle against Marbod. Whilst he, the sophisticated career-diplomat, understands that the Romans' long-term aim is to dominate Cheruska, the plodding Varus is simply content to carry out his orders unquestioningly: 'It is not my job to speculate about the Emperor's plans' ('Es ist nicht meines Amtes | Den Willen meines Kaisers zu erspähn'; *SW* I, 577; 1273–4). Once again, however, it is the desire to believe in a mythical picture of the Germans as a race of 'noble savages', all valour and no guile and thus quite removed from the sophisticated politics of palace intrigue that prevents him (and Varus) from taking seriously the possibility that Hermann could betray his Roman allies. This smug undervaluation of the forces of the enemy is shared by the ordinary rank and file, who dismiss as 'irrational' anything that does not fit in with their preconceptions of how an army should fight. These reactions are of course typical of the false sense of superiority that characterises the lower orders of a nation that the luck of history has placed 'in charge' of the world. Thus when, as a result of their 'primitive' opponents' skill, the Romans are led astray in the forests and are, obligingly, walking into a disastrous ambush, they still manage to blame the 'silly' language of their opponents for their own geographical incompetence:

Pfiffikon! Iphikon! – Was das, beim Jupiter!
Für eine Sprache ist! Als schlüg ein Stecken
An einen alten, rostzerfreßnen Helm!
Ein Greulsystem von Worten, nicht geschickt,
Zwei solche Ding, wie Tag und Nacht,
Durch einen eignen Laut zu unterscheiden.

(*SW* I, 601; 1897–902)[16]

(Pfiffikon! Iphikon! – By Jupiter, what kind of a language is that! it sounds like a stick banging against an old rusty helmet! An abominable series of grunts incapable of distinguishing in a word between two such things as night and day.)

Here Kleist contrasts the crude rationality of the Romans, misapplied in their iron system of discipline, with the more flexible – but no less rational – thinking of the Germans fighting in a forest terrain of which they have complete mastery. As we shall see, it was the flawed nature of such a system of iron discipline that Kleist was to explore more fully in his next play, *Prinz Friedrich von Homburg*.

THE GERMAN WAY

Hermann triumphs over the Romans because he makes an uncompromisingly realistic assessment of the situation with which he is confronted. Firstly, he recognises that there are very few individuals who understand the true nature of freedom and are prepared to sacrifice everything in the attempt to preserve it. More importantly, however, he sees how effectively propaganda has been used to create the overweening confidence of the soldiers and officers of Rome. He therefore decides to use the same weapon himself, and circulates a false, but highly credible rumour that there is no atrocity too diabolic for the hated Romans to commit. He even goes as far as to fabricate evidence in support of this propaganda war. The highpoint of his campaign comes in the 'Hally-episode' of act IV, scene 6. Hermann orders the body of a young girl who has been raped by Roman soldiers to be cut up, and he sends a piece of her flesh to each of the German chieftains. In the context of the struggle this rape is an isolated, minor incident, but he guesses correctly that it will have repercussions out of all proportion to its seriousness. And he is right, for it is this 'stunt' that convinces the other German leaders to take up arms:

> Hally, die Jungfrau, die geschändete,
> Die du, des Vaterlandes grauses Sinnbild,
> Zerstückt in alle Stämme hast geschickt,
> Hat unsrer Völker Langmut aufgezehrt.
>
> (*SW* I, 625; 2548–51)

(Hally the defiled Virgin it was – that horrific symbol of the fatherland whose body you dispersed in pieces to all the tribes – that finally exhausted the patience of our people.)

These lines, spoken by the sentimental Wolf, are important as much for what they do not say as for what they do. It cannot have escaped Hermann's notice that the same men who, in the opening scene of the play, were unwilling to sacrifice a single possession for the sake of freedom are now prepared to risk all for the sake of a smith's daughter who was, it must be remembered, killed by her own father. In short, he may have succeeded in persuading them to join the fight and take revenge, but not to fight for the cause of freedom.

ARISTAN

There is only one other character in the play, apart from Hermann, who understands the true nature of freedom, and that is Aristan. Unlike the other German princes, who have unsuccessfully tried to maintain their independence by allowing the Roman troops to occupy strategic positions within their borders, Aristan has committed himself unequivocally to the Roman cause right from the start. For as Wolf says in act I, scene I:

> Aristan hat, der Ubier,
> Der ungroßmütigste von allen deutschen Fürsten,
> In Varus' Arme treulos sich geworfen; (*SW* I, 535; 11–13)

(Aristan, the disloyal Ubian, the most ignoble of all the German princes has thrown himself into Varus's arms.)

Aristan never expresses any desire to be part of any German confederation, believing, quite understandably, that his own interests are better served by forming an alliance with the Romans. Indeed, when questioned about his absence from the Battle of Ariovistus, he is only too quick – especially in the presence of Varus – to make the point that he has never had any thoughts of helping the Germans, replying 'icily' ('kalt und scharf'):

> Aristan war in Ubien,
> Diesseits des Rheines, wo er hingehörte.
> Aristan hat das Schwert niemals
> Den Cäsarn Roms gezückt, und er darf kühnlich sagen:
> Er war ihr Freund, sobald sie sich
> Nur an der Schwelle von Germania zeigten.
>
> (*SW* I, 575; 1229–34)

(Aristan was in Ubia on this side of the Rhine where he belongs. Aristan has never raised his sword against the Romans and he may claim quite boldly that he was their friend as soon as they set foot in Germania.)

Hermann's ironic response – 'Arminius admires his prudence' ('Arminius bewundert seine Weisheit'; *SW* I, 575; 1235) – acknowledges Aristan as someone who also understands the nature of freedom. For Hermann, like Aristan, knows that to be genuinely independent, a leader must be free to conclude an alliance with whomsoever he pleases. He is equally aware that, though the others regard Aristan as a 'traitor', the truth of the matter is that there has never been a German cause to betray.

Hermann orders his execution at the end of the play not because he is a 'traitor', but because he insists on asserting his independence right to the last. And when Aristan is led on in chains, he publicly challenges his executioner's appeal to a notion of a 'Germania', saying:

> Ich las, mich dünkt, ein Blatt von deiner Hand,
> Das für Germanien in den Kampf mich rief!
> Jedoch was galt Germanien mir?
> Der Fürst bin ich der Ubier,
> Beherrscher eines freien Staats,
> In Fug und Recht, mich jedem, wer es sei,
> Und also auch dem Varus zu verbinden!
>
> (*SW* I, 627; 2604–10)

(I think I read a declaration of yours, appealing to me to take part in a struggle for Germania. But what do I care about Germania? I am the prince of Ubia, the ruler of an independent state, perfectly entitled to form an alliance with anyone I please, including Varus.)

In thus asserting his right to be an independent leader, he exposes the spuriousness of the concept of a 'Germania' to which Hermann appeals in order to justify his own preempted position of authority. Unfortunately for Aristan, in exposing Hermann's *mauvaise foi*, he signs his own death warrant. Hermann's reply:

> Du bist imstand und treibst mich in die Enge,
> Fragst, wo und wann Germanien gewesen?
> Ob in dem Mond? Und zu der Riesen Zeiten?
> (*SW* I, 627; 2611–14)

(I know, Aristan. I am familiar with this way of thinking. You are forcing me into a corner, asking me when and where this *Germania* is to be found? On the moon? When giants ruled the earth?)

makes it clear that whilst he acknowledges the validity of his rival's objections, he cannot tolerate them in the new world order that is emerging at the end of the play. Furthermore, Hermann knows that he has no choice but to condemn Aristan to death; only one man at a time can wield absolute power and he intends to be that man. So when Aristan cries: 'How dare you, you tyrant!' ('Wie, du Tyrann!' *SW* I, 628; 2619) we must take that epithet very seriously; indeed its significance is made yet more sinister by Hermann's chilling comment: 'What can he tell me that I do not already know?' ('Was kann er sagen, das ich nicht schon weiß?'; *SW* I, 628; 2623).

The Germans have thrown off the Roman yoke, but they have not won their freedom; they have merely exchanged the totalitarian rule of the Emperor Augustus for that of Emperor Hermann. Moreover, as Hermann's empire seeks to secure a position of total dominance for itself and begins to push its boundaries even as far as Rome, other nations will be subjected to the same colonial domination the Germans themselves experienced at the hands of the Romans. This is likely to result in the emergence of other Arminius-like leaders, prepared to commit equally horrific massacres in the attempt to assert their right to freedom from the new German imperialism. But as we saw in the case of the Romans, once a nation assumes a position of absolute power, it is in danger of mistaking the ideological 'fictions' that underpin its social structures for reality. The Romans saw themselves as a superior, civilised race with nothing to fear from a bunch of inferior, German savages, and there is a risk that Arminius's Germans will come to regard themselves as a master race invincible in the face of a bunch of primitive Italian peasants.

In the light of the play's ending, Hermann cannot be taken uncritically as the straightforward embodiment of Kleist's ideal political leader. Admirable though his realistic appraisal of Roman imperialism is, we cannot ignore the fact that the beginning of his reign heralds the birth of an authoritarian and autocratic state. His bleak vision of the future in which he anticipates his followers marching on Rome itself:

> Denn eh doch, seh ich ein, erschwingt der Kreis der Welt
> Vor dieser Mordbrut keine Ruhe,
> Als bis das Raubnest ganz zerstört,
> Und nichts, als eine schwarze Fahne,
> Von seinem öden Trümmerhaufen weht!
>
> (*SW* I, 628; 2632–6)

(For the world will enjoy no respite from these murderous hordes until their nest itself has been completely destroyed and nothing remains except a black flag fluttering over its ruins.)

could not be further from Kleist's ideal of a benevolent confederation of states in which the autonomy of each member would be respected by the others. Thus the play can be read as a warning to those of Kleist's contemporaries who believed that it would be necessary or wise to resort to such (Arminius-like) tactics in the struggle against the French.[17] Any political leader who successfully employs such tactics risks turning himself into a Napoleonic despot. And, since most people are not genuinely concerned about their freedom, he will find this all too easy.

KLEIST AND THE QUESTION OF NATIONALISM

Clearly *Die Hermannsschlacht* is not a straightforward patriotic play glorifying a war of liberation and endorsing the use of violence and deception. On the contrary, Kleist is at pains to depict the horrific consequences of any war for victors and vanquished alike and wanted to dispel the sentimental notion that the struggle against Napoleon and the French would be a chivalrous display of courage between noble antagonists. The temptation to indulge in obscene reprisals – the temptation to which Thusnelda succumbs in her 'punishment' of Ventidius – will be overwhelming, and the remorse that follows no less unendurable. Kleist seems anxious to avoid the unrealistic treatment of revolution that we find in such works as Schiller's *Wilhelm Tell*[18] and Klopstocks's *Hermanns Schlacht.* In the latter, the hero is a model of humane restraint, refusing to indulge his mother's unnatural lust for revenge and declaring: 'I will not draw my sword on defenceless prisoners' ('Ich zücke das Schwert gegen waffenlose Krieger nicht!'; *Werke* IV, 143), whereas Kleist's Hermann, despite Septimius's reminding him of his responsibilities as victor, condemns his helpless captive to a brutal and ignominious death: 'Take a cudgel twice the normal size and club him to death' ('Nehmt eine Keule doppelten Gewichts, | Und schlagt ihn tot!'; *SW* I, 612; 2219–20). By portraying the national hero in so unattractive a light, Kleist invites his audience to take a critical view of the contemporary struggle for liberation from the French and its consequences, and to anticipate the excesses likely to attend it. The play is not anti-patriotic; rather it is a plea for moderation and statesmanship in the struggle for justice. Hermann's conception of freedom is noble and appealing, and he is no villain; but his despair of his country-men's resolve tempts him to use them as mere instruments with which to assert his own freedom without regard for theirs.[19]

In the course of the play, Hermann's notion of freedom becomes fundamentally flawed, and by the end of the play he has abandoned his vision of a benevolent confederation of states in favour of a nightmarish vision of a German Empire, no less oppressive than that which it is intended to replace.[20] In short, Hermann's view of freedom is one which can easily degenerate into a position of 'ethical egoism', claiming that perhaps only one individual has the right to be free. This is what Aristan (the only other character who understands Hermann's original conception of individual freedom) realises when he places his life in Hermann's hands by challenging him at the end of the play. Of course in defying Hermann, Aristan is making one last attempt to assert his own freedom; like Hermann, he would rather die than become a vassal. His death shows the others what will be in store for them unless this new 'Augustus' re-espouses his old idea of empire as a benevolent confederation. The play – had it been performed – can be interpreted as a warning to those of Kleist's contemporaries involved in the patriotic struggle: Hermann's notion of freedom may be far superior to that of the other German chieftains, but it also contains a serious defect which they ignore at their peril.

CHAPTER 9

Prinz Friedrich von Homburg

In the early part of 1809, Kleist borrowed from the Dresden *Staatsbibliothek* two works[1] dealing with the historical events behind what had come to be known as the Homburg legend.[2] This was concerned with a historical figure, the Landgrave of Hesse-Homburg, who it appears, was guilty of exactly the same breach of discipline as the hero of Kleist's play, and who, in like manner, was generously pardoned by his commander-in-chief, the Great Elector, Frederick William of Brandenburg. It was this historical legend that provided the inspiration for Kleist's *Prinz Friedrich von Homburg.*

By the time he started writing the play, fundamental changes were taking place in Prussian society. The devastating defeats at Jena and Auerstedt in 1806 proved that a full-scale reform of the Prussian army was long overdue. Even before 1806 it was already becoming apparent that the military strategies and tactics dating back to the times of Frederick the Great were no longer suited to contemporary warfare, and this prompted various members of the Prussian Reform Movement, such as Scharnhorst and Gneisenau to advocate a programme of army reform. These reformers were particularly critical of the prevailing style of discipline, which had shown itself to be counter-productive in that it produced soldiers who were blindly obedient rather than courageously committed to their cause. Just how crude this old-style military discipline was, is revealed in a letter written on 18 and 19 March 1799 by Kleist whilst himself a lieutenant in the Prussian army:

Die größten Wunder militärischer Disziplin, die der Gegenstand des Erstaunens aller Kenner waren, wurden der Gegenstand meiner herzlichsten Verachtung; die Offiziere hielt ich für so viele Exerziermeister, die Soldaten für so viele Sklaven, und wenn das ganze Regiment seine Künste machte, schien es mir als ein lebendiges Monument der Tyrannei. (*SW* II, 479)

(The greatest wonders of military discipline, while objects of awe to all the experts, became objects of my own most heartfelt contempt; the officers I regarded as so many drillmasters, the soldiers as so many slaves, and when the whole regiment was performing its tricks, it seemed to me like a living monument to tyranny.) [M, 22]

In the same letter he goes on to justify his decision to resign his commission: it was impossible, he maintained, given the current state of the army to be an officer and remain a human being.[3]

In the play, Kleist shows that the chief reason for maintaining this outmoded system of discipline was its spurious claim to be an unquestionably 'correct' code of conduct, whose exceptionless application would remove all 'grey areas' from the deliberations of commanders in the field, thereby making possible the creation of a self-regulating military machine. The play explores Kleist's belief that by abandoning this mechanical notion of discipline, it would be possible to reform the army and turn it into a flexible fighting-force capable of overthrowing the French invaders. In this sense the play has an unambiguous patriotic thrust; nonetheless, it met with great opposition. In fact it was not staged until 3 October 1821[4] at the Burgtheater, Vienna, and even then, was taken off after only five performances on the grounds that it was detrimental to the troops' morale. Critics and audience alike, it seems, were blinded as to its overall patriotic intention by Kleist's portrayal of the Prince being thrown into a panic at the sight of his own grave in act III, scene 5. One critic records the reactions of an outraged Prussian officer as follows: 'Then the lieutenant shouted, "It is quite impossible in a militaristic state like Prussia to portray an officer on stage who has so little sense of honour that he goes around pleading for his life; the whole thing would make our class look ridiculous and we can't have that"' ('In einem militärischen Staate, wie Preußen, ist es erstlich ganz unmöglich, einen Offizier auf das Theater zu bringen, der so wenig point d'honneur im Leibe hat, daß er um sein bißchen Leben bettelt, das würde unseren ganzen Stand ridikülisieren und das geht nicht'; *Nachruhm*, no. 554b). In the end, however, a more favourable opinion prevailed and – with the notable exception of Berlin – it was not long before numerous productions of the play were put on all over Germany, and today it is still part of the standard repertoire of the German stage.

It is often said that *Prinz Friedrich von Homburg* presents us with a conflict between 'two different realities' ('zwei Wirklichkeiten') each struggling to assert its supremacy over the other.[5] But as we shall see, the conflict is not between the world of the Prince and the world of the Elector ('Der Kurfürst'), but between the common-sense world – represented in the main by Natalie, the Electress ('Die Kurfürstin') and Kottwitz – and a make-believe world of heroic bravura and unworkable 'iron' discipline which the Prince and the Elector respectively typify. Paradoxically, it is on this unreal world that the whole edifice of the state is founded. However, there is an important difference between the Prince's and the Elector's involvement with the prevailing ideology. The Elector, by virtue of his age and experience, has become inured to, and is at one with, the system. And, since he stands at its pinnacle, he is in no sense threatened by it. (Nonetheless, he is, on occasion, quite capable of pretending that he is merely the 'instrument' of a 'higher' authority, *viz.* the 'Ten Commandments' of the State.) The Prince, on the other hand, as a junior member of the military hierarchy has to accept that there is always a possibility that the long reach of this iron discipline will extend to him. At the same time, however, brought up from his earliest years as the favoured protégé of the Elector, he has been encouraged to entertain the highest hopes of preferment. Accordingly, in one half of his mind he harbours fear and loathing of the system of iron discipline built into the world of the Elector, and in the other, he cherishes the near certainty that he will one day become Elector. This is reflected in his neurotic mood swings: one moment he is confident of his immunity from the worst rigours of this blind military machine and the next is seen cowering abjectly before it. This manifests itself in a dangerous game of bluff and counter-bluff played out according the rules of a preposterous system of *noblesse oblige* in which he and the Elector have become enmeshed. At stake is a life neither believes is really at risk, save perhaps when the Prince is assailed by his neurotic doubts or the Elector momentarily believes he is 'required' by a 'higher authority' to take a step which, on return to reality, he will see to be disastrous and irredeemable. The role of Natalie and her more common-sense confederates is to exploit and manipulate the rules of this game so as to obviate its potentially fatal consequences.

THE ELECTOR

The action of *Prinz Friedrich von Homburg* is set in a highly authoritarian society in which human beings, stripped of their individual autonomy, are reduced to playing purely functional roles within a rigidly organised military hierarchy. The members of the dominant class have been brought up to believe that, in its 'ideal' form, governed as it is by the exceptionless application of these regulations, their society constitutes a perfect unchangeable social order. However, we are soon shown that this delusion, which equates the mere *ad hoc* and often ill-chosen temporal living arrangements of fallible human beings with the operation of eternal laws of nature, is largely responsible for the difficult and potentially tragic predicaments with which the characters in the play are confronted.

At the pinnacle of this society stands the Elector who, as his decision to tear up the order for the Prince's execution in act V, scene 9 shows, has the power to make and unmake the rules that underpin the system. Nor does it escape our attention that the Elector's claim to be only the instrument of a perfect governmental machine, does not prevent his acting highly indulgently (in his more human moments) towards his young protégé. The Prince hints as much in act III, scene 1:

> Ich bin ihm wert, das weiß ich,
> Wert wie ein Sohn; das hat seit früher Kindheit,
> Sein Herz in tausend Proben mir bewiesen.
> (*SW* I, 668; 829–31)

(I know he loves me, loves me like a son; I've had a thousand proofs of it since I was little.) [G, 310]

There is further evidence of this protective bias in act II, scene 9. There the Elector declares that he has no option but to court-martial the officer who led the premature charge, but in the very next breath asks: 'The Prince of Homburg wasn't leading them?'

[G, 304] ('Der Prinz von Homburg hat sie nicht geführt?'; *SW* I, 663; 722).

The Elector asserts his absolute authority in the opening scene of the play; he thinks nothing of overriding the reluctance of the others to take part in the charade involving the Prince in the garden. Despite the Electress's plea, 'We should help him, so it seems to me, not spend our time in making fun of him!' [G, 272] ('Man sollt ihm helfen, dünkt mich, | Nicht den Moment verbringen, sein zu spotten!'; *SW* I, 632; 33–4) he orders his entourage to follow him into the garden where he will make Natalie subject the Prince to the indignities of his little joke, and neither she nor the Electress feels able to disobey. The Elector is unquestionably a puppet-master manipulating the Prince, even if in this instance, his little joke is innocent enough and prompted only by idle curiosity, the desire to see 'just how far he will go' ('wie weit ers treibt'; *SW* I, 633; 64). As the scene unfolds the audience gathers that the Elector knows full well what is on the Prince's mind; he says as much to Hohenzollern: 'Good heavens, but it's strange! And yet I'll give you odds I know what's causing all the agitation in this young fool's breast' [G, 273] ('Seltsam beim Himmel! Doch, was gilts, ich weiß, | Was dieses jungen Toren Brust bewegt?'; *SW* I, 633; 54–5). But, although he urges the Prince to attend to the matter in hand, namely to the battle, rather than to the victor's crown, and warns him that, 'Such things are never won in dreams!' [G, 274] ('Im Traum erringt man solche Dinge nicht!'; *SW* I, 634; 77), he never suggests that he is opposed to a match between his beloved Natalie and his protégé.[6] And it is clear that he shares the dream the Prince has been acting out in the garden that there will be a glorious victory in which the Prince will have played an outstanding part, a victory crowned by marriage to the Princess.

Although this opening scene ends with the Elector appealing to the Prince to take a more realistic attitude towards the task in hand, there are a number of points in the play where Kleist suggests that the Elector himself is not wholly free of those 'romanticising' tendencies that he so disapproves of in his young protégé. At the end of act I, scene 5, he urges the Prince to conduct himself properly in the battle,[7] but when the time comes for the Elector himself to enter the fray, despite his greater experience, he displays an equally foolhardy attitude to the realities of war, when, contrary to his officers' advice, he declares his intention of riding into battle, conspicuous on his fine white horse. In act II, scene 8, Sparren reports that:

> Der Landesherr, der, jeder Warnung taub,
> Den Schimmel wieder ritt, den strahlendweißen,
> Den Froben jüngst in England ihm erstand,
> War wieder, wie bis heut noch stets geschah,
> Das Ziel der feindlichen Kanonenkugeln. (*SW* I, 660; 641–5)

(Our monarch who, deaf to every warning, was riding his white horse again, the pure white stallion Froben bought him a short time ago in England, was once again, as always, the target of the enemy's cannonades.) [G, 301]

Moreover, this 'romanticising tendency' on the Elector's part is responsible for the death of his loyal equerry, Froben.[8] Count Sparren obligingly describes the unfortunate Froben as 'a sacrifice to his fidelity' [G, 302] ('ein Opfer seiner Treue'; *SW* I, 661; 676), but the fact is that his death is an easily foreseeable consequence of reckless bravura in a person in command who should have known better. And, of course, the episode reminds us that it is usually those at a lower level of the hierarchy (such as the equerry)[9] who pay for their superiors' folly.

Despite his position of absolute power, the Elector would like to believe that he too is subject to another authority, 'higher' than his own, namely an allegedly 'transcendent' concept of military discipline which, because it is 'infallibly' correct, makes it unnecessary to take into account the special circumstances of any particular instance of its infringement. Accordingly, when Natalie pleads for the life of her beloved in act IV, scene I, he claims that whilst he would be quite willing (as an ordinary person) to pardon the young man, it does not lie within his power (as head of state) to do this:

> Wär ich ein Tyrann,
> Dein Wort, das fühl ich lebhaft, hätte mir
> Das Herz schon in der erznen Brust geschmelzt.
> Dich aber frag ich selbst: darf ich den Spruch
> Den das Gericht gefällt, wohl unterdrücken? –
> Was würde wohl davon die Folge sein? (*SW* I, 679; 1112–17)

(If I were simply a tyrant, what you say, I feel this very strongly, would already have made my heart melt in its iron cage. But *I* ask you: May I suppress the verdict of the Court? What consequences would that have?) [G, 320]

Here the Elector is guilty of *mauvaise foi* on two accounts: firstly, he denies having the freedom to override the 'inviolable' laws of this 'higher' system of 'perfect' military discipline; secondly, he refuses to acknowledge the fact that even the exceptionless application of these laws cannot exclude the possibility of similar acts of insubordination occurring in future. The Elector cannot see that it is neither possible nor wise to attempt to turn an army of real men into a perfectly-functioning military machine and that there is a strong possibility that this rigid system of discipline will produce the very type of erratic behaviour recently displayed by the Prince (and, as we have seen, from time to time by the Elector himself). The response of those individuals (such as the Prince), for whom this concept of discipline is too restrictive and, above all, unworkable in actual military engagements, is to revere it in theory, but override it in practice whilst hoping that (somehow) their actual behaviour will give an impression of being in accordance with it. For as Kleist shows, this rigid code of practice, far from providing a fool-proof guide to military decisions, actually conceals the reality of combat and offers standard 'solutions' of interest only to would-be strategic perfectionists (such as the Elector). This is precisely what Kottwitz points out in act v, scene 5.

In the final analysis, what prompts the Elector to act is not Natalie's proof of the weakness of his arguments and her simple insistence that it does indeed lie within his capacity as a free agent to spare the Prince, but rather her description of the latter's broken spirit: 'All he thinks of now, the only thing, is being saved!' [G, 321] ('Der denkt jetzt nichts, als nur dies eine: Rettung!'; *SW* I, 680–1; 1148). When the Elector hears of the Prince's abject state of mind, he is, as the stage directions indicate, completely taken aback, and almost immediately offers to pardon him.[10] But, although the Elector's first impulse (as a human being) is to offer the Prince a pardon, he almost immediately resorts to yet another move in the grand game of *noblesse oblige* in which he is so expert – the victim will pass sentence upon himself: 'If he can find it in himself to say the sentence is unjust, I cancel it: he's free!' [G, 323] ('Wenn er den Spruch für ungerecht kann halten | Kassier ich die Artikel: er ist frei!'; *SW* I, 682; 1185–6). He is relying on the fact that, if the Prince adheres to the rules of their preposterous game, as the Elector knows he 'must', the Prince has 'no choice' but to order his own execution. Nonetheless, although his faith in the Prince's capacity to act wholly in accordance with these absurd conventions proves well-founded, he seriously under-estimates the risks involved. It is at this point that the rules of the game begin to elude the understanding of the players themselves. The Elector's plan is that, once the Prince has accepted his own execution and thereby proved his submission to the rules, he will withdraw him from the game (by pardoning him), thereby demonstrating his own 'grand-masterly' magnanimity. However, if the Elector were to examine the rules more closely, he would discover that the Prince has one further move at his disposal; for he can, quite legitimately, reject the Elector's pardon, insist that he has lost and demand his execution. This final insane move would render the Elector powerless to prevent the potential disaster that has lurked all along within this deadly game, obvious to all save the two obsessive contestants. Of course, there is a double-sense in which the Elector loses the game. If the Prince were indeed to insist on making this final move, the Elector would be confronted with an impossible choice: to execute the Prince (thus depriving himself of his favourite officer and condemning himself to a life of remorse), or to exercise his humanity (thereby having to admit that his exceptionless system of military discipline is, after all, not infallible). In the event, by being forced to have recourse to his humanity in the final act of the play, the Elector is obliged, in logic, to abandon this game which has manifestly failed to serve its purpose.[11]

THE PRINCE

Kleist goes to considerable lengths in his portrayal of the Prince to undermine the audience's preconceptions regarding the 'appropriate' behaviour of a young military hero. In the opening scene, for example, Hohenzollern tells the incredulous Elector of the extent to which the Prince has neglected his duties:

Da nun die Stunde schlägt,
Und aufgesessen schon die ganze Reuterei
Den Acker vor dem Tor zerstampft,
Fehlt – wer? der Prinz von Homburg noch, ihr Führer.
(*SW* I, 631; 18–21)

(And now the hour has struck, the cavalry mounted up and trampling the field outside the gate, who should it be that's missing? The Prince no less, their own commanding officer!) [G, 271–2]

Not only has the Prince failed to appear to lead his troops into position but, as Hohenzollern says, when finally tracked down, he was discovered behaving in what his military colleagues clearly regard as a most 'un-soldierly' fashion:

Als ein Nachtwandler, schau, auf jener Bank,
Wohin, im Schlaf, wie du nie glauben wolltest,
Der Mondschein ihn gelockt, beschäftiget,
Sich träumend, seiner eignen Nachwelt gleich,
Den prächtgen Kranz des Ruhmes einzuwinden.
(*SW* I, 632; 25–9)

(Look there, on that bench, our somnambulist, where the moonlight drew him (though you won't believe me) in his sleep – lost in dreams, he acts posterity's part and himself weaves the glorious crown of fame to set on his own head.) [G, 272]

The Elector's reluctance to revise his romanticised impression of his young favourite is highlighted by his exclamation of disbelief: 'He's fast asleep! But that's impossible!' [G, 272] ('Im Schlaf versenkt? Unmöglich!'; *SW* I, 632; 30). And the Electress and Natalie can only account for the Prince's aberrant behaviour in terms of ill health;[12] but, as Hohenzollern tells them, there is nothing physically wrong with the Prince. Moreover, this is not his first lapse, but just one more example of his inveterate tendency to view the world through the distorting categories of a hopelessly romantic imagination. For the Prince appears lost in a moon-lit reverie, weaving a victory garland and enjoying a conventional fantasy of success in the fields of love and war, all thoughts of the impending battle far from his mind.[13] The origin of these fantasies is hinted at by Hohenzollern, who, when asked by the Elector what sort of garland the Prince was weaving, replies:

Der Lorbeer ists,
Wie ers gesehn hat, an der Helden Bildern,
Die zu Berlin im Rüstsaal aufgehängt. (*SW* I, 633; 47–9)

(A laurel wreath is what it is, just like the ones he's seen on the brows of heroes' portraits hanging in the Berlin Arsenal.) [G, 273]

This is the stuff from which the Prince's fantasies are made,[14] but their cause lies in the de-humanising effects of the arbitrary code of discipline imposed upon him (and, we may assume, his fellow officers). Stripped of their autonomy and reduced to mere instruments within the chain of command, they enjoy scant personal satisfaction from the activities in which they are involved, so instead of focusing their thoughts on the task in hand, they become preoccupied with visions of the glorious military successes, which, they have been led to believe, their unquestioning obedience cannot fail to produce. Accordingly, the import of the opening scenes is to show that it is precisely when human beings are subjected to severe (and unnecessary) constraints, that they are most liable to indulge in this sort of 'hysterical posturing'.[15]

Kleist's handling of the briefing in act I, scene 5, where the Prince appears distracted, makes it clear to the audience that the young man's subsequent failure to obey orders is not a deliberate act of insubordination but the result of his inability to come to terms with the murderously inhuman kind of discipline he has to endure. His failure to confine his attention to the pre-arranged ('infallible') battle-plan and to ignore the opportunity of seizing victory that he sees opening up before him during the course of the real battle is the result of a psychological conflict within him. To a large extent, the Prince is a 'natural' product of his 'unnatural' upbringing in this absurd world and indeed, at a number of points in the play, Kleist suggests he is simply a younger and less experienced version of the Elector himself. There are moments, of course, when the immature Prince shows himself to be no less committed to the same disastrous misconception of discipline as the Elector. Having announced his intention to mount a premature charge against the Swedes in act II, scene 2, he is confronted (in an episode that anticipates his own treatment at the hands of the Elector) with an act of insubordination by the young First Officer

('Erster Offizier') who calls for him to be relieved of command. The Prince turns on him, appealing to the sanctity of the same law that he himself is flouting: 'Why, what impertinence! Did you forget the ten commandments of the March of Brandenburg?' [G, 294] ('Ei, du vorwitzger Knabe, der du noch | Nicht die Zehn märkischen Gebote kennst!'; *SW* I, 653; 486–7) and places him under arrest.

A further complication in the Prince's situation is that, at times, he can persuade himself that he has accepted the 'ten commandments of Brandenburg' only on the tacit (but self-contradictory) assumption that he is personally exempt from their ruthless jurisdiction because of his special relationship with the Elector. But of course he can never be sure of this. In consequence, he attempts to oust the dread 'commandments' from his mind by filling it with sentimental images of himself as conquering hero and Natalie's chosen one. Thus, when Hohenzollern visits him in the opening scene of act III, the Prince puts on an exaggerated display of confidence, taking it for granted that his friend has come with news of his impending release: 'Now look who's there – friend Heinrich! Welcome! Come to tell me I'm set free, I'm sure!' [G, 308] ('Sieh da! Freund Heinrich! Sei willkommen mir! | Nun, des Arrestes bin ich wieder los?'; *SW* I, 667; 791–2). Even when he learns that this is not the case, his euphoria is quite undampened and he remains supremely confident that it will only be a matter of time before he is pardoned:

> Der Kurfürst hat getan, was Pflicht erheischte,
> Und nun wird er dem Herzen auch gehorchen.
> Gefehlt hast du, so wird er ernst mir sagen,
> Vielleicht ein Wort von Tod und Festung sprechen:
> Ich aber schenke dir die Freiheit wieder – (*SW* I, 668; 820–4)

(The Elector did what he must do, according to his duty. But now he'll heed his heart. 'You've been at fault', he'll tell me very gravely, mention death, perhaps, imprisonment. 'However, I've decided to give you back your freedom –') [G, 309]

However, as Hohenzollern recounts the details of the court's proceedings, the Prince's confidence in his 'privileged' position begins to waver and is finally replaced by an equally blind panic, when on the way to visit the Electress, he catches sight of the grave that is being prepared for him:

> Ach! Auf dem Wege, der mich zu dir führte,
> Sah ich das Grab, beim Schein der Fackeln, öffnen,
> Das morgen mein Gebein empfangen soll.
> Sieh, diese Augen, Tante, die dich anschaun,
> Will man mit Nacht umschatten, diesen Busen
> Mit mörderischen Kugeln mir durchbohren.
> (*SW* I, 675; 981–6)

(Coming here, I saw my own grave, in the torchlight, being dug, which tomorrow morning will receive my bones. Look here at these eyes, Aunt, that look at you – their purpose is to drown them in everlasting night, drive bullets through this breast of mine.) [G, 316]

Here, the Prince is, perhaps for the first time in his life, compelled to take seriously the possibility that he is going to die. At this point good sense would suggest that the Prince should make a sober reappraisal of his situation. Instead – and this is symptomatic of the basic hysteria inherent in the Prince's struggle with 'the ten commandments of Brandenburg' – his mood swings from the overweening confidence (of act III, scene 1) to the abject despair (of act III, scene 5). This transformation occurs on the way to the women's apartments to plead with them to intervene on his behalf, an audience on whose feminine sensibility, his neurotic brain feels it can rely. For as he begs the Electress:

> O Gottes Welt, o Mutter, ist so schön!
> Laß mich nicht, fleh ich, eh die Stunde schlägt,
> Zu jenen schwarzen Schatten niedersteigen!
> [. . .]
> Seit ich mein Grab sah, will ich nichts, als leben,
> Und frage nichts mehr, ob es rühmlich sei!
> (*SW* I, 676; 995–7 & 1003–4)

(Mother, God's earth is so fair! I beg you, don't, before my hour comes, let me go down among the shadows! [. . .] since I've seen my grave my only thought is, Let me live, I don't care how!) [G, 316]

This is the first of a series of increasingly melodramatic gestures, the intensity of which does not fail to elicit the appropriate response from her and her niece. The Electress is so taken aback by the Prince's abject behaviour and, at the same time, so anxious to preserve her (conventional) heroic image of Natalie's future husband, that she begs him to stop: 'Stand up, my son – oh, do stand up! You're so unnerved you don't know what you're saying. Try to get a grip on yourself!' [G, 317] ('Steh auf, mein Sohn: steh auf! Was sprichst du da? | Du bist zu sehr erschüttert. Fasse dich!'; *SW* I, 676; 1005–6). Fortunately for the Prince, his impassioned plea, despite its disquieting and unflattering excesses (including a 'generous' offer to give up his beloved to another) does not fall on deaf ears, and Natalie goes to the Elector to plead for his life. She realises that she can exploit the Prince's current state of abject terror to arouse the compassion of her uncle, the Elector.

The support of Natalie and the Electress gives the Prince back some of his usual *sang froid*, but he has still to face his ultimate test, the letter from the Elector which Natalie gives him in act IV, scene 4, and in which he is called upon to pass sentence on himself. At first he thinks that the letter is granting him an outright pardon. But despite Natalie's attempts to rush the matter to its conclusion: 'And there it is! A line from you is all that's needed – !' [G, 328] ('Nun denn, da stehts! Zwei Worte nur bedarfs – !'; *SW* I, 687; 1314) as well as her shrewdly inserted reminder: 'You saw your own grave in the churchyard yawning up at you with open jaws' [G, 329] ('Saht Ihr die Gruft nicht schon im Münster, | Mit offnem Rachen, Euch entgegengähn'n?'; *SW* I, 687; 1325–6), the Prince insists on reading the letter a second time. As he does so, he realises that the next round of the grand game has begun and that he must consider his counter-move. He is now back in the 'higher' world of make-believe, and this does not escape the experienced eye of Natalie whose obvious frustration is underlined by the stage-direction: she turns away to hide her tears.[16] And when the Prince tears up his first attempt with the words, 'Pooh! It's how a scoundrel goes about it, not a Prince' [G, 329] ('Pah! – Eines Schuftes Fassung, keines Prinzen'; *SW* I, 688; 1334) and examines the Elector's letter once more, saying, 'I only want to see how I should answer him' [G, 329] ('Ich will nur sehn, wie ich mich fassen soll'; *SW* I, 688; 1338) her worst fears are confirmed. She sees that her beloved has fallen headlong into the Elector's trap. Furthermore, she knows that he has been so steeped in the absurd conventions of this artificial military world that he is quite capable of losing sight of reality altogether and of agreeing with his superior that his execution is 'necessary'. Not without good reason does she say to herself, 'Good God, that's it, we've reached the end!' [G, 329] ('O Gott der Welt! Jetzt ists um ihn geschehn!'; *SW* I, 688; 1339). The Prince attempts to pacify her by pointing out; 'You don't consider what the letter says!' [G, 330] ('Du hast des Briefes Inhalt nicht erwogen!'; *SW* I, 689; 1354) but this is to assume – mistakenly – that she accepts the same absurd conventions as himself. Not only did Natalie strongly suspect what was in the Elector's letter, but she also had little doubt that as soon as the Prince saw what it really said, he would (as a military officer) be unable to resist acting in accordance with the rules of Elector's impossible game. Her suspicions prove well-founded when the Prince exclaims:

> Daß er mir unrecht tat, wies mir bedingt wird,
> Das kann ich ihm nicht schreiben; zwingst du mich,
> Antwort, in dieser Stimmung, ihm zu geben,
> Bei Gott! so setz ich hin, du tust mir recht!
>
> (*SW* I, 689; 1355–8)

(His stipulation: if I think I've been unjustly treated – I can't meet, and if you press me, in my present frame of mind, to answer him, by God, I'll write: with perfect justice yes, you've treated me!) [G, 330]

In complying with his superior's demands, the Prince abnegates his freedom to act according to his own moral dictates. His cry of bravado, 'He can do just as he pleases, let him – I must do just as I should!' [G, 331] ('Er handle, wie er darf; | Mir ziemts hier zu verfahren, wie ich soll!'; *SW* I, 690; 1374–5) merely underlines how completely he surrenders to the twisted etiquette of military life. Here we might adapt Kleist's image of the marionette and say that the Prince has now become the perfect 'toy-soldier', a marionette-like figure, whose movements are controlled by the Elector, his puppet-master. Accordingly, when Natalie gasps: 'A more unnatural man – ! Is that what you are writing there?' [G, 331] ('Du Ungeheuerster, ich glaub, du schriebst?'; *SW* I, 690; 1376) we share her exasperation that anyone could so far forget his essential humanity as to order his own execution, and that with such inhuman enthusiasm.

HOHENZOLLERN

In Hohenzollern, Kleist has created a character who is temperamentally quite different from the Prince and who responds in an altogether different way to the unrealistic system of military discipline in which both are obliged to operate. He understands its hierarchical structure rather better than the Prince and has learnt to modify his behaviour accordingly, and thus he displays far more diplomacy than his more impulsive colleague. He never challenges the rules directly, even when common-sense suggests he should, and always displays a prudent regard for the requirements of the hierarchical chain of command, no matter how nonsensical these may be. In act II, scene 2, he warns the Prince against disobeying the Elector's orders and urges him to listen to reason,[17] but as soon as the more junior First Officer attempts to have the Prince relieved of command, he jumps on this act of insubordination: 'Quiet! Are you mad?' [G, 294] ('Schweig! Bist du rasend?'; *SW* I, 653; 490). Similarly, when the Elector issues orders to arrest the Prince in act II, scene 10, Hohenzollern is equally quick to rebuke the latter for his disobedience: '*The law is: obedience!*' [G, 307] ('Der Satzung soll Gehorsam sein'; *SW* I, 666; 774). However, his is not a crude conformity; he merely displays a more controlled, diplomatic attitude towards his superiors. Thus, whereas the more naïve First Officer openly challenges the Prince's authority, Hohenzollern is more tactful: 'It was advice, no more, we offered' [G, 295] ('Es war ein Rat nur, den man dir erteilt'; *SW* I, 654; 495) thus covering himself against summary arrest for refusing an order (the First Officer's fate) or against court-martialling for disregarding the commander-in-chief's orders (the Prince's fate).

Hohenzollern's attitude towards the Prince is the sneaking admiration of a man who would never dream of taking the risks that the Prince does and who (quite correctly) assumes that he, the stolid Hohenzollern, could never get away with the kind of outrageous behaviour displayed by the Elector's favourite. In the opening scene of the play, Hohenzollern simply cannot believe the Prince's neglect of his duties:

> Der ganze Flecken könnt in Feuer aufgehn,
> Daß sein Gemüt davon nicht mehr empfände,

Als der Demant, den er am Finger trägt.

(*SW* I, 632; 43–5)

(All the village could go up in flames and he would pay it no more mind than the diamond on his finger does.) [G, 272–3]

Likewise, when the Elector's charade reveals that there are apparently no limits to the Prince's ambition, Hohenzollern (like the other bystanders) is completely amazed.[18] Throughout the first and third acts of the play, Hohenzollern's behaviour towards the Prince is prompted more by his curiosity to see how he will extricate himself from this particular predicament, than by straightforward compassion.[19] Of course, Hohenzollern may argue that it is precisely because the Prince is the Elector's favourite that he can afford to take the risks he does. By the same token, it is the Prince's romantic temperament and his inclination to take risks that appeals to a similarly sentimental streak in the Elector (as well as in the audience) and thereby ensures that he enjoys the Elector's favour. Indeed, it is this capacity for risk-taking that singles him out from the other officers and makes him (as against the less flamboyant Hohenzollern) a possible candidate for the highest office of state. Thus by showing how the Prince ultimately emerges 'triumphant' from the 'test' set for him by the Elector, the play both upholds and – by virtue of its patently artificial ending – adroitly subverts the myth that in the last resort, those of a 'genuinely' noble disposition will stand firm while other 'lesser' beings fall – yet another 'noble lie' propping up this artificial regime.[20]

The tone of Hohenzollern's speech to his colleague in act III, scene I, suggests he believes that this time the Prince has gone too far, though there is nothing to suggest that Hohenzollern is maliciously hoping for the Prince's downfall. Indeed, quite the opposite appears to be the case; he describes himself as 'dismayed' [G, 312] ('bestürzt'; *SW* I, 671; 892) by the court's verdict and we have no reason to doubt his sincerity. However, lest it be thought that Hohenzollern represents an ideal product of this military establishment, we should note that the fact that he tries to help the Prince escape his punishment is a (heartening) sign that he is not wholly committed to the system: a truly committed officer would have felt obliged to agree that the Prince deserved to die.

Hohenzollern's lack of genuine commitment has already been exposed in act II, scene 10: there he insists that the Prince conform to the letter of the law – '*the law is: obedience*' – but in the very next breath is attempting to reassure his colleague with the words: 'It doesn't mean your neck' [G, 307] ('Es wird den Hals nicht kosten'; *SW* I, 666; 776). Even a man like Hohenzollern – a man who ostensibly endorses the 'ten commandments of the March of Brandenburg' – would nonetheless like to see the Prince pardoned: another tacit condemnation of the system, whose deficiencies are so ruthlessly exposed whenever it is put to the test in real-life situations.

Hohenzollern never actually questions the assumption that the Elector is, at least in a technical sense, acting quite 'correctly' in ordering the Prince's execution, but at a number of points in act III, scene 1, he shows a more pragmatic interpretation of the prevailing code of discipline. And, although he warns the Prince that a pardon is at best only a 'technical possibility', he nonetheless, immediately tries to bring about a practical solution to the dilemma. Convinced that his colleague's amorous intentions towards Natalie lie at the root of the problem, because they stand in the way of one means of making peace with the Swedes, he puts the Prince to the test:

> Graf Horn traf, der Gesandte Schwedens, ein,
> Und sein Geschäft geht, wie man mir versichert,
> An die Prinzessin von Oranien.
> Ein Wort, das die Kurfürstin Tante sprach,
> Hat aufs empfindlichste den Herrn getroffen;
> Man sagt, das Fräulein habe schon gewählt.
> Bist du auf keine Weise hier im Spiele? (*SW* I, 672; 917–23)

(The Ambassador from Sweden has arrived and his business, I am told, concerns the Princess Natalie. But something the Electress said provoked His Lordship mightily; the talk is, the young lady's made her choice already. You don't play a part in this, do you?) [G, 313]

Here Hohenzollern shows himself in his true colours, for the course of action he tacitly suggests – the renunciation of Natalie – is an attempt to arrive at a satisfactory solution within the parameters of the prevailing system. At the same time, the type of solution he proposes underlines the essential difference between the pragmatic career-officer, Hohenzollern, and the 'noble' Prince who, in complying with the terms of the letter in act IV, scene 4, selects (almost intuitively) the one solution that will not only bring about his salvation, but will also ensure that he continues to enjoy the Elector's favour. We can be sure that had the Prince opted instead for Hohenzollern's proposed course of action, the Elector would have been deeply disappointed in his young protégé. For whilst the army contains many officers like Hohenzollern, who have accepted this artificial system for what it is and have worked out a means of getting by in it without ever quite embracing its full implications, there are very few, who, like the Prince, are willing to commit themselves so whole-heartedly to that system that they are prepared to order their own execution rather than see it called into question. This crucial difference between these two types of officer is underlined once again at the end of the play, when the Prince prepares to face the firing squad. Hohenzollern continues to maintain that: '*The law is: obedience*', but when he is confronted with an officer prepared to do just this – even to the point of requesting his own execution – far from admiring his colleague's 'commitment' he assumes that he has simply lost his wits. His exclamation in act V, scene 7: 'Does he *want* to die – ?' [G, 345] ('Er will den Tod – ?'; *SW* I, 704; 1747) is not of awe, but of sheer incomprehension.

KOTTWITZ

Kottwitz is an elderly officer who, through his long years of service, has gained a far more realistic insight into the nature of military combat than any of the others. His more realistic approach contrasts sharply with the naïve enthusiasm of the younger officers in the scenes at the beginning of act II. The less experienced Hohenzollern can hardly contain his eagerness for the battle: 'Shoot! Shoot all you like, and rip the womb of earth to dig your bodies' graves!' [G, 293] ('Schießt! Schießt! Und macht den Schoß der Erde bersten! | Der Riß soll eurer Leichen Grabmal sein'; *SW* I, 652; 461–2); Kottwitz, on the other hand, speaks as one who has had considerably more experience of the horrors of combat:

Ein schöner Tag, so wahr ich Leben atme!
Ein Tag von Gott, dem hohen Herrn der Welt,
Gemacht zu süßerm Ding als sich zu schlagen!
(*SW* 1, 649; 384–6)

(As I live and breathe, a glorious day! A day the Lord God made for better things than killing one another!) [G, 290]

At the same time, he has the advantage over the younger, less experienced officers such as Hohenzollern and the Prince, of having already proved himself a loyal (and respected) servant of the Elector. This makes him considerably less anxious than the other commanders in matters of military discipline and, like the Prince, he is more willing to take risks when the situation warrants it. We see this when the Prince gives the premature order to charge; Kottwitz first reminds him, quite properly, of the Elector's instructions: 'According to his Lordship's orders yesterday, we mustn't move except upon command' [G, 294] ('Des Herrn Durchlaut, bei der Parole gestern, | Befahl, daß wir auf Order warten sollen'; *SW* 1, 652–3; 471–2) and then obeys – as indeed he must – the orders of his superior, the Prince. Having done so, he commits himself whole-heartedly to the attack, thereby demonstrating his qualities as an experienced soldier. Hohenzollern and the First Officer worry about possible charges of insubordination; Kottwitz is primarily concerned with the battle that is being fought. He knows that from time to time risks have to be taken; he has backed the Prince's decision to attack and if this is to be successful, those taking part must put all distracting thoughts of possible court-martials out of their minds and focus on the task in hand. He assumes (incorrectly as it turns out) that the Elector will take a similar view of the situation and will not concern himself unduly about questions of 'insubordination' provided the engagement is a success. The Elector's decision to court-martial the Prince produces widely differing reactions in Kottwitz and the other officers: Hohenzollern accepts the Elector's decision almost without demur, whereas Kottwitz is so taken aback that he immediately attempts (unsuccessfully) to intervene on the Prince's behalf.[21] The others (timidly) leave the Prince's victory trophies lying on the ground; Kottwitz, following his common-sense conviction that the Prince's success on the battle-field will outweigh any charge of insubordination, boldly picks them up.

Kottwitz may not agree with the Elector's treatment of the Prince, but this does not mean that he is against an appropriate degree of discipline in military life. He is essentially an experienced soldier, not a diplomat, and the further he is from his preferred sphere of operation (the battle-field), the more convention-bound he reveals himself to be. He is prepared to organise a petition in support of the Prince, but he is too much a part of the system to march to Fehrbellin to collect more signatures, as such an act could be misconstrued as mutiny.[22] It is Kottwitz's military mentality that leads him to misjudge this situation. As it turns out, it is the very fact that – thanks to the shrewder Natalie's intervention – he does go to Fehrbellin and collects the signatures of all the officers that prevents this act of insubordination from turning into an insurrection and transforms it into a peaceful (because unanimous) protest. It is Natalie who best understands the contradictions in Kottwitz's character; as she says to Count Reuss: 'He's odd, he is, that gentleman! So bold, and then so careful!' [G, 326] ('Der wunderliche Herr! Bald kühn, bald zaghaft!'; *SW* I, 685; 1264).

NATALIE

Natalie and, to a lesser degree, the Electress, stand some way outside the artificial world in which the action takes place.[23] In the opening scene the two of them show their reluctance to take part in the Elector's charade, suggesting that instead of making fun of the Prince, Hohenzollern and the Elector would do better to show more compassion towards the young man.[24] Like the Prince, Natalie enjoys the Elector's favour. In act IV, scene I, he refers to her as his 'dear child' [G, 320] ('mein süßes Kind'; *SW* I, 679; 1112), and her heart-felt appeal on the Prince's behalf touches him profoundly:

> Fürwahr, mein Töchterchen, mein Nichtchen, weinte!
> Und ich, dem ihre Freude anvertraut,
> Mußt ihrer holden Augen Himmel trüben!
>
> (*SW* I, 682; 1191–3)

(Weeping so, she was, my darling daughter, little niece! And I, whose duty is to make her happy, am the one who caused the clouds to gather in the bright blue weather of her eyes!) [G, 323]

Natalie is deeply in love with the Prince and she shows the depth of her feeling not only in the risks she takes in her attempt to rescue him, but also in her impassioned speech in act IV, scene I:

> Ich will ihn nicht für mich erhalten wissen –
> Mein Herz begehrt sein und gesteht es dir;
> Ich will ihn nicht für mich erhalten wissen –
> Mag er sich welchem Weib er will vermählen;
> Ich will nur, daß er da sei, lieber Onkel,
> Für sich, selbständig, frei und unabhängig,
> Wie eine Blume, die mir wohlgefällt: (*SW* I, 679; 1083–9)

(I don't want to have him for myself – though my heart is filled with longing for him, I confess; oh, I don't want him for myself – let him marry whom he pleases; all I wish, dear uncle, is that he should go on living as he is, a free and self-sufficient being, who gives me pleasure simply by existing, like a flower.) [G, 319]

This speech of Natalie's comes closer than perhaps any other in Kleist's work to articulating his ideal of selfless love. At the same time, it is important to note that Natalie's feelings for her beloved are strengthened by the loyalty and courage he has displayed in the past. However, unlike the male members of this society, who subscribe to a spurious notion of courage – an alleged 'inability' to experience fear – Natalie takes a more realistic view. When the Prince is terrified by the prospect of his impending execution in act III, scene 5, she does not make fun of him, but looks upon him with compassion,[25] pledging her loyalty in life as in death and thereby inspiring him to recover his composure:

> Geh, junger Held, in deines Kerkers Haft,
> Und auf dem Rückweg, schau noch einmal ruhig
> Das Grab dir an, das dir geöffnet wird!
> Es ist nichts finstrer und um nichts breiter,
> Als es dir tausendmal die Schlacht gezeigt!
> Inzwischen werd ich, in dem Tod dir treu,
> Ein rettend Wort für dich dem Oheim wagen:
> Vielleicht gelingt es mir, sein Herz zu rühren,
> Und dich von allem Kummer zu befrein!
> (*SW* I, 677; 1053–61)

(Go, my hero, back into your cell! And on your way back, look again, composed and calm, at the grave they've dug for you. It's not the least bit darker, deeper than those that yawned beneath your feet a thousand times on the battlefield! I am true to you come life, come death. And meanwhile I myself will try with our uncle to see if I can find the words to touch his heart and rescue you from all this misery.) [G, 318]

The fact that the Prince has, quite understandably, given in to fear on this occasion does not (at least in her eyes)[26] make him a coward or cause her to forget his courageous behaviour on other occasions. She knows that true courage can only be displayed by those who conquer their fear. And, no matter how much the high command of the Prussian army (and indeed the lower-ranking officers themselves) would like to believe the contrary, the members of this army cannot be turned into fearless fighting machines. For Natalie, the fact that the Prince gives in to fear on this occasion is not only proof that he is capable of true courage, but is exactly what makes him so appealing to her, and to the Elector. She rejects all pretentious and unrealistic versions of 'heroism' and 'bravery', but recognises and values the real thing. We see this most clearly at the end of act IV, scene 4, when she cannot help but admire her beloved's courage (however foolishly misplaced she may believe it to be) in agreeing to the 'necessity' of his own execution:

> Nimm diesen Kuß! – Und bohrten gleich zwölf Kügeln
> Dich jetzt in Staub, nicht halten könnt ich mich,
> Und jauchzt und weint und spräche: du gefällst mir!
> (*SW* I, 690; 1386–8)

(Here, I must kiss you, oh I must! Even if a dozen bullets bore you down into the dust right now, I still could not, amid my tears, keep back the exultation I should feel and I would say: you please me, very much!) [G, 331–2]

Natalie has a far more realistic appraisal of human potential and of basic human values than either the Prince or the Elector, but at the same time understands the peculiar conventions on which authorities in her society rely. Indeed it is her understanding of these *bizarreries* that enables her to manipulate them to her advantage, for example, when she hits upon the expedient of sending out an order 'on behalf of' the Elector, summoning Kottwitz to

Fehrbellin. However, her main function in the drama is to alert the Prince and the Elector to the catastrophe which will almost certainly ensue from their deadly game of *noblesse oblige*. When she exclaims 'God will send me the shafts to hit the mark!' [G, 318] ('Gott wird die Pfeile mir, die treffen, reichen!'; *SW* I, 678; 1068) before setting off to see the Elector in act IV, scene I, she is referring to the arguments she will deploy to remind her uncle that, however much he may deny it, he is not obliged by any 'higher authority' to give up his freedom to act with humanity and compassion. For as she says to him:

> Erst, weil er siegt', ihn kränzen, dann enthaupten,
> Das fordert die Geschichte nicht von dir;
> Das wäre so erhaben, lieber Onkel,
> Daß man es fast unmenschlich nennen könnte:
> Und Gott schuf nichts Milderes, als dich.
>
> (*SW* I, 679; 1107–11)

(To crown his head because he conquered, then cut off his head – oh, surely that's not something history demands you do. Dear uncle, that would be an action *so* sublime one would almost have to call it cruel, inhuman: yet God has made no milder man than you.) [G, 320]

Similarly, when, in a further act of *mauvaise foi*, he spuriously invokes the notion of the Fatherland in an attempt to maintain that he has 'no choice' in the matter, Natalie gently points out the weakness of his argument:

> O Herr! Was sorgst du doch? Dies Vaterland!
> Das wird, um dieser Regung deiner Gnade,
> Nicht gleich, zerschellt in Trümmern, untergehn.
>
> (*SW* I, 680; 1122–4)

(Oh, Sir, why should you be so very fearful? The Fatherland indeed! It won't collapse on the spot because your heart is moved to mercy!) [G, 320]

Natalie knows, perhaps better then the Elector himself, that his obsession with 'the ten commandments of the March of Brandenburg' is capable of leading him to commit a crime which, because he is a human being and not the blind instrument of a system, he will regret for ever afterwards. At the same time, she knows that, despite his capacity for compassion, the Elector (as head of state) will wish to appear to have upheld the conventions of the artificial world over which he presides, so she is careful to add: 'the rules of war must never be allowed to fall into contempt' [G, 321] ('Das Kriegsgesetz, das weiß ich wohl, soll herrschen'; *SW* I, 680; 1129) before going on to say: 'nor must our tender feelings, equally!' [G, 321] ('Jedoch die lieblichen Gefühle auch'; *SW* I, 680; 1130). In addition, she goes to considerable lengths to reassure him by painting an extremely rosy picture of the future:[27]

> Das Vaterland, das du uns gründetest,
> Steht, eine feste Burg, mein edler Ohm:
> Das wird ganz andre Stürme noch ertragen,
> Fürwahr, als diesen unberufnen Sieg;
> Das wird sich ausbaun herrlich, in der Zukunft,
> Erweitern, unter Enkels Hand, verschönern,
> Mit Zinnen, üppig, feenhaft, zur Wonne
> Der Freunde, und zum Schrecken aller Feinde:
> (*SW* I, 680; 1131–8)

(The Fatherland we owe to you, good uncle, is a mighty fortress; it will weather heavier storms by far than a victory that didn't come exactly as was called for in the battle plan; the future years will see its walls extend on every side, the citadel enlarging still as heir succeeds to heir and battlement crowds battlement as if sprung up by magic to our friends' delight and enemies' dismay.) [G, 321]

It is highly likely (and Kottwitz will re-emphasise this point in act V, scene 5) that if the members of this society are reduced to automata acting from blind obedience rather than loyalty and patriotism, then the future of this state will be severely threatened not merely from without but also, and far more importantly, from within.[28]

Although the Elector, in one act of self-deception after another, tries to repudiate all of Natalie's arguments by invoking the 'sanctity' of such concepts as the Fatherland and the authority of the court, when she finally confronts him with her account of the Prince's broken spirit, her 'shaft' ('Pfeil') strikes home. The Elector now sees that if the grand game is to continue, the Prince will need a stiffener to restore his flagging *amour-propre*. It is then that he decides that he can 'relent' and offer the Prince a 'pardon'. However, the shrewd Natalie suspects that all is not well; she fears that the Elector, trapped as he is within his artificial world, may – as indeed he does – send out another challenge to the vaingloriously susceptible Prince. And the knowing way in which she expresses her 'hope and belief' that her uncle would never stoop to deceiving amounts to a covert attempt to let him know that she considers him quite capable of this:

> Was deine Huld, o Herr, so rasch erweckt,
> Ich weiß es nicht und untersuch es nicht.
> Das aber, sieh, das fühl ich in der Brust,
> Unedel meiner spotten wirst du nicht:
> Der Brief enthalte, was es immer sei,
> Ich glaube Rettung – und ich danke dir!
> (*SW* I, 682–3; 1200–5)

(I've no idea, and shan't inquire, what it was that moved you to be merciful so suddenly. But I am sure, Sir, in my heart I'm sure you would never descend to playing jokes on me. Let the letter say whatever it may say, my faith is, he is saved – and for that I have yourself to thank!) [G, 324]

After these words, it can come as no surprise that Natalie, ever the realist, immediately takes the added precaution of signing Kottwitz's petition in the following scene, referring to it as a document:

> Das, in des Herrn Entscheidung, klug gebraucht,
> Als ein Gewicht kann in die Waage fallen,
> Das ihm vielleicht, den Ausschlag, einzuleiten,
> Sogar willkommen ist . . . (*SW* I, 684; 1232–5)

([which] if used in the right way, could tip the scales of our Sovereign's judgement; he would even welcome it, perhaps, as helping him to arrive at a decision.) [G, 325]

She signs the petition believing that if public opinion can be mobilised in this way, it will provide the Elector with the excuse he needs: he will be able to claim that, in pardoning the Prince, he did not give in to 'human weakness' but was 'compelled' to act as he did by the wishes of the people. This episode also shows that Natalie sets little store by the conventions underpinning this artificial military world, especially when they stand in the way of a common-sense solution to the problem in hand. For when Count Reuss tells her that Kottwitz cannot follow his personal inclinations for want of an official order summoning him to Fehrbellin, she wastes no time in drawing one up 'on behalf of' the Elector:

Zum Glück trug mir der Kurfürst, fällt mir ein,
Bedrängt von anderen Geschäften, auf,
An Kottwitz, dem die Stallung dort zu eng,
Zum Marsch hierher die Order zu erlassen!

(*SW* 1, 685; 1265–8)

(Luckily I just remembered that the Elector, who had many other matters on his mind, asked me to send an order to Kottwitz instructing him to leave his current stabling there that is too cramped and move his troops here instead.)

Of course the fact that she is able to do this so simply highlights yet another flaw in this would-be robotic army, namely that once the chain of command has been accessed, however deviously, the instructions pass through the system unimpeded by any commonsense considerations.

THE DENOUEMENT: NATALIE'S 'REVOLUTION'

In the opening scene of act v, the Elector is taken aback to learn of Kottwitz's unexpected arrival in Fehrbellin, though his remarks show that he is surprised rather than afraid. For the fact that this 'mutiny' has been instigated by the faithful Kottwitz convinces him that the situation cannot be too serious:

Doch weils Hans Kottwitz aus der Priegnitz ist,
Der sich mir naht, willkürlich, eigenmächtig,
So will ich mich auf märksche Weise fassen:
Von den drei Locken, die man silberglänzig,
Auf seinem Schädel sieht, faß ich die eine,
Und führ ihn still, mit seinen zwölf Schwadronen,
Nach Arnstein, in sein Hauptquartier, zurück.
Wozu die Stadt aus ihrem Schlafe wecken?

(*SW* 1, 692; 1417–24)

(But since it's Hans Kottwitz out of Priegnitz comes upon me in this way, unauthorised and unallowed, I'll do it as we do such things in Brandenburg: take hold of him by one of his three silver hairs and lead him quietly, with his twelve squadrons, back to Arnstein, where old Hans belongs. Why wake the sleeping town?) [G, 333]

In this assessment of the situation he is quite correct. Kottwitz is no less taken aback than the Elector himself, but what troubles him most is that he may, unwittingly, have done something disloyal. And so when the Elector asks him who ordered him to Fehrbellin, Kottwitz exclaims: 'Good Lord, Prince, I hope it comes as no surprise to you!' [G, 336] ('Bei Gott, mein Fürst und Herr, ich will nicht hoffen, | Daß dir die Order fremd?'; *SW* I, 695; 1494–5). The Elector, who knows full well that he has not issued any such order, attempts to bluster it out ('in the Brandenburg manner'), pretending to have everything under control and deflects Kottwitz's question with a lie, maintaining that what he wanted to know was who had *delivered* the order, not who had *signed* it.[29]

KOTTWITZ'S DEFENCE OF THE PRINCE

In his defence of the Prince in act v, scene 5, Kottwitz, the experienced campaigner draws the audience's attention to the discrepancy between his own realistic, tactical view of military combat and the Elector's largely 'theoretical' strategic standpoint. Kottwitz does not even address the charge of 'insubordination' itself; he defends the Prince on the ground that, from a tactical point of view, he took the appropriate action at the right moment:

> Dem Prinzen, der den Krieg gar wohl versteht,
> Hätt ich mich ruhig unterwerfen sollen.
> Die Schweden wankten, auf dem linken Flügel,
> Und auf dem rechten wirkten sie Sukkurs;
> Hätt er auf deine Order warten wollen,
> Sie faßten Posten wieder, in den Schluchten,
> Und nimmermehr hättst du den Sieg erkämpft.
>
> (*SW* I, 696–7; 1530–6)

(The Prince knows war, he understands it; I was wrong, I should have bowed at once to his decision. The Swedish left was giving way – they started marching over reinforcements from their right to bolster it. If he had waited for your order, time would have been allowed them to re-establish their position in the ravines – and then you might have kissed good-bye forever, Sir, to all your hopes of victory.) [G, 338]

The Elector attempts to counter this, claiming that the Prince's premature action prevented the total annihilation of the Swedish forces, but Kottwitz's response highlights once again the gulf that lies between the amateur with his desire for perfection and the experienced campaigner with his more realistic outlook. And although he takes care to flatter his superior with the words:

> Es ist der Stümper Sache, nicht die deine,
> Des Schicksals höchsten Kranz erringen wollen;
> Du nahmst, bis heut, noch stets, was es dir bot.
> (*SW* 1, 697; 1547–9)

(Sir, only hopeless amateurs, not soldiers like yourself, imagine they'll reach out and seize, at once, the greatest crown that Fortune has to give; until today you always took whatever she might offer.) [G, 338]

it is clear to anyone with eyes to see that the Elector himself is one of the 'hopeless amateurs' ('Stümper') to whom Kottwitz refers. Furthermore, as the old soldier goes on to explain, there is no guarantee that the Swedes would have been defeated in the way that the Elector claims would – of necessity – have been the case, had his 'grand strategy' been followed to the letter. Thus, although the Elector may protest: 'I've no desire for a victory that's a bastard child of the slut chance' [G, 339] ('Den Sieg nicht mag ich, der, ein Kind des Zufalls, | Mir von der Bank fällt'; *SW* 1, 697; 1566–7) this is at best wishful thinking, the view of a remote theoretician, and certainly not a cogent argument against Kottwitz's position. Kottwitz's defence of the Prince is based on the fact that the Prince has been successful and inevitably it addresses the vital question of how a modern fighting-force should be organised:

> Was kümmert dich, ich bitte dich, die Regel,
> Nach der der Feind sich schlägt: wenn er nur nieder
> Vor dir, mit allen seinen Fahnen, sinkt?
> Die Regel, die ihn schlägt, das ist die höchste!
> Willst du das Heer, das glühend an dir hängt,
> Zu einem Werkzeug machen, gleich dem Schwerte,
> Das tot in deinem goldnen Gürtel ruht? (*SW* 1, 698; 1575–81)

(Why, I ask, should you be so concerned about the enemy's being beaten exactly as the rule book calls for, if only he is overthrown with all his banners and rolling at your feet? The rule that beats him is the only rule! The army whose delight it is to serve you – you would have it be a senseless instrument, a dead thing, like the sword you've got tucked in your golden belt?) [G, 339]

Here he points out that an army composed of real human beings cannot be made to function with the exceptionless regularity of a machine. Furthermore, the fact that this is impossible is not, as the Elector might suppose, a disadvantage – quite the opposite. The effectiveness of an army is not based upon the blind obedience of each of its 'pre-programmed' members, but upon each individual's unique, whole-hearted commitment to the cause for which he is fighting. For as Kottwitz reminds his sovereign:

> Schütt ich mein Blut dir, an dem Tag der Schlacht,
> Für Sold, seis Geld, seis Ehre, in den Staub?
> Behüte Gott, dazu ist es zu gut!
> Was! Meine Lust hab, meine Freude ich,
> Frei und für mich im Stillen, unabhängig,
> An deiner Trefflichkeit und Herrlichkeit,
> Am Ruhm und Wachstum deines großen Namens!
> (*SW* 1, 698; 1588–94)

(Do I, you think, pour out my blood upon the battlefield for pay – for gold coin or for honours? God forbid, my blood comes at a dearer price than that! Oh no! My joy and my delight, for which I am beholden to no man, which I possess without the need to speak a word, I have in your great goodness, glory, the fame, continually growing, of your great name!) [G, 339–40]

Towards the end of his speech, he makes two further important points. Firstly, he reminds the Elector that the unpredictable nature of warfare (and of human behaviour generally) makes it impossible to say for certain what the outcome of any given course of action will be;[30] a flash of inspiration which, in one situation will secure victory, in another, may lead to defeat. To believe that every flash of ('insubordinate') inspiration will – of necessity – result in success is to take a wholly unrealistic view of warfare. By the same token, to punish every instance of failure is not only unrealistic; it is profoundly wasteful:

> Die schlechte,
> Kurzsichtge Staatskunst, die, um eines Falles,
> Da die Empfindung sich verderblich zeigt,
> Zehn andere vergißt, im Lauf der Dinge,
> Da die Empfindung einzig retten kann! (*SW* 1, 698; 1583–7)

(What bad, short-sighted policy, because quick-acting instinct comes to grief in one case, to rule it out thereafter in instance after instance in which spontaneous impulse, it alone, can save the day!) [G, 339]

Secondly, he concludes his defence by pointing out the paradoxical (and indeed absurd) nature of the death sentence in the present case: the Elector is demanding something which the Prince is all too willing to give him. And citing his own behaviour by way of example, Kottwitz demonstrates that this is precisely what loyalty means:

> Und sprächst du, das Gesetzbuch in der Hand:
> 'Kottwitz, du hast den Kopf verwirkt!' so sagt ich:
> 'Das wußt ich Herr; da nimm ihn hin, hier ist er:
> Als mich ein Eid an deine Krone band,
> Mit Haut und Haar, nahm ich den Kopf nicht aus,
> Und nichts dir gäb ich, was nicht dein gehörte!'
> (*SW* I, 698–9; 1603–8)

(And if you took the regulations out and said: 'Kottwitz, you've just forfeited your head,' I'd answer: 'Yes, I know, Sir, here it is, it's yours. I bound myself to defend your throne with all my heart and soul – my head was not excepted. So I don't give you more than what's your own!') [G, 340]

And when he has finished, the Elector good-humouredly passes over his arguments on the grounds that he is all too ready to be seduced by them by reason of his affection for both Kottwitz and the Prince:

> Mit dir, du alter, wunderlicher Herr,
> Werd ich nie fertig! Es besticht dein Wort
> Mich, mit arglistger Rednerkunst gesetzt,
> Mich, der, du weißt, dir zugetan . . . (*SW* I, 699; 1609–12)

(An extraordinary fellow, yes, you are – you're more than I can deal with! I find my mind suborned by all your cunning arts of rhetoric, who am too much inclined already, as you know, to sympathise with what you feel.) [G, 340]

The fact is, however, that the old soldier's arguments cannot be so simply dismissed as 'mere rhetoric'; they have exposed serious weaknesses in the kind of military discipline the Elector reveres, and it would be surprising if the latter has not noticed this.

HOHENZOLLERN'S DEFENCE OF THE PRINCE

Whilst Kottwitz's defence of the Prince constitutes a serious attack on the myth that a proper use of discipline can over-ride human freedom and initiative entirely and create a 'perfect', self-regulating military machine, Hohenzollern takes the opposite line, accepting unquestioningly the principles of discipline so dear to the heart of the Elector. When he reminds the Elector of the events of act I, scene I, he implies that it is the Elector himself who is to blame for the Prince's distracted state of mind – a point not lost on the Elector:

> Und nun, wenn ich dich anders recht verstehe,
> Türmst du, wie folgt, ein Schlußgebäu mir auf:
> Hätt ich, mit dieses jungen Träumers Zustand,
> Zweideutig nicht gescherzt, so blieb er schuldlos:
> Bei der Parole wär er nicht zerstreut,
> Nicht widerspenstig in der Schlacht gewesen.
> Nicht? Nicht? Das ist die Meinung? (*SW* I, 702; 1706–12)

(And so, unless I quite mistake your words, what must follow for me, with inexorable logic, is: if I had not allowed myself a dubious amusement with the young dreamer in his helpless state, he never would have proved delinquent in his duty: at the briefing, his mind would not have been on other things; in the fighting, he never would have failed to follow orders. Right? Confess it! Isn't that your meaning?) [G, 343]

True to type, however, Hohenzollern avoids openly accusing his superior, opting instead for a more tactful, diplomatic approach: 'Draw your own conclusions, Sire' [G, 344] ('Mein Gebieter, | Das überlaß ich jetzt dir, zu ergänzen'; *SW* I, 702; 1712–13). In this line of defence, Hohenzollern exploits the rigidly hierarchical nature of the chain of command which makes it easy to shift the blame from one party to another. Essentially he accuses the Elector of having behaved irresponsibly towards the Prince (though of course not intentionally) and thus of having 'caused' the latter to behave irresponsibly in turn. The Elector's complacent ridicule of this argument, serves only to reveal its essential correctness:

> Tor, der du bist, Blödsinniger! hättest du
> Nicht in den Garten mich herabgerufen,
> So hätt ich, einem Trieb der Neugier folgend,

Mit diesem Träumer harmlos nicht gescherzt.
Mithin behaupt ich, ganz mit gleichem Recht,
Der sein Versehn veranlaßt hat, warst du!
(*SW* I, 702; 1714–19)

(What a fool you are, an idiot! If you had not said, Come down to the garden, Sir, and see! – my curiosity would not have been aroused and I shouldn't have played that harmless joke of mine on the dreaming Prince. And so, with equal justice I declare: The one who is to blame for his mistake was you!) [G, 344]

The Elector has virtually sawn off the very branch he is sitting on. For in attempting to defend himself against Hohenzollern's 'accusation' he inadvertently draws attention to the fact that within a hierarchical structure of this kind, identifying the guilty party in any given situation is an almost wholly arbitrary affair. By showing that essentially the same arguments can be deployed to defend the Prince as were used to condemn him, Kleist reveals the emptiness of the system as a means of governing the actions of free human beings with minds to see beyond the letter of the law.

THE SUMMING UP

In act v, scene 5, the Elector faces two quite different sets of arguments in support of the Prince. On the one hand there is Kottwitz, who exposes the unsuitability of the Elector's brand of discipline for real military engagements, and who argues that the issue of the Prince's alleged insubordination is not relevant here. And on the other, there is Hohenzollern who exploits the very notion of military discipline that condemns the Prince to prove the latter's innocence, and who argues that the cause of this act of insubordination is the Elector himself. Kottwitz's defence rejects the Elector's system of military discipline altogether; Hohenzollern's upholds the system but seeks to apportion blame at a different point within it. Thus the Prince's innocence is proved twice-over and it is this two-fold protection, which appears to cover every eventuality, that prompts the Elector's reference to the 'Delphic wisdom' [G, 344] ('die delphsche Weisheit'; *SW* I, 702; 1720) of his officers. And as if that were not enough, there is the peaceful appeal for clemency towards the Prince made by all the army officers. For, as the Field Marshall ('Feldmarschall') warns him in act v, scene 3:

> Herr, ich beschwöre dich, wenns überall
> Dein Wille ist, den Prinzen zu begnadigen:
> Tus, eh ein höchstverhaßter Schritt geschehn!
> Jedwedes Heer liebt, weißt du, seinen Helden;
> Laß diesen Funken nicht, der es durchglüht,
> Ein heillos fressend Feuer um sich greifen.
>
> (*SW* I, 693–4; 1457–62)

(I beg you, Sir, if you mean to grant a pardon to the Prince, then do it now before some dreadful thing occurs! An army as you know full well – it loves its heroes! Don't, however, let this spark which warms its courage turn into a conflagration devouring all around it.) [G, 335]

Moreover, aware as he is that the Elector will not wish to be seen to be giving in to public pressure, he tells him that he can still act without losing face: 'Kottwitz and the men he has collected don't know yet that you've been warned, most loyally, by me' [G, 335] ('Kottwitz weiß und die Schar, die er versammelt, | Noch nicht, daß dich mein treues Wort gewarnt'; *SW* I, 694; 1463–4).

THE FINAL MOVE: THE PRINCE AND THE ELECTOR

In the end, however, the Elector does not choose to be moved by the arguments of Kottwitz, Hohenzollern or the Field Marshall. Instead, he summons the Prince himself to make the decision for him, and addresses Kottwitz, saying:

> Der wird dich lehren, das versichr' ich dich,
> Was Kriegszucht und Gehorsam sei! Ein Schreiben
> Schickt' er mir mindstens zu, das anders lautet,
> Als der spitzfündge Lehrbegriff der Freiheit,
> Den du hier, wie ein Knabe, mir entfaltet.
>
> (*SW* I, 699; 1616–20)

(Believe me, he will teach you what obedience and discipline should be! I've got a letter here from him, at any rate, that has a different ring indeed from all those sophistries you've spun out, like a clever schoolboy, for my benefit.) [G, 340]

Of course the Elector does ultimately spare the Prince, but not, he claims, because his hand has been forced, but because the Prince has (as the Elector was confident he would) shown himself to be so committed to the over-riding authority of military discipline, that rather than breach it, he is prepared to order his own execution. When the Prince appears on stage in act v, scene 7, the Elector shows him Kottwitz's petition.[31] But whilst the Prince gratefully acknowledges the (not inconsiderable) risks that Kottwitz has run on his behalf, he declines to avail himself of the latter's help, for he has now reached the disastrous stage of self-deception at which he is willing to sacrifice his own life in order to preserve the integrity of this make-believe world. As he says:

> Ich will das heilige Gesetz des Kriegs,
> Das ich verletzt, im Angesicht des Heers,
> Durch einen freien Tod verherrlichen! (*SW* I, 704; 1750–2)

(I wish to glorify, before the eyes of the whole army, the sacred rules of war against which I offended, by freely choosing death!) [G, 345]

As the final scene unfolds, it becomes increasingly obvious that what we are witnessing is little more than a public relations exercise, stage-managed by the Elector, to prop up the hollow structures on which his authority rests. From his point of view, the Prince's performance ('before the eyes of the whole army') could not be surpassed; the latter's words of farewell provide a ringing endorsement of his glorious rectitude:

> Nun fleh ich jeden Segen dir herab,
> Den, von dem Thron der Wolken, Seraphin
> Auf Heldenhäupter jauchzend niederschütten:
> Geh und bekrieg, o Herr, und überwinde
> Den Weltkreis, der dir trotzt – denn du bists wert!
> (*SW* I, 705; 1795–9)

(I pray that every blessing may be yours which seraphim, on their cloudy thrones pour down, with loud exulting cries, on heroes' heads! Go forth, great Sovereign, to fight and, even if the whole world should defy you, conquer – for you are worthy of no less!) [G, 347]

The Prince has indeed been 'educated', a fact to which the Elector is careful to allude, when he says: 'it has been an education for him' [G, 348] ('die Schule dieser Tagen'; *SW* I, 706; 1822). But in what does this education consist? Has he, as the Elector believes, been educated to a state of blind compliance with the nightmarish system of rules that constitute 'the sacred rules of war', and to suppress all sense of his own autonomy and initiative? Or has the Prince come to see (like Natalie, Kottwitz and the other more common-sense members of the Elector's entourage) that whilst strict discipline is an essential component of the art of war, it must be a flexible kind of discipline that allows for individual initiative and takes into account the strengths and weaknesses of ordinary human beings? The ending of the play shows that the reasonable balance of discipline and initiative implied in the second of these alternatives has not been achieved; the old, rigid order is still firmly in place. The Prince will be able to escape from his neurotic preoccupation with this inhuman system of discipline only by becoming Elector and thus ceasing to be personally at risk from it. However, as we have seen, the Elector has been able to conceal the absurdity of this system only by breaking its rules and introducing new 'moves': pardoning is an action not permitted by the rules. Consequently, the Prince, if he inherits the system, will be faced with an endless series of similar dilemmas in which he can salve his conscience only by resorting to pardons and other expedients wholly contrary to the system he will have undertaken to maintain. And one day, perhaps, he will recall the sinister pronouncement of Kottwitz, that a truly committed member of the system might be prepared to allow even the demise of its sovereign rather than break one of its 'sacred laws':

Bei dem lebendgen Gott,
Du könntest an Verderbens Abgrund stehn,
Daß er, um dir zu helfen, dich zu retten,
Auch nicht das Schwert mehr zückte, ungerufen!
(*SW* I, 707; 1825–8)

(By the living God, if you were tottering on the brink of ruin, about to plunge into the abyss, he wouldn't even *think* of drawing his sword to help you, rescue you, unsummoned!) [G, 348]

Bearing all this in mind, we are obliged to look more sceptically at the Prince's behaviour in the last scenes of the play. His 'death-monologue' in act v, scene 10, beginning with the words: 'Now immortality, you're mine, entirely mine!' [G, 349] ('Nun, o Unsterblichkeit, bist du ganz mein!'; *SW* I, 707; 1830) is yet another virtuoso display of heroic bravado for the assembled onlookers that suggests he is once more under the spell of his romantic delusion. But this pretence of heroic indifference to death cannot 'protect' him from the (decent) human feeling of fear, and thus when Natalie holds out the garland and the chain and he realises that he is not going to be executed after all, then, like a 'mere' man, he faints from relief – an anti-climactic lapse back into the real world.

CONCLUSION

And thus the play ends in the same fashion as it began: as 'a dream, what else?' [G, 350] ('Ein Traum, was sonst?'; *SW* I, 709; 1856). The artificial resolution at the end of *Prinz Friedrich von Homburg* is highly reminiscent of the (equally contrived) ending of the earlier drama, *Das Käthchen von Heilbronn*,[32] and invites the audience to adopt a similar attitude of sceptical detachment. There still remains the question of the Prince's fate, for he is still young and has the opportunity to modify his behaviour in the light of his (horrific) experiences should he wish to do so. Essentially, he can develop in one of two ways: either he can choose to forget what he has undergone in the past twenty-four hours and commit himself fully to 'the ten commandments of the March of Brandenburg', in which case he will eventually turn into another version of the old Elector; or he can modify the system along the sensible lines which Kottwitz, Natalie and the others could easily indicate. For, as Kleist has shown, a system that requires so many running repairs is in permanent danger of collapsing under the weight of its own contradictions.

Kleist breaks new ground in his characterisation of the Prince. For he presents many of the symptoms of the classic psychoneurotic personality. His frequent 'absences' are remarked upon in the play, and his sado-masochistic involvement with 'the sacred laws of war' are typical of the anxiety-neurotic's vain attempt to deal with the conflict within himself. All his fellow-officers have difficulties with the Elector's code, but none of them attempts to deal with his difficulties by making an all-out commitment to its 'infallible correctness' as the Prince does. The others know they can never escape the long arm of this code, but the Prince can imagine himself in the privileged position of the Elector, able to believe the unbelievable because he is exempt from its menace. However, he cannot be certain that he will reach the haven of the Elector's position, and remains in a limbo of doubt. Hence his neurotic ambivalence: one day an advocate of total submission to the law, the next, the worst offender against its simplest tenets.

CHAPTER 10

Conclusions

In the present study, I have examined each play separately on the ground that Kleist's characters can be properly understood only in their respective social contexts. Nowhere is this more true than in *Penthesilea*, where to judge the queen's behaviour in isolation from the Amazon state is to run the risk of seeing it through the uncomprehending eyes of the (boorish) Greeks.[1] It is a central component of Kleist's basic thesis that all individuals are, to a greater or lesser extent, products of their societies. If for a moment we step back to consider the plays as a whole, we can discern essentially three distinct levels of conditioning. In the first place there are the older and more experienced members of these societies, usually the leaders, who have been so steeped in its conventions that there is little hope of their redemption. In the second place, there are the more youthful (but usually high-born) individuals whose indoctrination, although at a relatively advanced stage, is not yet complete. Finally, there are those who inhabit the margins of these societies and have, to varying degrees, escaped the stranglehold of convention. As we shall see, the members of this last group are often very different from one another; nevertheless, in the essentially aristocratic male-oriented worlds in which the plays are set, Kleist suggests that women, the young and those of humble origins are more likely to see through the prevailing conventions than adult, high-ranking males.

In the first of these groups, we find those whose ancestors provided the links between the prevailing social arrangements and their allegedly transcendent models. Since these individuals are not the creators of such systems, but have simply inherited them from their forebears, they are more or less unaware of the arbitrary historical processes which have brought them into being. And, having little appreciation of the original impulse that wove them into the very fabric of society, they have neither an interest in, nor any means of, questioning their validity. Thus, Amphitryon (in *Amphitryon*), the Kaiser (in *Das Käthchen von Heilbronn*) and the Elector (in *Prinz Friedrich von Homburg*) all preside over what have become quasi self-regulating societies, which, because they manifestly favour the interests of the ruling elite, are all too easily regarded by them as enshrining in their basic prejudices profound insights into what is 'natural' and what is not. By plunging these figures into a series of peculiarly bizarre and paradoxical situations, Kleist exposes the ideological character of these allegedly natural ways of life, revealing their inherent contradictions and, more importantly, the essentially flawed approach to human progress contained in the underlying philosophies. Furthermore, Kleist's critique is not solely confined to those authoritarian societies favouring the interests of the dominant class, but also embraces societies founded on more benevolent (essentially Christian) precepts of love and forgiveness, such as Warwand in *Die Familie Schroffenstein* and the Amazon State in *Penthesilea*.[2] In *Die Familie Schroffenstein*, for example, he shows how Sylvester, though essentially a well-intentioned man, has only acquiesced, however willingly, in a system that is not of his own making. This leads to a state of idle complacency where the appeal to tradition replaces argument. This gradual process of decline is hinted at in the contrast between the elderly Sylvius and his son, Sylvester, of whom the former has a far better understanding of the original ideological precepts underpinning Warwand society. A similar process can be discerned in *Penthesilea*: the original (revolutionary) impulse behind the founding of the Amazon state (the work of Tanaïs) now lies in the distant past and has, over the years, been reduced to the status of an accepted 'faith', which, however 'unnatural' it may seem to the Greeks, is regarded as perfectly 'natural' by the Amazons. It is safe to assume that the original conception of the precepts underpinning Amazon society was more explicitly thought through than is its contemporary day-to-day application by the High Priestess. And Kleist leaves us in no doubt that, despite some serious flaws (which he points out), the structure of society in both Warwand and Themiscyra represents a genuine advance on all the other societies presented in his plays. Indeed, in his depiction of the Amazon state, Kleist makes a bold attempt to portray certain features of a post-revolutionary society set up for the benefit of all its members. Although some of the Amazons have titles, these are, for the most part, mere formalities and there is little evidence of a qualitative distinction between the treatment of the 'higher' and 'lower' ranked Amazons.[3] Furthermore, Amazon society is unique in another important respect in that, although restricted to women, membership of this society is voluntary. Penthesilea is not forced to comply with its conventions, and when, in scene 19, it appears that she no longer wishes to accept them, she is simply invited by the High Priestess to leave and join the Greeks. By contrast, in Greek 'society' (here, the army) total obedience is required and exacted through the use of force on any would-be dissenters. Kleist's preference for Warwand and Themiscyra is obvious. But in keeping with his views on education generally,[4] he does not give in to the temptation to set up either as an example of 'perfection' and the catastrophic denouements of *Die Familie Schroffenstein* and *Penthesilea* are intended to act as a warning for those who believe that such 'transcendent' models exist and are available for human beings to 'copy' in reforming their existing institutions.

The contrast in Kleist's plays between the older, more experienced members of society and their younger, less experienced counterparts, enables him to draw our attention to the important role played by processes of social indoctrination in maintaining the *status quo* (and the defects inherent therein). For the most part, literary critics have ignored the extent to which Kleist's young 'heroes' are the products, albeit as yet imperfect ones, of the system against which they are said to 'rebel'. As we have seen, Ottokar does not really rebel against his father, Rupert; Achilles' attitude to women is not fundamentally different from that of Odysseus and the other Greek commanders; and in *Prinz Friedrich von Homburg*, the Prince's behaviour is not a considered act of insubordination against the Elector. All three of these youthful figures are members of the dominant class, obviously destined for positions at the head of their respective societies, and for this reason none of them seriously challenges the prevailing conventions. Any disparity, therefore, between their behaviour and that of their superiors is not due to a conscious rejection of the prevailing norms, but to the fact that these have not yet been properly absorbed. Moreover, these young men, precisely because they have not been exposed to social indoctrination for as long as their superiors, have a better chance of turning out differently. And Kleist constantly hints at this possibility through the open-ended character of his individual works. The same may be said of some of Kleist's younger female characters, such as Alkmene in *Amphitryon*; she is of noble birth, yet she occupies a somewhat marginalised position in her society by reason of her youth and the fact that she is a woman in a patriarchal culture. Similarly, in *Prinz Friedrich von Homburg*, of all the high-born characters, it is Natalie who most clearly sees through the web of convention that constitutes the life of the court.

Before considering the role of those characters, who for various reasons, have remained largely untainted by the prevailing norms of social convention, we should note the existence of another class of individual, represented by the likes of Walter in *Der zerbrochne Krug* and Kottwitz in *Prinz Friedrich von Homburg*. Both these characters are essentially pragmatists, experienced men who are forced by circumstances to take a more realistic view of justice and war respectively than do their masters. As such, both men play an important role in averting some of the disasters latent in the flawed systems espoused by their superiors. Thus, Walter's brief is to ensure that the corrupt features behind the painted face of 'perfect justice' are not too often or for too long exposed to the eyes of her devotees – or of her victims. And Kottwitz's task is to oversee the successful management of an army in the field, whilst paying lip-service to his commander-in-chief's unrealistic conception of military discipline and perfectionist ambitions as a master-strategist. Of course, both Walter and Kottwitz are, to a certain extent, guilty of *mauvaise foi*; both have seen through the system yet neither directly challenges it, preferring instead, to work to ensure that some of its worst excesses are avoided.

Finally we come to the most interesting and diverse group of Kleist's characters: those who have managed to avoid almost completely the more pernicious effects of conventional society or who have seen through these conventions to the extent that they either reject them outright or attempt to manipulate them to their own advantage. Perhaps the best example is Johann in *Die Familie Schroffenstein*, whose inclusion in the play seems explicable only on the assumption that his behaviour highlights the contrasting artificiality of that of Ottokar and Agnes. As an illegitimate child, Johann is effectively excluded from the power structures of Rossitz and, as a result, has not been required to comply with the prevailing conventions there to the same extent as Rupert's legitimate heir, Ottokar. However, his intelligence together with his daily experience of the world of Ottokar and Agnes, puts him at an advantage over the members of the lower orders. As we have seen, Johann's understanding of love is close to the essentially Christian, selfless view of love favoured by Kleist, and Johann's 'madness' at the end of the play constitutes a rejection of the 'sane' world of the Schroffensteiner. Like Johann, Kunigunde and Aristan are also outsiders. Kunigunde's marginalisation is symbolised by her unmasking and banishment at the end of *Das Käthchen von Heilbronn*, Aristan's by his execution at the end of *Die Hermannsschlacht.* Kunigunde has the intelligence to see through the prevailing stereotype of 'perfect womanhood' and has had some success in subverting the system from within. Aristan has no illusions about Hermann's imperialistic ambitions, and in insisting on his right to retain his autonomy as a self-determining individual, forfeits his life. The gloomy fates of Johann, Kunigunde and Aristan all highlight the difficulties faced by those who (like Kleist himself) live within such worlds without ever truly belonging to them.

The characters from the lowest ranks of society, such as Eve, Marthe, Sosias and the like, are in a rather different situation. Usually they have not been educated to the same degree as their superiors and have had little direct experience of the way of life of the elite and so have less to lose by rebelling against the establishment than do the higher-ranking Johann, Kunigunde and Aristan. Eve in *Der zerbrochne Krug* (at least in the original, longer version of the play) is a woman in whom the 'advantages' of lowly rank are combined with a shrewd understanding of the mechanisms of power. Because of her youth, Eve is not burdened with her mother's notion of the over-riding importance of 'feminine virtue' and, as a result, is able to challenge the district magistrate, Walter, and obtain what she requires. Of course, belonging to the lower ranks is not in itself an absolute guarantee against falling prey to convention. In fact the more the lower orders are able to move up the social scale and away from the hard facts of reality, the more liable they are to ape the grand manners of their betters. And this is not simply a question of rank, but also of age. The older Frau Marthe, for whom sexual escapades are, it is safe to assume, a thing of the past, can indulge in the luxury of insisting on fancy notions of feminine purity, but in her younger days it is quite probable that she would have taken a view more in line with that of her daughter, Eve. The same reaction is even more predictable in the case of the servants, whose work brings them into daily contact with the 'noble' behaviour of their high-ranking masters and who, by association, acquire a degree of snobbish regard for it. Charis in *Amphitryon* cannot help hoping that her husband, the slovenly Sosias, will become a little more genteel. And, as we have seen, even Sosias himself has moments (as in act III, scene 9, for example) when he imagines himself to be the 'loyal butler' supportively involved with his master in matters of great moment – the seduction of high-born women and that sort of thing.

The target of Kleist's critique is fundamentally the same in all his plays. He warns of the catastrophic consequences that ensue when human beings close their eyes to reality and rest complacently upon the rotting supports of ill-founded and out-moded conventional dogmas that promise certainty but deliver disaster. For as he shows, most notably in *Der zerbrochne Krug* and *Prinz Friedrich von Homburg*, the uncritical acceptance of such cliché-ridden codes of practice may result in tragedy – in each case the death of an innocent young man. And, as we have seen, in both cases tragedy is avoided largely by the common-sense intervention of a young woman – Eve (aided by Walter) in *Der zerbrochne Krug* and Natalie (aided by Kottwitz) in *Prinz Friedrich von Homburg*. In *Die Familie Schroffenstein* and *Penthesilea* common-sense circumspection is ignored with tragic results.

So what, if anything, do Kleist's characters learn from their experiences? The open-ended nature of Kleist's work, and the fact that the characters themselves cannot really be said to undergo a process of development on stage make this a difficult question to answer, particularly in the case of the four plays which appear to end on a note of reconciliation: *Der zerbrochne Krug*, *Amphitryon*, *Das Käthchen von Heilbronn* and *Prinz Friedrich von Homburg*. As we have already seen, Walter does not restore Eve's 'trust' in the authorities any more than Jupiter 'educates' Alkmene to a better understanding of the nature of love. Nor does Käthchen 'teach' Strahl to trust his instincts any more than the Elector 'guides' the Prince to a genuine understanding of the importance of 'the sacred laws of war'. Instead, Kleist presents us with a series of characters each of whom pursues an intrinsically flawed 'ideal' to its limit (and it is perhaps not insignificant that Alkmene, Käthchen and the Prince all collapse at the end of their respective 'ordeals'). In short, Kleist reveals the contradictions inherent in the prevailing concepts of love, justice and freedom by forcing his characters to pursue these 'ideals' to their logical (and usually absurd) conclusion, and whilst his plays may end with the prevailing structures of society still intact, the flawed nature of these 'ideals' has been cunningly exposed. And we, the audience, are left to draw our own conclusions. Will Alkmene learn from her painful experiences, or will she simply become a loyal wife to the boorish Amphitryon? Will the Prince learn from his lucky escape, or will he too one day put some unfortunate young man through the same ordeal? Will society change, or will things just carry on as before? No one can say for certain and Kleist himself provides no answers. His approach is oblique and he inserts many doubts into the minds of his audience, but along with those doubts, he also deftly inserts prospects of improvement.

In the past, critics have been inclined to regard Kleist's work as dominated by a conflict between the subjective and objective world, a conflict which he is said to have resolved in his last play, *Prinz Friedrich von Homburg*.[5] More recently, critics have started to question whether the alleged resolution at the end of even this play can be accepted uncritically, but there does appear to be some consensus that Kleist's last work is also his most advanced and that in it, some sort of synthesis is achieved. However, as I have tried to show, the denouement of *Prinz Friedrich von Homburg* is no less ironic than that of *Das Käthchen von Heilbronn* and the society with which we are left is anything but utopian. It is, therefore, perhaps appropriate to ask in what sense, if any, Kleist's work as a whole shows evidence of a 'development'. Although I have dealt with the plays in chronological order,[6] I do not believe that there is a clear line of development (at least of the sort alluded to above) running from one play to the next. For, as I have tried to demonstrate, all Kleist's plays share the same underlying theme, namely the difficulties that arise when human beings look to metaphysical 'insights' embodied in the prescriptive conventions of their societies to protect themselves against the inroads of uncertainty in their relations with one another. This fundamental problem is explored in relation to a variety of themes: justice in *Der zerbrochne Krug*, love and fidelity in *Amphitryon*, love and femininity in *Penthesilea* and *Das Käthchen von Heilbronn*, freedom and patriotic feeling in *Die Hermannsschlacht*, and military discipline in *Prinz Friedrich von Homburg*. It will be clear from this list that many of these themes are foreshadowed in *Die Familie Schroffenstein*, a not untypical first play with its abundance of rather schematically presented material. But to say that Kleist's work need not be regarded as a series of attempts to 'overcome' an epistemological crisis resulting from his encounter with Kant's philosophy,[7] is not to say that there is no difference between his first and last works. Such development as there is, however, should be seen in terms of his attempts to improve his technical skills as a writer,[8] and indeed it is this line of development that can be traced from *Die Familie Schroffenstein* through to *Prinz Friedrich von Homburg*.

The fact that his plays are often concerned with similar themes should not obscure their rich variety; Kleist was an astute observer of public taste and, as his remarks on *Penthesilea* and *Das Käthchen von Heilbronn* show, he knew what the theatre would and would not tolerate, even if he often chose to ignore this. Moreover, the wide variety of theatrical forms which he tried out, ranging from the classical comedy of Molière (in *Amphitryon*) to the popular chivalrous drama (in *Das Käthchen von Heilbronn*), bears witness to his continual willingness to experiment with dramatic form. It was Kleist's misfortune to live at a time when the German theatre was dominated at one end of the scale by the sentimental farces of Iffland and Kotzebue, and at the other, by the idealising aesthetics of Weimar Classicism and the dramas of Goethe and Schiller.[9]

It is in the early part of Kleist's life, roughly speaking the period from 1799 up until the publication of *Die Familie Schroffenstein* in early 1803 that the most clearly discernible developments take place. We can see him oscillate between his heady enthusiasm for, and crushing disappointment with, the ideals of his upbringing in the tradition of the eighteenth-century Enlightenment. In his earliest letters we witness his faith in the absolute power of reason to emancipate the individual from the caprices of fate and chance, an insight which encouraged him to leave the army and made him unwilling to take up a position in the Prussian civil service. His desperate search for certainty is everywhere visible: it lies behind his postulation that the practice of virtue must of necessity lead to happiness; it lies behind the formulation of a life-plan ('Lebensplan') which, if followed, would guide the individual infallibly towards his or her goal. But Kleist's encounter with Kant in the early part of 1801 was to put an end to his involvement with such wish-fulfilling, utopian panaceas. At this point in his life, it would appear that the sudden removal of such metaphysical 'certainties' was a crushing blow. For now it seemed to Kleist that the individual was inescapably trapped within the conventional forms of society that he so abhorred. In addition, his trip to post-revolutionary Paris merely confirmed his scepticism regarding the alleged benefits conferred on the ordinary members of society by technological 'progress'. All this resulted in a withdrawal from society altogether to a Rousseauesque retreat on the island of Thun, and it is there that he set to work on the first drafts of *Die Familie Schroffenstein.*

Many critics have claimed that Kleist's plays reflect the sense of despair that emerges from his private correspondence. For example, *Die Familie Schroffenstein* is often regarded as a fate-tragedy, a testament to Kleist's belief that the world is ruled only by fate and chance and that even the best-laid plans go awry. As we have seen, this view of Kleist's work is partly correct, but it is far from being the whole truth. For whilst in his plays and stories nothing is certain, equally not everything is purely a matter of chance. Similarly, it is often claimed that the 'heroine' of *Das Käthchen von Heilbronn* represents Kleist's 'ideal' woman. But such an assertion takes no account of the element of irony that is unmistakably at work in the play. In *Das Käthchen von Heilbronn*, Kleist criticises the conventional notions of femininity that he himself had harboured in his youthful (and illusory) quest for certainty in love. And thus his plays and stories bear witness to a critical reappraisal of the 'transcendent' ideals of his youth. The same development can be seen in his attitude to art and literature generally. For although his correspondence is full of echoes from the works of his eighteenth-century forebears, most notably those of his idols, Goethe and Schiller, in time Kleist came to see that despite their excellence, the way forward lay not in the imitation but in the *emulation* of such works. For as he writes in the fictional *Brief eines jungen Dichters an einen jungen Maler (Letter from a young writer to a young painter)*, 'the object . . . is not to become someone else, but to be yourself' [M, 238] ('denn die Aufgabe . . . ist ja nicht, ein anderer, sondern ihr selbst zu sein'; *SW* II, 336).

Notes

1 INTRODUCTION

1 See, for example, Klaus Müller-Salget, 'Das Prinzip der Doppeldeutigkeit in Kleists Erzählungen', *Zeitschrift für deutsche Philologie*, 92 (1973), 185–211; Walter Müller-Seidel, 'Die Struktur des Widerspruchs in Kleists *Marquise von O . . .*', *DVjs*, 28 (1954), 497–515; Denys Dyer, 'Kleist und das Paradoxe', *Kleist-Jahrbuch* (1981/2), 210–19.

2 For example, Wilhelm Emrich, 'Kleist und die moderne Literatur', in Walter Müller-Seidel, ed., *Heinrich von Kleist: vier Reden zu seinem Gedächtnis* (Berlin, 1962), pp. 9–25.

3 Franz Kafka, *Briefe an Felice und andere Korrespondenz aus der Verlobungszeit*, ed. Erich Heller and Jürgen Born (Frankfurt, 1967), p. 460.

4 See Wolfgang Wittkowski, 'Der neue Prometheus: Kleists *Amphitryon* zwischen Molière und Giraudoux', and Lawrence Ryan, 'Amphitryon: doch ein Lustspielstoff!', in Walter Müller-Seidel, ed., *Kleist und Frankreich* (Berlin, 1969), pp. 27–82 and pp. 83–121.

5 Wittkowski, 'Der neue Prometheus', p. 35.

6 Ryan, 'Amphitryon', p. 87.

7 The fact that Kleist calls his play a comedy ('ein Lustspiel') is, in Wittkowski's view, a reflection of the way in which both Jupiter's 'triumph' and Amphitryon's 'honour' at the end of the play are heavily ironised. See Wittkowski, 'Der neue Prometheus', p. 35.

8 Ryan, 'Amphitryon', pp. 83–5.

9 In this way, the Wittkowski–Ryan debate suggests that Kleist's play cannot be so straightforwardly subsumed under the genres of comedy and tragedy.

10 See chapter 5 below.

11 See, for example, Günter Blöcker, *Heinrich von Kleist oder Das absolute Ich* (Berlin, 1960).

12 See, for example, Hermann Reske, *Traum und Wirklichkeit im Werk Heinrich von Kleists* (Stuttgart, 1969).

13 Walter Müller-Seidel, *Versehen und Erkennen: eine Studie über Heinrich von Kleist* (Cologne, 1961), p. 7.
14 Ibid., p. 90.
15 Ibid., p. 131.
16 Ibid., p. 131.
17 Ibid., p. 214.
18 See Benno von Wiese, 'Das verlorene und wieder zu findende Paradies: eine Studie über den Begriff der Anmut bei Goethe, Kleist und Schiller', in Walter Müller-Seidel, ed., *Kleists Aufsatz über das Marionettentheater: Studien und Interpretationen* (Berlin, 1967), pp. 196–220.
19 Ilse Graham, *Heinrich von Kleist. Word into flesh: a poet's quest for the symbol* (Berlin; New York, 1977), pp. 1–7.
20 Ibid., p. 5.
21 John Ellis, *Heinrich von Kleist: studies in the character and meaning of his writings* (Chapel Hill, 1979), p. 145.
22 Ibid., p. 120.
23 See especially Kleist's letter of 5 February 1801 to his sister, Ulrike (*SW* II, 626–7 and M, 90–1).
24 See, for example, the contributions of Hermann Reske, 'Die Kleistsche Sprache', *German Quarterly*, 36 (1963), 219–35; Jakob Spälti, *Interpretationen zu Heinrich von Kleists Verhältnis zur Sprache* (Bern; Frankfurt, 1974) and J. M. Lindsay, 'Faulty communication in the works of Kleist', *GLL*, ns 31 (1977), 57–67.
25 Hans Heinz Holz, *Macht und Ohnmacht der Sprache: Untersuchungen zum Sprachverständnis und Stil Heinrich von Kleists* (Frankfurt, 1962), p. 91. In his book, Holz claims that Kleist's literary *œuvre*, taken in its entirety, reflects the 'dialectical character' of language itself and argues that whilst Kleist's narrative discourse is characterised by its syntactic precision and lack of ambiguity, in the plays we witness how human beings come to grief as a result of the inadequacies of language (see p. 23). In the light of a number of studies on the role of the narrator – for instance, John Ellis, *Narration in the German Novelle: theory and interpretation* (Cambridge, 1974) – the claim that Kleist's narrative style is characterised by a sober, objective rendering of the facts (see p. 117) seems highly contentious. Ultimately, Holz's characterisation of Kleist's stylistic technique in his prose fiction seems to be prompted more by the need to find a correlate to the stylistic techniques deployed in the dramas than by a close examination of the texts themselves. As a result, the book ends up being not so much a study of the role of language in Kleist's work, but rather an exposition of Holz's own views on the nature of language.
26 Anthony Stephens, '"Eine Träne auf den Brief": Zum Status der

Ausdrucksformen in Kleists Erzählungen', *JbDSG*, 28 (1984), 315–48, (p. 315).

27 In his polemical review of Kleist criticism, John Ellis dismisses Kommerell's essay on the grounds that 'it soon abandons any attempt to go beyond very well-known interpretative views to concentrate on developing its own linguistic texture per se'. See Ellis, *Heinrich von Kleist*, p. 150. Once again, however, the aggressive tone of Ellis's rhetoric leads one to suspect that his own approach is rather closer to that of Kommerell than he would care to admit.

28 Max Kommerell, *Geist und Buchstabe der Dichtung: Goethe, Schiller, Kleist, Hölderlin* (Frankfurt, 1944), p. 309.

29 Ibid., p. 309.

30 See, above all, Helmut Arntzen, 'Heinrich von Kleist: Gewalt und Sprache', in Wieland Schmidt, ed., *Die Gegenwärtigkeit Kleists: Reden zum Gedenkjahr 1977 im Schloß Charlottenburg zu Berlin* (Berlin, 1980), pp. 62–78; Gerhard Neumann, 'Hexenküche und Abendmahl: die Sprache der Liebe im Werk Heinrich von Kleists', *Freiburger Universitätsblätter*, 25 (1986), 9–31; and Stephens, '"Eine Träne auf den Brief"'.

31 Arntzen, 'Gewalt und Sprache', pp. 233–5.

32 Anthony Stephens, *Heinrich von Kleist: the dramas and stories* (Oxford, 1994), p. 5.

33 On this, see Seán Allan, '"Liederlichkeit, Spiel, Trunk, Faulheit und Völlerei, behalte ich mir bevor": Heinrich von Kleist's last word on modern educational theory', *GLL*, ns 48 (1995), 353–61.

2 THE QUEST FOR 'GLÜCK'

1 It is important to be aware of the difficulties inherent in drawing too hard and fast a distinction between Kleist's correspondence and his more explicitly literary works, since very often his letters display a high degree of literary self-consciousness. For a discussion of the reproduction of literary genres in Kleist's *Brautbriefe* – and in particular of his use of pietistically charged vocabulary – see Hans-Jürgen Schrader, 'Unsägliche Liebesbriefe: Heinrich von Kleist an Wilhelmine von Zenge', *Kleist-Jahrbuch* (1981/2), 86–96 and '"Denke du wärest in das Schiff meines Glückes gestiegen": widerrufene Rollenentwürfe in Kleists Briefen an die Braut', *Kleist-Jahrbuch* (1983), 122–79.

2 The contents of Kleist's essay are partially reproduced in a letter of 18 March 1799 to his former tutor, Christian Ernst Martini (*SW* II, 472–86). For a translation of selected excerpts from this letter, see M, 19–25.

3 For a discussion of the possible influences on Kleist during the writing of this essay, see Ulrich Gall, *Philosophie bei Heinrich von Kleist* (Bonn, 1977), pp. 11–32.

4 The essay is addressed to his friend – and literary confidant – Otto Rühle von Lilienstern.

5 As the argument unfolds, it becomes increasingly clear that the problem which Kleist wishes to address is that which Goethe, in an essay on the poem, *Harzreise im Winter*, later termed the 'pathological condition of sentimentality so prevalent at that time' ('den damals herrschenden Empfindsamkeitskrankheit'; *GA* II, 592).

6 Once again, we must be wary of taking Kleist's 'neutral account' at face value, for there is a striking similarity between his reflections of those around him and that expressed by Goethe in the poem *Warum gabst du uns tiefe Blicke? (Why did you give us deep insight?)*:

> Ach, so viele tausend Menschen kennen,
> Dumpf sich treibend, kaum ihr eigen Herz,
> Schweben zwecklos hin und her (*GA* II, 44)

(Oh there are so many thousands of men and women with scarcely any knowledge of their own hearts, drifting insensitively through life, floating aimlessly hither and thither) [*SV*, 70]

7 Kleist's ideal of *Bildung* is a thinly-disguised version of that put forward by Serlo in book V, chapter I of *Wilhelm Meisters Lehrjahre (Wilhelm Meister's apprenticeship)*: '"And therefore," he would add, "we should form the habit of hearing a little song, reading a good poem, seeing an excellent painting, or uttering a sensible observation everyday."' [*WM*, 263] ('Man sollte, sagte er, alle Tage wenigstens ein kleines Lied hören, ein gutes Gedicht lesen, ein treffliches Gemälde sehen und, wenn es möglich zu machen wäre, einige vernünftige Worte sprechen'; *GA* VII, 305).

8 In his letter, Kleist comes close to embracing an almost Burkean concept of the sublime.

9 At this stage of his development, Kleist's reception of Kant's work is coloured by his reading of the *Anthropology* – a work written some years before the development of the transcendental method that informs the *Critique of pure reason* – in which the author is writing in the tradition of (rather than against) the dualism of the Enlightenment.

10 See *SW* II, 624.

11 It is this very constellation of images which Kleist invokes in order to describe this process of 'refinement' – ore ('Erz'), gold ('Gold') and trial by fire ('Feuerprobe') – that are subjected to critical scrutiny in the play, *Das Käthchen von Heilbronn*.

12 For an interesting discussion of paradigms of femininity and their reproduction in the literature of the *Goethezeit*, see Julie Prandi, *Spirited women heroes: major female characters in the dramas of Goethe, Schiller and Kleist* (Bern; Frankfurt; New York, 1983).

13 For an up-to-date discussion of the (highly controversial) question of Kleist's reception of Kant's philosophy, see Gall, *Philosophie*, pp. 108–34, who suggests that Kleist's knowledge of Kant's ideas derives from their presentation in a more accessible form in Karl Leonard Reinhold's *Versuch einer neuen Theorie des menschlichen Vorstellungsvermögens* (Jena, 1789).

14 Of course, in drawing such a distinction between the noumenal and phenomenal world, it was not Kant's intention to demonstrate that objective knowledge was impossible. Indeed quite the reverse was the case.

15 There are some critics who take a more sceptical view of Kleist's 'Kant crisis', suggesting that it was merely a piece of melodramatic posturing on Kleist's part, designed to elicit approval for his decision to abandon his work for the *Technische Deputation* and travel to Dresden and Paris. See, for example, Wolfgang Binder, *Aufschlüsse: Studien zur deutschen Literatur* (Zürich, 1976), pp. 311–29 (especially p. 319).

16 In his letter to Ulrike of 5 February 1801, Kleist writes of his despair at being asked to prepare a report for the commission on a new French treatise on mechanics: 'My state of mind as I heard these words, I could never describe to you' [M, 91] ('Was in diesem Augenblicke alles in meiner Seele vorging kann ich Dir wieder nicht beschreiben'; *SW* II, 627).

17 Amongst those to visit post-revolutionary Paris at around the same time as Kleist were Joseph Görres, Jens Baggesen, Dorothea and Friedrich Schlegel and Wilhelm von Humboldt. For an informative study of eighteenth-century epistolary accounts of Paris, see Ingrid Oesterle, 'Werther in Paris? Heinrich von Kleists Briefe über Paris', in Dirk Grathoff, ed., *Heinrich von Kleist: Studien zur Werk und Wirkung* (Opladen, 1988), pp. 97–116. Similarly, in visiting the Dresden art gallery, Kleist was following in the footsteps of Tieck and Wackenroder who had been there some five years previously. On the Romantics and the Dresden art gallery, see Roger Paulin, *Ludwig Tieck: a literary biography* (Oxford, 1985), especially pp. 71–3.

18 See *SW* II, 650–1.

19 See his letter of 25 November 1800 to Ulrike, where he reproduces his answer to a question that is repeatedly put to him: '"If you will not apply your knowledge, why then strive so hard for Truth?" My only answer to this is: because it *is* Truth! – but who among them understands this?' [M, 81] ('"Wenn du dein Wissen nicht nutzen willst, warum strebst du denn so nach Wahrheit?" . . . Die einzige Antwort dis es gibt, ist diese: *weil es Wahrheit ist!* – Aber wer versteht das?'; *SW* II, 603).

20 For an excellent account of the rise of the novel in Germany in the

eighteenth century see Albert Ward, *Book production, fiction and the German reading public, 1740–1800* (Oxford, 1974).

21 For a translation of excerpts from this letter see M, 58–64 (especially p. 61).

22 Kleist saw that the inclusion of certain 'low-brow' anecdotes in his newspaper might have the effect of getting the ordinary member of the populace to look at other articles of a more challenging kind. See for example, Kleist's letter of 23 October 1810 where he defends himself against Eduard Prinz von Lichnowsky's accusation of vulgarity on the grounds that: 'Articles like the one about the drummer please the populace and stimulate it to peruse the other articles as well, which are not so directly written for them' [M, 190] ('Aufsätze, wie der vom Tambour . . . das Volk vergnügen und dasselbe reizen, auch wohl die anderen Aufsätze, die nicht unmittelbar für dasselbe geschrieben sind, zu überlesen'; *SW* II, 840).

23 See especially part II, letter XIII.

24 For a discussion of Kleist's relationship to this tradition see Oesterle, 'Werther in Paris?'.

25 Kleist's depiction of Parisian street life in his letter of 29 July 1801 to Adolfine von Werdeck is taken – almost verbatim – from the 24th Letter of Montesquieu's *Lettres Persanes*.

26 See *SW* II, 651.

27 Clearly we must be wary of taking Schlegel's aphorisms in the *Athenaeum* as a series of programmatic statements for Romantic aesthetics; nonetheless, it seems not unreasonable to regard them as indicative of the general tendencies of the movement as a whole.

28 For an extended discussion of the relationship of Kleist's aesthetics to Romantic theories of irony, see Bernd Fischer, 'Irony ironised: Heinrich von Kleist's narrative stance and Friedrich Schlegel's theory of irony', *European Romantic Review*, 1 (1990), 59–74.

29 As Kleist wrote in a subsequent essay *Von der Überlegung: eine Paradoxe (On thinking things over: a paradox)*, 'Reflection, or thinking something over, finds its proper moment *after* rather than *before* an act' [M, 217] ('Die Überlegung, wisse, findet ihren Zeitpunkt weit schicklicher *nach*, als *vor* der Tat'; *SW* II, 337).

30 Thus in his review of Achim von Arnim's *Halle und Jerusalem*, Kleist makes a plea for artistic experimentation, defending the writer's occasional departure from conventional literary forms, saying: 'If now and then an expression of this marvellous work strikes us as strange, surely we are not such philistines as to regard the literary conventions of poetry to which we have become so accustomed as a set of inviolate rules for all poetry. For this writer has something to say to us that goes beyond the artificial notions of what is good and beautiful propagated

by narrow-minded literary circles' ('Wenn hier oder dort uns eine Wendung des wunderbaren Gedichtes befremdete, so sind wir doch nicht Barbaren genug, um irgend eine angewöhnte, unserm Ohr längst eingesungene poetische Weise für die Regel alles Gesanges zu halten. Der Dichter hat mehr auszusprechen, als das besondere uns in engen Schulen anempfundene Gute und Schöne'; *SW* II, 422–3).

3 'DIE FAMILIE SCHROFFENSTEIN'

1 One such reviewer was L. F. Huber in his review published in *Der Freimüthige* of 4 March 1803. See *Lebensspuren*, no. 98a.

2 For a detailed commentary on the stage history of this and other plays by Kleist, see William C. Reeve, *Kleist on stage: 1804–1987*, (Montreal and Kingston, London, Buffalo: 1993).

3 For a helpful overview (in English) of the secondary literature up to 1978 on Kleist's work, see the notes in James McGlathery's book, *Desire's sway: the plays and stories of Heinrich von Kleist* (Detroit, 1983), pp. 157–219. For a more up to date review (in German) of the secondary literature, see the extensive notes to the plays and stories to be found in *Heinrich von Kleist. Sämtliche Werke und Briefe*, edited by Ilse-Marie Barth, Klaus Müller-Salget, Stefan Ormanns, and Hinrich C. Seeba, 4 vols. (Frankfurt, 1991).

4 Writing in the *Dramaturgische Blätter für Hamburg* in February 1821, F. G. Zimmermann suggests that it would be quite possible to stage the play 'if someone would go over the manuscript and make some changes, especially to the ending' ('wenn jemand das Ganze sichten und insbesondere den *Schluß* umarbeiten wollte'; *Nachruhm*, no. 265a).

5 Thus Hinrich Seeba in his highly influential article, 'Der Sündenfall des Verdachts: Identitätskrise und Sprachskepsis in Kleists *Familie Schroffenstein*', *DVjs*, 44 (1970), 64–100, regards the collapse of the idyll in the cave as symptomatic of Kleist's pessimistic attitude towards the teleological theories of history espoused by his contemporaries. Having been expelled from their original state of paradisical innocence, Kleist's young lovers are forced to recognise that the 'earthly paradise' of the idyll in the final act is merely an illusion, a poetic fiction that cannot be sustained in the world of reality (p. 100). Seeba's discussion of the relationship between language and subjectivity has been taken up and developed by Anthony Stephens, who also regards the play as a quest for a utopian realm of transparent communication in which Man would be restored to a condition of full subjectivity. Accordingly the demise of Ottokar and Agnes is the first example of what, for Stephens, is a recurrent theme in Kleist's work, namely 'the destruction of the future through the abrupt curtailment of any

emancipatory tendency' ('das Motiv der Zerstörung der Zukunft durch das jähe Abschneiden sämtlicher emanzipatorischer Tendenzen'). See Stephens, '"Eine Träne auf den Brief"', p. 347.

6 In this respect it is not unlike the 'idyll' in *Das Erdbeben in Chili (The Earthquake in Chile)* which is similarly described as the product of poetic fantasy – possessing a degree of beauty 'such as only a poet might dream of' [L, 57] ('wie nur ein Dichter davon träumen mag'; *SW* II, 149) – and which also collapses in an orgy of violence. In addition, the use of the term courtly-love ('Minnesang') may contain a further irony insofar as the theme of 'Minnesang' is always unfulfilled love.

7 My own interpretation of *Die Familie Schroffenstein* is thus diametrically opposed to those readings of the play which regard it as a 'fate-tragedy' ('Schicksalsdrama') in the manner of Zacharias Werner's *Der 24. Februar (February the 24th)*. See, for example, Valentine Hubbs, 'The concept of fate in Kleist's *Schroffenstein*', *Monatshefte*, 56 (1964), 339–45 (especially p. 339).

8 For example, Hubbs claims that: 'Rupert is unable to subordinate his actions to an ethical code.' See Hubbs, 'The concept of fate', p. 343.

9 Eustache also makes the same error. Although she too advocates a policy of restraint, she never goes as far as to claim that revenge *per se* is morally indefensible, but merely suggests that there is, as yet, insufficient evidence to pin the blame on Sylvester. Thus when she attempts to persuade her husband to give the matter more consideration, she does not try to dissuade him from actually taking revenge, but points out that a clear-sighted appraisal of the situation is essential if Peter's death is to be effectively avenged:

> Könntst du nicht prüfen mindestens
> Vorher, aufschieben noch die Fehde. – Ich
> Will nicht den Arm der Rache binden, leiten
> Nur will ich ihn, daß er so sichrer treffe. (*SW* I, 53; 81–4)

(Could you not at least examine the facts beforehand, postpone the feud. – I do not wish to restrain the hand of revenge, merely direct it that it strike home all the more effectively.)

Whilst she – like Sylvester – may hope that the lack of clear-cut evidence may obviate the need to take revenge, one (albeit indirect) consequence of her failure to grasp that there are *no* circumstances that would justify taking revenge is the death of her remaining son, Ottokar.

10 Here the pun on 'Hölle' (hell) and 'Höhle' (cave) seems more than coincidental.

11 See, for example, Stephens, *Heinrich von Kleist*, p. 42, where he speaks of 'the dubious reconciliation of the fathers'.

12 The symmetry of the play's dramatic structure, together with the motif of the young lovers suggests a number of parallels with the novella, *Die Verlobung in St. Domingo (The betrothal in St. Domingo)* where the love affair between Gustav and Toni is put forward as a potential – but ultimately unsuccessful – means of transcending the conflict between two mutually hostile groups, the indigenous inhabitants of Haiti and the French colonists.

13 It is particularly striking that the importance of Johann's role in the play has been almost completely ignored in the secondary literature, although it is perhaps understandable given that his presence in the drama undermines any attempt to present Ottokar and Agnes as straightforward embodiments of 'uncorrupted innocence'.

14 Compare the opening scene of Goethe's *Die natürliche Tochter (The natural daughter)* in which Eugenie also falls from her horse.

15 See *SW* I, 59; 241.

16 See *SW* I, 81; 857–8.

17 In this respect my own view is diametrically opposed to that of James McGlathery who suggests that the love affair between Ottokar and Agnes corresponds to an ideal Kleist had hoped to realise in his own relationship with Wilhelmine. This leads McGlathery to view Ottokar in a wholly uncritical light and thus he ends up suggesting that 'Ottokar's trust in Agnes' love is so basic and instinctive that jealous feelings are not kindled in him for a moment. It is Johann, the undesired lover, who is seized by jealousy.' See McGlathery, *Desire's sway*, p. 42.

18 The similarity between this episode and that at the end of *Penthesilea* where the queen commits suicide with a 'dagger' fashioned from 'a killing feeling' [G, 268] ('ein vernichtendes Gefühl'; *SW* I, 427; 3027) suggests a number of parallels between Johann and Penthesilea, both of whom subscribe to essentially the same concept of love.

19 Despite drawing attention to the wholly artificial character of Agnes's 'monologue' in act II, scene I, Peter Michelsen is still inclined to view the 'idyll' in the mountains as a locus situated 'beyond the conventions of society' ('außerhalb menschlicher Konventionen'). See Peter Michelsen, 'Die Betrogenen des Rechtgefühls: zu Kleists *Die Familie Schroffenstein*', *Kleist-Jahrbuch* (1992), 64–80 (p. 73). In my view, the only area that is genuinely isolated from the conventions of the respective Schroffenstein dynasties is the peasants' hut inhabited by Barnabe and Ursula. On this, see Neumann, 'Hexenküche', pp. 15–16 and Stephens, *Heinrich von Kleist*, pp. 18–19.

20 See *SW* I, 77; 741–5.

21 In the light of this, it is not possible to see Jeronimus, as Hubbs does, as 'the only character in the drama whose behaviour seems to be directed

by a well-developed faculty of thinking'. See Hubbs, 'The concept of fate', p. 340.

22 In her lengthy discussion of the religious motifs that are reproduced during the course of the *Höhlenszene*, Ingeborg Harms follows those who take the 'cave-idyll' at face value, suggesting that 'In the scene in which she undresses, Agnes is not exposed in her nakedness. She casts off the veils of convention and emerges clothed only in the veil of her natural beauty' ('Die Entkleidungsszene zeigt Agnes nicht in ihrer Nacktheit. Sie tritt aus den Umhüllungen hervor im natürlichen Schleier ihrer Schönheit'). See Ingeborg Harms, '"Wie fliegender Sommer": eine Untersuchung der "Höhlenszene" in Heinrich von Kleists *Familie Schroffenstein*', *JbDSG*, 28 (1984), 270–314 (p. 298). As a result Harms is obliged to ignore the way in which the seemingly transcendent rhetoric of the scene is mercilessly (at times even comically) undermined by the action taking place on stage.

4 'DER ZERBROCHNE KRUG'

1 See, for example, Rolf N. Linn, 'Comical and humorous elements in Kleist's *Hermannsschlacht*', *Germanic Review*, 47 (1972), 159–67.

2 For two excellent studies of the use of irony in Kleist's prose fiction see Michael Moering, *Witz und Ironie in der Prosa Heinrich von Kleists* (Munich, 1972) and Bernd Fischer, *Ironische Metaphysik: die Erzählungen Heinrich von Kleists* (Munich, 1988).

3 Anthony Stephens speaks for many, when he says: 'None of Kleist's works moves very far away from tragedy, and his two comedies develop a tragic sub-plot around the main female character'. See Stephens, *Heinrich von Kleist*, p. 59.

4 In his letter of 25 April 1811 to Friedrich de la Motte Fouqué, Kleist describes it as being 'suggested by a Teniers' [M, 192] ('nach dem Tenier gearbeitet'; *SW* II, 862).

5 These sentiments are echoed in Falk's own review of the Weimar première. See *Lebensspuren*, no. 249.

6 As Peter Horn, quite correctly, points out, 'the real scandal is not so much Adam's behaviour *per se*, but rather the structure of this society that makes his behaviour possible in the first place' ('Der wirkliche Skandal ist aber nicht eigentlich die Verhaltensweise Adams: der eigentliche Skandal ist aber die Struktur dieser Gesellschaft, die seine Verhaltensweise möglich macht'). See Peter Horn, 'Das erschrockene Gelächter über die Entlarvung einer korrupten Obrigkeit: Kleists zwiespältige Komödie *Der zerbrochne Krug*', in Dirk Grathoff, ed., *Heinrich von Kleist*, pp. 149–62 (p. 158).

7 It is perhaps significant that those critics who have adopted a more

metaphysical approach to the play have tended to concentrate on the later (shortened) version. The classic study of this kind is to be found in Ilse Appelbaum Graham's article 'The broken pitcher: hero of Kleist's comedy', *Modern Language Quarterly*, 16 (1955), 99–113. Drawing on her teleological reading of Kleist's essay *Über das Marionettentheater* (*On the puppet theatre*), she interprets the play as a re-working of the myth of Man's fall from grace and sees it as depicting a world in which 'the gates of paradise are shut' (p. 112). My own reading of the play runs directly contrary to metaphysical interpretations of this sort.

8 Peter Michelsen is amongst the more recent critics who are inclined to view Walter as an essentially benevolent figure: 'Walter is not concerned with the privileges of the ruling authorities . . . but with the welfare of the community as a whole' ('Nicht um den "Vorteil" der Obrigkeit geht es Walter . . ., sondern um das Wohl des Ganzen'). See Peter Michelsen, 'Die Lügen Adams und Evas Fall: Heinrich von Kleists *Der zerbrochne Krug*', in Herbert Anton, Bernhard Gajek and Peter Pfaff, eds., *Geist und Zeichen: Festschrift für Arthur Henkel* (Heidelberg, 1977), pp. 268–304 (p. 297, n. 64). Anthony Stephens also takes an uncritical view of Walter and criticises Eve for her failure to see 'that Walter is different' and as such, worthy of her trust. See Stephens, *Heinrich von Kleist*, p. 61. A more sceptical view of Walter's behaviour is to be found in Wolfgang Wittkowski's article '*Der zerbrochne Krug*: Juggling of authorities', in Alexej Ugrinsky, ed., *Heinrich von Kleist Studien* (Berlin, 1981), pp. 69–79. In keeping with his view that the play 'is a satire . . . on authority and on uncritical obedience to authority' (p. 69), Wittkowski goes to some lengths to point out how 'Walter is not the paragon of virtue he seems to be' (p. 73). For two similarly sceptical views of Walter's role in the play, see Dirk Grathoff, 'Der Fall des Krugs: zum geschichtlichen Gehalt von Kleists Lustspiel', *Kleist-Jahrbuch* (1981/2) 290–314, and Bernd Leistner, 'Heinrich von Kleists *Der zerbrochne Krug:* die tragische Aufhebung eines Lustspielvorgangs', *Weimarer Beiträge*, 30 (1984), 2028–47.

9 See *SW* I, 243; 1936–7 and G, 156.

10 Thus Wittkowski claims that Eve is a victim of 'her pious devotion to the authorities' and that the apparently 'harmonious' ending with the restoration of the villagers' faith in the judiciary is merely an example of 'man's inclination to have faith in all and any authorities and . . . to restore this faith whenever it has been undermined.' See Wittkowski, '*Der zerbrochne Krug*', pp. 72–3.

11 In this way, the play has certain affinities with the novella *Michael Kohlhaas*. For just as Eve's knowledge of the letter shown to her by Adam puts her in a position of strength vis-à-vis the state authorities,

so too the scrap of paper given to Kohlhaas by the gypsy woman gives him a similar hold over his enemy, the Elector of Saxony.

12 Those critics who regard Eve as an essentially naïve, innocent figure, are inclined to see the shortened version of the text as an improvement upon the original version. Thus Ilse Appelbaum Graham warns that the longer *Variant* disturbs the poetic unity of the play and suggests that in it, 'Eve is too conscious, too articulate, to be comic'. See Appelbaum Graham, 'The broken pitcher', p. 113. Although arguing from rather different premises, Siegfried Streller also finds fault with the *Variant*, on the grounds that Eve lacks the naïvety of the earlier scenes and appears 'too worldly-wise' ('welterfahren'). See Siegfried Streller, *Das dramatische Werk Heinrich von Kleists* (Berlin, 1966), p. 17.

13 See *SW* 1, 241; 1891 and G, 155.

14 See *SW* 1, 854; 2378.

15 Thus I am unable to agree with Peter Horn when he suggests that nothing has changed by the end of the play since 'Rupert's body will still remain the property of the state and the armed forces, whilst Eve's body will remain subject to the restrictions of provincial morality' ('Der Körper Ruprechts wird weiterhin dem Staat und der Armee gehören, der Körper Eves den Zwängen der dörflichen Moral unterworfen bleiben'). See Horn, 'Das erschrockene Gelächter', p. 160.

16 It is important to note that the later version of the play also ends with the rehabilitation of Adam. See *SW* 1, 244; 1960–1 and G, 157.

17 See *SW* 1, 227; 1509 and G, 140.

18 For a detailed discussion of Licht's role in the play – though one which, in my view, portrays him as having a greater (and more sinister) influence on events than is compatible with his essential mediocrity, see William C. Reeve, 'Ein dunkles Licht: the court secretary in Kleist's *Der zerbrochne Krug*', *Germanic Review*, 58 (1983), 58–65.

19 See *SW* 1, 189; 327–8 and G, 10.

20 For a discussion of the play's relationship to legal issues in Prussia at the end of the eighteenth century, see Hans-Peter Schneider, 'Justizkritik im *zerbrochenem Krug*', *Kleist-Jahrbuch* (1988/9), 309–26.

5 'AMPHITRYON'

1 The first performance of the play did not take place until 1899.

2 In it, Müller writes. 'There is one wish that the editor of this volume cannot suppress, namely that in the last act, the Thebans should be reminded of the difference between the earthly Amphitryon and his divine counterpart just as Alkmene is in the second. The author's *intention* was to expose not only the flawed nature in the temporal character of Alkmene's love for her husband, but also the same flaw in the

Thebans' love for their leader – but the author did not actually spell this out' ('Einen Wunsch kann der Herausgeber nicht unterdrücken, nämlich den, daß im letzten Akte das thebanische Volk an den Unterschied des göttlichen und irdischen Amphitryon gemahnt werden möchte, wie Alkmene im zweiten Akt. Gewollt hat es der Autor, daß die irdische Liebe des Volks zu ihrem Führer ebensowohl zu Schanden werde, als die Liebe der Alkmene zur ihren Gemahl – aber nicht ausgedrückt'). See Helmut Bachmaier and Thomas Horst, eds., *Heinrich von Kleist: 'Amphitryon'. Erläuterungen und Dokumente* (Stuttgart, 1983), p. 7.

3 For a most comprehensive survey (in German) of the secondary literature on the play up to the mid-seventies, see Karl-Heinz Wegener, *'Amphitryon' im Spiegel der Kleist-Literatur* (Frankfurt; Bern, 1979).

4 In the modern era, the critical reception of Kleist's *Amphitryon* has been dominated by essentially three distinct critical approaches. The first of these, usually associated with the work of Gerhard Fricke sees the play as a demonstration of Kleist's faith in the supremacy of human intuition ('innerstes Gefühl'). See Gerhard Fricke, *Gefühl und Schicksal*, pp. 60–96. Yet of all Kleist's plays, *Amphitryon* would appear to be the one in which the limitations of this approach are most clearly revealed, for the fact remains that ultimately Alkmene's intuition lets her down and she chooses the 'wrong' Amphitryon. More recently, critics have abandoned this approach in favour of one in which the play is regarded as an exploration of Man's relationship to the gods. Under this heading there are essentially two views, which, at first sight, appear to be diametrically opposed to one another, namely that of Wolfgang Wittkowski and that of Lawrence Ryan. As I have already suggested in chapter 1 (see pp. 1–3 above) these critics differ in respect of which of the two characters – Jupiter or Alkmene – they believe is upheld in the play. See Wolfgang Wittkowski, 'Der neue Prometheus' and Lawrence Ryan, 'Amphitryon'. In Ryan's view, Jupiter educates Alkmene to a better understanding of the difference between her love for her husband and her love for the god ('Amphitryon', p. 88). For Wittkowski, however, the spirit of the play is far closer to that of Molière insofar as it consists in a satirical treatment of religious authority. Accordingly, it is Alkmene who is ultimately upheld as a 'Promethean' figure questing for ethical autonomy in the face of the oppressive structures of institutionalised religion. ('Der neue Prometheus', p. 35). For an illuminating discussion of the dispute between Ryan and Wittkowski, see Bernd Fischer, 'Wo steht Kleist im *Amphitryon?*', *Studia Neophilologica*, 56 (1984), 61–8. The third critical approach to be brought to bear on *Amphitryon* views the play from the perspective of the Idealist tradition in German philosophy and

regards it as an exploration of the dialectical nature of human subjectivity. For the best-known proponent of this view, Hans Robert Jauss, the play ends on a profoundly pessimistic note: 'As [Jupiter] departs, all that remains scattered over the battle-field on which he has forced his victory are identities that have been destroyed . . . At the end of Kleist's *Amphitryon*, there is no longer any prospect of human happiness' ('Der entschwindende Gott läßt auf dem Feld seines erzwungenen Triumphes nur noch gebrochene Identitäten zurück . . . Die Möglichkeit menschlichen Glücks ist im Ausgang von Kleists *Amphitryon* nicht mehr vorgesehen'). See Hans Robert Jauss, 'Von Plautus bis Kleist: *Amphitryon* im dialogischen Prozeß der Arbeit am Mythos', in Walter Hinderer, ed., *Kleists Dramen: neue Interpretationen* (Stuttgart, 1981), pp. 114–43 (pp. 139–40). Leaving aside the question as to how far the subject matter of *Amphitryon* can be said to be directly concerned with the question of human subjectivity (as opposed to the nature of love and fidelity), the negative conclusions that Jauss draws from his study seem to me to be contrary not only to the ending of *Amphitryon*, but also to the spirit of Kleist's work generally. What Jauss fails to appreciate is that Kleist's critique of allegedly 'transcendent' notions of subjectivity is no different from his critique of 'transcendent' notions of love and fidelity. Thus although Alkmene is indeed forced to confront her 'fractured sense of identity' ('gebrochene Identität') at the end of the play, what she actually experiences is the collapse of a fundamentally misguided image of herself. Seen from this perspective, the denouement of Kleist's play is anything but pessimistic, for the collapse of these false beliefs is essential if there is to be any prospect of embarking on a programme of genuine self-improvement.

5 Ryan, 'Amphitryon', p. 88.

6 Wittkowski, 'Der neue Prometheus', p. 35.

7 In this respect, he is not unlike Rupert in *Die Familie Schroffenstein*.

8 See *SW* I, 299; 1720–1 and G, 61.

9 See *SW* I, 307; 1943–4 and G, 69–70.

10 For example, Helmut Bachmaier and Thomas Horst suggest that 'it should not be overlooked that Amphitryon too undergoes a process of transformation. He is transformed into a genuinely loving husband' ('Doch darf nicht übersehen werden, daß Amphitryon eine Wandlung durchmacht. Er wandelt sich zum Liebenden'). See Helmut Bachmaier and Thomas Horst, 'Die mythische Gestalt des Selbstbewußtseins: zu Kleists *Amphitryon*', *JbDSG*, 22 (1978), 404–41 (p. 437; n. 47).

11 Like Helmut Bachmaier and Thomas Horst, Walter Müller-Seidel also detects a change in Amphitryon: 'Amphitryon too rediscovers his

humanity. He has learned a great deal . . . and above all, he has discovered the truth of love' ('Auch Amphitryon kehrt in die Grenzen seines Menschentums zurück. Er hat viel gelernt . . . vor allem die Wahrheit der Liebe'). See Walter Müller-Seidel, 'Die Vermischung des Komischen mit dem Tragischen in Kleists Lustspiel *Amphitryon*', *JbDSG*, 5 (1961), 118–35 (p. 130). For a similar view, see Helmut Arntzen, *Die ernste Komödie: das deutsche Lustspiel von Lessing bis Kleist* (Munich, 1968), pp. 240–1.

12 Even Wittkowski is obliged to 'rescue' the boorish Amphitryon at the end of the play. See Wittkowski, 'Der neue Prometheus', p. 53.

13 Ryan's 'education thesis' obliges him to discount the possibility of any erotic motivation underlying Jupiter's seduction of Alkmene on the grounds that he is 'a transcendent being whose essence lies beyond all human understanding' ('eine für die Menschen ungreifbare und unfaßliche Transzendenz'). See Ryan, 'Amphitryon', p. 90.

14 See *SW* I, 288; 1352–3 and G, 49.

15 We shall encounter essentially the same notion of 'love-as-conquest' when we consider the character of Achilles in Kleist's next play, *Penthesilea*. Like Jupiter, Achilles is confronted with the same (irresolvable) paradox, when, in scene 14, he tells Prothoe that he 'loves' the queen, 'Like men love women: . . . in innocence and yet desiring to take hers from her' [G, 213] ('Wie Männer Weiber lieben; | . . . in Unschuld, | Und mit der Lust doch, sie darum zu bringen'; *SW* I, 375; 1522–4).

16 In *Das Käthchen von Heilbronn*, Graf Wetter von Strahl will be confronted with a similar dilemma (though he lacks the insight to recognise it as such). For since the robotic Käthchen is incapable of *not* 'loving' Strahl, her 'love' for him is rendered meaningless.

17 Peter Szondi takes Alkmene's Rousseauesque gesture at face value and regards this as a crucial difference between her and Molière's heroine: 'In contrast to [Molière's] Alcmène, who partakes of [Amphitryon's] fame, Kleist's Alkmene – like the author himself – has no truck with the conventional trappings of society' ('Gegen Alcmènes Teilnahme an dem Ruhm des Feldherrn, gegen dies Einverständnis der Liebenden mit der Gesellschaft lehnt sich Kleists Alkmene wie der Dichter selber auf'). See Peter Szondi, '*Amphitryon*: Kleists "Lustspiel nach Molière"', *Euphorion*, 55 (1961), 249–59, (p. 253).

18 Alkmene's persistent attempts to assert the integrity of her reputation in the face of empirical evidence to the contrary, suggests a number of parallels between her predicament and that of the Marquise in the novella, *Die Marquise von O . . .*

19 In this respect, Charis's function in the play is to offer the audience a critical perspective on Alkmene's extravagant rhetoric and in this

respect, the maid's function is not dissimilar to that of the midwife in *Die Marquise von O...* See especially *SW* II, 123–4 and L, 90–1.

20 See *SW* I, 284; 1243–4 and G, 45.

21 Most commentators seem to have overlooked the fact that this scene is played out in front of the servants, Charis and Sosias.

22 See *SW* I, 287; 1337–9 and G, 48–9.

23 See also the lines: 'sooner will I go down to my grave than come back, while there's breath still in my bosom, to your bed' [G, 48] ('Eh will ich meiner Gruft, als diesen Busen, | So lang er atmet, deinem Bette nahn'; SW I, 287; 1331–2).

24 See *SW* I, 258; 373–5 and G, 16.

6 'PENTHESILEA'

1 See chapter 2, pp. 27–32 above.

2 The first full-length production of the play, albeit in an adapted version, did not take place until 1876. See Reeve, *Kleist on stage*, p. 80.

3 Reviewing the publication of the 'Organisches Fragment' in *Der Freimüthige* of 5 February 1808, Karl Böttiger writes: 'Nowadays people are complaining about the so-called sensationalist dramas . . . But nowhere are you likely to come across anything wilder than the action in this particular tragedy . . . Oh! Poor old Kotzebue, you who have been so criticised for all your *coups de théatre*, if you had dared anything like this you would have been run out of town by all and sundry!' ('Man schimpft auf die jetzigen sogenannten Spektakelstücke . . . Aber so toll, wie der Spektakel in diesem Trauerspiele getrieben wird, dürfte er doch wohl nirgends ausgeführt sein . . . Ach! Du armer Kotzebue, über dessen Theatercoups man so sehr herzieht, hättest du das gewagt, ausgetrommelt wärest du von jedem Buben geworden!'; *Lebensspuren*, no. 225a).

4 It is striking that at the time, Goethe should have preferred to stage Zacharias Werner's *Wanda*, a play which, though highly Romantic in style, deals with themes not dissimilar to Kleist's *Penthesilea*. Although Goethe disapproved of Werner's mystical leanings and was suspicious of the Romantic *Liebestod* with which *Wanda* ends, he clearly felt more at home in what he saw as the more dramatically coherent work of Werner (See *GA* XIX, 536), than he did in the 'unfamiliar territory' of *Penthesilea*. For an illuminating discussion of Goethe's relationship to Zacharias Werner, see Elizabeth Stopp, '"Ein Sohn der Zeit": Goethe and the Romantic plays of Zacharias Werner', *PEGS*, ns 40 (1970), 123–50.

5 Few critics have commented on the relationship of Kleist's epigrams

to his work as a whole. A notable exception in this respect is Moering, *Witz und Ironie*, pp. 96–106.

6 Much of the material for *Penthesilea* was almost certainly taken from Benjamin Hederich's *Gründliches mythologisches Lexikon*. On this, see Roger Paulin, 'Kleist's metamorphoses: some remarks on the use of mythology in *Penthesilea*', *OGS*, 14 (1983), 35–53 (especially pp. 37–8).

7 In the modern era, the critical debate concerning the play has tended to focus upon the relationship of Penthesilea to the Amazon state, a debate which, as usual, sees the participants divided into two mutually opposed camps. On the one hand, there are those, like Walter Müller-Seidel, who see the Amazon state in purely negative terms as an institution which has been responsible for the perpetuation of a version of femininity that is 'unnatural'. Accordingly, the death of Achilles comes about as the result of Penthesilea's misguided attempt to comply with the dictates of her 'inhuman' society. See Walter Müller-Seidel, '*Penthesilea* im Kontext der deutschen Klassik', in Hinderer, *Kleists Dramen*, pp. 144–71. Gerhard Kaiser takes a more positive view of the Amazon state, seeing it as a more advanced society than its Greek counterpart, but noting that it contains contradictory elements within itself, insofar as 'it merely reproduces – albeit in a different guise – the situation it was originally set up to overcome' ('der Zustand, der überwunden werden soll, wird unter verkehrten Vorzeichen reproduziert'). See Gerhard Kaiser, *Wandrer und Idylle: Goethe und die Phänomenologie der Natur in der deutschen Dichtung von Geßner bis Gottfried Keller* (Göttingen, 1977), p. 210. Like many others, Kaiser suggests that Achilles' death cannot be reduced to the simple matter of Penthesilea's uncritical acceptance of an inhuman law, but is the inevitable result of the contradictions inherent in their respective societies. And thus he concludes that the realisation of this love affair can take place only in death. Both he and Müller-Seidel see the play as heralding the end of the Amazon state and regard this as a necessary stage in the dialectical progress of history. Despite certain differences in emphasis, the basic positions of Müller-Seidel and Kaiser are considerably closer than appears to be the case at first sight. For in each, there is a tacit assumption that the love of Achilles and Penthesilea constitutes an emancipatory tendency in the play by means of which the contradictions inherent in their respective societies might be transcended.

More recently, some critics have questioned the alleged 'unnaturalness' of the Amazon state, claiming that it is presented in the play as a perfectly viable form of social organisation. By far the best account of this aspect of the play is to be found in Ruth Angress's article, 'Kleist's nation of Amazons', in Susan L. Cocalis and Kay Goodman, eds.,

Beyond the eternal feminine: critical essays on women and German literature (Stuttgart, 1982), pp. 99–134. Yet whilst Angress comments, quite correctly, that 'we weaken the impact of the play if we treat the state of the Amazons as a ridiculous construct, perverse to start out with and doomed from the start' (p. 111), her reading fails to take sufficient account of the fact that the Amazon state is itself not exempt from Kleist's critique. For a similarly positive reading of the Amazon state, see Julie Prandi, 'Woman warrior as hero: Schiller's *Jungfrau von Orleans* and Kleist's *Penthesilea*', *Monatshefte*, 77 (1985), 403–14.

Finally, a number of critics working within an explicitly Lacanian paradigm have seen the relationship between Achilles and Penthesilea as an exploration of the dialectical construction of human subjectivity in language. Foremost amongst these is Helga Gallas, who sees the obstacle to the realisation of this love affair not in terms of the social structures to which the combatants belong, but rather in the relentless efforts of the participants to postpone the satisfaction of desire: 'Desire is sustained by continually postponing the moment of satisfaction; it is the desire to live in a state of unsatisfied desire' ('Das Begehren wird durch die dauernde Verhinderung der Befriedigung aufrechterhalten; es ist das Begehren, ein unbefriedigtes Begehren zu haben'). See Helga Gallas, 'Kleists *Penthesilea* und Lacans vier Diskurse', in Inge Stephan and Carl Pietzcker, eds., *Frauensprache – Frauenliteratur: Für und Wider einer Psychoanalyse literarischer Werke* (Tübingen, 1986), pp. 203–12 (p. 204). Under this interpretation of the play, Gallas suggests that for Penthesilea, the fascination of Achilles lies in the fact that, by virtue of having defeated Hector, he knows what it is to occupy the position of victor (see p. 210). Accordingly when she desecrates Achilles' corpse, she assumes the position of conqueror within the discursive structure, but in so doing she destroys the very structure underpinning her own sense of self. For another explicitly Lacanian reading see Chris Cullens and Dorothea von Mücke's article, 'Love in Kleist's *Penthesilea* and *Käthchen von Heilbronn*', *DVjs*, 63 (1989), 461–93.

8 In this respect my reading of the play is diametrically opposed to those which operate in terms of archetypal notions of femininity, such as Valentine Hubbs who sees Penthesilea as an 'atavistic manifestation of a more primitive stage of man's development'. See Valentine Hubbs, 'The plus and minus of Penthesilea and Käthchen', *Seminar*, 6 (1970), 187–94 (p. 194).

9 See *SW* I, 328; 179–186 and G, 165.

10 Calchas had prophesied that the walls of Troy would never fall without the active participation of Achilles.

11 The exaggerated impression made by Achilles on his devoted admir-

ers is further underlined in scene 7, when he is described in very similar terms, by the young, gawking Amazon girls. See *SW* I, 356; 1033–5 and G, 193.

12 This is one of a number of similarities between Achilles and the Prince in *Prinz Friedrich von Homburg*. The terror Achilles displays here, when he realises that he is going to die is not unlike the Prince's reaction in act III, scene 5, after he has seen his grave.

13 See *SW* I, 325; 92 and G, 163.

14 My reading of the play runs contrary to those which attempt to locate the emancipatory tendency of the play in the allegedly 'utopian' love-affair of Achilles and Penthesilea. One such interpretation is that put forward by Hélène Cixous in her essay, 'Sorties', in Hélène Cixous and Catherine Clément, *The newly-born woman*, tr. Betsy Wing (Manchester, 1986), pp. 63–132. In order to sustain this reading of the play, however, Cixous not only has to take the idyll of scene 15 at face value, but is also compelled to see Achilles as undergoing a fundamental transformation: 'Achilles . . . under Penthesilea's influence . . . really becomes another man: the new lover' (p. 113). In a not dissimilar vein, Lilian Hoverland – drawing on the utopian feminism of Luce Irigaray – views the final clash between the lovers as the reconciliation of the dualistic antagonism between male and female elements in an ideal (because androgynous) space. See Lilian Hoverland, 'Heinrich von Kleist and Luce Irigaray: visions of the feminine', in Marianne Burckhardt, ed., *Gestaltet und gestaltend: Frauen in der deutschen Literatur* (Amsterdam, 1980), pp. 57–82. In my view, however, Kleist's presentation of the 'love affair' highlights the weaknesses of both Cixous's and Irigaray's critique of patriarchal culture. For despite their desire to expose the ideological character of essentialist notions of masculinity and femininity, ultimately it is their concern with the concept of a transcendent 'utopia' that results in their endorsement of equally essentialist notions of femininity, albeit at a higher level in the argument.

15 See *SW* I, 387; 1905–8 and G, 226.

16 In the light of this, I cannot agree with Anthony Stephens's claim that 'the Amazon state is an efficient war-machine'. See Stephens, *Heinrich von Kleist*, p. 122.

17 See *SW* I, 426; 3000 and G, 266.

18 The selfless character of the mother's love for her child is also the subject of the anecdote *Mutterliebe* (*Mother love*). See *SW* II, 277 and M, 289.

19 It is important to note that the reverse does not hold. Since the child gains a distinct advantage from the mother's affections, its love for the mother is, from the outset, corrupted by self-interest. In this respect we

might recall Kleist's letter to his sister, Ulrike, in which he observes: 'You have already done so much for me that my feelings of friendship, mixed with those of gratitude, are no longer pure' [M, 90] ('Du hast zu viel für mich getan, als daß meine Freundschaft, in welche sich schon die Dankbarkeit mischt, ganz rein sein könnte'; *SW* II, 625).

20 The unfavourable depiction of Asteria underlines the fact that although the structure of Amazon society may *encourage* its members to act in a more altruistic manner, it cannot *guarantee* that this will be the case.

21 I am unable to detect the 'qualities of nobility and magnanimity' which Hilda Brown attributes to the Greeks in her discussion of the play. See Hilda Brown, *Kleist and the tragic ideal: a study of 'Penthesilea' and its relationship to Kleist's personal and literary development, 1806–1808* (Bern; Frankfurt; Las Vegas, 1977), p. 65.

22 See *SW* I, 343; 649 and G, 181.

23 It was these lines which – according to Johann Daniel Falk – Goethe described as worthy of a boulevard theatre in Naples. See *Lebensspuren*, no. 281.

24 It is precisely to prevent such exploitation that the Amazons are compelled to break off relations with their male partners after the Festival of Fertile Mothers. The fact that Penthesilea (in common with the other young Amazons) does not understand why this should be thought necessary – see *SW* I, 392; 2085–7 and G, 231 – shows how the original revolutionary vigour of this concept has deteriorated with the passage of time.

25 See *SW* I, 399; 2291–2 and G, 238.

26 See Christa Wolf, *Die Dimension des Autors* (Berlin; Weimar, 1986), vol. II, p. 204.

27 It is sometimes claimed that in writing *Penthesilea*, Kleist deliberately set out to produce a play diametrically opposed in spirit to Goethe's *Iphigenie auf Tauris*. This reading of *Penthesilea* has, in part, been prompted by Katharina Mommsen's highly biographically oriented interpretation of the dramatic conflicts in Kleist's work in terms of an agonistic rivalry between Kleist and Goethe. See Katharina Mommsen, *Kleists Kampf mit Goethe* (Heidelberg, 1974). A similarly agonistic view of the relationship between the two plays is to be found in Helga Gallas's essay, 'Antikenrezeption bei Goethe und Kleist: Penthesilea – eine Anti-Iphigenie?', in Linda Dietrick and David G. John, eds., *Momentum dramaticum: Festschrift for Eckehard Catholy* (Waterloo, 1980), pp. 209–20. For Gallas, the action of *Penthesilea* revolves around the ('imperfect') queen's search for an ideal of 'perfection' that she sees embodied in Achilles (see pp. 214–15), a search that ends with the recognition of the illusory nature of her quest. Thus

Gallas suggests that 'the ending of *Penthesilea* can, therefore, be regarded as a gesture of humility towards Goethe: I [i.e. Kleist] strove to attain the highest ideal, the impossible – but I cannot live up to it and no longer desire it. Goethe perceived only a challenge in these words of Kleist, not an act of humility' ('Der Schluß der *Penthesilea* kann deshalb auch als Demutsgeste Goethe gegenüber verstanden werden: ich wollte das Höchste, das Unmögliche – aber ich gleiche diesem Ideal nicht, ich will es auch gar nicht. Goethe hatte nur ein Ohr für die Herausforderungen Kleists, für die Demut nicht'; p. 218).

In addition to the reservations I have in respect of Gallas's psychoanalytical reading of the play and Mommsen's biographically oriented approach, I do not see Kleist's *Penthesilea* as an 'anti-*Iphigenie*'. For as I have tried to show above, Kleist in no way repudiates the concept of humanity put forward in *Iphigenie auf Tauris*. The chief difference between the two plays lies in the fact that it is the 'barbarian' Amazons, rather than the 'civilised' Greeks who display the qualities more usually associated with Goethe's heroine. Indeed Iphigenie's qualities – frankness, mutual trust (based on personal experience of human decency and generosity) and the courage to place reliance on one's fellow human beings – are precisely those that the Amazon state has been set up to promote. But whereas Iphigenie triumphs because King Thoas (the 'barbarian') responds to her gesture of humanity, Penthesilea's downfall is a reflection of the 'civilised' Achilles' inability to reciprocate her superior concept of love.

28 See my discussion of Kleist's observations on the nature of human disappointment in chapter 2, pp. 18–19 above.

7 'DAS KÄTHCHEN VON HEILBRONN'

1 Ernst Stahl speaks for many when he suggests that, 'Kleist was not at his best when he tried his hand at this kind of drama'. See Ernst Stahl, *Heinrich von Kleist's dramas* (Oxford, 1948), p. 98.

2 For a discussion of some of the better known parodies in the first half of the nineteenth century see Dirk Grathoff, ed., *Heinrich von Kleist: 'Das Käthchen von Heilbronn oder die Feuerprobe'. Erläuterungen und Dokumente* (Stuttgart, 1977), pp. 122–30 and 157–8. It is, of course, highly ironic that the authors of these parodies failed to appreciate the subversive nature of the material from which they drew their inspiration.

3 See chapter 2, pp. 38–40 above.

4 In his letter of 1 February 1808, Goethe adds the following comment to his criticism of *Penthesilea*: 'perhaps you will permit me to say that it always saddens me and fills me with consternation when I see intelligent and talented young men waiting for a form of theatre that does

not as yet exist' ('erlauben Sie mir zu sagen . . . daß es mich immer betrübt und bekümmert, wenn ich junge Männer von Geist und Talent sehe, die auf ein Theater warten, welches da kommen soll'; *Lebensspuren*, no. 224).

5 Hans Wolff has attempted to account for what he regards as the 'series of discontinuities and structural weaknesses that considerably detract from the effectiveness of the play' ('Reihe von Unstimmigkeiten und strukturellen Schwächen, die die Wirkung des Dramas erheblich beeinträchtigen') in terms of the discrepancies between the different versions of the play. See Hans Wolff, 'Käthchen von Heilbronn und Kunigunde von Thurneck', *Trivium*, 9 (1951), 214–24 (p. 214). Wolff's dissatisfaction with the version of the text that has survived, however, is a reflection of his uncritical acceptance of the (commonly-held) view that the play is a straight-faced testimony to the power of love and feminine innocence.

6 Not all critics in the twentieth century have been as forthright as Charlotte von Schiller. Of the critics who have dealt with the play in any detail, the majority have taken their cue from Gerhard Fricke. Fricke regards Käthchen in a wholly uncritical light, seeing her as the 'human' counterpart of the Kleistian marionette, as a perfect embodiment of an idealised state of infinite grace. And thus he suggests that: 'Käthchen follows her pure intuition, thereby acting totally in accordance with God's will' ('Käthchen . . . folgt ihrem reinen Gefühl und ist eben dadurch in Übereinstimmung mit Gott'). See Fricke, *Gefühl und Schicksal*, p. 155. For not dissimilar views of the play based upon the essay, *Über das Marionettentheater (On the puppet theatre)*, see Müller-Seidel, *Versehen und Erkennen*, p. 100, and, more recently, Rolf-Peter Janz, 'Die Marionette als Zeugin der Anklage: zu Kleists Abhandlung *Über das Marionettentheater*', in Hinderer, *Kleists Dramen*, pp. 31–51 (especially pp. 42–3). Given that the effect of this type of reading is to render the heroine – at least from a dramatic point of view – essentially uninteresting, critics have shifted the focus of their attention to Strahl, to the question of the class barrier separating the lovers and to the implications of this for Kleist's own political views. The most recent full-scale discussion of this is to be found in William C. Reeve, *Kleist's aristocratic heritage and 'Das Käthchen von Heilbronn'* (Montreal and Kingston; London; Buffalo, 1991). However, I find Reeve's view that 'Kleist . . . remained at heart an aristocrat whose heritage determined not only his basic values, but, not surprisingly, his very thought patterns' (p. 16) not only overly deterministic, but explicitly contradicted by the obvious elements of irony and parody in the play itself. Those who would see the play as a glorification of the nobility are obliged to take its 'happy' ending at face value, and indeed Reeve confesses that

he feels 'very uncomfortable with Strahl's behaviour, especially in the last two scenes' (p. 100), though this does not prompt him to question the basic premises of his interpretation. A more incisive account of the political and philosophical issues in the play is to be found in Dirk Grathoff's essay, 'Beerben oder Enterben? Probleme einer gegenwärtigen Aneignung von Kleists *Käthchen von Heilbronn*', in Walter Raitz and Erhard Schütz, eds., *Der alte Kanon neu: zur Revision des literarischen Kanons in Wissenschaft und Unterricht* (Opladen, 1976), pp. 136–75.

7 In her otherwise illuminating study, Julie Prandi ignores the ironic dimension of Kleist's play and hence arrives at the conclusion that Käthchen embodies not only 'a feminine ideal that would find applause throughout the nineteenth century, but one endorsed by the author himself'. See Prandi, *Spirited women heroes*, p. 40.

8 See Heinrich Meyer-Benfey, *Das Drama Heinrich von Kleists* (Göttingen, 1913), vol. II, p. 49.

9 Accordingly, my own view of the play is diametrically opposed to those whose approach is based upon archetypal notions of femininity such as Hubbs, 'Plus and minus'; Robert M. Browning, 'Kleists *Käthchen* and the monomyth', in Donald H. Crosby and George Schoolfield, eds., *Studies in the German drama: a Festschrift in honor of Walter Silz* (Chapel Hill, 1974), pp. 115–24, and Edith Borchardt, *Mythische Strukturen im Werk Heinrich von Kleists* (New York; Bern; Frankfurt; Paris, 1987).

10 Although Kleist's use of comic names in the play has been commented on by a number of critics – on this aspect of the play see, above all, William C. Reeve '"O du – wie nenn ich dich?": names in Kleist's *Käthchen von Heilbronn*', *GLL*, ns 41 (1988), 83–98 – the significance of Kunigunde's name appears not to have been commented on. St. Cunigunde was renowned as a virgin queen who, when called upon to do so, also 'proved' her innocence in a 'Test by Fire', by walking upon red-hot plough-shares.

11 See *SW* I, 900–3.

12 The 'catalogues' of these desirable qualities are to be found in Theobald's speech at the beginning of act I (domestic), and in Strahl's speech at the beginning of act II (erotic).

13 This desire for a 'domesticated' version of 'nature' is most clearly exemplified by Strahl's wish (in act V, scene 12) to set up a 'summer-house' ('Sommersitz') under the elder boughs where he was first 'enlightened' as to Käthchen's 'true' identity (see *SW* I, 528; 2614–8 and P, 341). It is impossible to ignore the similarity between Strahl's wish here and the Duke's plan to erect 'a shrine to the restorative powers' ('ein Tempel . . . der Genesung') of Eugenie in Goethe's play, *Die natürliche Tochter (The natural daughter)*. See *GA* VI, 333–4 and 610–31.

14 For a discussion of the comic dimension of the play, see Fritz Martini, '*Das Käthchen von Heilbronn* – Heinrich von Kleists drittes Lustspiel?', *JbDSG*, 20 (1975), 420–7.

15 In this respect, her automaton-like behaviour closely resembles that of Rupert's equally 'devoted' servant, Santing, in *Die Familie Schroffenstein*.

16 In order to clarify the point I am making, I have used my own translations. For a full translation of act IV, scene 2, see P, 317–23.

17 The same description might well be applied to Sylvester's society in *Die Familie Schroffenstein*, a society whose *modus operandi* is symbolised by the gardener (rather than by the hunter as is the case in Rossitz).

8 'DIE HERMANNSSCHLACHT'

1 For a discussion of Goethe's views on Napoleon, see Richard Samuel, 'Goethe – Napoleon – Heinrich von Kleist', *PEGS*, ns 14 (1939), 43–75.

2 See Richard Samuel, 'Kleists *Hermannsschlacht* und der Freiherr vom Stein', *JbDSG*, 5 (1961), 64–101 (pp. 69–72).

3 During his dispute with Hardenberg over the content of the *Berliner Abendblätter*, Kleist was to gain first-hand experience of the workings of 'French journalism' in his native Prussia. See Dirk Grathoff, 'Die Zensurkonflikte der Berliner Abendblätter: zur Beziehung von Journalismus und Öffentlichkeit bei Heinrich von Kleist', in Klaus Peter, Dirk Grathoff, Charles N. Hayes, and Gerhard Loose, eds., *Ideologische Studien zur Literatur: Essays I* (Frankfurt, 1972), pp. 37–168.

4 See Samuel, 'Kleists *Hermannsschlacht*', pp. 72–3.

5 It is perhaps hardly surprising that Napoleon himself greatly admired Stein for his political acumen.

6 See Samuel, 'Kleists *Hermannsschlacht*', p. 85.

7 For a discussion of the relationship between historical events and the reception of *Die Hermannsschlacht* and *Prinz Friedrich von Homburg*, see Hans Joachim Kreutzer, 'Die Utopie vom Vaterland: Kleists politische Dramen', *OGS*, 20/1 (1981/2), 69–84.

8 Taking their cue from Kleist's own remarks, the majority of scholars have tended to approach the play as a straightforward work of political propaganda with the result that its critical fortunes have risen and fallen with the course of German history in the twentieth century. In 1922, Friedrich Gundolf had few qualms in expressing his enthusiasm for it – see Friedrich Gundolf, *Heinrich von Kleist* (Berlin, 1922), especially pp. 126–7. Walter Müller-Seidel, however, writing some thirty years later, reflects the views of many of his post-war colleagues when he suggests that 'only with a continual reminder of the need for caution can the play be included in the canon of Kleist's literary

works' ('Nur mit immer erneut auszusprechenden Vorbehalten wird man dieses Stück in das dichterische Werk Kleists einbeziehen dürfen'). See Müller-Seidel, *Versehen und Erkennen*, p. 53. One of the first critics to present a more balanced view of *Die Hermannsschlacht* was Richard Samuel in his painstaking attempt to link the events of the play with the activities of Stein and the Prussian Reform Movement in the summer of 1808. See Samuel, 'Kleists *Hermannsschlacht*', pp. 43–75. Yet readings of this kind – in which the play is seen as a thinly-disguised allegory of contemporary political events – often raise more difficulties than they resolve, not least that of assigning the correct roles to the main characters. Thus whilst Samuel suggests that Hermann and Cheruska are to be identified with Prussia, with Marbod standing for Austria (p. 84), the (Austrian) critic Josef Nadler sees Marbod as a representative of Prussia and Hermann as a symbol of Austrian salvation. See Josef Nadler, *Die Berliner Romantik 1800–1814: ein Beitrag zur gemeinvölkischen Frage. Renaissance, Romantik, Restauration* (Berlin, 1921), especially p. 184. More recently, Anthony Stephens has drawn attention to the difficulties inherent in an uncritical acceptance of Hermann as the embodiment of an ideal political leader when he notes that he 'corresponds much more closely to Kleist's portrait of Napoleon as a demonic figure than he does to any of the rulers or generals on the German side.' See Anthony Stephens, 'Kleists mythicisation of the Napoleonic era', in J. C. Eade, ed., *Romantic nationalism in Europe* (Canberra, 1983), pp. 165–79 (p. 168). Nonetheless, despite the ambivalent light in which Hermann is presented, a number of critics have argued for a more favourable view of the play's central protagonist. Ruth Angress speaks for many when she states that in writing *Die Hermannsschlacht*, Kleist set out to demonstrate 'the incompatibility of . . . traditional ethics' in the revolutionary situation. See Ruth Angress, 'Kleist's treatment of imperialism: *Die Hermannsschlacht* and *Die Verlobung in St. Domingo*', *Monatshefte*, 69 (1977), 17–33 (p. 19). Lawrence Ryan, in his article 'Die "vaterländische Umkehr" in der *Hermannsschlacht*', in Hinderer, ed., *Kleists Dramen*, pp. 188–212, also sees the play as demonstrating the primacy of political action over moral values (p. 202). For William C. Reeve, the play is seen as a dramatisation of many of the practical political recommendations outlined in Niccolò Machiavelli's *Il Principe*. See William C. Reeve, *In pursuit of power: Heinrich von Kleist's Machiavellian protagonists* (Toronto, Buffalo, London, 1987). Rather than see the play as a critique of such political practices, however, Reeve claims that 'Kleist together with Machiavelli would seem to be arguing in favour of moral relativity in the political arena where the only thing that really counts is success' (p. 83). Hans-Dieter Loose, in his full length study of the play, *Kleists 'Hermannsschlacht': kein Krieg für Hermann und seine Cherusker. Ein paradoxer Feldzug aus dem Geist der Utopie gegen den Geist besitzbürgerlicher und feudaler Herrschaft* (Karlsruhe, 1984), sees Hermann as a figure engaged on a utopian mission, *viz.* the implementation of 'a society based on the principle of a universal humanity' ('eine menschheitsumfassende Gemeinschaft'; p. 92) and suggests that Hermann corresponds to Kleist's concept of an ideal political leader (p. 225).

Those critics who see in Hermann an 'ideal' figure, are left with the problem of Aristan's execution at the end of the play. Significantly, neither Loose nor Angress devote any space to this episode at all. The difficulties posed by the play's ending have been commented upon by two critics: Sigurd Burckhardt in his book, *The drama of language: essays on Goethe and Kleist* (Baltimore, 1970) and Peter Michelsen, '"Wehe, mein Vaterland, dir!": Heinrichs von Kleist *Die Hermannsschlacht*', *Kleist-Jahrbuch* (1987), 115–36. But whilst Burckhardt suggests that 'we may feel, as Aristan does, that this is not law but *ex post facto* violence, since obviously there can be no treason against a not yet existing state' (p. 154), he fails to follow up the implications of his own insights and sees Kleist as simply putting forward 'the bitter truth that a state is a structure of laws claiming a capital jurisdiction' (p. 155). Nonetheless, in pointing out that Aristan can – with good reason – feel that he has been unjustly treated, Burckhardt has isolated a key moment in the drama which critics ignore at their peril. For his part, Michelsen interprets the treatment of Aristan as an indication that 'Hermann clearly does not subscribe to a notion of freedom which seeks to preserve itself by recognising the freedom of the *other*' ('das Prinzip einer Freiheit, deren Wahrung sich darin erweist, daß man die des *anderen* achtet, ist offenbar nicht das Freiheitsprinzip Hermanns'). See Michelsen, '"Wehe, mein Vaterland, dir!"', pp. 135–6. More contentious, however, is Michelsen's view that Thusnelda's revenge should be seen as the final stage in her education to a 'state of barbarism' ('Inhumanität'), p. 133. As we shall see, Thusnelda's despair in act v, scene 23, demonstrates that her humanity is very much intact.

9 See *SW* I, 544; 297–9.

10 The difference betwen Wolf and the others does not escape Hermann's attention either. In act IV, scene 3, he shows little interest in hearing about the contributions of the other princes to the national cause, but makes an exception in Wolf's case, saying: 'Wolf is the only one of them who is sincere' ('Wolf ist der einzge, der es redlich meint'; *SW* I, 585; 1503).

11 See *SW* I 537; 72–4.

12 In this respect, she closely resembles the queen in *Penthesilea.*

13 See *SW* I, 551; 511.

14 Friedrich Dahlmann reports a conversation in which Kleist is reputed to have said, 'my Thusnelda is a respectable enough figure, but a little naïve and vain, rather like those girls nowadays who are so impressed by the French; when they come to their senses again, they feel obliged to exact a terrible revenge' ('meine Thusnelda ist brav, aber ein wenig einfältig und eitel, wie heute die Mädchen sind, denen die Franzosen imponieren; wenn solche Naturen zu sich zurückkehren, so bedürfen sie einer grimmigen Rache'; *Lebensspuren*, no. 319).

15 There is a strong similarity here between Hermann's cultivation of feelings of hatred towards the Romans and Rupert's cultivation of his hatred for Sylvester in *Die Familie Schroffenstein* . See *SW* I, 54; 90–5.

16 It seems likely that the '-kon' suffix was intended to evoke memories of Napoleon's Swiss campaign.

17 Of course it was a 'warning' that was never heard, since, for political reasons, the play was not performed until 1860.

18 On this aspect of the play, see Burckhardt, *The drama of language*, pp. 134–40.

19 In so doing he violates the Kantian maxim, to use other human beings always as an end and never as a means.

20 Interestingly, this marks out Hermann as one of the few characters in Kleist's plays who undergoes an overt development in the course of the action.

9 'PRINZ FRIEDRICH VON HOMBURG'

1 The works in question were: *Œuvres de Fréderic II roi de Prusse*, vol. I, (Berlin, 1789) and K. H. Krause, *Mein Vaterland unter den Hohenzollerischen Regenten: ein Lesebuch für Freunde der Geschichte*, vol. II, (Halle, 1803). The relevant extracts (together with a wealth of background material on the play) are reproduced in Richard Samuel's excellent annotated edition of the play. See, Richard Samuel, ed., *'Prinz Friedrich von Homburg': ein Schauspiel by Heinrich von Kleist* (London, 1962), pp. 187–93.

2 See Samuel, ed., *Prinz Friedrich*, pp. 27–9.

3 See chapter 2, pp. 19–20 above.

4 Even so, the director, Josef Schreyvogel, was obliged to remove a number of the more controversial lines and change the title to *Die Schlacht von Fehrbellin (The battle of Fehrbellin)*. On the reception of *Prinz Friedrich von Homburg* see Rolf Busch, *Imperialistische und faschistische Kleist-Rezeption 1890–1945: eine ideologische Untersuchung* (Frankfurt, 1974).

5 A useful – though far from impartial – account (in English) of the secondary literature is to be found in John M. Ellis, *Kleist's 'Prinz Friedrich von Homburg': a critical study* (Berkeley, 1970), pp. 3–11. The main critical

approaches are also detailed (in German) in Klaus Kanzog's invaluable edition of the play. See Klaus Kanzog, ed., *Heinrich von Kleist: 'Prinz Friedrich von Homburg'. Text, Kontexte, Kommentar* (Munich, 1977). See also, Fritz Hackert, ed., *Heinrich von Kleist: 'Prinz Friedrich von Homburg'. Erläuterungen und Dokumente* (Stuttgart, 1979).

It is not possible to deal here in detail with the now massive amount of critical literature relating to the play. Broadly speaking, it is possible to detect two mutually opposed critical approaches, each of which has its origins in Max Kommerell's succinct summary of the play's dramatic structure: 'Two realities compete to discover which is the more real' ('Zwei Wirklichkeiten streiten, welche wirklicher ist'). See Kommerell, *Geist und Buchstabe der Dichting*, p. 252. For as in the case of *Amphitryon*, critics are sharply divided as to which of the two value-systems presented in the play – that of the Prince or that of the Elector – is ultimately upheld. Does Kleist endorse the individualism of the Prince as a quality that transcends military law; or does he present the Elector as a god-like creature, the perfect embodiment of Kantian values and the 'Prussian ethos'? A good example of the first type of reading is offered by Alfred Schlagdenhauffen in his book, *L'univers existentiel de Kleist dans le Prince de Hombourg* (Paris, 1953), where he writes 'how absurd is this world in which . . . the law is tyrannical and grace merely arbitrary' ('Absurde cet univers . . . où la loi est tyrannique et la grâce arbitraire'; p. 102). For an example of a reading favouring the opposite view, see Hans M. Wolff, *Heinrich von Kleist: die Geschichte seines Schaffens* (Berkeley, Bern, 1954), pp. 225–48. The difficulties in upholding either protagonist as an idealised figure in the play has prompted most critics to see the play as ending in a synthesis of the two positions, a view which is sometimes referred to as the 'education thesis'. Thus the play is said to depict a process of education in which the (naïve) Prince is 'educated' by the (benevolent) Elector to a proper understanding of the nature of military discipline. See Müller-Seidel, *Versehen und Erkennen*, especially pp. 204–5. A not dissimilar reading of the play is to be found in John Gearey's book, *Heinrich von Kleist: a study in tragedy and anxiety* (Philadelphia, 1968), pp. 149–81. However, the view of the play as ending with a harmonious reconciliation between the Prince and the Elector has not passed unchallenged. Wolfgang Wittkowski detects a note of 'sceptical resignation' ('skeptische Resignation') in the face of a reality which refuses to accommodate the products of the imagination. See Wolfgang Wittkowski, 'Absolutes Gefühl und absolute Kunst in Kleists *Prinz Friedrich von Homburg*', *Der Deutschunterricht*, 13 (1961), 27–71 (p. 71). John Ellis, in his psychological reading of the play in terms of a conflict in which the (ageing) Elector is portrayed as the jealous rival of the (younger) Prince, also sees the play as ending on a dissonant note: 'the end of the play, instead of solving problems, leaves them open'. See John Ellis, *Kleist's 'Prinz Friedrich von Homburg'*, p. 99. Another critic to question whether the alleged reconciliation does indeed take place at the end of the play is Erika Swales. For in her view, the multiplicity of perspectives at work in the play continually subverts any attempt on the part of the reader to impose his or her reading of the text: 'in Prinz Friedrich von Homburg willed harmony and fragmentation . . . are provocatively fused'. See Erika Swales, 'Configurations of irony: Kleist's *Prinz Friedrich von Homburg*', *DVjs*, 56 (1982), 407–30. For other views which emphasise the dissonant aspects of the play, see Bernd Leistner, 'Dissonante Utopie: zu Kleists *Prinz Friedrich von Homburg*', *Impulse*, 2 (1979), 259–317, Johannes Harnischfeger, 'Der Traum vom Heroismus: zu Kleists *Prinz Friedrich von Homburg*', *Jahrbuch des Freien Deutschen Hochstifts*, 1989, 244–80, and Dieter Liewerscheidt, '"Ich muß doch sehen, wie weit ers treibt!": die Komödie in Kleists *Prinz Friedrich von Homburg*', *Wirkendes Wort*, 40 (1990), 313–23. For a reading of a rather different type, which views the play in terms of a rejection of existing literary paradigms, see Benjamin Bennett, *Modern drama and German classicism: renaissance from Lessing to Brecht* (Ithaca and London, 1979), pp. 22–56 (especially pp. 48–51).

6 Hohenzollern is quite mistaken in act III, scene 3, when he suggests that the Prince's affections for Natalie are responsible for the crisis in which he finds himself.

7 See *SW* I, 647; 350 and G, 288.

8 See *SW* I, 661; 673–7 and G, 302.

9 In this respect one might compare Froben's fate with that of the First Officer ('Erste Offizier'), who is arrested at the Prince's behest in act II, scene 2. Froben dies on the battlefield and the fate of the young officer remains uncertain. It is tempting to ask whether the Elector's pardon at the end of the play will 'oblige' the Prince to offer a similar pardon to the young officer who disobeyed him earlier.

10 See *SW* I, 681; 1175–6 and G, 322.

11 Amusingly enough, the logic of the situation outlined above is identical with that of Kleist's humorous anecdote, *Der verlegene Magistrat* (*The perplexed magistrate*). There a magistrate is confronted with a criminal who has committed a trivial offence but insists on his right, under an ancient law, to be put to death (rather than pay the customary fine). In the circumstances, the magistrate decides he has no choice but to let him off altogether. See *SW* II, 262–3 and M, 267.

12 See *SW* I, 632; 32–3 and G, 272.

13 Kleist's critical view of such sentimental posturing is suggested by the dismissive tone he adopts in the essay *Was gilt es in diesem Kriege?* (*What*

are we fighting for in this war?) when he writes: 'Has this war got anything to do with the fame of a young and resourceful prince, who has been dreaming of victory garlands in the sweet fragrance of a beautiful summer's eve?' ('Gilt es den Ruhm eines jungen und unternehmenden Fürsten, der, in dem Duft einer lieblichen Sommernacht, von Lorbeern geträumt hat?'; *SW* II, 377).

14 Here the Prince resembles Strahl in *Das Käthchen von Heilbronn*, who is equally in awe of the portraits of his ancestors in the armoury at Schloß Wetterstein. See *SW* I, 454; 702–6 and P, 271.

15 Another example of such hysterical posturing is to be found in the 'Fortuna scene' of act I, scene 6, itself an extension of the moon-lit reverie in the garden.

16 See *SW* I, 688 and G, 329.

17 See *SW* I, 653; 477 and G, 294.

18 See *SW* I, 634; 69 and G, 274.

19 The fact that he acts more out of curiosity than compassion need not imply that, as William Reeve would have it, Hohenzollern is the 'unsung villain of the play'. See Reeve, *In pursuit of power*, p. 112.

20 In this respect there is a striking parallel between *Das Käthchen von Heilbronn* and *Prinz Friedrich von Homburg*.

21 See *SW* I, 665; 759 and G, 306.

22 See *SW* I, 685; 1262–3 and G, 326.

23 The crucial importance of Natalie's role in the play seems to have been overlooked by many critics. Walter Silz is a notable exception – see Walter Silz, 'Kleist's Natalie', *Modern Language Notes*, 91 (1976), 531–7. Nonetheless, I cannot agree with Silz that her mission in act IV, scene 4, is to 'induce him to do what in her heart she does not want him to do' (p. 535), i.e. to sign the Elector's letter and assent to his execution.

24 See *SW* I, 632; 33–4 and G, 272.

25 Note the contrast between the way the women treat the Prince in this scene and the way in which he is treated by Hohenzollern and the Elector in the opening scene of the play.

26 In this respect Natalie displays a rather better understanding of the nature of heroism than did many of Kleist's contemporaries.

27 Strictly speaking, Natalie has no right to hold out such an appealing vision of the future. Nonetheless, Kleist's contemporaries – had they had an opportunity to see the play – would no doubt have recalled that the Great Elector's act of clemency all those years ago had not led to the collapse of the state either.

28 Hence the reason why the Prussian Reform Group was just as much concerned with the transformation of the institutions of state as it was with combating the external threat posed by France.

29 See *SW* I, 695; 1496 and G, 336. Although not taken to the same (absurdly comic) degree as in *Das Käthchen von Heilbronn*, there is a marked similarity between the Elector's behaviour here and the Kaiser's behaviour in act V, scene 2 of the earlier play. For just as the Kaiser wishes to throw a veil over the improprieties of imperial paternity, so too in this scene, the Elector is worried in case word gets out that his armies are no longer carrying out his orders, but those of a 'mere' woman.

30 Here we might recall Kleist's advice to Rühle von Lilienstern as to the impossibility of knowing for certain what the result of any given artistic experiment will be: 'It's no better than a throw of the dice, but that's all there is' ('Es ist ein Wurf, wie mit dem Würfel; aber es gibt nichts anderes'; *SW* II, 770).

31 It is interesting to note that Hohenzollern's arguments are never put to the Prince. This may reflect the fact that they do not represent as radical an assault on the prevailing norms of military discipline as those of Kottwitz.

32 It is striking that in each case, the central protagonists – Käthchen and the Prince – faint in the final scene.

10 CONCLUSIONS

1 Hence the reason why Kleist selected scene 15 (in which Penthesilea explains the conventions of the Amazon state to Achilles) for advance publication in his own literary journal, *Phöbus*.

2 There is one other 'Amazon-type' society in Kleist's plays, namely the all-female household of Ursula and Barnabe, in act IV, scene 3, of *Die Familie Schroffenstein*.

3 Similarly, whilst distinctions of rank have not been abolished altogether in Sylvester's society, there is a considerable difference in the way subordinates are treated in Warwand and in Rossitz.

4 See Allan, '"Liederlichkeit"'.

5 Thus Ernst Stahl writes, '*Prinz Friedrich von Homburg* . . . represents the final dissolution of [Kleist's] disharmonies'. See Stahl, *Heinrich von Kleist's dramas*, p. 113.

6 For further details of the chronology of Kleist's works, see Helmut Hermann, 'Daten zur Werkgeschichte', in Hinderer, *Kleists Dramen*, pp. 24–30.

7 This is essentially the teleological model underlying Ilse Graham's study. See Graham, *Heinrich von Kleist*.

8 See chapter 2, pp. 46–7, above.

9 Much has been made of the rivalry between Goethe and Kleist, most notably by Katharina Mommsen. See Mommsen, *Kleists Kampf*. The

fascinating question of how far Kleist's works can be regarded as specifically literary responses to other literary works has vexed Kleist scholars over the years, and does not really lie within the scope of the present study. As I suggested in my brief discussion of the relationship between *Penthesilea* and *Iphigenie auf Tauris*, (see notes to chapter 6, pp. 289–90, n.27, above), it may be more productive to look at what Kleist's works have in common with those of Goethe, rather than to see the two writers as locked in diametrically opposed positions to one another.

Select bibliography

(1) PRIMARY SOURCES

Gneisenau, Neithardt von, *Denkschriften zum Volksaufstand von 1808 und 1811*, Kriegsgeschichtliche Bücherei, Heft 10 (Berlin: Junker und Dünnhaupt, 1936).

Goethe, Johann Wolfgang, *Gedenkausgabe der Werke, Briefe und Gespräche*, edited by Ernst Beutler, 24 vols. (Zürich: Artemis, 1949).

Selected Verse, edited and with an introduction by David Luke (London: Penguin, 1986).

Wilhelm Meister's apprenticeship: a novel from the German of Goethe, translated by R. Dillon Boylan (London: Bohn, 1855).

Kafka, Franz, *Briefe an Felice und andere Korrespondenz aus der Verlobungszeit*, edited by Erich Heller and Jürgen Born (Frankfurt: Fischer, 1967).

Kleist, Heinrich von, *Sämtliche Werke und Briefe*, edited by Helmut Sembdner, 7th extended and revised edition, 2 vols. (Munich: Hanser, 1984).

Sämtliche Werke und Briefe, edited by Ilse-Marie Barth, Klaus Müller-Salget, Stefan Ormanns, and Hinrich C. Seeba, 4 vols. (Frankfurt: Deutscher Klassiker Verlag, 1991).

An abyss deep enough: letters of Heinrich von Kleist with a selection of anecdotes, edited, translated and introduced by Philip B. Miller (New York: Dutton, 1982).

Five plays, translated from the German with an introduction by Martin Greenberg (New Haven and London: Yale University Press, 1988).

Kaethchen of Heilbronn, translated by Frederick E. Peirce, in Frederick E. Peirce and Carl F. Schreiber, *Fiction and fantasy of German Romance: selections from the German Romantic authors, 1790–1830, in English translation* (London, Toronto, Melbourne and Bombay: Oxford University Press, 1927), pp. 248–344.

The feud of the Schroffensteins, translated from the German by Mary J. Price and Lawrence M. Price, *Poet Lore*, 27 (1916), 457–576.

The Marquise of O . . . and other stories, translated and with an introduction by David Luke and Nigel Reeves (London: Penguin, 1978).

Klopstock, Friedrich Gottlieb, *Klopstocks Werke*, edited by R. Hamel, 4 vols. (Berlin, Stuttgart: Speman, 1883).

Rousseau, Jean-Jacques, *Emile*, translated by Barbara Foxley and with an introduction by P. D. Jimack (London: Dent, 1911, repr. 1989).

Schlegel, Friedrich, *Kritische Friedrich-Schlegel-Ausgabe*, edited by Ernst Behler with the collaboration of Jean-Jacques Anstett, Hans Eichner, and other specialists, 35 vols. (Munich, Paderborn, Vienna: Schöningh; Zürich, Thomas, 1958–).

Philosophical Fragments, translated by Peter Firchow; foreword by Rodolphe Gaché (Minneapolis: University of Minnesota Press, 1991).

Tieck, Ludwig, *Kritische Schriften. Zum erstenmale gesammelt und mit einer Vorrede* (Leipzig: Brockhaus, 1848–52. [Photomechanical reproduction, Berlin, New York: de Gruyter, 1974])

(II) SECONDARY SOURCES

Allan, Seán, '"Liederlichkeit, Spiel, Trunk, Faulheit und Völlerei, behalte ich mir bevor": Heinrich von Kleist's last word on modern educational theory', *GLL*, ns 48 (1995), 353–61.

Angress, Ruth K., 'Kleist's treatment of imperialism: *Die Hermannsschlacht* and *Die Verlobung in St. Domingo*', *Monatshefte*, 69 (1977), 17–33.

'Kleist's nation of Amazons', in Susan L. Cocalis and Kay Goodman, eds., *Beyond the eternal feminine: critical essays on women and German literature*, Stuttgarter Arbeiten zur Germanistik, no. 98 (Stuttgart: Hans-Dieter Heinz, 1982), pp. 99–134.

Appelbaum Graham, Ilse: see under Graham.

Appelt, Hedwig, and Maximilian Nutz, eds., *Heinrich von Kleist: 'Penthesilea'. Erläuterungen und Dokumente* (Stuttgart: Reclam, 1992).

Arntzen, Helmut, *Die ernste Komödie: das deutsche Lustspiel von Lessing bis Kleist* (Munich: Nymphenburger, 1968).

'Heinrich von Kleist: Gewalt und Sprache', in Wieland Schmidt, ed., *Die Gegenwärtigkeit Kleists: Reden zum Gedenkjahr 1977 im Schloß Charlottenburg zu Berlin*, Jahresgabe der Heinrich-von-Kleist-Gesellschaft, 1977 (Berlin: Erich Schmidt, 1980), pp. 62–78.

'*Prinz Friedrich von Homburg*: Drama der Bewußtseinsstufen', in Walter Hinderer, ed., *Kleists Dramen: neue Interpretationen* (Stuttgart: Reclam, 1981), pp. 213–37.

'Kleists kleine Prosa', *Freiburger Universitätsblätter*, 25 (1986), 45–56.

Bachmaier, Helmut, and Thomas Horst, 'Die mythische Gestalt des Selbstbewußtseins: zu Kleists *Amphitryon*', *JbDSG*, 22 (1978), 404–41.

Bachmaier, Helmut, and Thomas Horst, eds., *Heinrich von Kleist: 'Amphitryon'. Erläuterungen und Dokumente* (Stuttgart: Reclam, 1983).

Bennett, Benjamin, *Modern drama and German classicism: renaissance from Lessing to Brecht* (Ithaca and London: Cornell University Press, 1979).

Binder, Wolfgang, *Aufschlüsse: Studien zur deutschen Literatur* (Zürich: Artemis, 1976).

Blöcker, Günter, *Heinrich von Kleist oder Das absolute Ich* (Berlin: Argon, 1960).

Borchardt, Edith, *Mythische Strukturen im Werk Heinrich von Kleists*, American University Studies, Series 1; Germanic Languages and Literature, no. 40 (New York, Bern, Frankfurt, Paris: Peter Lang, 1987).

Borcherdt, H., ed., *Schiller und die Romantiker: Briefe und Dokumente* (Stuttgart: Cotta, 1948).

Brown, Hilda, 'Penthesilea: nightingale and Amazon', *OGS*, 7 (1972), 24–33.

Kleist and the tragic ideal: a study of 'Penthesilea' and its relationship to Kleist's personal and literary development, 1806-1808, European University Papers, Series 1; German Language and Literature, no. 203 (Bern, Frankfurt, Las Vegas: Peter Lang, 1977).

Browning, Robert M., 'Kleist's Käthchen and the monomyth', in Donald H. Crosby, and George Schoolfield, eds., *Studies in the German drama: a Festschrift in honor of Walter Silz* (Chapel Hill: University of North Carolina Press, 1974), pp. 115–24.

Burckhardt, Sigurd, *The drama of language: essays on Goethe and Kleist* (Baltimore: Johns Hopkins Press, 1970).

Busch, Rolf, *Imperialistische und faschistische Kleist-Rezeption 1890–1945: eine ideologische Untersuchung* (Frankfurt: Akademische Verlagsgesellschaft, 1974).

Cixous, Hélène, and Catherine Clément, *The newly born woman*, translated by Betsy Wing, and with an introduction by Sandra M. Gilbert, Theory and history of literature, no. 24 (Manchester: Manchester University Press, 1986).

Cullens, Chris, and Dorothea von Mücke, 'Love in Kleist's *Penthesilea* and *Käthchen von Heilbronn*', *DVjs*, 63 (1989), 461–93.

Durzak, Manfred, 'Das Gesetz der Athene und das Gesetz der Tanaïs: zur Funktion des Mythischen in Kleists *Penthesilea*', *Jahrbuch des Freien Deutschen Hochstifts* (1973), 653–84.

Dyer, Denys, 'Kleist und das Paradoxe', *Kleist-Jahrbuch* (1981/2), 210–19.

Ellis, John M., *Kleist's 'Prinz Friedrich von Homburg': a critical study*, University of California Publications in Modern Philology, no. 97 (Berkeley: University of California Press, 1970).

Narration in the German Novelle: theory and interpretation (Cambridge: Cambridge University Press, 1974).

Heinrich von Kleist: studies in the character and meaning of his writings, University of North Carolina studies in the Germanic languages and literatures, no. 94 (Chapel Hill: University of North Carolina Press, 1979).

Emrich, Wilhelm, 'Kleist und die moderne Literatur', in Walter Müller-Seidel, ed., *Heinrich von Kleist: vier Reden zu seinem Gedächtnis*, Jahresgabe der Heinrich-von-Kleist-Gesellschaft, 1962 (Berlin: Erich Schmidt, 1962), pp. 9–25.

Fischer, Bernd, 'Wo steht Kleist im *Amphitryon*?', *Studia Neophilologica*, 56 (1984), 61–8.

Ironische Metaphysik: die Erzählungen Heinrich von Kleists (Munich: Fink, 1988).

'Irony ironised: Heinrich von Kleist's narrative stance and Friedrich Schlegel's theory of irony', *European Romantic Review*, 1 (1990), 59–74.

Fischer, Peter, *Heinrich von Kleist*, Preußische Köpfe (Berlin: Stapp, 1982).

Fricke, Gerhard, *Gefühl und Schicksal bei Heinrich von Kleist: Studien über den inneren Vorgang im Leben und Schaffen des Dichters*, Neue Forschung: Arbeiten zur Geistesgeschichte der germanischen und romanischen Völker, no. 3 (Berlin: Junker und Dünnhaupt, 1929).

Gadamer, Hans G., 'Der Gott des innersten Gefühls: zu Kleists *Amphitryon*', *Die neue Rundschau*, 72 (1961), 340–9.

Gall, Ulrich, *Philosophie bei Heinrich von Kleist: Untersuchungen zu Herkunft und Bestimmung des philosophischen Gehalts seiner Schriften*, Abhandlungen zur Philosophie, Psychologie und Pädagogik, no. 123 (Bonn: Bouvier, 1977).

Gallas, Helga, 'Kleists *Penthesilea* und Lacans vier Diskurse', in Inge Stephan, and Carl Pietzcker, eds., *Frauensprache – Frauenliteratur: Für und Wider einer Psychoanalyse literarischer Werke*, Kontroversen, alte und neue: Akten des VII. Internationalen Vereinigung der germanistischen Sprach- und Literaturwissenschaft, vol. 6 (Tübingen: Niemeyer, 1986), pp. 203–12.

'Antikenrezeption bei Goethe und Kleist: Penthesilea – eine anti-Iphigenie?', in Linda Dietrick, and David G. John, eds., *Momentum dramaticum: Festschrift for Eckehard Catholy* (Waterloo, University of Waterloo Press, 1980), pp. 209–220.

Gearey, John, *Heinrich von Kleist: a study in tragedy and anxiety* (Philadelphia: University of Philadelphia Press, 1968).

Gönner, Gerhard, *Von 'zerspaltenen Herzen' und der 'gebrechlichen Einrichtung der Welt': Versuch einer Phänomenologie der Gewalt bei Kleist* (Stuttgart: Metzler, 1989).

Gossman, Lionel, 'Molière's *Amphitryon*', *PMLA*, 78 (1963), 201–13.

Graham, Ilse (Ilse Appelbaum Graham), 'The broken pitcher: hero of Kleist's comedy', *Modern Language Quarterly*, 16 (1955), 99–113.

Heinrich von Kleist. Word into flesh: a poet's quest for the symbol (Berlin, New York: de Gruyter, 1977).

Grathoff, Dirk, 'Die Zensurkonflikte der Berliner Abendblätter: zur Beziehung von Journalismus und Öffentlichkeit bei Heinrich von Kleist', in Klaus Peter, Dirk Grathoff, Charles N. Hayes, and Gerhard Loose, eds., *Ideologische Studien zur Literatur: Essays 1*, These: New York Ottendorfer Series, Neue Folge, no. 5, (Frankfurt: Athenäum, 1972), pp. 37–168.

'Beerben oder Enterben? Probleme einer gegenwärtigen Aneignung von Kleists *Käthchen von Heilbronn*', in Walter Raitz, and Erhard Schütz, eds., *Der alte Kanon neu: zur Revision des literarischen Kanons in Wissenschaft und Unterricht*, Lesen 2 (Opladen: Westdeutscher Verlag, 1976), pp. 136–75.

'Der Fall des Krugs: zum geschichtlichen Gehalt von Kleists Lustspiel', *Kleist-Jahrbuch* (1981/2), 290–314.

Grathoff, Dirk, ed., *Heinrich von Kleist: 'Das Käthchen von Heilbronn oder die Feuerprobe'. Erläuterungen und Dokumente* (Stuttgart: Reclam, 1977).

Heinrich von Kleist: Studien zu Werk und Wirkung (Opladen: Westdeutscher Verlag, 1988).

Gundolf, Friedrich, *Heinrich von Kleist* (Berlin: Bondi, 1922).

Gustafson, Susan E., '"Die allmähliche Verfertigung der Gedanken beim Reden": the linguistic question in *Amphitryon*', *Seminar*, 25 (1989), 104–26.

Hackert, Fritz, ed., *Heinrich von Kleist: 'Prinz Friedrich von Homburg'. Erläuterungen und Dokumente* (Stuttgart: Reclam, 1979).

Harms, Ingeborg, '"Wie fliegender Sommer": eine Untersuchung der "Höhlenszene" in Heinrich von Kleists *Familie Schroffenstein*', *JbDSG*, 28 (1984), 270–314.

Harnischfeger, Johannes, 'Der Traum vom Heroismus: zu Kleists *Prinz Friedrich von Homburg*', *Jahrbuch des Freien Deutschen Hochstifts* (1989), 244–80.

Heiseler, Bernd von, *Gesammelte Essays zur alten und neuen Literatur*, 2 vols. (Stuttgart: Steinkopf, 1966).

Hellmann, Hanna, '*Über das Marionettentheater*', in Walter Müller-Seidel, ed., *Kleists Aufsatz über das Marionettentheater: Studien und Interpretationen*, Jahresgabe der Heinrich-von-Kleist-Gesellschaft, 1965–6 (Berlin: Erich Schmidt, 1967), pp. 17–31.

Hermann, Helmut G., 'Daten zur Werkgeschichte', in Walter Hinderer, ed., *Kleists Dramen: neue Interpretationen* (Stuttgart: Reclam, 1981), pp. 24–30.

Hinderer, Walter, ed., *Kleists Dramen: neue Interpretationen* (Stuttgart: Reclam, 1981).

Hoffmeister, Elmar, *Täuschung und Wirklichkeit bei Heinrich von Kleist*, Abhandlungen zur Kunst- Musik- und Literaturwissenschaft, no. 59 (Bonn: Bouvier, 1968).

Holz, Hans H., *Macht und Ohnmacht der Sprache: Untersuchungen zum*

Sprachverständnis und Stil Heinrich von Kleists, Bücher zur Dichtkunst (Frankfurt: Athenäum, 1962).

Horn, Peter, 'Das erschrockene Gelächter über die Entlarvung einer korrupten Obrigkeit: Kleists zwiespältige Komödie *Der zerbrochne Krug*', in Dirk Grathoff, ed., *Heinrich von Kleist: Studien zu Werk und Wirkung* (Opladen: Westdeutscher Verlag, 1988), pp. 149–62.

Hoverland, Lilian, 'Heinrich von Kleist and Luce Irigaray: visions of the feminine', in Marianne Burkhardt, ed., *Gestaltet und gestaltend: Frauen in der deutschen Literatur*, Amsterdamer Beiträge zur neueren Germanistik, no. 10 (Amsterdam: Rodopi, 1980), pp. 57–82.

Hubbs, Valentine C., 'The concept of fate in Kleist's *Schroffenstein*', *Monatshefte*, 56 (1964), 339–45.

'The plus and minus of Penthesilea and Käthchen', *Seminar*, 6 (1970), 187–94.

Jancke, Gerhard, 'Zum Problem des identischen Selbst in Kleists Lustspiel *Amphitryon*', *Colloquia Germanica*, 3 (1969), 87–110.

Janz, Rolf-Peter. 'Die Marionette als Zeugin der Anklage: zu Kleists Abhandlung *Über das Marionettentheater*', in Walter Hinderer, ed., *Kleists Dramen: neue Interpretationen* (Stuttgart: Reclam, 1981), pp. 31–51.

Jauss, Hans R., 'Von Plautus bis Kleist: *Amphitryon* im dialogischen Prozeß der Arbeit am Mythos', in Walter Hinderer, ed., *Kleists Dramen: neue Interpretationen* (Stuttgart: Reclam, 1981), pp. 114–43.

Kaiser, Gerhard, *Wandrer und Idylle: Goethe und die Phänomenologie der Natur in der deutschen Dichtung von Geßner bis Gottfried Keller* (Göttingen: Vandenhoek and Ruprecht, 1977).

Kanzog, Klaus, ed., *Heinrich von Kleist: 'Prinz Friedrich von Homburg'. Text, Kontexte, Kommentar*, Reihe Hanser Literatur-Kommentare, no.7 (Munich: Hanser, 1977).

Kayser, Wolfgang, 'Kleist als Erzähler', *GLL*, ns 8 (1954), 19–29.

Kittler, Wolf, *Die Geburt des Partisanen aus dem Geist der Poesie: Heinrich von Kleist und die Strategie der Befreiungskriege* (Freiburg: Rombach, 1987).

Kluge, Gerhard, 'Der Wandel der dramatischen Konzeption von der *Familie Ghonorez* zur *Familie Schroffenstein*', in Walter Hinderer, ed., *Kleists Dramen: neue Interpretationen* (Stuttgart: Reclam, 1981), pp. 52–72.

Kommerell, Max, *Geist und Buchstabe der Dichtung: Goethe, Schiller, Kleist, Hölderlin*, 3rd revised and extended edition (Frankfurt: Klostermann, 1944).

Kreutzer, Hans Joachim, 'Die Utopie vom Vaterland: Kleists politische Dramen', *OGS*, 20/1 (1991/2), 69–84.

Leistner, Bernd, 'Dissonante Utopie: zu Kleists *Prinz Friedrich von Homburg*', *Impulse*, 2 (1979), 259–317.

'Heinrich von Kleists *Der zerbrochne Krug:* die tragische Aufhebung eines Lustspielvorgangs', *Weimarer Beiträge*, 30 (1984), 2028–47.

Liewerscheidt, Dieter, '"Ich muß doch sehen, wie weit ers treibt!": die

Komödie in Kleists *Prinz Friedrich von Homburg*', *Wirkendes Wort*, 40 (1990), 313–23.

Lindsay, J. M., 'Faulty communication in the works of Kleist', *GLL*, ns 31 (1977), 57–67.

Linn, Rolf N., 'Comical and humorous elements in Kleist's *Hermannsschlacht*', *Germanic Review*, 47 (1972), 159–67.

Loose, Hans-Dieter, *Kleists 'Hermannsschlacht': kein Krieg für Hermann und seine Cherusker. Ein paradoxer Feldzug aus dem Geist der Utopie gegen den Geist besitzbürgerlicher und feudaler Herrschaft*, (Karlsruhe: von Loeper, 1984).

Lugowski, Clemens, *Wirklichkeit und Dichtung: Untersuchungen zur Wirklichkeitsauffassung Heinrich von Kleists* (Frankfurt: Diesterweg, 1936).

Maas, Joachim, *Kleist: die Geschichte seines Lebens* (Bern, Munich: Scherz, 1977).

Martini, Fritz, '*Das Käthchen von Heilbronn*: Heinrich von Kleists drittes Lustspiel?', *JbDSG*, 20 (1976), 420–47.

Mathieu, G. 'Kleist's Hermann: the portrait of an artist in propaganda', *GLL*, ns 7 (1953), 1–10.

'Heinrich von Kleist's primer for propaganda analysis', in *Monatshefte*, 46 (1954), 375–82.

McGlathery, James M., *Desire's sway: the plays and stories of Heinrich von Kleist* (Detroit: Wayne State University Press, 1983).

Meyer-Benfey, Heinrich, *Das Drama Heinrich von Kleists*, 2 vols. (Göttingen: Hapke, 1913).

Michelsen, Peter, 'Die Lügen Adams und Evas Fall: Heinrich von Kleists *Der zerbrochne Krug*', in Herbert Anton, Bernard Gajek, and Peter Pfaff, eds., *Geist und Zeichen: Festschrift für Arthur Henkel* (Heidelberg: Carl Winter, 1977), pp. 268–304.

'"Wehe, mein Vaterland, dir!": Heinrichs von Kleist *Die Hermannsschlacht*', *Kleist-Jahrbuch* (1987), 115–36.

'Die Betrogenen des Rechtgefühls: zu Kleists *Die Familie Schroffenstein*', *Kleist-Jahrbuch* (1992), 64–80.

Moering, Michael, *Witz und Ironie in der Prosa Heinrich von Kleists* (Munich: Fink, 1972).

Mommsen, Katharina, *Kleists Kampf mit Goethe*, Poesie und Wissenschaft, no. 27 (Heidelberg: Lothar Stiehm, 1974).

Müller-Salget, Klaus, 'Das Prinzip der Doppeldeutigkeit in Kleists Erzählungen', *Zeitschrift für deutsche Philologie*, 92 (1973), 185–211.

Müller-Seidel, Walter, 'Die Struktur des Widerspruchs in Kleists *Marquise von O . . .*', *DVjs*, 28 (1954), 497–515.

Versehen und Erkennen: eine Studie über Heinrich von Kleist (Cologne: Böhlau, 1961).

'Die Vermischung des Komischen mit dem Tragischen in Kleists Lustspiel *Amphitryon*', *JbDSG*, 5 (1961), 118–35.

'*Penthesilea* im Kontext der deutschen Klassik', in Walter Hinderer, ed., *Kleists Dramen: neue Interpretationen* (Stuttgart: Reclam, 1981), pp. 144–71.

Müller-Seidel, Walter, ed., *Heinrich von Kleist: vier Reden zu seinem Gedächtnis*, Jahresgabe der Heinrich-von-Kleist-Gesellschaft, 1962 (Berlin: Erich Schmidt, 1962).

Kleists Aufsatz über das Marionettentheater: Studien und Interpretationen, Jahresgabe der Heinrich-von-Kleist-Gesellschaft, 1965–6, (Berlin: Erich Schmidt, 1967).

Heinrich von Kleist: Aufsätze und Essays, Wege der Forschung, no. 147 (Darmstadt: Wissenschaftliche Buchgesellschaft, 1967).

Kleist und Frankreich, Jahresgabe der Heinrich-von-Kleist-Gesellschaft, 1968 (Berlin: Erich Schmidt, 1969).

Kleists Aktualität: neue Aufsätze und Essays 1966–1978, Wege der Forschung, no. 586 (Darmstadt: Wissenschaftliche Buchgesellschaft, 1981).

Nadler, Josef, *Die Berliner Romantik 1800–1814: ein Beitrag zur gemeinvölkischen Frage. Renaissance, Romantik, Restauration* (Berlin: Erich Reiss, 1921).

Neumann, Gerhard, 'Hexenküche und Abendmahl: die Sprache der Liebe im Werk Heinrich von Kleists', *Freiburger Universitätsblätter*, 25 (1986), 9–31.

'"... Der Mensch ohne Hülle ist eigentlich der Mensch": Goethe und Heinrich von Kleist in der Geschichte des physiognomischen Blicks', *Kleist-Jahrbuch* (1988/9), 259–75.

Oesterle, Ingrid, 'Werther in Paris? Heinrich von Kleists Briefe über Paris', in Dirk Grathoff, ed., *Heinrich von Kleist: Studien zu Werk und Wirkung* (Opladen: Westdeutscher Verlag, 1988), pp. 97–116.

Paulin, Roger, 'Kleist's metamorphoses: some remarks on the use of mythology in *Penthesilea*', *OGS*, 14 (1983), 35–53.

Ludwig Tieck: a literary biography (Oxford: Clarendon, 1985).

Pfeiffer, Joachim, *Die zerbrochenen Bilder: gestörte Ordnungen im Werk Heinrich von Kleists*, Epistemata: Reihe Literaturwissenschaft, no. 45 (Würzburg: Königshausen and Neumann, 1989).

Politzer, Heinz, 'Auf der Suche nach Identität: zu Heinrich von Kleists Würzburger Reise', *Euphorion*, 61 (1967), 383–99.

Prandi, Julie D., *Spirited women heroes: major female characters in the dramas of Goethe, Schiller and Kleist*, European University Papers, Series 1; German Language and Literature, no. 750 (Bern, Frankfurt, New York: Peter Lang, 1983).

'Woman Warrior as Hero: Schiller's *Jungfrau von Orleans* and Kleist's *Penthesilea*', *Monatshefte*, 77 (1985), 403–14.

Reeve, William C., 'Ein dunkles Licht: the court secretary in Kleist's *Der zerbrochne Krug*', *Germanic Review*, 58 (1983), 58–65.

In pursuit of power: Heinrich von Kleist's Machiavellian protagonists (Toronto, Buffalo, London: University of Toronto Press, 1987).

'"O du – wie nenn ich dich?": names in Kleist's *Käthchen von Heilbronn*', *GLL*, ns 41 (1988), 83–98.
Kleist's aristocratic heritage and 'Das Käthchen von Heilbronn', (Montreal and Kingston, London, Buffalo: McGill's University Press, 1991).
Kleist on stage: 1804–1987 (Montreal and Kingston, London, Buffalo: McGill's University Press, 1993).
Reske, Hermann, 'Die Kleistsche Sprache', *German Quarterly*, 36 (1963), 219–35.
Traum und Wirklichkeit im Werk Heinrich von Kleists, Sprache und Literatur, no. 54 (Stuttgart: Kohlhammer, 1969).
Ryan, Lawrence, 'Die Marionette und das "unendliche Bewußtsein" bei Heinrich von Kleist', in Walter Müller-Seidel, ed., *Kleists Aufsatz über das Marionettentheater: Studien und Interpretationen*, Jahresgabe der Heinrich-von-Kleist-Gesellschaft, 1965–6 (Berlin: Erich Schmidt, 1967), pp. 171–195.
'*Amphitryon*: doch ein Lustspielstoff!', in Walter Müller-Seidel, ed., *Kleist und Frankreich*, Jahresgabe der Heinrich-von-Kleist-Gesellschaft, 1968 (Berlin: Erich Schmidt, 1969), pp. 83–121.
'Die "vaterländische Umkehr" in der *Hermannsschlacht*', in Walter Hinderer, ed., *Kleists Dramen: neue Interpretationen* (Stuttgart: Reclam, 1981), pp. 188–212.
Samuel, Richard, 'Goethe – Napoleon – Heinrich von Kleist', *PEGS*, ns 14 (1939), 43–75.
'Kleists *Hermannsschlacht* und der Freiherr vom Stein', *JbDSG*, 5 (1961), 64–101.
Samuel, Richard, and Hilda M. Brown, *Kleist's lost year and the quest for 'Robert Guiskard'* (Leamington Spa: Hall, 1981).
Samuel, Richard, ed., *Prinz Friedrich von Homburg': ein Schauspiel by Heinrich von Kleist*, revised edn. (London: Harrap, 1962).
Schlagdenhauffen, Alfred, *L'univers existentiel de Kleist dans le Prince de Hombourg* (Paris: Belles Lettres, 1953).
Schmidt, Wieland, ed., *Die Gegenwärtigkeit Kleists: Reden zum Gedenkjahr 1977 im Schloß Charlottenburg zu Berlin*, Jahresgabe der Heinrich-von-Kleist-Gesellschaft, 1977 (Berlin: Erich Schmidt, 1980).
Schneider, Hans-Peter, 'Justizkritik im *zerbrochenem Krug*', *Kleist-Jahrbuch* (1988/9), 309–26.
Schrader, Hans-Jürgen, 'Unsägliche Liebesbriefe: Heinrich von Kleist an Wilhelmine von Zenge', *Kleist-Jahrbuch* (1981/2), 86–96.
'"Denke du wärest in das Schiff meines Glückes gestiegen": widerrufene Rollenentwürfe in Kleists Briefen an die Braut', *Kleist-Jahrbuch* 1983, 122–79.
Schwerte, Hans, 'Das Käthchen von Heilbronn', *Der Deutschunterricht*, 13 (1961), 5–26.

Seeba, Hinrich C., 'Der Sündenfall des Verdachts: Identitätskrise und Sprachskepsis in Kleists *Familie Schroffenstein*', *DVjs*, 44 (1970), 64–100.

Sembdner, Helmut, *Das Detmolder 'Käthchen von Heilbronn': eine unbekannte Bühnenfassung Heinrich von Kleists*, Beihefte zum *Euphorion*, vol. 17 (Heidelberg: Carl Winter, 1981).

Sembdner, Helmut, ed., *Heinrich von Kleist: 'Der zerbrochne Krug'. Erläuterungen und Dokumente* (Stuttgart: Reclam,1973).

Heinrich von Kleists Lebensspuren: Dokumente und Berichte der Zeitgenossen (Frankfurt: Insel, 1984).

Heinrich von Kleists Nachruhm: Eine Wirkungsgeschichte in Dokumenten (Frankfurt: Insel, 1984).

Silz, Walter, 'Kleist's Natalie', *Modern Language Notes*, 91 (1976), 531–7.

Spälti, Jakob, *Interpretationen zu Heinrich von Kleists Verhältnis zur Sprache*, European University Papers, Series I; German Language and Literature, no. 110 (Bern: Herbert Lang; Frankfurt: Peter Lang, 1974).

Stahl, Ernst L., *Heinrich von Kleist's dramas*, Modern Language Studies, IV (Oxford: Blackwell, 1948).

Stephens, Anthony, 'Zur Funktion der Metapher beim frühen Kleist', in Heinz Rupp, and Hans-Gert Roloff, eds., *Akten des VI. Internationalen Germanisten-Kongresses, Basel 1980*, Jahrbuch für Internationale Germanistik, Series A, vol 8 (Bern, Frankfurt, Las Vegas: Peter Lang, 1980), pp. 371–7

'Kleist's mythicisation of the Napoleonic era', in J. C. Eade, ed., *Romantic nationalism in Europe*, Humanities Research Centre Monograph, no. 2 (Canberra: Australian National University; Humanities Research Centre, 1983), pp. 165–79.

'"Eine Träne auf den Brief": Zum Status der Ausdrucksformen in Kleists Erzählungen', *JbDSG*, 28 (1984), 315–48.

'"Was hilfts, daß ich jetzt schuldlos mich erzähle?": zur Bedeutung der Erzählvorgänge in Kleists Dramen', *JbDSG*, 29 (1985), 301–23.

'Name und Identitätsproblematik bei Kleist und Kafka', *Jahrbuch des Freien Deutschen Hochstiftts* (1985), 223–59.

'"Das nenn ich menschlich nicht verfahren": Skizze zu einer Theorie der Grausamkeit im Hinblick auf Kleist', in Dirk Grathoff, ed., *Heinrich von Kleist: Studien zu Werk und Wirkung* (Opladen: Westdeutscher Verlag, 1988), pp. 10–39.

'"Wie beim Eintritt in ein andres Leben": Geburtsmetapher und Individualität bei Kleist', in Ulrich Fülleborn and Manfred Engel, eds., *Das neuzeitliche Ich in der Literatur des 18. und 20. Jahrhunderts: zur Dialektik der Moderne. Ein internationales Symposium* (Munich: Fink, 1988), pp. 195–214.

Heinrich von Kleist: the dramas and stories (Oxford: Berg, 1994).

Stern, Martin, 'Die Eiche als Sinnbild bei Heinrich von Kleist', *JbDSG*, 8 (1964), 199–225.
Stopp, Elizabeth, '"Ein Sohn der Zeit": Goethe and the Romantic plays of Zacharias Werner', *PEGS*, ns 40 (1970), 123–50.
Streller, Siegfried, *Das dramatische Werk Heinrich von Kleists*, Neue Beiträge zur Literaturwissenschaft, no. 27 (Berlin: Rütten and Loening, 1966).
Swales, Erika, 'The beleaguered citadel: a study of Kleist's *Die Marquise von O . . .*', *DVjs*, 51 (1977), 129–47.
'Configurations of irony: Kleist's *Prinz Friedrich von Homburg*', *DVjs*, 56 (1982), 407–30.
Szondi, Peter, '*Amphitryon*: Kleists "Lustspiel nach Molière"', *Euphorion*, 55 (1961), 249–59.
Ueding, Gerd, 'Zweideutige Bilderwelt: *Das Käthchen von Heilbronn*', in Walter Hinderer, ed., *Kleists Dramen: neue Interpretationen* (Stuttgart: Reclam, 1981), pp. 172–87.
Ugrinsky, Alexej, ed., *Heinrich von Kleist Studien* (Berlin: Erich Schmidt, 1981).
Ward, Albert, *Book production, fiction and the German reading public, 1740–1800* (Oxford: Clarendon, 1974).
Wegener, Karl-Heinz, *'Amphitryon' im Spiegel der Kleistliteratur*, European University Papers, Series 1; German Language and Literature, no. 302 (Frankfurt, Bern, Cirencester: Peter Lang, 1979).
Weigand, Hermann J., 'Zu Kleists *Käthchen von Heilbronn*', in Anna G. Hatcher, and Karl L. Selig, eds., *Studia Philologica in Honorem L. Spitzer* (Bern: Francke, 1958), pp. 413–30.
Wiese, Benno von, 'Das verlorene und wieder zu findende Paradies: eine Studie über den Begriff der Anmut bei Goethe, Kleist und Schiller', in Walter Müller-Seidel, ed., *Kleists Aufsatz über das Marionettentheater: Studien und Interpretationen*, Jahresgabe der Heinrich-von-Kleist-Gesellschaft, 1965–6 (Berlin: Erich Schmidt, 1967), pp. 196–220.
Wittkowski, Wolfgang, 'Absolutes Gefühl und absolute Kunst in Kleists *Prinz Friedrich von Homburg*', *Der Deutschunterricht*, 13 (1961), 27–71.
'Der neue Prometheus: Kleists *Amphitryon* zwischen Molière und Giraudoux', in Walter Müller-Seidel, ed., *Kleist und Frankreich*, Jahresgabe der Heinrich-von-Kleist-Gesellschaft, 1968 (Berlin: Erich Schmidt, 1969), pp. 27–82.
'Die Verschleierung der Wahrheit in und über Kleists *Amphitryon*', in Wilhelm Pelters and Paul Schimmelpfennig, eds., *Wahrheit und Sprache: Festschrift für Bert Nagel*, Göppinger Arbeiten zur Germanistik, no. 60 (Göppingen: Kümmerle, 1972), pp. 151–70.
'*Der zerbrochne Krug*: Gaukelspiel der Autorität, oder Kleists Kunst, Autoritätskritik durch Komödie zu verschleiern', *Sprachkunst*, 12 (1981), 110–30.

'*Der zerbrochne Krug:* juggling of authorities', in Alexej Ugrinsky, ed., *Heinrich von Kleist Studien* (Berlin: Erich Schmidt, 1981), pp. 69–79.

Wittkowski, Wolfgang, ed., *Heinrich von Kleists 'Amphitryon': Materialien zur Rezeption und Interpretation*, Quellen und Forschungen zur Sprach- und Kulturgeschichte der germanischen Völker. Neue Folge, no. 72 (Berlin, New York: de Gruyter, 1978).

Wolf, Christa, *Die Dimension des Autors: Essays und Aufsätze, Reden und Gespräche, 1959-85*, 2 vols. (Berlin, Weimar: Aufbau, 1986).

Wolff, Hans M., 'Käthchen von Heilbronn und Kunigunde von Thurneck', *Trivium*, 9 (1951), 214–24.

Heinrich von Kleist: die Geschichte seines Schaffens (Berkeley: University of California Press; Bern: Francke, 1954).

Index

(This index excludes proper names within Kleist's works and references to secondary literature on Kleist.)